G000093665

Preface

In 1998 I was commissioned by Unilever to research and write an independent and critical history between 1965 and 1990 based on unrestricted access to corporate archives and executives. Unilever has a unique record of openness to scholarly research. It was the first major European company to commission such a corporate history in the 1950s. Charles Wilson's two-volume *History of Unilever*, published in 1954, examined the history of the company before the Second World War. Unlike most company histories of the era, this was not a piece of public relations, but a critical study based on confidential records written by an independent historian at Cambridge University. Wilson went on to publish a third volume in 1968 which dealt with the years between 1945 and 1965. Subsequently, Unilever opened its archives to major studies of Unilever's business outside Europe and the United States by David Fieldhouse. *Unilever Overseas* (1978) told the story of Unilever's manufacturing and plantations businesses before 1968, while *Merchant Capital and Economic Decolonization* (1994) provided a study of Unilever's trading company, the United Africa Company, between its foundation in 1929 and its demise in 1987. The existence of this book has meant that UAC has received less attention in this *History* than would otherwise have been the case. This present study, therefore, builds on a long tradition. It begins where Wilson ends, and takes the history forward until 1990.

Unilever lived up to the commitment to permit unrestricted access to archives and people. The research team was allowed access to every document we sought. Over the course of the project hundreds of thousands of pages have been read. A large number of present and former Unilever employees were interviewed, and extensive use was made also of many interviews conducted at the end of the 1980s.

Much of the research for this book was undertaken by a dedicated team of research assistants, who have made a major contribution to the final work. Peter Miskell undertook outstanding research on innovation in detergents, foods, and personal products; human resource management; marketing; and plantations. Alison Kraft used her scientific background to excellent effect in studies on margarine, chemicals, and research. Lina Gálvez-Muñoz painstakingly reconstructed the scattered historical data on acquisitions, and also wrote reports on Latin America and relations with European regulators. Kim Prudon got the project off to a fine start with her research on Unilever in Europe. Finally, Anna Tijsseling explored with enthusiasm corporate culture, gender, and human resource management in the Netherlands. A number of researchers worked on the project for shorter periods. Rita Klapper wrote on the origins and impact of Co-ordination, and Anne-Marie Kuijlaars described the growth of Unilever in the United States. Fabienne Fortanier and Judith Wale undertook statistical analysis of data. In Britain and the United States, Margaret Gallagher, Yvonne Green, and Katrina Piehler provided administrative support which helped to keep me sane.

A steering committee read and commented on every draft chapter. The Joint Secretaries of Unilever, Stephen Williams, Jos Westerburgen, and subsequently Jan van der Bijl, have been pillars of support. Valerie Roberts served on the committee during the start of the project, and Jaap Winter for most of its duration, and their help was also greatly appreciated. David Ewing and Wouter Mulders played important roles in guiding the book to publication. The final member of the committee was Professor Barry Supple, who was closely involved in the origins of the project, and thereafter served as Historical Adviser to Unilever, in addition to his duties as director of the Leverhulme Trust. His guidance, scholarly advice, and personal support to the author have been exceptional, and beyond the call of duty.

The archivists of Unilever played a major role in facilitating the research. In Rotterdam, Ton Bannink was a pillar of strength. He was unfailingly helpful, supportive, and knowledgeable about Unilever, Dutch business, and Rotterdam. In Central Archives, René Trommelen and his colleagues, especially Rob Ultee, Saskia Rebers, and Marlies van Leersum, were formidably efficient. In the United States, Mary Pfeil and Todd Braisted facilitated the research at Lipton's archives at Englewood Cliffs. In London and Port Sunlight, Phaedra Casey, Sophie Clapp, Gary Collins, Lesley Owen-Edwards, Melanie Peart, Robert Pickering, Michael Thomas, Jeannette Strickland, and Philip Waterhouse took time off from their busy schedules to find documents. Beverly Tyson and Lorna Meecham were helpful in accessing other research materials. Lesley Dumphreys provided administrative support. Sue Meeson performed outstanding service in locating the photographs for this book.

Over the four years of the research, I have been employed at three educational institutions. Each has been supportive of my involvement in this project. At the University of Reading in the UK, I would like to thank the former Vice Chancellor Roger Williams for allowing me to take time away from teaching to research Unilever, and my former colleagues at the Centre for International Business History for their stimulating academic support. I held a Special Chair at Erasmus University, Rotterdam, between 2000 and 2002. I would like to thank my former colleagues in the CBG, especially Joop Visser and Ferry de Goey, for many insights about the

Netherlands. Finally, in 2000 I became a visiting professor at the Harvard Business School in the United States, which became a permanent appointment in 2002. I would like to thank Dean Kim Clark for his support, alongside with my colleagues Alfred D. Chandler Jr., Tom McCraw, and Richard Tedlow.

G. J.

Harvard Business School

Contents

List of Plates   x
List of Illustrations   xii
List of Figures   xv
List of Tables   xvii

Introduction   1

Part I   **Strategy and Performance**

1   Heritage and Challenges   5
2   Managing Diversity, 1965–1973   17
3   New and Old Worlds, 1974–1983   54
4   Rethinking Unilever, 1984–1990   88

Part II   **Dynamics and Routines**

5   Adding Value: Marketing and Brands   115
6   Risk and Reward in Emerging Markets   152
7   Trading, Plantations, and Chemicals   185
8   Human Resources   215
9   Corporate Culture   247
10   Innovation   267
11   Acquisitions and Divestments   298
12   Corporate Image and Voice   322

     Epilogue   352

Appendix 1   The Special Committee and its Successors   368
Appendix 2   Unilever and its Major International Competitors   369

     Notes   378
     Bibliography   416
     Index   425

List of Plates

between pages 46 and 47

1 Rama, the leading German margarine brand, in 1967

2 Flora margarine in Britain in 1977

3 A sale van for Stork margarine in 1981

4 Sana margarine in Turkey in 1980

5 Promotion for I Can't Believe It's Not Butter in 1986

6 Street advertisement in Paris for Boursin cheese in 1990

7 Wall's meat pies in Britain, 1977

8 Vesta ready made meals in Britain, 1974

between pages 110 and 111

9 Viennetta ice cream gateaux in Greece, 1988

10 Cornetto ice cream in Arabia in the early 1990s

11 Magnum ice cream in Germany in the early 1990s

12 Birds Eye Fish Fingers in Britain in 1987

13 Lipton tea in the United States in 1986, featuring the tennis player Chris Everett Lloyd

14 Chimps advertising PG Tips in 1989

15 Etah rural development project in India in 1983

between pages 174 and 175

16 Supermarket demonstration for Zwan meat products in Mexico in 1987

17 Unox sponsorship of the Dutch Elfstedentocht in the mid-1990s

18 Cup-A-Soup in the United States in 1987

19 Ragu pasta sauce in the United States in 1988

20 Advertisement for turkey feed sold by BOCM Silcock

21 A Ben & Jerry's ice cream street vendor in Britain in 2000

22 Drinking Slim-Fast on North Shore beach, O'ahu, Hawaii in 2000

23 Enjoying a Knorr Cubitos seasoning cube, sold in the Caribbean and Brazil, in 2004

List of Figures

2.1 Unilever organization, 1960   39

2.2 Unilever organization, 1974   48

3.1 Unilever profits and sales by region, 1969–1984   58

3.2 Unilever yields by region, 1969–1984   58

3.3 Sales of Unilever's European businesses by product group, 1969–1984   59

3.4 Capital employed in Unilever's European businesses by product group,
     1969–1984   60

3.5 Profits of Unilever's European businesses by product group, 1969–1984   60

3.6 Yields on Unilever's European businesses by product group, 1969–1984   61

3.7 Sales of Unilever's North American businesses by product group, 1969–1984   70

3.8 Capital employed in Unilever's North American businesses by product group,
     1969–1984   70

3.9 Profits of Unilever's North American businesses by product group, 1969–1984   71

3.10 Yields on Unilever's North American businesses by product group, 1969–1984   71

3.11 Sales of Unilever's Overseas businesses by product group, 1969–1984   80

3.12 Capital employed in Unilever's Overseas businesses by product group,
     1969–1984   80

3.13 Profits of Unilever's Overseas businesses by product group, 1969–1984   81

3.14 Yields on Unilever's Overseas businesses by product group, 1969–1984   81

4.1 Unilever profits and sales by region, 1985 and 1989   94

4.2 Unilever yields by region, 1985 and 1989   95

4.3 Unilever yields by product category, 1985 and 1989   95

4.4 Unilever Co-ordinations, 1987   108

5.1 Unilever expenditure on marketing and research and development as a
     percentage of sales, 1966–1990   149

7.1 Sales of UAC, Plantations, and Chemicals as a proportion of Unilever total,
     1969–1984   187

7.2 Profits from UAC, Plantations, and Chemicals as a proportion of Unilever total,
     1969–1984   188

List of Figures

7.3 Capital employed in UAC, Plantations, and Chemicals as a proportion of Unilever total, 1969–1984   189

7.4 Yields on UAC, Plantations, and Chemicals and Unilever average, 1969–1984   190

7.5 Unilever Plantation profits, 1965–1990   199

8.1 Total employment in Unilever, 1965–1990   216

8.2 Definitions of categories on Unilever's Management Lists   229

12.1 Unilever's position in national and European trade associations   334

List of Tables

2.1 Unilever operating companies with £30 million and over sales, *c.* 1970   42

5.1 Unilever branding strategies by product group, *c.* 1977   131

6.1 Government constraints on Unilever operations in overseas countries, at end 1971   155

6.2 The relationship between products sold and consumption per capita, *c.*1990   162

7.1 Unilever Chemicals business, 1966–1980   205

7.2 Unilever Chemicals business, 1987–1990   211

10.1 Unilever's position in new product development, 1950–1972   268

Introduction

It is hard to imagine a world without Lux and Dove soap, Sunsilk shampoo, Impulse and Axe deodorants, Pond's Cream, Mentadent toothpaste, Omo and Surf washing powders, Cif cleaners, Rama and Flora margarine, Iglo frozen foods, Lipton tea, and Ben & Jerry's and Wall's ice cream. It is almost as hard to imagine that they are produced by a single company. Yet this is the reality. These brands, which are familiar parts of the daily lives of tens of millions of people worldwide, are made and sold by Unilever, a unique global company whose origins lay in Britain and the Netherlands. It is the world's largest ice cream, tea, and margarine company, and one of the world's largest home and personal care companies. Yet although the brands are part of everyday life, Unilever's own name has historically been far better known to investors than to consumers.

Unilever originated in an Anglo-Dutch merger in 1929. This book picks up the history of Unilever in the middle of the 1960s, and takes it forward to 1990. There is no simple way to examine a business which operates in most countries of the world and employs around 300,000 people. The history of one major brand, or of one individual country, could fill a volume. The approach taken here is selective. The book takes the perspective of Unilever as a whole. It provides a unique 'inside' study of how that company functioned and changed over time. And it explores the impact of Unilever on the world in which it operated.

The book has two parts. Part I shows how and why Unilever's strategy and organization changed between the 1960s and 1990. Any perception of Unilever as a grey corporate monolith disintegrates as it is shown how decision-making was constrained and shaped by the complex internal dynamics within the organization. Unilever evolved through a complex process of success and failure, triumph and disaster, action and inaction. These chapters provide the context for Part II, which explores key themes in more depth. Chapters 5, 6, and 7 consider Unilever's brands, its franchise in emerging markets, and non-consumer businesses. Chapters 8 to 12 examine human resources, corporate culture, innovation, acquisitions and divestments, and corporate image. An Epilogue summarizes the main conclusions, and provides an overview of Unilever's recent past. Appendix 1 provides a list of Unilever's chief executives. Appendix 2 provides statistical data on Unilever and its major international competitors since the 1960s.

trolled activities across countries. They accounted for most of the flows of foreign direct investment which began to grow in size from the 1960s, and which resulted in accelerating cross-border flows of capital and ideas. The same firms were responsible for much of world trade, which increasingly took the form of 'intra-firm trade' inside the same large corporation. They created much of the world's new technology, and were responsible for transferring it across borders. Unilever in 1990 estimated that it accounted for over 0.7 per cent of total personal consumption in a range of diverse countries from Britain, the Netherlands, and Sweden in Europe, to Mexico and Chile, Nigeria and South Africa, Australia and Malaysia.[3]

Unilever provides a microcosm of many of the processes which transformed the world. It was a 'global firm' par excellence. Its products affected the daily lives of a large proportion of the world's population in what and how they ate, how they washed and cleaned their houses and themselves, and how they presented themselves to others. Unilever's history offers compelling insights into the part played by large corporations in the great changes of recent decades, and provides answers to key questions about this process.

How did large multinational firms such as Unilever arise, who runs them, and what are their aims? How do such firms allocate resources between different products and between the different countries in which they operate? How do they organize themselves? How can such enormous and diverse companies function? What kind of choices are made between the interests of shareholders, employees, suppliers, and customers? What are the implications of such firms as Unilever? Do they follow fashion and tastes, or create them? Are they responsible for a wasteful, image-obsessed consumer society, or have they played a beneficial role in providing consumers with choice? Have such firms improved, through their research and innovation, the lives of millions of consumers, or have they distorted consumption patterns? In essence, have they enhanced global welfare, or detracted from it?

Unilever's Origins

Unilever was created in 1929 by a merger between the British firm of Lever Brothers, a pioneer of branded soap manufacture founded by William Hesketh Lever (later Viscount Leverhulme), and the Margarine Unie of the Netherlands, itself a merger of leading Dutch margarine manufacturers including Van den Bergh and Jurgens, Hartog's meat business at Oss, and the central European firm of Schicht.

This historical legacy exercised a powerful influence on Unilever's subsequent development. Soap (and later detergents) and margarine, both initially derived from edible oils, were to remain at the heart of Unilever's business. However, Leverhulme also left a wider legacy. He diversified around the time of the First World War on a massive scale into West African trading and plantations, seeking security of raw material supplies. This was the origin of the United Africa Company (hereafter UAC), formed through another merger at the end of the 1920s, which grew as a vast trading and subsequently manufacturing business in Africa. Leverhulme's private ventures also ultimately led Lever Brothers in the 1920s into ice cream and sausage manufacture, fish shops and trawling fleets, and tinned salmon. These diversifications were rarely profitable, and—in the case of the West African trading companies—almost bankrupted Lever Brothers after the end of the First World War. Virtually all of these businesses were swept into Unilever, which, by some estimates, was the largest company in Europe on its formation.[4]

Unilever proved remarkably resilient. The merger which created the firm took place in the same year as the American stock market crashed, and the world economy fell into the Great Depression. The first decade of its existence saw collapsing incomes and high unemployment in many countries, but demand for Unilever's products expanded rather than contracted. People continued to eat and wash even if they lost their jobs. Meanwhile the collapse of the world economic system had the perverse result of encouraging further diversification. The profits from Unilever's large German business, trapped by Nazi controls over dividend remittances abroad, were invested in cheese, ice cream, hair dyes, and even shipping companies.

Unilever's historical development included a uniquely wide geographical spread. The firm's predecessors had been among the first 'multinational' firms which, during the second half of the nineteenth century, had begun to build factories in foreign countries rather than merely export products to them. The Dutch margarine companies had extensive operations not only in the Netherlands, but also in Germany and central Europe, as well as in Britain. Lever Brothers had expanded far beyond Europe. During the 1890s the firm began to switch from exporting its soap to building factories in foreign markets. Factories were built in other European countries, in the richer markets of the British Empire such as Canada and Australia, and in the United States. A factory was opened in Japan in 1909. The search for raw materials took Lever Brothers into Africa as plantation owner and trader.

Unilever's predecessors were thus important participants in the making of the world's first 'global economy' before the First World War, but unlike many firms their international growth was not halted by the subsequent political and economic shocks. During the inter-war years new factories were opened in, among other countries, India, Thailand, Indonesia, China, Argentina, and Brazil. By the end of the 1930s no US corporation, and almost certainly no other European company either, could match Unilever in the sheer geographical spread of its business.

The 'international' flavour of Unilever was enhanced by its dual nationality. Following the merger in 1929, Unilever retained a structure of two holding companies.

1 Unilever House in Blackfriars, London, Ltd/PLC's head office since 1932 (*c.* 1970).

Unilever Ltd (PLC after 1981) was British and capitalized in sterling. Unilever NV was Dutch and capitalized in guilders. Ltd and NV had different shareholders, but identical Boards. An 'Equalization Agreement' between them provided that they should at all times pay dividends of equivalent value in sterling and guilders. There were two chairmen and two head offices, in London and Rotterdam. It thus became an extremely rare case of a large company owned and managed in two countries. The only comparison—at least before the wave of cross-border mergers of the 1990s—was Unilever's Anglo-Dutch twin Royal Dutch Shell.

Unilever's bi-national ownership structure proved resilient to external shocks. During the Second World War the Dutch and other European businesses of Unilever were cut off from the British and remaining parts of the group by the Nazi occupation of continental Europe. However, at the end of the war unity was again restored to the business. Unilever had continued to expand even during the Second World War. In the United States, Unilever acquired T. J. Lipton, a leading tea company. It already owned Lever Brothers, which had been established in the late nineteenth century, and acquired a large share of the US soap market. In Britain, Unilever acquired Batchelors Peas, one of that country's largest vegetable canners.

2 Unilever House at Museumpark, Rotterdam, NV's head office between 1931 and 1992 *(taken in 1986).*

It also purchased from General Foods in the United States the right to manufacture and sell quick frozen foods under the Birds Eye name. During the 1930s Birds Eye had convinced Americans that frozen foods were a quality product, and in the early 1950s it was to be a leader in the movement to shift the industry from serving a privileged market segment into a mass marketing business, which sought to give Americans quality and convenience at a low price.[5] In the post-war decades Unilever expanded further into foods, and new factories were opened in Turkey, south-east Asia, and tropical Africa.[6]

While Unilever's historical legacy had made it one of the most 'global' of multinationals, it also contributed to making it one of the most decentralized. Unilever had grown through repeated mergers of companies who usually retained their names and brands, and this encouraged a strong belief in the virtues of 'local initiative and decentralised control'.[7] The decentralized nature of Unilever was strikingly manifested in its portfolio of brands. The corporate name was not used as a brand, nor was it found on the packaging of any of its goods. Unilever resembled a 'virtual company'. Its manufacturing and other activities were conducted by numerous 'operating companies'. It was their names, such as Van den Bergh & Jurgens, Langnese, and Birds Eye, that were known to employees and consumers. They owned thousands of different brands, most of them sold only in one country, and often originating with a local firm which had been acquired. Each brand had a distinctive franchise, many of which were—by later standards—remarkably small.

Unilever's business spanned an extraordinary range of industries. In the mid-1960s 'Edibles'—the term used for margarine and other edible oils—and soap and detergents each accounted for over a fifth of total sales, and a slightly higher proportion of profits. A further fifth of sales, and a rather lower share of profits, were in what Unilever called 'Foods', a category which excluded edible oils but included everything else, from frozen peas to ice cream to fresh meat. Unilever's remaining sales were derived from all sorts of things, from personal care—then known as Toilet Preparations (and later Personal Products) and including toothpaste, shampoos, deodorants, and cosmetics—to animal feeds and chemicals manufacturing. UAC accounted for nearly 15 per cent of Unilever sales. Unilever's businesses were supported by high levels of vertical and horizontal integration, which had led the firm into owning fishing fleets, fish restaurants, river and road transport businesses, packaging and printing operations, and advertising and market research agencies. In geographical terms, Unilever made two-thirds of its sales in Europe, another tenth in the United States, and the remainder in the rest of the world.

Markets and Competitors

Unilever's diverse business meant that it faced a spectrum of market structures and competed against many of the world's leading consumer goods firms. In some products Unilever operated in oligopolistic markets, dominated by a small number of international firms, while in other products markets and competitors remained overwhelmingly local. Nor was this the only element of competition faced by Unilever. Some of its major products, such as margarine and tea, were in competition with near-substitutes, such as butter and coffee.

Detergents and soap were a classic oligopolistic market. In the immediate postwar years the soap industry had been transformed by the development of synthetic detergents. Although there were significant local firms in particular markets, four large international firms dominated the world industry. These were Unilever, Procter & Gamble (hereafter P & G), Colgate, and Henkel. Unilever estimated in 1961 that these four firms accounted for 60 per cent of world sales of soap and detergents. P & G and Unilever held the largest shares, with 25 per cent and 22 per cent respectively, in that year. Colgate and Henkel accounted for a further 9 and 4 per cent respectively.[8] The position of these firms derived from the barriers to entry arising from economies of scale in production, research, and marketing.

Strategy and Performance

This was an advertising-intensive industry with regular 'soap wars' breaking out between the major participants. Given the structure of the industry, entry, other than by acquisition, was not really an option. Competition took the form of fierce rivalry between incumbent firms which had a long experience of one another.

The four international firms had different profiles. Unilever was the biggest firm in terms of sales and employment, but its product range was much wider. Unilever made around one-half of its sales of detergents in western Europe, where it held almost one-third of the total market in the 1960s, and the remainder in North America and many emerging markets. Its fiercest competitor in world detergents was P & G. This American firm was less diversified than Unilever, with its non-detergents businesses confined, in the 1960s, to shampoos, toothpaste, and paper products. It was also largely focused on developed markets, especially its North American home region, which accounted for nearly 90 per cent of total profits even in the 1980s. In contrast to Unilever, decision-making was heavily centralized on the Cincinnati head office.[9]

Colgate and Henkel were smaller firms. Colgate's main business was household and personal care products, and it competed against Unilever mostly in household cleaners, soap, and toothpaste. Although US based, Colgate only accounted for 10 per cent of the US detergents market in the 1960s. Its foreign sales exceeded those in the United States, and it occupied the number two or three position in a number of emerging markets, including South Africa and Thailand. Quite different again was the German family-owned firm of Henkel, with whom Unilever shared for historical reasons the ownership of the famous Persil brand name. Henkel had originated as a detergents company, but then integrated backwards into chemicals. In the 1960s around one-half of the firm's sales were in detergents and cleaning products, and two-thirds of its total sales were in Germany. It was the market leader in the German detergents market, and a major competitor in a number of other European markets.[10]

Unilever faced a range of market situations in personal care products, in which it held a modest 4 per cent of the world market in the 1960s. This product category had begun to grow from the late nineteenth century as discretionary incomes rose, and as branding and mass production techniques were applied. During the inter-war years shampoos began to be used to wash hair in preference to soap and water—though their use long remained confined to women—and there was also a new concern for body odours—Unilever's American subsidiary Lever Brothers had invented the concept of 'BO' in the 1920s—though the solution at that stage was found in soap or cologne lotions rather than deodorants. However, the real growth of the industry came after the Second World War. 'Luxuries' began a transition into 'essentials'. The process was most dramatically seen in the United States, which accounted for one-half of total sales of personal care products during the first two post-war decades.[11]

Toothpaste shared many of the characteristics of the detergents industry. The level of research, distribution, and marketing required to support successful brands served as barriers to entry. Four firms together accounted for three-quarters of total world toothpaste sales outside the Communist countries. These were Unilever, P & G, Colgate, and Beechams, the British-based pharmaceuticals company, which had built a substantial stake in the industry since it acquired Macleans in 1938. Hair products, including shampoos, were much more fragmented, although by the 1960s a number of firms, including Colgate, Helene Curtis, and the German company Schwarzkopf, had international brands.[12] In deodorants, Unilever's worldwide competitors included Gillette, which had a large US deodorant business based on Right Guard and Soft & Dri brands, and which held substantial market shares in Latin America and Britain, and Bristol-Myers, which had worldwide presence with brands such as Mum.

In the skin and hair care businesses there were a cluster of US firms, including large consumer goods companies such as Chesebrough-Pond's and Richardson Vicks, and specialist cosmetics firms, including firms selling to mass markets like Avon, Revlon, and Max Factor, and others selling to the prestige sector, including Elizabeth Arden, Helena Rubinstein, and Estée Lauder. A number of these firms began to expand internationally on a considerable scale from the 1950s.[13]

Beyond the United States, the French company L'Oréal, founded in 1909 to sell hair colourants to hairdressers, expanded into hairsprays, and subsequently into perfume, cosmetics, and deodorants. During the 1960s L'Oréal acquired several other French cosmetic and perfume brands, including Lancôme and Garnier, and launched its first really successful international product, the hairspray Elnett. Yet it remained a small company which still earned three-fifths of its profits in France in 1970.[14] In Japan, cosmetics companies were also growing rapidly along with disposable incomes. Shiseido, the market leader, had been founded as early as 1872, but its modest international expansion into the United States and Europe only began during the 1960s.

Edible fats were at the heart of Unilever's foods business. Unilever accounted for 12 per cent of total edible fats consumption in the world in the 1960s. In margarine, Unilever was a giant in Europe, with market shares in Germany, the Netherlands, and Britain—the main consumers of the product—of over two-thirds. Its main competitors were smaller local companies, though its most serious competition was butter.

There was a high degree of fragmentation in the food industry as a whole. The market for foods was characterized by diversity in consumer tastes and national regulations. There were no economies of scale to encourage large-scale rationalization of production or marketing across borders. The major international firm was

Strategy and Performance

Nestlé, an early multinational investor, which by 1914 had widespread manufacturing operations in Europe, the United States, and Australia. Nestlé's product range was initially confined to milk products—and it began manufacturing chocolate during the 1900s—but in 1938 the firm introduced a revolutionary instant coffee, Nescafé. It proved to be a 'global' product which could be sold to consumers with widely different consumption habits.

Nestlé, based in neutral Switzerland, did not suffer the wartime disruption experienced by Unilever, and during the post-war decades expanded through acquisition into soups and seasonings, canned foods, and frozen foods, though coffee—in which Nestlé held the number one position in instant coffee worldwide—still contributed at least two-fifths of its profits in the 1980s. Unilever and Nestlé competed directly in frozen foods, processed foods, and soups, but they did not clash over the full range of their products. Unilever hovered on the fringes of dairy products, chocolate, and other Nestlé products, but never became more than a marginal player, while Nestlé did not confront Unilever in oils and fats.

Unilever also competed to some extent in foods with large US firms. General Foods, the world's largest coffee company, also manufactured frozen foods, beverages, and other foodstuffs. General Foods held strong positions in a number of Latin American markets such as Brazil, which made them direct competitors of Unilever. CPC—the name used between 1969 and 1998 when it was changed to Bestfoods—had originated as the Corn Products Refining Company, a leading US corn refiner whose products included Mazola corn oil. It acquired a share in the German-owned Knorr soup and bouillon company in 1926, which became wholly owned thirty-three years later. In 1958 Corn Products merged with the Best Foods, whose foods business included Hellmann's mayonnaise. The Corn Products Refining Company had extensive European and Latin American corn refining businesses from the inter-war years, and from the early 1960s foods brands such as Knorr and Hellmann's began to be introduced into Latin America. Kraft claimed to be the world's largest food processing company. Manufactured dairy products and processed foods provided the core of the business. From the 1920s Kraft had built extensive international operations in Europe, especially in Germany and Britain, but the United States and Canada still accounted for 85 per cent of sales in the mid-1970s. Unilever competed against Kraft in processed cheese products, margarine, salad creams and dressings, and ready meals.

In terms of sales and employment, if not market capitalization, Unilever was much larger than its major international competitors in the mid-1960s. In US dollars it sold more than P & G, Colgate, Nestlé, and Henkel together, while its workforce dwarfed those of these four firms and Kraft combined. None of those firms faced the diversity of competitive situations and market structures faced by Unilever.

14

Competitive Challenges and the Legacy of the Past

Unilever's historical development had given it formidable competitive advantages by the mid-1960s. It held strong market share positions in many countries, based on numerous well-established brands. It was large enough to be an unlikely takeover target and big enough to buy all but very large competitors. Unilever had an unusually extensive experience of operating in foreign countries. It even had two home countries with different cultures to help it understand the complexity of operating internationally.

All of these advantages might be summarized as 'knowledge'. During the 1990s the importance of knowledge as a competitive advantage and the concept of 'knowledge-based' organizations became the latest management fashion.[15] It was often assumed that such arguments applied essentially to firms in 'knowledge industries', such as biotechnology or computer software, rather than what became known as 'old economy' firms. It was also usually assumed that the rise of 'knowledge' as a competitive advantage was a new phenomenon.

In fact, Unilever had already conceptualized itself as a 'knowledge organization' in the early 1970s. As the chairmen told Unilever's Annual General Meetings in 1972, 'the competitive advantages on which our success depends all rest in the last resort on knowledge'. The chairmen recognized that this 'knowledge' was the result of cumulative learning, both multifaceted and tacit:

It may be the combination of technological, mathematical and computer skills which is used to change the composition of a margarine without loss of quality when there is a shift in relative prices of the wide range of oils and fats. It may lie in an understanding of how the retailer makes his profit . . . It may be knowledge of the most minor details of how to distribute and handle in the shop fresh, chilled or frozen products in such a way that they do not lose quality . . . much of the knowledge which is important to a firm like Unilever cannot be found in books. It has to be acquired often expensively, sometimes painfully, by experience and deliberate enquiry. . . . The knowledge Unilever has is both extensive and complex. It is the source of its profits and of the main benefits Unilever brings to the peoples of the countries in which it operates.[16]

The central theme in Unilever's history from 1965 was to be the struggle to gain full advantage from its formidable knowledge base, and to learn how to acquire new knowledge resources through buying other firms. Unilever's depth and range of knowledge needed to be matched by the appropriate strategy, organization, corporate culture, and managers who could exploit this knowledge, and translate it into competitive advantage in the market and returns to shareholders. This involved continual choices, over the allocation of resources between different products and countries, between different strategies, between different organizational forms, between who to recruit, and who to promote. These choices in turn had profound implications for the millions of consumers of Unilever products, its tens of thousands of employees, its numerous shareholders, and for the many countries in which Unilever operated.

an attractive industry with 'no effective price control'. There was no suggestion that Unilever companies would make use of the acquired facilities.[65]

Unilever's own advertising and market research businesses also diversified. Lever Brothers had established an internal advertising agency in 1925, and this evolved into Lever's International Advertising Service—universally known as Lintas—in 1930. By the 1950s Lintas had agencies in over twenty countries, and the firm began evolving its own non-Unilever business. Despite Unilever's experience in the United States, the introduction of commercial television in Britain found Lintas rather unprepared. This was the background to an alliance formed in 1962 of Lintas with the US-based agency SSC&B, designed to facilitate access to US advertising expertise. There was no great transfer of information until 1970, when the American firm acquired a 49 per cent shareholding in Lintas.[66] Unilever's market research units in Europe, gathered together in the European Market Research Group in 1973, also began to search for outside business.

If roll-on/roll-off ferries seemed far removed from Unilever's traditional margarine and detergents businesses, the position of the United Africa Company within Unilever was even more extraordinary. In the mid-1950s UAC provided 15 per cent of Unilever's total profits. A decade later UAC remained a giant enterprise, but profits had dwindled. Like Unilever itself, it was a business under pressure. Its vast business had been built on exporting West African commodities, especially palm oil and cocoa, and importing almost everything required by the region. However, the growth of state intervention in the West African economies progressively curbed such traditional activities. UAC responded by focusing on activities which were less vulnerable to the growing state intervention in economies, such as automobile distribution. Joint ventures were formed with manufacturing and brewing firms.[67]

UAC responded to growing political risk in Africa by geographical diversification, setting up companies to sell alcohol in the Arabian Gulf and engaging in logging in the Solomon Islands. Concerned to provide employment for UAC's large number of expatriate managers in Africa, UAC was encouraged to adopt a strategy known as 'redeployment' which involved investing in Europe. An ill-advised joint venture with Heineken to brew beer in Burgos in Spain resulted in large losses before the brewery was sold in 1969.[68] This was a first warning, which was not to be heeded, that UAC's managerial skills were not easily transferable from Africa.

Despite the pursuit of diversification, Unilever's business portfolio in 1974 was not radically different from that of 1965. The share of edibles, detergents, and foods in Unilever's total sales fell only marginally from 67 to 64 per cent. Unilever's reliance on 'the rest of the world' for profits had grown greatly, however, reflecting poor performance in the United States and a downturn in profits in Europe. The managerial tasks of steering the 'several different fleets' had also intensified.

Unilever's Organization: Decentralization and Fragmentation

Unilever's growth prompted a growing debate about the appropriate organizational structures required to manage the firm effectively and to respond to changes in its external environment. However, the process of identifying and adopting the 'best model' proved difficult. Unilever had become so complex that even its identity and purpose had become clouded. 'Is Unilever a conglomerate or a definable business?', one director asked in 1969. 'What are its contours and limitations?'[69]

The central difficulty revolved round getting the right balance between 'centralization' and 'decentralization', and between 'products' and 'geography', but there were trade-offs whatever the approach taken. A consumer goods manufacturer needed intimate knowledge of each market in which it operated, but if each country was managed as an independent entity the potential economies of scope possible from cross-border transfers of knowledge would be lost. Finding the right balance was complicated because there were major differences in the markets faced by different products—some were mature, and others growing—while the nature and intensity of competition also varied. Because of the diverse layers of decision-making within Unilever, starting at the top with the twin head offices, there were always likely to be 'winners' and 'losers' from any major organization change.

Unilever's post-war organization was built on decentralization and geographically based management. Most large European-based companies functioned as what have been called 'decentralized federations'. They tended to rely on personal relationships and informal contacts rather than formal structures and systems to control affiliates, while national affiliates were managed as independent units. This reflected not only historical growth patterns, but also the slow development of professional management in Europe, and cultural orientations which stressed the importance of 'relationships' in business affairs. This model contrasted with that used by US firms, which had a greater preference for more formal management systems which were used to exercise much greater central control over overseas affiliates.[70]

A belief in the value of local decision-making was natural for a consumer goods company. Its managers were aware that food and washing products were imbued with cultural meaning, and that they needed to be sensitive to differences in taste and preference caused by geography and culture. Although P & G was always seen within Unilever as highly centralised, in practice its European affiliates were also given a high degree of autonomy to develop products and marketing programmes in recognition of the strong differences in consumer habits and market conditions. P & G only gradually adopted a regionalization strategy in Europe, beginning with more coordinated R & D, following the oil crises of 1973/4.[71]

The historical events through which Unilever had passed reinforced the belief in decentralization. During the Second World War, Unilever's affiliates found themselves isolated from each other, and from the head offices. After 1945, the need to reconstruct Unilever businesses quickly in post-war Europe led to a reliance on local initiative and autonomy, with responsibilities largely delegated to national managements. Centralization seemed not only unworkable for such a large company, but also most unwise, as it might stifle 'entrepreneurship' and innovation, which was best found at the 'local' level.

Fig. 2.1 describes the basic organizational structure of Unilever around 1960. Below the level of the Board there were four principal management groups. Each was organized separately. The Continental European Group in Rotterdam had six directors—four of whom were nominated 'Contact' Directors for individual countries—and was responsible for all business in continental Europe. There were national managements for each country. In the 1950s Dutch managers had often controlled these posts, but subsequently local appointments became more usual. National managers in Europe were extremely powerful with, in most cases, responsibility for profits and operational management. National managements also represented Unilever in their countries in relations with governments and public relations, in industrial relations, and in management recruitment.

The United Kingdom had a different system. The British business was more diversified than elsewhere, and a form of product management was established early on. The functions performed by national managements in continental Europe were

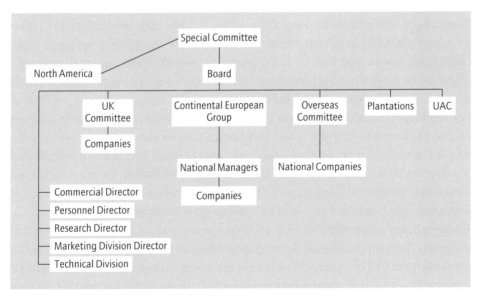

Fig. 2.1 Unilever organization, 1960.

from the late 1940s performed by 'Executives' for margarine, foods, detergents, and oil milling. The UK Committee comprising these Executives reported directly to the Special Committee. Each Executive was charged with making available relevant knowledge of their business to other countries,[72] but in practice the UK's operations were largely isolated from elsewhere in Europe. This was in part because they were so large—in 1964 Unilever employed around 85,000 people in the UK compared to just over 80,000 elsewhere in Europe—but the Group Management in Rotterdam was also protective of its authority on the European continent.

The Overseas Committee was responsible for most of the companies outside Europe, who employed nearly 55,000 people in 1964. Its business spanned an enormous range of countries in Asia, Australia, the Middle East, Africa, and Latin America, with a collective population of over 2,000 million. The thirty or so national companies reporting to the Overseas Committee were for the most part single integrated companies, though in Australia and South Africa there were national managements supervising around eight separate and mostly small companies. As in Europe, there was a heavy emphasis on local decision-making. The stronger and bigger the company, the more autonomy it exercised. The Overseas Committee saw its role as both representing the interests of the Overseas companies within Unilever, and promulgating new ideas for products and other matters for the companies.

The Overseas Committee was composed of four people, of whom three were likely to be directors, supported by a specialist staff of around twenty. Each member was allocated countries on a 'random' basis, so that one person might be responsible for a group of companies on each of the four continents. This 'random' system of allocation of countries had existed in the 1930s, and was then reintroduced as a matter of explicit policy in the late 1950s to avoid directors becoming geographical specialists who would 'lose interest in the rest of the world'.[73] This meant that specific 'regional' strategies hardly developed, and managers were not encouraged even to ask what was happening in neighbouring countries.[74]

Unilever's US companies, Lever Brothers and T. J. Lipton, were nominally part of the Overseas Committee, but in practice autonomous. There was no US national management, and virtually no contact between Lever Brothers and T. J. Lipton. Both had their own Board of directors, and their presidents reported directly to the Special Committee. The Special Committee's operational control over them was tangential at best. The autonomy of Lever and Lipton reflected the Unilever belief in decentralization. However, it was part of a wider phenomenon reflecting the high prestige of American management after the war, as well as the disinclination of US managers to accept direction from abroad, which resulted in many European companies experiencing difficulties exercising control over US affiliates.

A further influence was the strength at the time of US anti-trust law, and the prevailing interpretation of it. P & G faced an anti-trust action after its acquisition in 1957 of Clorox Chemical, the largest US manufacturer of household bleach, and it was forced to divest ten years later. Anti-trust action was also begun against Unilever following the acquisition of the All detergent from Monsanto in 1957. Unilever won the case in 1963, using the argument that Lever Brothers was so weak that it offered no competitive threat to anyone, but its US lawyers before and after the suit repeatedly warned that if Unilever appeared to exercise close control over its US affiliates the whole company might be exposed to anti-trust investigation, as had happened to the British chemicals company ICI previously. Unilever's chief legal adviser for many years, Abe Fortas, was a major figure in the corporate law profession in the United States and an adviser to many large corporations; he became a Supreme Court judge in 1965 and was unsuccessfully nominated to be chief justice in 1968. It was not surprising that his advice was taken very seriously in Europe.[75]

UAC's autonomy was almost as great as that of the US affiliates, even though it was far more integrated into Unilever's financial and reporting systems. It was organized as a private company with its own chairman and Board. In 1960 UAC, which had formerly been located inside Unilever's London head office, moved across the River Thames to its own building. Before 1960 the Special Committee were automatically members of UAC's Board. In that year it was decided that the Special Committee would attend only one meeting of UAC's Board a month, and in 1963 they resigned altogether from the Board. Thereafter the normal Unilever system of regular meetings between the Special Committee and UAC's Board was adopted, but although the latter reported to the Special Committee, it was sometimes unclear who was the dominant party.[76] UAC held a peculiar position. It was large—employing over 80,000 people in the 1960s—yet its business was far removed from consumer goods. The Dutch, even at director level, had little knowledge of its affairs, which some regarded as an example of British eccentricity.

Beneath Unilever's management groups and national managements were the operating companies. In the 1960s Unilever had around 500 operating companies. These were the main profit centres. They were owned by and transmitted dividends either to Ltd or NV, but this had almost no impact on their reporting relationships or control. The US affiliates were transferred to NV in 1937, and remained wholly owned until 1987 (when PLC was given a 25 per cent shareholding), but during the post-war decades North America was regarded as a 'British' area of responsibility.

Table 2.1 lists twenty-two operating companies with sales of £30 million or over in 1970, excluding UAC operations. These twenty-two companies accounted for over half of Unilever's sales in 1970, but many of the remaining companies had small

Table 2.1 Unilever operating companies with £30 million and over sales *c.* 1970

Company	Country	Sales (£ million)	Products
Lever Brothers	USA	219.8	D, Ed, PP
BOCM/Silcock	UK	167.4	Animal feeds
UDL	Germany	144.2	Ed
T. J. Lipton	USA	115.4	F
Birds Eye	UK	85.1	Frozen foods
V. d. B. & Jurgens	UK	83.0	Ed
Hindustan Lever	India	77.0	Ed, D, PP
Langnese Iglo	Germany	62.7	Frozen foods
Lever Bros. Ltd	UK	58.5	D
Savonneries Lever	France	50.8	D
Walls Drings	UK	46.9	Meat
Sunlicht	Germany	45.7	D
Lever Brothers	Canada	44.3	D
Astra Calvé	France	44.3	Ed
Zwanenberg	The Netherlands	36.9	Meat
V. d. B. en Jurgens	The Netherlands	34.8	Ed
Unox	The Netherlands	33.3	Meat
Liva/MB	Sweden	32.5	Ed
Union Group	Belgium	31.9	Ed
Frozen Group	Italy	31.7	Frozen foods
Gessy Lever	Brazil	31.3	D, Ed, PP
Nordsee	Germany	30.4	Fish
All Unilever		2,960.5	

Notes: D = detergents; Ed = edible fats and dairy; PP = personal products; F = foods other than frozen, fish, and meat.

turnovers. The degree of autonomy of the companies varied with their size and profitability. The largest of them, such as the Union Deutsche Lebensmittelwerke (UDL), whose sales of margarine in Germany were large and profitable, were powerful voices with great freedom of action. In contrast, a chairman running a small and loss-making company would have little bargaining power with higher levels of management.[77]

Although there were plenty of organization charts within Unilever, in practice it was the web of relationships and personal networks which kept Unilever functioning. There was much to be said for the flexibility which resulted from such informal arrangements rather than the strict organizational rules characteristic of US corporations. However, it was not always a recipe for decisive action, nor for knowledge to flow easily within the organization. Unilever consisted of numerous subgroups linked by partial communication channels, which functioned in part by forming loose, transient coalitions with one another. The different product categories had little contact with one another, being organized in different operating companies and possessing different subcultures. There was poor communication between functional areas also, including marketing and research.

Co-ordination

The development of 'Co-ordination' was the most important organiza-tional innovation within Unilever in the second half of the twentieth century. It played a key role in the development of international, even global, brands. The story of the introduction of Co-ordination was also illustrative of Unilever's decision-making. There was an early perception of the nature of the changing environment, and the problems it caused for the traditional organization, but it took an inordinate amount of time to effect radical change.

The origins of Co-ordination lay with Unilever's strategy of diversification. In 1952 it was decided to appoint two directors with 'overall responsibility for stimulat-ing the development of operations respectively in the Foods (other than margarine and cooking fats) and Toilet Preparations business'.[78] The rationale was straightfor-ward. Unilever wanted to develop businesses in these areas yet felt its internal knowledge resources were limited. Consequently it made no sense to rely on national managements and a more product-oriented structure had to be con-sidered.[79] On 1 January 1952 two directors were appointed 'World Foods (2) Co-ordinator'—with responsibility for foods other than edible fats, termed Foods (1)—and 'World Toilet Preparations Co-ordinator'. Although the titles were grandiose, the reality was not. The World Co-ordinators had no executive powers, and their very name emphasized that their function was to advise and guide, not to command. The power of national managers and operating companies continued to reign supreme. Yet the World Co-ordinators were important, nonetheless, in stimulat-ing strategic thinking about product strategies. They were largely behind influential 'study groups' set up in 1958 to investigate trends and future strategies in detergents, edible fats, and foods across Europe, and they became catalysts for further organiza-tional change based around a greater emphasis on product rather than geography.

From the late 1950s there were new pressures to move towards a more product-oriented management. The growth of the US detergents firms in European markets alarmed Unilever. An analysis of the comparative performance of Unilever, Colgate, and P & G in 1961 led to the conclusion that 'the Unilever policy of decentralisation of responsibility for taking decisions could lead to delays which were not encoun-tered by the competitors, who took their decisions centrally and imposed them on the operating companies'.[80] There was a perceived need for more professional man-agement. The need for a more professional competence was the central argument employed by Harold Hartog, a strong exponent of Co-ordination, who argued that Unilever was losing ground to P & G because it lacked 'sufficient "professionals" of a high enough calibre'. He blamed this situation on Unilever's regional management system, whereby 'promising young men—often before they have become fully-fledged "professionals" in their particular type of business are taken away from their jobs in order to be "de-specialised" for national management functions in Continental Europe or Overseas'.[81]

The growth of European integration after 1957 added to the momentum to expand Co-ordination. It became possible to rationalize production and research facilities, and to foresee a convergence of consumption patterns between European countries in ways which could not have been envisaged a decade previously.[82] The proponents of a shift to product-oriented management were anxious to seize these opportunities by operating on a more regional basis.[83] The problem was Unilever's legacy of multiple factories and brands scattered in each European country.

During 1959 and 1960 'product committees' were established in Rotterdam for detergents, toilet preparations, foods, and edible fats. The Product Committees undertook advisory roles for the Continental European Group countries. In 1962 Co-ordination was extended with the appointment of World Co-ordinators for Foods 1 (i.e. edible fats, as distinguished from Foods 2, or other foods), Detergents, and Paper, Printing, and Packaging. Each Co-ordinator was to be either a main board director or senior manager, and each had a marketing and a technical member appointed to their staff. At the same time their roles were changed from stimulating new business activities into a wider responsibility 'for policy, including long-term policy, for international lines and for advice on products in general'. Their most important role concerned 'international lines' which were defined as products being or intended 'to be sold in a number of countries and for which performance characteristics, brand name, design of package and theme of advertising conform reasonably closely to an agreed specification'. The World Co-ordinators were given the authority to decide which products were to be included in this category and 'by operating through the Regional Organisations ensure adherence to a common policy for international lines'. Regarding non-international products, their roles remained advisory.[84]

This new structure disturbed the equilibrium within Unilever. The result was a decade of internal debate about the nature of Co-ordination. The problem for the World Co-ordinators was that their power even over 'international products' remained advisory. They could persuade, but they could not direct.[85] The Co-ordinators had virtually no staff of their own, and were left to persuade managers to follow their wishes in systems where operating companies reported to national managers who reported to their regional Contact Directors. Hartog, and others who supported his views, argued that profit responsibility had to be given to the Co-ordinators for strategy and brand development in at least the key markets of Unilever. The Detergents Co-ordinator repeatedly warned of the dangers coming from the 'extremely aggressive' P & G and Colgate, and argued in 1963 for Co-ordinators to be given profit responsibility for Britain, France, Germany, and the United States 'at the earliest practicable time'.[86]

Any extension of executive roles for Co-ordinators met opposition, particularly from the Continental national managers—who had most to lose in terms of their power—

and among senior Dutch managers in general, who often held strong senior positions in national managements in Europe.[87] The London-based Co-ordinators coexisted uneasily with the four Product Committees in the Rotterdam Group Management until 1964, when they were made responsible to the World Co-ordinators.[88] The extension of Co-ordination was widely perceived as an attempt by the British to interfere with the preserves of the Dutch. There was strong opposition from a number of the Dutch directors who stressed the importance of national managements in Unilever's crucial relations with governments and trade unions in Europe, and the continued great differences between countries.[89] This group included members of the founding Dutch families of Unilever, one of whom considered it 'a matter of life and death for the future of Unilever that Co-ordinators should remain purely advisory'.[90]

Progress was stalled, as the Special Committee declined to take action unless there was consensus.[91] Towards the end of 1964 it was agreed that the Detergents Co-ordinator could become a part-time member of both the UK Committee and Rotterdam Group Management, with responsibilities for operational policies of the detergents companies in Britain, France, and Germany.[92] This set a precedent for the further expansion of Co-ordination, though Cole ruled out the exercise of any control over the United States as unacceptable 'for the time being'.[93] Finally, in 1966, the Special Committee felt ready to move forward, and Co-ordinators were given responsibility for turnover and profits for a number of 'executive countries': Britain, the Netherlands, Germany, Belgium, and France. Italy was added in 1968. National managements were to retain representational roles for Unilever in those countries, but 'responsibility for decision on operating matters will lie either with the Chairman (of operating companies) or the Co-ordinator'.[94] Beyond the executive countries, Co-ordinators were to retain their advisory roles.

By the end of 1966 five executive Co-ordinations—no longer with 'World' in their titles—were in place for Foods 1, Foods 2, Detergents, Toilet Preparations, and Paper, Printing, and Packaging. In 1967 a Chemicals Co-ordination was established. However, the fact that only the first Co-ordinator was Rotterdam based caused alarm in Rotterdam.[95] Anglo-Dutch tensions came to a head in a dispute concerning Foods 2 Co-ordination, where the new Co-ordinator—who was British—found himself in charge of an amorphous collection of food products including frozen foods, ice cream, convenience foods, fish, and meat. He argued that four sub-co-ordinators should be appointed for each of the main groups in order to develop more effective strategies. The problem was that all the nominated sub-co-ordinators were British. This caused great annoyance in Rotterdam. The Special Committee obliged the Co-ordinator to move the planned headquarters of Foods 2 Co-ordination to Rotterdam in response to what he termed the 'prejudice' of 'some of our Dutch colleagues that in the development of the Foods business in Europe the Rotterdam hand must be on the wheel'.[96] However, such was the feeling in Rotterdam that further moves were made to limit the executive power of the Co-ordination. The Co-ordinator resigned, a rare instance of a Unilever main board director resigning, going on to have a successful career as a senior executive of Mars.

The dispute over the nature of Foods 2 Co-ordination had serious repercussions. The new Co-ordinator was Dutch—the future NV chairman Gerrit Klijnstra—but in a typical compromise, the British were assuaged by placing the meats business under a separate Foods 3 Co-ordination under a London-based director, while the planned expansion into beer was placed under UAC.[97] It was not long before confusion had developed concerning the borders of the different Food Co-ordinations, and Unilever's hesitant development in foods can in part be related to these organizational problems.[98] More generally, the role of Co-ordination beyond Europe was left unclear. Co-ordinations lacked the resources to become involved in the affairs of the Overseas companies, especially after assuming profit responsibility in Europe. Several attempts by Co-ordinators to become more involved in the United States were rebuffed.[99] When Woodroofe broached the subject of involving Co-ordinators in strategy discussions in the United States in 1971, T. J. Lipton's president replied that 'he would not want anyone who did not know the American market instructing him on how he should conduct the business'.[100]

Even in Europe, the decisions of the mid-1960s on Co-ordination had been left unclear. Ambiguity had been used to prevent open conflict. However, because the Co-ordinators sought to use their powers, ambiguity intensified tensions, for key issues such as the relationship between national managers and the Co-ordinators were not spelled out. To some extent the legitimacy of Unilever's culture was thrown in doubt by the introduction of Co-ordination, 'by its very nature more centralistic than management by regional Contact Directors'.[101] An internal report stressing the adverse effects on national managements advised against further extension of Co-ordinators policies. This in turn provoked a strong reaction from the directors in favour of increased Co-ordination.[102]

It was evident that the best recourse was to call in external consultants to break the deadlock. Hartog had advocated their use as early as 1965.[103] Subsequently Unilever had begun to use the US firm of McKinsey on several projects, and the decision to commission that firm in 1970 to examine Unilever's organization represented a victory for those who favoured an unambiguous move towards product divisions. During the 1960s McKinsey and other US consulting firms began to be widely employed by European firms, and their advice was invariably the adoption of divisionalization, with a preference for product rather than geographical divisions.[104]

The McKinsey report was finally delivered in February 1972. The most important recommendation was to maintain and extend executive Co-ordination to other Western European countries. National managers were to be retained, but with their roles redefined and integrated with the Co-ordinations. A European Liaison

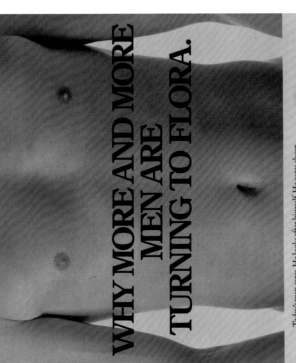

WHY MORE AND MORE MEN ARE TURNING TO FLORA.

Today's man cares. He looks after himself. He cares about what he eats.

Flora is part of healthy eating.

And that's why more and more women are choosing it for their men.

Flora is higher in polyunsaturated fat than any nationally available spread because it's made with pure sunflower oil.

Flora margarine contains no animal fats and men prefer its light, delicate taste.

FLORA. THE MARGARINE FOR MEN.

Schmeckt "prima! Davon möchte ich noch mehr..."

"Rama geb' ich für gern – denn Rama ist ja so gesund!"

RAMA weil sie uns am besten schmeckt

1 Advertisement for Rama, the leading German margarine brand, in 1967. Rama had been launched by Jürgens, Unilever's predecessor, in 1924.

2 Advertisement for Flora margarine in Britain in 1977. The brand was first launched in Britain in 1964, and from the beginning its importance in maintaining good health was stressed. During the mid-1970s its role in preventing heart disease in men was the main theme in advertising.

En çok satılan margarin sizlere teşekkür eder.

Sana, Türkiye'de margarinin adı.

3 A sales van for Stork margarine, pictured 20 miles outside Salisbury, Zimbabwe, in

4 Sana margarine was launched in Turkey in 1953. The photograph shows

5 Unilever acquired the I Can't Believe It's Not Butter brand in 1986 when it acquired J.H. Filbert in the United States. This was a promotion for the brand that year.

6 A street advertisement near the Arc de Triomphe, Paris, for Boursin cheese, acquired by Unilever in 1990.

Brenda's baby-sitting evening.

Brenda Jones, the baby-sitter,
Didn't know quite what had hit her:
Baby Annie screamed blue murder!
(Half the neighbours must have heard her.)

Then worn-out Brenda found they'd left her
A delicious pack of Vesta-
Beef Risotto, all complete,
Rice and vegetables and meat.

"Makes a tasty change." she thought,
"Helps me while I hold the fort."
With Baby Annie tucked in cot,
Brenda sat and ate the lot.

Beef Risotto ready meal
With chopped and shaped beef

This recipe contains dried
ingredients, all keyed on back.

Simple moral: fun to eat. These Vesta dishes are complete.

Sunday Circle Nov 1974.

158

8 Vesta ready made meals were launched nationally in Britain in 1962 by Batchelors, and became a feature of British life. This advertisement dates from 1974. The Vesta brand was sold by Unilever in 2001.

A
Wall's MEAT REPORT

HOW TO BE A MORE PROFITABLE PIEMAN

....A GROCER'S GUIDE TO
CAPITALISING ON A
YEAR-ROUND GROWTH MARKET

7 An advertisement for Wall's meat pies in Britain in 1977.

Committee (ELC), an idea first proposed by Hartog among others in the early 1960s,[105] was to bring together national and product managements, regional directors, and Co-ordinators with the overall aim of ensuring that 'the working relationships between regional and industrial groups are smooth'. McKinsey also recommended the

11 Built in the late 1940s and located on Park Avenue in New York City between 53rd and 54th Streets, Lever House set the standard for glass and steel office towers in the United States in this era, and became one of New York's best known architectural landmarks (*taken in 1972*).

formation of 'national conferences', several of which had already been held, in order to align more closely the interests of national and operating company managements. McKinsey confirmed the consensus within Unilever that Co-ordination should not be extended to the Overseas countries, arguing that the problems Unilever faced in most of these markets, such as government intervention, inflation, and currency instability, meant that geographical rather than product management was more appropriate. The consultants were not even asked to consider its extension to the United States.[106]

Fig. 2.2 shows the basic organizational structure of Unilever in 1974 following the implementation of the McKinsey recommendations. The major changes concerned

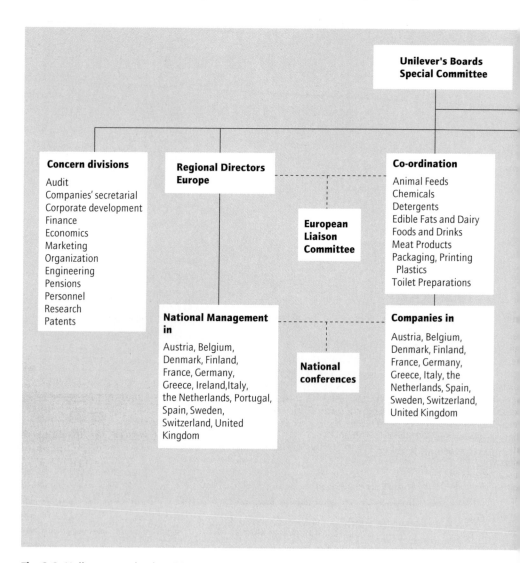

Fig. 2.2 Unilever organization, 1974.

Europe. Britain and the Continent were now integrated, and Co-ordinations had profit responsibility for the operating companies in thirteen European countries. The latter were linked to national managements through the national conferences, while national managements reported to the European regional directors who in turn had to a link to Co-ordination through the ELC.

Co-ordination did not transform Unilever into a centralized company. The belief in the value of local decision-making continued and the operating companies remained key components of Unilever. However, it did put in place a structure which enabled the accumulation of product-based competencies and a more

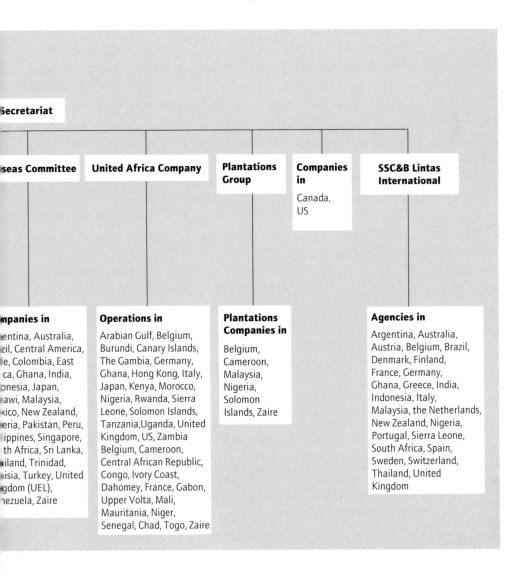

regional approach to be taken to products, brands, and factories. Meanwhile, during the long process of internal debate 'World' Co-ordinators had become European Co-ordinators, confirming the compartmentalization of Unilever's knowledge base. In Europe the creation of new Co-ordinations for every activity, in line with the 'parliamentary system', resulted in a new momentum for diversification.

'Unilever has a Problem'

'Unilever has a problem'. These were the opening words of a memorandum sent to senior management following a conference of directors and senior managers in Rotterdam in November 1970. The conference had heard speeches by Hartog and Woodroofe—who six months previously had replaced Cole as the chairman of Ltd.—and it represented a major new stage in thinking about Unilever's purpose and organization.

The immediate cause of concern was that between 1968 and 1970 Unilever's cash flow position had deteriorated rapidly and unexpectedly. A cash outflow of £20 million in 1968 rose to £56 million in the following year, with higher yet predictions for 1970.[107] Unilever lacked an effective system of financial control or planning. Financial plans were made by the companies or national managements using different assumptions and procedures. This lack of financial control became an issue as the businesses encountered more difficult trading conditions towards the end of the decade. A further complication was that the Finance Director, a close confidant of Cole, had lost the confidence of the Dutch. As a result, by the late 1960s Rotterdam was virtually running its financial affairs without reference to London.[108]

Trading margins were falling. Unilever's calculation of its post-return on capital employed—termed the 'yield' within the company—had slipped from 8.2 per cent to 7.3 per cent between 1968 and 1969, and was estimated to be heading towards 6.8 per cent in 1970. Woodroofe and Hartog saw the main culprit as deteriorating external conditions, especially growing inflation. While both wage bills and oils and fats prices were rising, they argued, many of Unilever's products were subject to price control.[109] There was certainly a problem with raw material prices. During the 1950s and the first part of the 1960s the market prices for edible oils showed an overall downward trend of about 1 per cent per annum, but thereafter the market became more erratic for a number of reasons, including climatic variations and currency movements. In 1969/70 there were sharp increases in key oils, with the price of soya oil increasing 30 per cent, sunflower oil by 75 per cent, and fish oil doubling over the previous year.[110]

At the Rotterdam conference the problem was seen within a Unilever context. 'We are not making enough money to provide for inflation,' Woodroofe told managers, 'to give our shareholders the return to which they are entitled, and to finance the expansion without which the business will stagnate.'[111] Unilever did not as yet compare its overall position to its major competitors, but if it had done the view that it had a 'problem' would have been much reinforced. While Unilever's growth of sales and profits between 1965 and 1973 was remarkably similar to that of its major international competitors, its return on sales and capital employed was consistently lower than that of P & G and Nestlé.

Unilever's 'problem' ran much deeper than the stresses of inflation and raw material price rises. There were wide variations in the performance of different parts of the business. The imbalances were both geographical and product. The United States business was making a declining contribution to profits, reflecting the weakness of Lever Brothers' detergents and edible fats businesses. Other underperformers included a cluster of businesses in Europe, such as animal feeds and chemicals. By the end of the 1960s detergents profits in Europe had also fallen away because of growing competition. UAC's profitability fell sharply as the business was restructured.[112]

The significance of the Rotterdam conference was that Woodroofe and Hartog showed a new readiness to acknowledge Unilever's problems. Profit and cash targets aimed at bringing Unilever's yield to 8.2 per cent by 1973. This resulted in substantial cost-cutting during the following years, but perhaps the most striking change was the Special Committee's declaration that they would be 'much quicker than in the past to disinvest in activities whose return is consistently poor, they will look with considerably greater suspicion on the promise of large returns on new investment from people who have failed to produce such returns on their existing investment, they will be less willing to accept yields no better than the Unilever average'.[113] In practice it was to be well over another decade before Unilever geared itself up to face the full implications of such a strategy, but in retrospect this can be said to mark a new era—one when the importance of profitability and earnings per share began at least to be discussed.

Woodroofe and Hartog worked to exert more central direction over strategy. Woodroofe wanted to make Unilever 'more than the sum of its parts'.[114] They pushed the cause of Co-ordination, and the need for more professional management. This was especially evident in financial matters. In 1969 Cob Stenham, then the finance director of a small diversified industrial company and with a background in merchant banking, was recruited by Cole, primarily to improve Unilever's acquisition skills in the wake of the Allied Breweries episode. Stenham was given a year to prove himself, and if he did so, he was promised a place on the Board as Finance Director. It was agreed that if he was not successful after a year he would leave the company. It was almost unprecedented for Unilever to make such mid-career appointments, especially someone like the Eton- and Cambridge-educated Stenham, whose tastes and interests were noticeably different from the staid style of

Unilever directors of the era. Stenham later became chairman of the Institute of Contemporary Arts in London, an appointment which the then Unilever chairman David Orr was rumoured to have given him permission to take up on the misunderstanding that it was the Institute of Chartered Accountants. In 1970 Stenham was made Finance Director of Ltd at the age of 38, the first 'outsider' ever to be appointed to the Unilever Boards.

The most pressing task was to install an effective management accounting system which laid more emphasis on monitoring performance against forecasts. Unilever previously had almost no idea how to invest cash resources, and there was little financial control. During the early 1970s an effort was made to control cash flows out of the company, while in the longer term a working relationship began to be built between London and Rotterdam in order to provide central direction over Unilever's financial resources. It was to take most of the decade to integrate fully the quite separate accounting and financial functions in the two head offices. Stenham also brought a closer knowledge of the financial community. He began talking to the financial community about the business and future plans, assisted by his 'pupil' Niall FitzGerald, who had joined Unilever Ireland in 1967 and served as Stenham's personal assistant between 1972 and 1974.[115]

The Special Committee also sought to develop longer-term thinking into the business. In London, a new 'Long Term Planning Unit' was formed which began to collate plans of individual parts of the business, beginning with the financial data, and then evolved into a wider strategic role. In Rotterdam, Han Goudswaard was appointed to head a new one-man Corporate Development department in 1970. Goudswaard was asked to identify one or two new areas of business which Unilever might enter to increase its rate of growth of earnings per share. This led to a wider investigation of Unilever's competitive strengths and weaknesses, and the lessons of the past decade.

Perspectives

During the 1960s and early 1970s Unilever had continued its post-war momentum of growth, both through internal innovation and new product development and through acquisitions. The pursuit of both related and unrelated diversification was broadly similar to those followed by other European and US firms. In Unilever's case, there were considerable achievements, especially with regard to building a 'third leg' in foods. Less positively, Unilever had continued to struggle with the competitive onslaught on its European detergents market, the Lever Brothers business in the United States drifted downwards, and the planned expansion of personal products remained unfulfilled. A series of major mergers failed either through bad tactics, as in the case of Smith & Nephew, or because different parts of the organization objected to them, as in the case of L'Oréal and Rowntree. The attempted merger with Allied Breweries displayed a spectacular failure of corporate governance.

Unilever's strategies reflected in part that it was a fragmented organization consisting of a coalition of different groups and interests held together by ambiguity, and by avoiding making priorities. Decentralization was regarded as a major competitive advantage, but it was also a necessity because the alternatives risked serious conflict. Knowledge was compartmentalized within the company. Growth was the best means to hold together this fragmented organization, while central intervention in, or disinvestments from, underperforming parts of the business were not options.

Unilever's organizational legacy of strong national companies with their own numerous brands and products came under pressure from the late 1950s, with the start of European integration and the impact of the US detergents firms on its European markets. Hartog and Woodroofe were organizational modernizers who began to address seriously the managerial consequences of Unilever's growth and diversity. The creation of Co-ordinations was a major step towards enhancing the product-specific knowledge of its managers. After nearly running out of cash, Unilever also took steps to modernize its financial systems and to enhance its financial acumen. There was a new awareness that profitability needed to be considered along with growth, and that the interests of shareholders mattered.

However, the legacy of Unilever's traditions remained. The Unilever 'fleets', now organized into Co-ordinations, continued to head in all sorts of directions with limited signs of purposeful direction. That imprecision of central direction was inevitably associated with a lack of adequately vigorous purpose in the organization itself. Change was under way, but slowly. In spite of what had been achieved, Unilever was not in the best condition to deal with the transformation of the world economy caused by the oil price shock of 1973.

3

New and Old Worlds, 1974–1983

The Decade of Lost Growth

Unilever faced a dramatic deterioration in the world economy after 1973. Inflation soared, and there was a major world recession. At the end of the decade a second oil price shock was followed by another major recession. The era of economic miracles gave way to one of cyclical volatility. In many emerging markets, the political environment for large foreign firms also deteriorated sharply, as governments sought to restrict or control their operations. This harsh external environment was difficult for all firms, but Unilever's wide span of businesses posed an almost unique managerial challenge, especially as its organizational culture constrained the prioritization of resource allocation.

Unilever was to experience a decade of lost growth. Adjusting for inflation, after an initial fall in sales and profits there was a brief recovery, but then a serious decline, which began to bottom out only in the early 1980s. Unilever's sales and profits in 1983 were the same in constant prices as in 1971. Between 1972 and 1980 the market capitalization of Ltd fell in constant prices by over 60 per cent, and that of NV by over 50 per cent. This was a period of general weakness on the European stock markets. In Amsterdam, a prolonged trend decline in share prices (again adjusted for inflation) set in around 1962, and this decline persisted through the 1970s, but NV's share price fell more than the average.[1] In London, Ltd's share price moved with the market until around 1977, but then began to turn down as the market as a whole

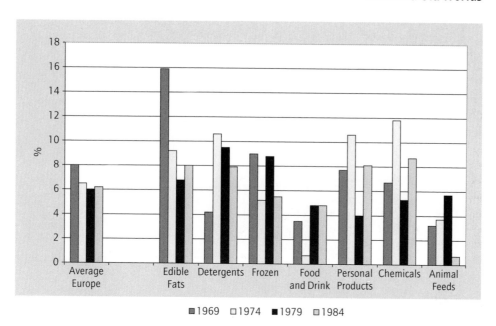

Fig. 3.6 Yields on Unilever's European businesses by product group, 1969–1984 (%).

was labour intensive, and left Unilever trying to dispose of all the parts of animals it did not want for its own products.[9] In Britain, Wall's had a particular problem in that it had built its business around a particular type of pig—the 'heavy hog'—which was believed suitable for producing the leanest bacon at the lowest cost, and set up large factories able to process such pigs. This business became particularly problematic following Britain's accession to the European Union in 1973, when it became possible for Unilever's competitors to benefit from European pig subsidies and import cheaper Danish pigs.[10]

The largest product groups were also in trouble. Unilever's largest European business in terms of sales was Edible Fats, which was also a substantial contributor to profits, but this contribution fell away sharply after 1974. A serious issue was the continued decline of the European yellow fats market. In terms of tonnage, the British and German yellow fats market declined by 27 per cent between 1968 and 1986, and that of the Netherlands by 14 per cent.[11] Yields were further taken down by the unsuccessful ventures in fresh dairy, including yoghurt, and underperforming cheese businesses. The profitability of oil milling also collapsed, in part because of structural shifts in the soya bean market. Unilever had erected new large oil milling facilities in Britain, the Netherlands, and Germany in the early 1970s, but this business only provided yields of 4 per cent over the following decade.[12]

The yields on Unilever's Detergents business also moved downwards from the early 1970s. Between 1968 and 1984 Unilever's share of the European market fell

16 The oil milling factory at Thörl supplied by Elbe boats in 1971. The Seehafen factory was one of the biggest oil milling plants in Europe. It was sold by Unilever in 1986.

from 24 to 22 per cent, while P & G's rose from 15 to 20 per cent.[13] Unilever remained strong in Britain, and a number of other countries including France and Portugal. In Britain, Unilever held market share leadership in all detergent products except washing-up liquid. Unilever's largest fabrics wash brand, Persil, held a 40 per cent share of the British market, and was that country's largest grocery brand. However Unilever was weak in Germany and other large markets such as Italy. In Germany—whose detergent market was twice the size of Britain's—Unilever was unable to recover from the collapse of market share following P & G's entry. Henkel's Persil and P & G's Ariel dominated the premium German fabrics wash market. Unilever's Detergents Co-ordination remained stoically convinced that Henkel and P & G could be overcome in the German market. Omo was launched onto the German market even though it had no clear differentiation from the other brands, and then an attempt was made to build market share by price discounting. An arrangement made with the Aldi cut price supermarket chain to distribute Omo and other products achieved modest share gains at the cost of low margins.[14] From the mid-1970s until the mid-1980s Unilever's German detergents business was loss making.

A third major product area which ran into profitability problems was frozen products. Despite a large amount of investment which this product category received, and the joint venture with Nestlé, yields were not high, and declined seriously from the late 1970s. Between 1979 and 1983 the European frozen products business lost 1 per cent of its market share per annum—in the context of rapidly growing markets—and faced low profit margins. At the heart of the problem was Birds Eye. The British company, once Unilever's champion performer and still accounting for about half of all the quick frozen products sold by Unilever in Europe, was loss making by the end of the decade.[15] Profits from ice cream, especially the take-home sector, also fell away in this decade.

The deterioration in Unilever's performance was the result in part of difficulties facing all business. While the German GDP had grown at almost 6 per cent per annum between 1950 and 1973, it slumped to fewer than 2 per cent between 1973 and 1984. In some European countries, there were high inflation rates—reaching 25 per cent in Britain in 1975—while by the 1980s European unemployment had almost trebled compared to the 1960s.

Unilever's products were for the most part in mature markets. There were always growth opportunities, but Unilever was not especially good at finding them. There were problems both in making appropriate acquisitions, and in turning research into successful products.[16] The category of foods and beverages remained a disparate collection of mainly national-based products and brands. Unilever did begin to develop a European tea business on the basis of the acquisition of Lipton, whose facilities were modernized with heavy investment, but attempts to purchase leading firms in the British and German tea markets came to naught.[17]

In personal care, Unilever launched successful new brands. It built on the earlier success of Rexona to pioneer the concept of perfumed deodorants, launching Impulse, a women's perfume deodorant. Timotei, launched as a shampoo in 1976, secured 5 per cent of the European shampoo market by 1984, by which time the brand represented over one-fifth of Unilever's total worldwide shampoo sales. During the early 1980s the Axe body spray for men was launched. In toothpaste, Close-Up was transferred from the United States, and the new brand Mentadent launched. Yet Unilever's market share in the European dental market fell from 23 to 16 per cent in the ten years after 1971. Growth in the mass skin care and cosmetics markets remained elusive. Greenfield entry was hard because of the strong franchises held by well-established, reliable, and trusted brands, while there were few acquisition opportunities. Unilever did acquire the medium-sized Swedish-based cosmetics house Pierre Robert in 1976, which offered a strengthening of its prestige business, but it proved difficult to use this as a basis for a much larger cosmetics business.[18] Overall, Unilever's sales of personal products fell—in constant money—by one-third between 1974 and 1981.

Unilever was adversely affected, along with all manufacturers, by the growing power of European retailers. From the 1960s retailing—and food retailing in particular—was transformed with the growth of large super- and hypermarkets. From a position when food retailing was conducted primarily through small retail outlets, often still with counter service rather than self-service, and daily shopping trips were predominant, food retailing became focused on large-scale, off-centre, self-service-based food superstores operated by large-scale firms. By the beginning of the 1980s the top five supermarkets' share of their national market's grocery trade had reached over 50 per cent in France, 46 per cent in Britain, and the Netherlands, and 36 per cent in Germany.[19]

The growth of large retailers shifted the balance of power between them and manufacturers in the supply chain. While in the 1950s and 1960s TV advertising in particular had given branded manufacturers such as Unilever great bargaining power with retailers, the growth of the retailers and their own use of advertising to build customer loyalty reversed this relationship. By virtue of their closeness to the consumer, food retailers were able to adapt to their changing tastes and desires and develop their own knowledge, securing the edge in the marketing channel. Manufacturers needed to offer low-price products in order to get the shelf space needed, and discount stores such as Aldi and Kwik Save confronted Unilever and other manufacturers with relentless demands for lower prices and more advertising support. A handful of buyers for the large retailers decided whether or not manufacturers' products were stocked. The difficulties of manufacturers were intensified by the growth of the own brands or private labels offered by European retailers, which had a serious impact on Unilever's market share in some product categories including margarine, take-home ice cream, and frozen vegetables.[20]

A third general problem was that Europe did not possess the flexible labour markets seen in the United States which permitted rationalization in response to changed competitive conditions. There were social, legal, and political constraints in almost all continental European countries hindering extensive redundancies. This ruled out large-scale redundancies even in businesses, such as meat slaughtering in the Netherlands, which were seriously loss making. In Britain there was more of a 'free market' tradition, but that country experienced severe labour disputes throughout the 1970s, and between 1974 and 1979 had a Labour government which was distinctively sympathetic to trade unions. In continental Europe, closing factories and discharging workers was painful, expensive, and opposed by governments.

Unilever's attempts at European rationalization were deeply constrained by such social and political considerations. The Special Committee was aware that many businesses were not profitable, and agonized over what to do about it, but felt its options were limited by circumstances. The closing down of unprofitable businesses, such as the oil mills, was effectively ruled out because of the social consequences.[21] The process of extracting the company from unprofitable businesses needed to be carried out almost by stealth. By the mid-1970s, while the Nordsee's

17 An advertisement for *Rexona* toilet soap in Margriet, a women's magazine in the Netherlands, in 1965.

restaurants and shops in Germany were quite profitable, the company's large trawler business was barely profitable at all, despite accounting for one-half of the entire capital employed by Nordsee. The problem lay with falling international fish prices and an enormous web of quotas and regulations.[22] The trawler business helped lower Nordsee's overall yield to less than 2 per cent by 1980. By 1976 Unilever was convinced that it should get out of trawling, and that it made more sense to buy fish on the open market. However, it was considered impractical to divest as 'the German government would probably regard the industry as essential for providing

18 Nordsee's fishing trawler Bremerhaven in 1974.

employment'. Instead, the business had to be run down by stealth, by not replacing existing ships. By 1981 Nordsee's ships were down to eleven from forty in 1976.

Unilever had its own specific problems. It often paid above average wages, and provided staff with many benefits. Past vertical integration strategies had resulted in high-cost structures, such as elaborate distribution systems employed in frozen products. In Britain, Birds Eye was burdened by owning a large distribution system preoccupied with supplying products to small retailers at a time when large supermarkets were changing the face of retailing, and investing in their own distribution systems, undermining the original vertical integration strategy.[23] Unilever's costs were too high because it had too many factories and far too little rationalization. Lux and Rexona toilet soap was produced in eleven factories in Europe in the mid-1970s, which differed widely in size and complexity. Over half the annual soap production

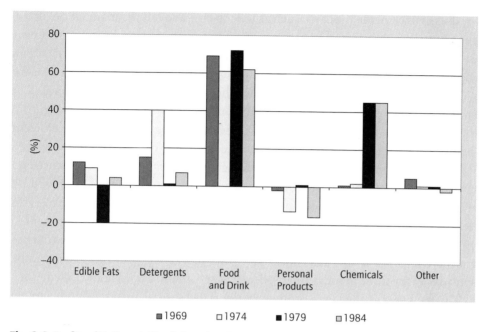

Fig. 3.9 Profits of Unilever's North American businesses by product group, 1969–1984 (%).

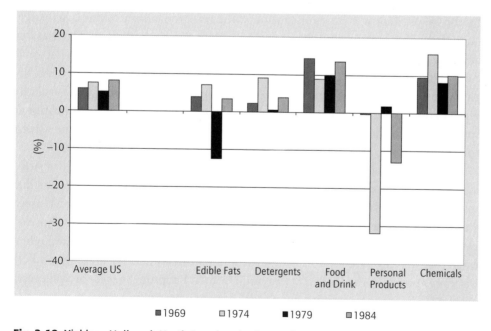

Fig. 3.10 Yields on Unilever's North American businesses by product group, 1969–1984 (%).

products which made money—such as toilet bars—and left the main fabrics detergents business dominated by P & G. The edible fats business was worse. Lever Brothers had bought a Chicago margarine manufacturer in the 1940s, and, after a rocky start, a new Imperial brand introduced in the mid-1950s became for a time the second largest brand in the United States. Thereafter the situation deteriorated. A core problem was poor quality and an uncompetitive cost structure arising from high production, plant overhead, and plant warehousing costs at a very inefficient factory at Hammond, Indiana.[38] Personal care sales were confined to toothpaste. As P & G's Crest dominated the 'therapeutic' sector of the market, Lever focused on cosmetic products, and in 1970 launched a new gel called Close-Up—based on research in the United States—positioned on a breath-freshness platform. This helped to raise Lever's share of the US toothpaste market to almost 24 per cent in 1977, which put it alongside Colgate in second place in the market, but this did not translate into profits because advertising and marketing promotions had to be spread over the three brands of Pepsodent, Close-Up, and a third brand called Aim.

The weakness of the Lever Brothers business had several causes. After the immediate post-war loss of momentum, the management of Lever Brothers lacked the resources, confidence, and capability to invest on a sufficient scale in new products to reverse its position. Lever became trapped in a cycle of trying to sustain income by cutting expenditure on both brand support and manufacturing plant. A lack of strong brands left Lever with high marketing costs, while cost-cutting at factories and the lack of sufficient funds for depreciation gave it higher manufacturing costs. By the 1970s there was little innovation at the research laboratory at Edgewater, New Jersey.[39] A lack of confidence and resources diminished interest in making acquisitions, for which there were a number of opportunities, especially in personal care, as the founders of some of the pioneering American specialist cosmetics companies retired. As Lever's performance deteriorated, so it was harder and harder to recruit good-quality managers in the United States. Lever's unitary organizational structure meant that senior managers were responsible for a span of products from soap to margarine, but full divisionalization was not implemented until 1980.[40]

There was, as the profits and yields figures for Food and Drink suggested, a striking contrast between T. J. Lipton and Lever Brothers. The former was a smaller, but much more successful company, whose businesses were well managed in a closely knit fashion. By the late 1970s T. J. Lipton, whose sales were 15 per cent of those of Lever in 1945, had sales approaching 75 per cent of Lever. Its profits were higher each year. By the late 1970s Lever Brothers had become loss making, and all Unilever's profits in the United States came from T. J. Lipton. Success bred success, enabling T. J. Lipton to recruit a good cadre of managers.

Tea accounted for four-fifths of T. J. Lipton's profitability between the 1960s and the 1980s. T. J. Lipton was the only national marketer of both bagged and instant tea, and held the leading market share in the southern states where most iced tea was consumed. The Lipton tea brand was a high-quality brand franchise on which high profit margins could be earned. The brand was exploited by line and brand extensions supported by extensive advertising and technical innovation. Building on Sir Thomas Lipton's early involvement in yacht racing, Lipton tea commercials in the 1970s used sports personalities to enhance the image of tea. Lipton also supplied tea to the Olympic Games, and to tennis and golf tournaments, and towards the end of the 1970s to the North American Soccer League. The smaller successful businesses were in soup—T. J. Lipton held over 90 per cent of the US instant soup market in the mid-1970s—and salad dressings, based on the Wish-Bone brand acquired in 1957.

Lipton's long-term strategy to diversify further was much less successful. By the 1970s other foodstuffs amounted to a third of total sales, but collectively made a negative profit contribution. A series of attempts to introduce new products flopped with substantial losses. Lipton pursued a persistently unsuccessful strategy of buying small regional companies in many products, including noodles, cat foods, spaghetti, and snacks, which it hoped could be expanded to sell in the national market, but then failed to expand the brand beyond its regional area. The most serious failure was in ice cream. The United States was the world's largest ice cream market, with per capita consumption four times the European average, but the Good Humor brand, acquired in 1961, withered under Lipton's ownership. Good Humor became loss making in 1968, and then lost money every year until 1984.

Unilever, then, found itself with a profitable tea company, but one with limited capabilities or desire to expand further into the giant US foods markets. It was evident that T. J. Lipton's management did not want to make big acquisitions or major investments in product areas such as frozen foods. Incentives were seriously misaligned with those of their European parent. A particular problem was the shadow stock option scheme provided to Lipton's senior management, which was driven by the percentage increase in derived net profit, calculated without regard for inflation. This provided a positive disincentive to undertake bold ventures beyond tea and soup.[41]

Unilever continued to maintain a hands-off relationship with its US affiliates despite the problems of performance. The Special Committee confined itself to expressions of alarm at falling profits at Lever, and discomfort at cuts in spending on plant and brand support.[42] Visits by Unilever executives to the United States were closely regulated, and even rationed on the American side. Many Unilever executives later remembered that senior European managers who did manage to visit the United States would be left sitting in waiting rooms with their US counterparts 'too busy' to see them.[43] There was a minimal interchange of personnel across the Atlantic, and almost no transfer of knowledge about the manufacture and sale of margarine, detergents, and ice cream from Europe to the United States.

20 *Make a Better Burger* was launched by T. J. Lipton in 1975. It contained a soya protein additive which was said to enhance the flavour of the minced beef, but the product did not succeed in the marketplace.

It was as if Unilever had replicated within its own boundaries the Iron Curtain which then divided Europe. The lack of knowledge-sharing across the Atlantic within Unilever can be regarded as a major constraint on its overall competitive advantage.[44]

There were, however, some knowledge flows outwards from the United States to other parts of the corporate network. Lever's toothpaste brands were transferred to Europe, while T. J. Lipton helped Unilever to develop its tea and soup businesses elsewhere. The more co-operative attitude of Lipton probably reflected its greater self-confidence compared to Lever, as it was acknowledged as the best company in the Co-ordination and the primary source of expertise on tea.[45]

By the 1970s there was mounting resentment within Unilever about the US situation. Margarine managers were appalled by what they saw in the United States. The Detergents Co-ordination complained that Lever's weakness handicapped Unilever in fighting P & G in Europe.[46] Personal Product Co-ordinators knew that an acquisition in the flourishing US industry offered one of the best opportunities to build a worldwide business in that category. From the early 1970s the Corporate Development directors began to stress the need for Unilever to reverse its decline in the United States. Given that the autonomy of Lever and Lipton appeared sacrosanct, attention became focused on making a large acquisition which could be used to enhance Unilever's position.[47] However the fact that acquisitions had to be pursued through the existing US affiliates, whose managements were more or less uninterested, tended to slow down the whole process. The momentum for change increased as Lever's performance deteriorated. A special Board meeting devoted to corporate strategy in January 1976 saw a break with the tradition of Unilever directors not speaking on matters other than their own responsibilities, with a number expressing their concerns on the situation at Lever Brothers.[48]

Although the Special Committee remained reluctant to take radical steps without 'the whole hearted co-operation of top Americans',[49] a two-pronged strategy was implemented during 1976. First, Lever Brothers was offered substantial investment and assistance, but the existing management still found it hard to suggest realistic plans to turn the business around.[50] Secondly, there was a more determined search for an acquisition, leading to the purchase of the speciality chemicals company National Starch for $487 million in 1978. This acquisition was the largest yet made by a foreign company in the United States. It proved a defining moment in Unilever's history, for although National Starch only added about 2 per cent to corporate sales, Unilever showed itself not only able successfully to acquire a large firm, but to acquire one in the United States.[51]

At least two aspects of the acquisition were curious. It was the culmination of a long search across a spectrum of industries, highlighting the fact that Unilever's strategy at this time was geographical rather than product based. The acquisition of a personal products or foods company, many of which were looked at, might have seemed a more logical step. There was no synergy with Unilever's current small chemicals business in Europe, the existence of which had no bearing on the acquisition.[52] Chemicals Co-ordination was only marginally involved in the acquisition. It had tried for years to secure another US company, Emery—a large producer of fatty acid—with which it had a joint venture in Europe, and from which Lever Bros. purchased all its supplies for the production of synthetic detergents.[53] It was the willingness of the family owner of National Starch to make an agreed deal, provided the price was right and that a tax-free arrangement could be made for large stockholders, and the lack of any anti-trust complications, which finally led to the acquisition of that firm instead.[54]

Secondly, as part of the acquisition agreement Unilever promised that for ten years National Starch would keep its own report and accounts, no one from Unilever would sit on its board, and that Unilever and National Starch research would be kept separate, or rather that for ten years National Starch could have access to Unilever research but not vice versa. The purchase would never have been consummated without such guarantee. Moreover 'Chinese walls' were necessary because P & G and other competitors to Unilever were major clients of National Starch. By granting autonomy, Unilever also hoped to retain the senior and well-respected executives at National Starch. If many of them had left the company, the consequences would have been serious, given that Unilever lacked managerial expertise in both chemicals and operating in the United States. Nevertheless, the almost total independence guaranteed to National Starch's management was not helpful to the Unilever directors seeking a more active role in the United States.

The National Starch acquisition did provide a momentum to the effort to address the problems of the American business. In 1977 Unilever decided to set up a holding company—UNUS—which would hold the shares of Lever and Lipton. The initial purpose was to facilitate an acquisition by enabling cheaper borrowing on the basis of a stronger balance sheet, and to achieve greater tax efficiency by offsetting Lever losses against Lipton profits.[55] A small head office was established in New York. Initially Stenham was asked to combine the posts of Finance Director and UNUS chairman, but after the regular commuting across the Atlantic resulted in his hospitalization with serious medical problems, he was replaced by Michael Angus. Angus, who since visits to the United States in the late 1960s as a member of Personal Products Co-ordination had wanted to be involved in rebuilding and expanding Unilever's American business,[56] was appointed chairman of UNUS and, at the beginning of 1980, became chairman of Lever also. The retirement of Lever's existing chief executive was a radical step, but one which the newly appointed 'third man' on the Special Committee, Durham, insisted was taken.[57] This was one of the first cases when a large European company intervened so directly in its US business. It was only in the mid-1980s that Shell and BP moved decisively in the same direction. Philips, which made its first large US acquisition when it purchased Signetics in 1975, took a further fifteen years to begin to exercise effective managerial control.

Angus stayed in the United States until 1984. His appointment marked the real turning point in the relationship between Unilever in Europe and its US affiliates. He faced a formidable task given Lever's lack of strong brands, run-down plant, and weak management. However, Angus had the full confidence of the Special Committee, which was now prepared to allocate the resources necessary to rebuild the Lever business. A large programme of capital investment was launched, along with the renewal of the research facilities, financed both by reinvestment and by borrowing from Unilever. Lever's expenditure on new product development rose from $9.6 million in 1980 to $42 million in 1982, most of which was spent on household products. Unilever received no dividends from its US business at all between 1978 and 1984, as the earnings of Lipton and National Starch were retained to meet the investment requirements of Lever, as well as the cost of servicing over $300 million of borrowing required to finance the National Starch acquisition.[58]

An urgent priority was to strengthen the management, and there was some head-hunting for outsiders as well as transfers from Europe. Angus took a nuanced approach to the US companies, involving a delicate balancing act of seeking to overcome the excesses of American parochialism, while going to considerable lengths to retain senior managers, and treading softly with the sensitivities of Americans.[59] The reorganization of Lever's management was by necessity a disrupting exercise. Angus made a great effort to visit plants and communicate directly with employees, sometimes standing on soap boxes to address workers, and frequently meeting with the unions to keep them informed.

The most remarkable turnaround was in margarine. In 1980 McKinsey had recommended that Lever Brothers should withdraw altogether from the product.[60] This suggestion was successfully blocked by the Edible Fats Co-ordinator at the time, Floris Maljers, who memorably observed that if Unilever 'can't sell margarine in the United States, we shouldn't be in margarine at all'.[61] Instead the decision was taken to close the Hammond, Indiana, plant, and to have Lever's margarines largely made by co-packers, the Shedd division of Beatrice Foods, which was the largest US manufacturer of margarine and concentrated on private label manufacture.[62] Over the following two years Lever Brothers was able to purchase and distribute margarine from co-packers for less than it would have cost to manufacture and distribute it itself, even after paying the co-packer a profit. Product quality and freshness improved also. However, a change of plan was dictated by unwanted leakage of Unilever's margarine know-how combined with Shedd's own entry into branded products. In 1983 Shedd launched its own Country Crock brand, a low-fat spread which took a 6 per cent market share within nine months.[63] Unilever's thoughts turned to an acquisition, and in 1984 Shedd was acquired from its parent for $89.5 million.[64] The acquisition transformed Unilever from a high-cost and inefficient manufacturer to market leader and lowest-cost margarine manufacturer in the United States.

The strength of P & G in its home market made a turnaround of the US detergents business much tougher. There was heavy investment in making manufacturing facilities more efficient. A new toilet soap facility was opened at Hammond, Indiana, in 1980, which led to greatly improved productivity, comparable to Unilever's European plants.[65] Unilever initially transferred European brands such as Shield toilet soap (launched 1980) and Sunlight dish detergent (launched 1981), which Lever sought to adapt to US market conditions. Surf washing powder, launched in 1984, was also based on research in Europe on products that deodorized and perfumed at the same time, but the product was actively developed in the United States, and the formulation, presentation, and advertising was entirely American. The high cost of product launches and brand expenditure meant that Lever's detergents business in the United States became seriously loss making during the early 1980s. Unilever was able in these years to raise its market share in some products such as toilet soaps and fabric conditioners, but not in the largest sector, laundry, where P & G remained pre-eminent.[66]

Lever's small personal care business also struggled. The total market share of toothpaste brands collapsed from 22 per cent in 1980 to 11 per cent in 1985.[67] This was primarily the result of diverting funds from the toothpaste business—marketing appropriations for toothpaste were halved between 1982 and 1985—in an attempt to expand other products. Timotei shampoo was transferred from Europe in 1982, but with no success. Two years later an American shampoo—Dimension—was launched as a pioneering combined shampoo and conditioner, but it also was rapidly overtaken by P & G using its recently acquired Vidal Sassoon brand. Unilever remained becalmed in the world's largest personal care market.

By 1984 the share of the United States in Unilever's total sales and profits was approaching its level in 1945. While yields were not high, they were improving in key categories such as detergents and edibles. Moreover the acquisition of National Starch, and the subsequent decision to take control of the Lever business, signalled a new way of doing business, and a new willingness to prioritize the use of resources. It was the first stage of the renewal of Unilever.

UAC and Overseas

During the 1970s the UAC and Overseas markets became extraordinarily profitable compared to Europe and North America. Unilever, Van den Hoven told the Board in October 1976, was 'living on OSC and UAC'.[68] Unilever, therefore, presented an unusual case of a large Western consumer goods manufacturer making a substantial proportion of its profits from developing countries. Indeed, it was an even rarer instance of a Western corporation which continued a large and profitable business in Africa, many of whose countries were already experiencing political and economic instability by the 1970s. Nigeria at times accounted for nearly three-fifths of Unilever's total sales outside the United States and Europe.

By the mid-1970s the most profitable part of Unilever was the UAC. During 1975, when Europe went into loss, UAC earned a yield of over 19 per cent and transferred over £40 million to the parent companies in remittances. Despite the post-war 'reinvention' of itself from commodity trader to mini-industrial and trading conglomerate, such profits would have seemed unlikely a few years previously, when it was obliged by governments to sell substantial shares of the equity of its African affiliates to local interests. However, the situation was changed out of recognition by the world oil crisis. While the consequences of the rise of oil prices for Unilever in Europe were extremely negative, Nigeria and the Gulf states were oil-producing countries which suddenly experienced huge flows of income. UAC boomed alongside its host economies.

There was an understandable mesmerization by UAC's large profits. As a result, UAC was allowed to pursue its 'redeployment' into Europe. This strategy was pursued by many European trading companies active in former African and Asian colonies,[69] but in UAC's case the logic was curious. It was not an independent company overexposed to high-risk regions, but a wholly owned affiliate of Unilever, which already possessed worldwide interests. However, at that time UAC's profitability carried great weight. The confidence felt in its ability to undertake aggressive product and geographical diversification was signalled by the change of name to UAC International in 1973. It was only in the early 1980s that the deteriorating position of West Africa, and Nigeria in particular, drove home the fragility of UAC's position, as profits and yields plummeted.[70]

While the UAC's business was far removed from consumer packaged goods, and its existence within Unilever provided the strongest support for those who thought the company had become a 'conglomerate', the Overseas business was broadly the same as that conducted in Europe and the United States, except that it was very profitable. Figs. 3.11–3.14 describe the nature of Unilever's Overseas business between 1969 and 1984. The Overseas markets had yields far higher than the corporate average, and provided a significant share of total Unilever sales. They included a spectacular spectrum of size, income levels, political regime, and culture, but there were a number of common characteristics to Unilever's position. Unilever's business was dominated by soap and detergents. Yields were high, and rose during the 1970s. In many countries the Unilever business had begun as a detergents one, and the emphasis on detergents was reinforced because the Overseas Committee, like

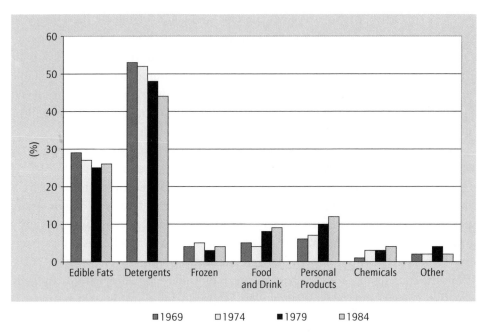

Fig. 3.11 Sales of Unilever's Overseas businesses by product group, 1969–1984 (%).

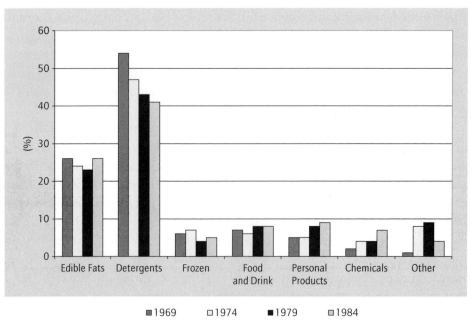

Fig. 3.12 Capital employed in Unilever's Overseas businesses by product group, 1969–1984 (%).

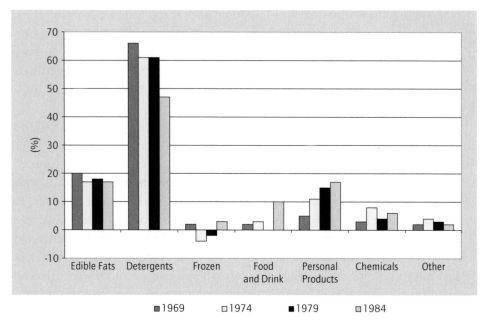

Fig. 3.13 Profits of Unilever's Overseas businesses by product group, 1969–1984 (%).

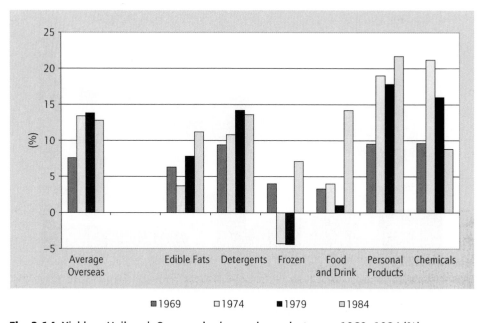

Fig. 3.14 Yields on Unilever's Overseas businesses by product group, 1969–1984 (%).

the Detergents Co-ordination, was London based. Many Overseas managers had their early careers in detergents.[71] Unilever had often been a first mover in modern manufacturing, and international competitors were only present in a few countries. Unilever calculated that it accounted for around 26 per cent of total detergent sales in the 'Overseas world' in 1971. The P & G and Colgate shares were estimated at 5 per cent and 9 per cent respectively.[72]

There was a profitable business also in shampoos, toothpaste, and deodorants, but the failure to grow the personal products business as a whole meant that Unilever lacked the product range to expand its business beyond a certain size. In contrast, Unilever's foods business was not a great success. Yields on edibles were modest, while frozen products were loss making. Unilever products such as margarine, black tea, ice cream, and frozen foods were not readily transferable to many Overseas countries. The consumption of margarine was largely confined to bread-eating Western countries such as Australia, where the dairy lobby was able to put limitations on its sales, while Unilever's businesses in other edible oils in developing countries were mass consumption items often subject to price controls. Low per capita income countries were not good markets for processed foods or instant soups, or expensive ice creams.[73]

The largest Overseas foods market was in Australia. During the early 1950s Unilever diversified into Lipton's tea and soup and Birds Eye frozen foods in Australia, though with little success, and both businesses were sold. However, from

21 An ice cream van owned by Streets in Australia in 1960, the year of acquisition by Unilever.

1959 a number of ice cream companies were acquired, including Streets of Sydney, and a number of other foods interests developed in order to diversify beyond detergents.[74] In the mid-1970s Australia alone accounted for 60 per cent of sales of sundry foods in the Overseas countries. It was the only sizeable business, and the one best suited for sales of European foods products.[75]

Unilever's Overseas business had to navigate through a welter of challenges, extending from hyperinflation to insistence on local equity participation. Exchange controls hindered remittances, and price controls turned best-selling brands into loss makers. Unilever pursued a policy of dogged persistence in the face of such difficulties, taking advantage of its knowledge of markets and systems, and seldom withdrawing from countries. Government intervention in markets was not always bad for Unilever either, for it benefited from high tariff walls which protected domestic manufacturing.

The Overseas Committee's remit included Japan, which became the world's second largest economy during the 1970s, but success in that market proved elusive. Lever Brothers had been an early multinational investor in Japan, opening a soap factory near Kobe in 1913, but heavy losses led to its being sold at the end of the 1920s.[76] Unilever sent a manager to occupied Japan as early as 1947 to investigate the prospects of reopening.[77] However, it took nearly twenty more years of negotiations with prospective partners and the Japanese government—which sought to persuade all foreign firms either to license their technology to local firms, or else to enter joint ventures with them—before Unilever started a joint venture with Hohnen Oil, the owner of the largest milling and refining facilities in Japan. In 1965 a new factory was opened at Shimizu, located between Tokyo and Nagoya, and during the following year production of lard and Rama margarine started.

Unilever's Japanese business became persistently loss making over the next two decades. The joint venture was hedged in by government restrictions, which included a prohibition of promotions and the recruitment of staff from competitors. Government restrictions and cross-shareholdings ruled out acquisitions. Hohnen Oil was an oil miller with no experience of marketing, while Unilever knew nothing of the Japanese market. Unilever saw the joint venture as a vehicle to enter the Japanese market, initially in margarine, while Hohnen Oil wanted to find a partner to supply it with downstream consumer products into which to feed the vegetable oils refined in its refinery. Hohnen Oil also transferred into the affiliate a traditional personnel system, based on the seniority wage and promotion systems. As losses mounted, Unilever slowly increased its shareholding, which reached 80 per cent in 1977, when the name was changed to Nippon Lever.

It proved hard to build sustained volume in any product category. Hohnen-Lever had launched the first all-vegetable margarine in Japan—the product had previously been made from fish oils and had a poor quality image. Rama held a market share of

20 per cent by 1970, but within three years it had slumped to as low as 8 per cent as Japanese competitors overcame Unilever's initial technical lead and introduced new brands. Unilever entered a joint venture with two Japanese trading companies to sell Lipton Tea, which was profitable, but most Japanese drank green tea. Black tea was an upmarket product with high margins, but a low share of the beverage market.[78] There was no enthusiasm to achieve the scale of investment necessary to challenge the position of incumbent companies Lion and Kao in the heavy-duty detergents market.

Unilever progressed furthest in personal care. Although there were a number of large Japanese firms, including Shiseido and Kao, in the industry, the market for such products was large and growing, if also highly competitive and subject to constantly changing fashions. Hohnen-Lever began selling Lux toilet soap in 1972, which was successful, but attempts to expand the business further ran into difficulties through an insufficient appreciation that most toilet soaps were bought as gifts, requiring heavy investment in brand image and quality.[79] In 1977 Sunsilk shampoo was launched in Japan—manufactured by a third party—and was a quick success, becoming Unilever's first really successful brand in Japan.[80] However an attempt to widen the use of the Sunsilk brand into hairdressing salons with a set of hair treatment products failed, providing Kao with the opportunity to enter the market with a competing brand.[81]

Most foreign companies found the Japanese market challenging in the post-war decades, and few built large and profitable businesses.[82] An exception was Nestlé, in continuous operation since 1933, which built a successful business largely based on Nescafé. However, P & G made losses of over $250 million in the decade after its entry into Japan in 1972, as both its main brands—Cheer detergent and Pampers nappies—floundered in the face of tough competition and marketing problems. The company's fortunes only improved from the early 1980s after it dispatched some of its best young managers to the country, and raised the quality of its products and marketing to meet the exacting requirements of Japanese consumers.[83] All foreign companies, including Unilever, found it hard to recruit good-quality local managers, and this lack of depth in local management led to misjudgements of the market.

In Unilever's case, there was no willingness to spend the large sums of money necessary to break into the Japanese market. In 1974 an opportunity to buy a majority of the equity of a well-known Japanese ice cream manufacturer for £80 million was turned down by the Special Committee in the context of Unilever's overall financial problems.[84] This was in accordance with the conservative approach at the time to both its balance sheet and acquisitions,[85] but also reflected the Euro-centric outlook of executives. Unilever felt comfortable with former colonies in Asia, such as Indonesia and India, but Japan appeared as an unforgivingly alien culture. It was only from 1978 that Japan rose in corporate priorities, in part because of the international expansion of Japanese firms.[86] Overall, Unilever's business remained too small compared to its overheads, yet expansion through a major acquisition remained an unlikely proposition.[87]

co-packing contracts. Almost against their better judgement, the Special Com-mittee approved the purchase of the company.[52] The acquisition was to prove a turn-ing point. The experience, production facilities, and base business gained through the acquisition of Gold Bond provided a foundation for the subsequent acquisitions which led to Unilever's emergence as one of the giants of the US ice cream business.

Towards the end of the 1980s Unilever's senior management began to be con-cerned about T. J. Lipton's overall performance. It had long been accepted wisdom that Lipton was a success.[53] Yet a closer examination showed a business with high margins, but little real growth. The US market for instant tea entered a trend decline from the mid-1980s of around 6 per cent per annum in the face of competition from carbonated soft drinks, bottled waters, and fruit-based drinks, while new product development remained insignificant. There was also a long-standing idiosyncratic feature that most profits were made in December of each year.[54] This was caused by 'trade loading', or the selling of large quantities of products to distributors towards the end of the year, and then in some cases buying them back at the beginning of the year. Unilever understood this to be part of normal trade practices in the United States, but it began to be realized that declining sales were being hidden by excessive trade loads, a practice which seemed to be getting out of control from around 1984.[55] The United States continued to hold surprises for Unilever.

The mid-1980s saw a new determination to build Unilever's business in Japan. In 1984 a 'Strategy for Japan' proposed by Nippon Lever set more ambitious growth targets for all product areas, and aimed to make the business marginally profitable by 1987. Unilever placed some hope on 'a "quantum leap" acquisition converting us into a first rank business',[56] though the availability and cost of acquiring a Japanese firm made this difficult. Nippon Lever remained burdened both by high fixed costs caused by an excessively large infrastructure built against the original hope that the margarine business would be much larger, and by a continuing lack of depth in local management. Unilever had around forty expatriate managers working in its Japanese business at this time.[57] Growth, if not profits, was achieved. Between 1983 and 1989 Nippon Lever achieved volume growth of 23 per cent per annum. Timotei emerged as the market leader in shampoos in 1987. Its 'natural' image and white bottle appealed to young Japanese female consumers, and for a time changed the traditional preference for evening bathing, becoming known as the 'morning sham-poo'.[58] The acquisition of Chesebrough-Pond's gave Unilever a personal products factory at Sagamihara, and two successful brands, Pond's Cream and Vaseline.

Unilever's strategy aimed at obtaining critical mass in personal products, deter-gents, and foods. Frozen fish and potato products were launched. In 1989 the Special Committee agreed to a major detergents—Surf—launch, though not without reser-vations because of the opportunity cost for investment elsewhere and for overall profitability.[59] By 1990 this growth strategy had once more run into problems. The

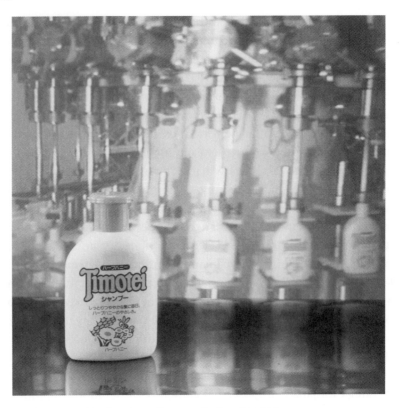

27 Production line for *Timotei* in Japan in the mid-1980s.

attempts to build frozen foods had to be abandoned in the face of difficulties in accessing distribution channels, as competitors owned freezers, as well as by the limited demand for 'Western' food products such as fish fingers and potatoes. Timotei's market share fell in a few months from nearly 13 per cent to around 4 per cent as competing products were launched.[60] Meanwhile the launch of Surf went wrong for several reasons, including the introduction of new automatic dosing machines which reduced the appeal of sachets, the failure to meet production standards of one of the third party factories used to produce sachets, and P & G's relaunch of Ariel with higher performance and a reduced price. At the centre of the problem was technical failure, as the powder in the sachets would not melt. There had been insufficient testing of the product, and a failure in the Port Sunlight research laboratories to appreciate that—in contrast to the United States and Europe—Japanese typically washed their clothes outside in cold rather than hot water.[61] Surf was unable to secure more than 5 per cent of the market, far less than the minimum of 15 per cent or so that had been envisaged, and a large loss followed.

Unilever's experience in the United States and Japan demonstrated the difficulty, even for a powerful consumer goods multinational, of competing against powerful incumbent firms in their home markets. In the pursuit of co-leadership in world detergents with P & G, Unilever underestimated those difficulties. In the United States, Unilever was able to use acquisitions in personal care and other categories to buy market positions, and it developed the skills to absorb the capabilities of acquired companies. In Japan it simply lacked the management resource and competitive strengths to make major inroads on the markets for foods and detergents. The large, if volatile, personal care industry appeared to offer the best prospects to build a profitable business.

Organizational Change and the Single European Market

These were years of further organizational change at Unilever, although the distinctive corporate governance system remained in place. There was no serious discussion of changing the structure of the two parent companies. The cost of two head offices was not especially easy to justify, but there were perceived advantages. The two head offices gave Unilever unique access to two cultures, strengthened the case for both British and Dutch diplomatic support, and meant that Unilever could recruit high-quality staff from two countries who could have expectations of achieving the highest levels within the company working in their own countries. Above all, there was too much sentiment, and too many vested interests, to make radical changes to Unilever's structure without a compelling justification, which was not forthcoming.

The issue of the right balance between centralization and local decision-making was more contentious. The Detergents Co-ordination wanted a more 'centralized' organization within Europe. In 1987 a step was taken to organize innovation more centrally with the formation of the Lever Development Centre. Subsequently the chairmen of the four largest detergent operating companies were brought together in a Lever Europe Executive. In contrast, the Foods Co-ordinations remained less centralized, reflecting their position in an industry in which both customers and competitors remained 'local'. The Special Committee remained committed to the view that Unilever's strength was being close to local markets.

Unilever's organizational structure remained a matrix of responsibilities by Co-ordinations, operating companies, and national management. Co-ordinations had a worldwide strategic responsibility and European profit responsibility, delegated usually to local operating companies. The only exception was Chemicals, where the Co-ordination had worldwide profit responsibility after 1986. The nature of Co-ordinations differed widely (Fig 4.4). Food and Drinks had twenty-nine reporting companies, most of them small. Detergents had fewer, but larger, companies.

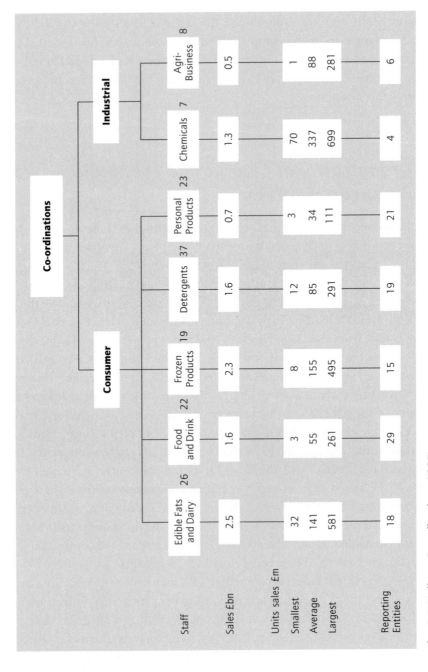

Fig. 4.4 Unilever Co-ordinations, 1987

Chemicals managed four large separate 'multinational' companies, each with worldwide responsibilities with many operating companies, none of which reported to national managements.

The EU's Single Market programme, launched in 1986, raised new doubts about Unilever's decentralized organization. There continued to be considerable differences in the formulation and packaging of the same product made by different Unilever companies in Europe, and there were differences—sometimes a factor of three—between the prices of the same product even in neighbouring countries. There was almost no European-wide buying. Unilever still had over 180 European factories in 1988. The numerous operating companies resulted in a high-cost structure, with so many marketing and buying departments, and they were often too small to pursue new opportunities or markets through large investments or acquisitions. There seemed to be a range of options. Co-ordinations might evolve into European companies, or assume global product mandates. The number of operating companies could be reduced, but the extent of rationalization, and whether it should be Europe-wide, was an open question,

All consumer goods manufacturers had to balance the potential for economies of scale and scope through centralization with the need to be informed and sensitive about local markets. By the late 1970s P & G had a European headquarters that exercised considerable control over national subsidiaries and sought to rationalize manufacturing, centralize research, and co-ordinate marketing on a Europe-wide basis.[62] However, country managers retained profit responsibilities within P & G's European organization and, despite strong central direction, there remained scope for local initiative by country and brand managers.[63] Nestlé had product groups, but territorial management had bottom line profit responsibilities. Considerable emphasis was placed on local decisions, but there was also extensive direction from Nestlé's head office in the 1980s from a 'senate' of product general managers and territorial market heads.[64]

Unilever edged towards changing its commitment to local decision-making with great caution. There was general agreement that Co-ordinations needed to determine their own structures given the variations in the market conditions which they faced, but by 1989 all Co-ordinators were seeking to create structures in Europe where they developed collective responsibility with a top management team involving major company chairmen. Mergers of operating companies were also encouraged.[65]

Foods presented particular organizational challenges. The division of responsibility into Edible Fats, Frozen Products, and Food and Drink Co-ordinations, which was based as much on history and technology as on consumer perceptions, had been under criticism for years for providing handicaps to growth opportunities. In 'health' products, low-calorie spreads were handled by Edible Fats, low-calorie soups were handled by Food and Drink, while low-calorie frozen foods were the responsibility of Frozen Foods.[66] The Foods Co-ordinations were also heavily European in their focus, yet Unilever had only a small foods business in the United States and a badly underdeveloped one in the Overseas world.

During 1988 it was agreed to form a new Foods Executive based in Rotterdam. Its purpose, harking back to the early 1950s, was to 'oversee the implementation of Unilever's world food strategy'.[67] The Foods Executive came into operation in 1990, replacing the three Co-ordinations with a new product and regional matrix structure. Five new product groupings were created: spreads, oils, and dressings; meals and meal components; ice cream and sweet snacks; beverages and savoury snacks; and professional markets. The Executive was composed of a regional director and chairman for the United States, and two Regional Directors for Europe. Each of those directors also represented Overseas regional managements in order to ensure strategies were consistent with Unilever's Global Foods Strategy.[68] As a response to regionalization in Europe and globalization, the creation of the Foods Executive might be best described as a form of halfway house. Further development of regional policies remained constrained by the continuing conviction of the business of the need for local decision-making in foods.

The reorganization of Unilever's detergents business went further. In 1989 Detergents Co-ordinator proposed the creation of Lever Europe. The vulnerability of Unilever's national company-based structure to the threat of competition drove the change.[69] The proposal had been mooted for some time, and arguably was long overdue, but the Detergents Co-ordination had been unable to generate sufficient support for the proposal, where many managers on the foods side of the business warned of the dangers of giving up its local strength and creating an over-complex structure.

Lever Europe was established in 1990. Brussels was chosen as the head office of the new company, which had around 10,000 employees. The chief executive, who was not a member of Detergents Co-ordination, was assisted by six general managers and the heads of Unilever's largest national businesses in France, Germany, Italy, and the UK. The European headquarters was focused on European business strategy, European brand marketing and development, and low-cost supply, while the national operating companies—which became divisions of the new entity—implemented innovation and brand development, managed national brand properties, and interpreted local market data.[70] It was to prove a time-consuming task to build a successful organization out of a loose federation of companies.

In the Overseas markets, Unilever continued to prefer country rather than product management. However, the new management structure put in place in 1987 after the merger of the Overseas Committee and the UAC could only be described as partly regional. An African and Middle East Group linked sub-Saharan Africa—

9 The Viennetta ice cream gateaux was first launched in Britain in 1982. This advertisement for the brand in Greece dates from 1988.

10 Advertisement for Cornetto ice cream in Arabia in the early 1990s. The Cornetto brand had been acquired with the Italian ice cream company Spica in 1962, and launched by Unilever in Belgium, the Netherlands and Germany in the following year.

11 Advertisement for Magnum ice cream in Germany in the early 1990s.

12 An advertisement for Birds Eye Fish Fingers in Britain in 1987. Captain Birds Eye (also known as Captain Iglo, Captain Frudensa, and Captain Findus) was invented by Lintas in 1967 in response to growing competition for Birds Eye fish fingers, which had been launched in Britain twelve years previously.

13 Lipton tea in the United States was traditionally promoted by sports personalities. This advertisement in 1986 features the tennis player Chris Evert-Lloyd.

14 Advertisement for PG Tips in 1989. Brooke Bond had started selling Pre-Gest-Te (PG Tips) in Britain in the 1930s, and chimps were first used on a TV advertisement on Christmas Day 1956. The chimps continued to be used in advertising until 2002.

15 Hindustan Lever started an integrated rural development programme in the backward district of Etah in the state of Uttar Pradesh in North India in 1976. The photograph illustrates work on the project in 1983.

except South Africa—and the Middle East, largely because it was considered that running down the UAC would be such a colossal job that larger responsibilities were not practical. The East Asia and Pacific Group was a regional group, but the Latin America and Central Asia Group, which included South Asia, Latin America, and South Africa, was a mini-Overseas Committee.

Perspectives

In 1984 the Special Committee launched a process of change which led to a deep rethinking of Unilever. Acquisitions, disposals, and restructuring led to a sharp improvement in performance which converged with major international competitors. Unilever finally achieved its long-held ambition to build a broadly based personal products business. By the end of the 1980s Unilever had sales of personal products of £2 billion, making it one of the largest firms in the world industry, with a market share of 10 per cent. Unilever had maintained its impressive record of innovation and marketing in edible fats. It held around one-half of the total world market for margarine and spreads, and was market leader in every country except the United States. The large past investment in ice cream had begun to deliver profits. Worldwide sales of £1.4 billion gave it 14 per cent—the largest single share—of the world 'industrial' ice cream market. A turnover of around £10 billion in foods made Unilever the world's third largest foods company after Nestlé and Philip Morris, though with less than 1 per cent of the world market. Unilever remained dependent for 70 per cent of its foods sales on Europe. In detergents, Unilever's sales of £4 billion made it just smaller than P & G, but with some notable weaknesses. In 1990 it continued to hold a distant second place in the United States, was in third place in Germany, and was heading towards a costly failed launch in Japan.

At the turn of the decade there were renewed debates about the pace of change. A Board meeting in May 1990 saw a division between those seeking further disposals of non-core businesses 'or indeed any business which was, and was likely to remain, low yielding', and those advocating 'caution on disposals', noting that 'some non-core businesses were good generators of cash'.[71] Unilever's European business still had costs above, and margins below, those of competitors. The 1990 accounts contained an 'Extraordinary Charge' of £195 million for restructuring—closing plants and reorganizing facilities—to take advantage of the Single Market in Europe, but some directors believed there was a case for more radical restructuring.

Unilever had made progress in trying to capture the benefits from its knowledge base. The organization had been reshaped, and time-consuming, loss-making, and inappropriate businesses divested. Unilever had manifested a growing ability to identify, acquire, and absorb other firms. However, there still appeared to be constraints on performance. There was still a plethora of different brands and product specifications. Unilever still appeared pedestrian at turning innovations into marketable products. The pace of change seemed slow. The corporate culture seemed to constrain innovation and entrepreneurship, even though the enterprise contained numerous innovative and entrepreneurial individuals. There remained many tasks ahead.

Part II
Dynamics and Routines

5

Adding Value: Marketing and Brands

The End of Mum

By the 1960s it was evident that Unilever's markets were undergoing a radical change. The economic boom of the post-war decades was creating a new affluence in western Europe as well as the United States. Western European incomes increased more in these two decades than in the previous 150 years. Accelerating social change accompanied the growth of incomes. Large numbers of young people were the first members of their families to go to universities. There was a great rise in the number of women working outside the home after marriage. Family structures began to weaken as divorce rates moved upwards. People lived longer.

These economic and social developments stimulated two apparently contradictory trends in consumer markets. The first was towards greater uniformity. As people travelled more, or else saw more of foreign—especially American—lifestyles on television and cinema, consumer tastes began to converge, albeit at different speeds in different countries and for different products. The second trend was towards fragmentation. Rising incomes, more education, and longer lives provided consumers with a much greater ability to make choices. There was a major generational shift. The post-war 'baby boomer' generation wanted to differentiate themselves from their parents' generation. During the 1960s Pepsi Cola made use of such feelings when it created the 'Pepsi generation'.[1] As mass consumer products and uniformity spread, the desire for individuality became stronger. Even as people drank cola or ate

115

burgers, they sought individual identities, which they hoped might distinguish them from others. The impact of social changes on women carried the greatest implications of all for Unilever for, it was observed in 1968, they were 'the great majority of our consumers and therefore, affect us most'.[2]

Within Unilever, in 1965 a Consumer Change Committee composed of senior executives was established to consider the nature of these changes and their impact on the company.[3] In 1967 the Committee produced an influential report on 'The Changing Consumer' which identified some major changes that appeared to be underway:

We have always thought of ourselves in Unilever as selling to the average housewife. In the UK we called her Mum; in France Madame Dupont; in other countries by a dozen different names, but whatever we called her she was always monolithic. . . . Mum . . . was working class, thirtyish, the mother of two or three young children, uneducated. . . . Her husband only came home from work or the pub in order to express sycophantic approval of her home-making. Her children were muddy, and she was much concerned with their energy and the colour of their shirts; but they had no complexes, never exercised any judgement of their own unless put up to it by an advertisement, and disappeared at adolescence into a whirl of hair-shampoos and glamour—respectable glamour. . . . Mum was conservative. Catch her in her 20s, hammer her with advertising, titillate her with promotions, and you had her for life.

By 1967, the Committee concluded, this stereotype Mum was getting badly out of date. The new Mums were more middle class, more educated, livelier, healthier, sexier, lived longer, more intimate with their husbands, more independent, more individual in their tastes. Unilever's market was no longer monolithic:

It is split into many different fragments, of many different sizes. The fragment may be by class or age or education or ownership of an automatic washing machine or colour of hair. Whatever it is, one now has to decide for each product at whom one is aiming; one can no longer simply always go for Mum.[4]

These changes in the consumer market had serious implications for Unilever. It was everywhere a local company whose products and brands were for local markets. The trend towards uniformity and convergence raised questions about which products and brands would become 'international', and which would remain local. The fragmentation of markets posed other problems. While Mum had been a clearly defined consumer, the desire for choice and individuality made future consumer tastes less certain. The new Mums might not be as loyal as in the past, and—moreover—men were increasingly recognized as grocery shoppers as well. Unilever needed to search for, or create, market segments for its goods, but this process was fraught with uncertainty. This chapter considers Unilever's responses to this more uncertain and challenging world.

Capabilities

In responding to the challenges of the changing consumer market, Unilever could draw on formidable capabilities in marketing. In 1968 Woodroofe identified Unilever's 'knowledge of the marketing of branded consumer goods' alongside research as one of the company's 'two major strengths'.[5]

There were separate marketing and sales departments. Sales managers tended to rise through the ranks within their individual operating companies, and as a result tended to be older than brand managers, and very practical in their outlook.[6] When Lever Europe was formed at the end of the 1980s, nearly two-thirds of its sales managers were over 40 compared to 20 per cent in marketing. Sales managers were often treated as second-class citizens by their marketing counterparts.[7] The task of selling to tens of thousands of small retailers could easily have been regarded as less than exacting or intellectually challenging in the 1960s. A problem was that the low status of sales persisted even as retailing became concentrated into large groups, dealing with buyers handling large budgets supported by extensive information technology.

Marketing managers typically had little or no sales experience, and they were more 'intellectual', more 'conceptualizers' than their sales counterparts. Brand managers were central components of the marketing departments. Unilever adopted a brand management system about three decades after it was developed by P & G in the 1930s. Initially the P & G system of appointing a manager for each brand was tried, but by the end of the 1970s it was 'almost universal practice' to have brand managers responsible for more than one brand.[8]

Marketing was extremely decentralized. Decision-making took place at the national and operating company level. By 1958 a Marketing Division was in place at the head offices whose function included providing 'advice on the marketing policy of the Concern as a whole and each country or unit',[9] but its role was advisory. It sought to deepen Unilever's knowledge of marketing through scanning ongoing research on the latest marketing trends, and through keeping informed of the actions of governments, consumer groups, and other influential bodies. It then disseminated this knowledge throughout Unilever, encouraging the adoption of best practice and also, so far as was possible, some uniformity in marketing matters. The research of the Marketing Division was largely concerned with social and economic trends, and by the mid-1980s there was growing discomfort about the gap between its work and the actual experience of marketing managers in operating companies.[10]

The changing nature of the consumer market was tracked at several different levels. The Consumer Change Committee, which had diagnosed the end of Mum, delivered over thirty reports to the Special Committee between 1965 and 1975 on matters ranging from the impact of an ageing population to the spending habits of British housewives. A constant theme was the unpredictable way consumer demand was changing, although the long-established practice of using boards of housewives to test new products remained in use.[11] There was particular interest in learning from the United States. The Committee's first report in 1965, on 'Using the Rich Countries as a Crystal Ball', considered how far changes and trends in the United States would eventually be followed in Europe and elsewhere. The Committee also dispatched people to talk to leading marketing scholars in US universities.[12]

At the level of the operating company, the marketing function began with market research. By the 1960s Unilever's market researchers were at the forefront of corporate market research. Lever Brothers in the United States was active in sophisticated analysis of panel data, an activity, it was proudly noted in 1970, that was no longer the preserve of 'a few baggy trousered intellectuals in a back room'.[13] By 1972 Unilever had over thirty market research units, including one in each of the major European markets and in some Overseas markets, including Australia and South Africa, usually under the control of national managements. They made use of discussion groups and extended interviews with small groups of consumers, and new products or product concepts were sometimes tested through 'mini-van testing'. This would involve a company representative taking a van to a supermarket or other location and setting up a mini sales outlet offering a new product, usually at a promotion price. Unilever was inclined to 'test market' more extensively than its competitors, contributing to a certain slowness in getting new products to the market place.[14] Although Unilever sold its own market research business in 1986, it continued to be a vast user of market research services, spending upwards of £80 million per annum during the second half of the decade. Unilever was probably the largest corporate client for market research worldwide.[15]

Marketing expenditure was spread over two elements—'promotions' and advertising. Unilever generally allocated around one-third of marketing expenditure to promotions, and the remainder to advertising.[16] Promotions in the form of free samples, gifts, and special displays had formed an important part of marketing from the early days of branded consumer goods. Their role had diminished after the Second World War, but then expanded once more with the growth of self-service shops, first in the United States and then in Europe.[17] In the new retailing environment, promotions assumed a new importance because catching the consumer's eye in the shop became essential. In self-service stores, brands had to compete directly on shelves for consumers to reach out and buy them. Simultaneously advances in packaging were used as new means to enhance the appeal of brands. Advances in plastics manufacture enabled packs to be moulded into varied shapes, while aluminium foils became available during the 1960s for packing products such as toilet soap. Promotions included a full spectrum of devices intended to persuade consumers to choose one brand rather than another in stores, including coupons to obtain price discounts, or the offer of a gift or a prize with purchases.

Advertising expenditure was less directed at persuading consumers to make immediate purchases than at creating a positive impression in consumers' minds about a brand long before they reached any store. There was a radical change in strategies as commercial television spread beyond the United States, where by 1945 there were already six commercial television stations, and a decade later over 400.[18] Commercial television arrived in Britain in 1955, and then spread to other European and Overseas countries. The consumer goods companies were amongst the most extensive users of the new medium. In 1972 14 per cent of all television advertising in the Netherlands was for detergents, almost entirely fabric washing powders.[19] Unilever became a major spender on television, which consumed around three-quarters of its total advertising budget in most European countries during the 1970s and 1980s. Press advertising, especially women's magazines, accounted for much of the remaining expenditure. As an advertiser, Unilever had the reputation, at least among one group of advertising agencies surveyed at the end of the 1970s, of being 'safe' rather than daring.[20]

Despite the size of Unilever's advertising expenditure, there was continuing uncertainty about its effectiveness. William Lever made the classic observation that one-half of all advertising expenditure was wasted, but the trouble was no one knew which half.[21] Measuring the returns to advertising continued to be difficult because there were so many variables affecting sales. In 1983 one large-scale study of the results of advertising on over 200 brands—largely detergents, but with a significant number of personal products and edible fats brands also—showed that the extra profit generated by advertising varied by a factor of 20 to 1, but that for the majority of brands the profit arising from extra sales was less than one-third of the cost of the advertising. There were some predictable factors behind such variations. The response to advertising was much higher for new brands and growing markets, for example, than for mature markets.[22] Still, the question of how much advertising was really required to support a brand remained open.

Unilever's advertising was created through the interaction of companies and their advertising agencies. The overall marketing strategy was the responsibility of the company, which also wrote the advertising brief in consultation with the agency. The writing of the advertising copy was the responsibility of the agency, though the company gave the final approval.[23] From 1964 the Marketing Division produced a 'Unilever Plan for Good Advertising' which gave guidelines for the most effective advertising. The role of Co-ordinations remained limited at least until the late 1970s, when the Detergents Co-ordination started to provide central advertising films for its companies, who were allowed only to make adaptations after consultation.[24]

Unilever made considerable, but not exclusive, use of Lintas, its own advertising agency. During the mid-1960s Unilever launched an international brand alignment policy with four advertising agencies. Lintas was joined by J. Walter Thompson,

Ogilvy & Mather, and McCann Erickson (owned by the US agency Interpublic), who were given responsibility for handling key brands on an international basis. At the end of the 1970s over half of Unilever's advertising outside the United States was still with Lintas, with proportions varying from two-thirds in edible fats to one-third in personal products. In the United States nearly two-thirds of Lipton's business was with Lintas, though less than one-fifth of Lever's.[25] Despite the sale of the Unilever shareholding, Lintas retained 40 per cent of Unilever's business worldwide through the 1980s, and Unilever remained Lintas's biggest client.[26]

The prominence of television advertising raised growing hostility in Europe from the 1960s. The initial focus was on the cost of advertising. In Britain detergents advertising was referred to the Monopolies Commission, which reported in 1966 that Unilever and P & G's dominant market positions were against the public interest, and that excessive advertising expenditure blocked new entrants. The two companies were obliged to introduce economy brands and freeze their prices for two years.[27] Unilever argued that high levels of advertising reflected the competitive nature of the industry, but it did agree to market one of its leading detergents brands, Surf, at a lower cost to the consumer, while reducing the amount of advertising support behind it. Square Deal Surf made little progress, and was eventually withdrawn. Unilever took away from the episode the view that customers were often reassured when buying leading branded products that they were getting the best product.[28] The Unilever position remained that advertising did not necessarily lead to higher prices, and that costs were naturally restrained by the need to maximize profits.

By the 1970s the rapid growth of consumer movements had led to a shift in criticism from the cost of advertising to the accusation that it was intrusive and manipulative, and lowered programme standards.[29] A study of advertising in Britain and Germany by European consumer associations identified the advertising of several Unilever brands as 'misleading', alongside those of P & G, Nestlé, and other leading companies. Claims that Flora margarine 'will result in increased health', and that it was the 'peaches' in Sunsilk shampoo which 'somehow make hair soft and healthy', were cited as examples.[30] There were concerns that negative attitudes to advertising could harm the reputation of Unilever companies.[31] Unilever was consistently opposed to regulatory interference with advertising, and instead hoped that a form of self-regulation would be sufficient to assuage anxiety about the honesty of advertisements. Unilever saw the maintenance of standards as a question of self-interest, as unless advertising was honest and credible it would lose its power to persuade.[32] Consequently, companies were encouraged to pass proposed television commercials through several levels of screening before receiving clearance. This may have contributed to their 'safe' nature.

Unilever was one of the world's foremost marketing companies, then, but it faced a growing challenge with the changing nature of markets from the 1960s. The strength of brands was dependent on advertising, but this became more complex as markets segmented, and as the rise of consumer movements raised the possibility of advertising becoming counter-productive for the corporate image, and ultimately the sales of its products. Over time Unilever responded to such growing complexities by turning to the market to supply specialist advertising and market research services rather than trying to provide them in-house.

Segmenting Markets

The first wave of branding of consumer products on a large scale had been in the late nineteenth century. As national markets replaced local markets, and companies grew in size exploiting new technologies, producers ceased to know consumers personally. Brands developed as means to inform consumers about products and to provide guarantees of quality. They reduced the risk of purchasing for consumers, and made such choices easier. Products which had been homogeneous began to be differentiated by brands, whose identities were created and developed through intensive advertising.[33] During the post-war decades Unilever was a major force behind a second great wave of branding, which involved the segmentation of markets on demographic and lifestyle lines. By the late 1950s American marketing specialists had begun to examine means of segmenting markets by social class and subsequently by consumer lifestyle, eventually using computers to identify and quantify different market segments. Unilever took the same route.

Brands signal reliability and consistency. They are based on accumulated reputations, and are thus less things in themselves than rewards for past investment in innovation and in marketing. Typically they possess both functional and emotional characteristics. The former, often based on a technological innovation, is important when a brand is first launched, and thereafter has to be kept relevant and perceivable to consumers. The emotional characteristics of a brand are accumulated over time. Strong emotional ties are formed with consumers. Brands develop personalities, and come to symbolize sets of values. The relationship between products and brands changed over time. Brands originate from an innovation and the 'product carries the brand'. Over time the intangible values of a brand become the dominant factor.[34]

Unilever shared with P & G and CPC a policy of using stand-alone brand names, rather than following the practice of Nestlé, Colgate Palmolive, Kraft, and Heinz of using their names on products as guarantors of quality and dependability. The name Unilever had no connotations for the millions who purchased its products every day. In Unilever's case even the 'small print' giving manufacturing information did not reveal the name of the ultimate parent. The disinclination to use the Unilever name reflected both the way the company had grown through numerous mergers of companies each with its own brand franchises, and the corporate preference for a low public profile.

To some extent brands had different characteristics across the range of consumer products. An important attribute of brands in detergents and toothpaste was their reputation for technical effectiveness, which could to some extent be scientifically tested. Detergents companies sought endorsements of their brands from washing machine manufacturers, while toothpaste endorsements from national dental associations were highly valued. Nevertheless detergents and toothpaste brands had emotional as well as functional associations, as consumers associated particular brands with feelings of safety or reliability.[35] In personal products such as cosmetics and fragrances, emotional feelings of image and aspirations lay at the core of brands. Exclusivity, variety, and individuality were important features of successful brands in these products.

Unilever's personal care brands increasingly emphasized image and aspirations more than functionality. Sunsilk was well advanced along this trend by the early 1970s. Targeted at 15–34 year-old women, the preferred brand images included 'Sunsilk is modern and forward looking, just right for the sort of life I want to lead in the 1970s'.[36] A subsequent attempt to develop a 'more functional range' of shampoos under the Harmony brand name in the late 1970s failed. This had been expected to grow as Unilever's key brand in the mildness/frequent wash shampoo sector, but it failed on launch, possibly because it was too 'functional'.[37] In contrast Timotei, which started as a deodorant in Finland and was relaunched as a shampoo in Sweden in 1976, flourished on an image as 'naturally mild for frequent hair washing with selected meadow herbs'. It was the strength and clarity of its brand image which made Timotei appealing. Images of innocence, youth, and purity turned out to have a wide international appeal.[38]

In foods, the more products were consumed in public, either as impulse purchases or served on dining tables, the more image and aspiration counted. Ice cream brands carried emotional associations of 'fun', while Lipton Tea carried images of heritage and tradition. At the other end of the spectrum, the emotional value of brands in frozen vegetables was limited. There was also little public prestige in buying a packet of Iglo frozen peas over those of a cheaper competitor, although consumers might be persuaded that they were fresher and better tasting.

Europe's margarine consumers provided the nearest Unilever equivalent to the 'Pepsi generation'. Margarine had been a branded product since its invention, but such branding remained at an elementary stage. Unilever relied on single brands, such as Blue Band, introduced in the Netherlands in 1923, and margarine remained positioned as a cheap substitute for butter.[39] During the mid-1950s Unilever began to introduce improved quality brands, including Rama in Germany and Blue Band in Britain, which were termed 'premium' brands, as opposed to 'standard' margarines,

28 Celebrating 50 years of *Blue Band* margarine in the Netherlands in 1973.

and intended as high-quality and more expensive products. However in the Netherlands the image of margarine was not helped in 1960 when a new emulsifier used in the manufacture of Planta margarine was implicated in widespread outbreaks of skin disease among the Dutch population. The Planta brand was never to reappear in the Netherlands, although it was sold elsewhere, including neighbouring Belgium.

By the 1960s Unilever had begun to explore more imaginative means of segmenting the margarine market. Becel, the pioneering 'health' margarine, was launched in the Netherlands in 1960. It was launched as a dietary spreadable fat made from maize oil and palm oil, vitaminized with vitamins A and D, and containing 50–55 per cent 'pufa'—polyunsaturated fats—which were claimed to benefit those at risk from coronary heart disease. The name stood for Blood Cholesterol Lowering, which left no doubt about the functional benefits of the brand. It was initially sold in tins at a premium price above standard margarines, and it was deliberately kept in the medical sphere by positioning it as a salt-free dietary product distributed through pharmacies and available only on prescription.[40] Having established an identity as a quasi-medical product, Becel was repositioned in 1963 as a diet margarine with minimum 50 per cent 'pufa' content, with distribution widened to include the grocery sector.

Origins Some fifty years after the invention of margarine, the market for this product in Germany was highly fragmented, with over a thousand different varieties available by the 1920s. In 1924 the leading margarine producers sought to end this situation by developing high-quality branded products that could be easily recognized and were available nationally. In a classic example of what later came to be known as market unification, Jurgens launched Rahma in August 1924 (at a price of 1 Reichsmark per pound), and Van den Bergh's launched Blue Band Schwan im Blauband at around the same time. Rahma quickly took off, and soon the biggest problem facing its producers was supply bottlenecks. Teams of salesmen were dispatched to even the remotest parts of Germany to ensure that the brand had a truly national distribution. Subsequently Rahma was renamed Rama to prevent misunderstanding with pure milk products. The integration of Jurgens and Van den Bergh's into Margarine-Verkaufs-Union in 1929 led to a merger of the two rival brands. For the next ten years Rama im Blauband was the leading margarine in Germany.

Growth During the war years Rama, like many other consumer brands across Europe, disappeared from grocery store shelves. Margarine-Union delayed the reintroduction of Rama into Germany until it was certain that its former high quality could be guaranteed. The relaunch in 1954 was a great success. During the 1970s the brand accounted for almost one-third of all margarine sales in that country. Rama found new success on a wider international stage, including Japan, and within a year of its launch in Russia in 1996, it had captured a fifth of the market. By 2002 Rama was available in sixteen countries worldwide.

Brand Identity Rama has always been positioned as a premium-quality margarine, with its key selling point being taste. It has traditionally been sold as a spreading product, rather than simply a commodity to be used in cooking, and it was among the first margarines to be sold in plastic tubs that could adorn the dining table. In the 1970s the brand was sold in Germany as Breakfast Rama, further reinforcing its identity as a tasty spread, and in the same decade a 'slightly salted' variant was also introduced. Rama has been able to build a reputation as a high-quality, pleasant-tasting product that can be enjoyed by the whole family.

By the mid-1960s the Edible Fats Co-ordination had a well-defined strategy in place focused on developing specialized brands along two main lines: improved quality and medical benefit.[41] A policy of 'Brand Intentions' laid down the essential characteristics of brands—or a series of brands given that margarine brand names remained largely country specific—with the same features.[42] Becel-like products were launched elsewhere, including Ceres in Germany, which was prescription only and aimed at people clinically diagnosed as having deficient fat metabolism. In Britain Flora was launched as a high 'pufa' health brand. However Unilever's desire to make health claims for its margarine remained tempered by the uncertain evidence linking the relative health benefits of saturated and polyunsaturated fatty acids, and instead Unilever promoted the image of a 'general aura of health'.[43] Unilever also began to introduce margarines which were low in calories, beginning with Era, launched in the Netherlands in 1969. As Era, later known as Linera, contained only half the amount of fat used in standard margarines, it was described as a 'halvarine'.

Market segmentation was facilitated by advances in packaging. In 1959 Unilever launched its first margarine—previously sold in greaseproof paper—in a tub, Blauband, in Germany, followed by Flora in Britain. The use of tubs made major changes in product formulation possible—specifically the use of more expensive vegetable oils instead of animal and other hard oils—which in turn made 'soft' margarines possible. This boosted spreading usage at a time when the ownership of refrigerators was increasing rapidly in Europe. The tub packs, most of which were manufactured by Unilever itself, augmented the development of high 'pufa' margarines by extending the use of raw materials with higher polyunsaturated fat content, such as sunflower oil, rather than palm oil which was high in saturated fat. Tubs were also used to improve the image and appeal of margarine; they could be used on family dining tables and in miniature form on hotel dining tables.[44] During the early 1970s some of Unilever's major brands—such as Blue Band, Stork, and Flora—were relaunched in tub formats. By 1973 86 per cent of Unilever margarine in Germany and two-thirds in Britain was sold in tubs, though at that stage the Dutch still consumed two-thirds of their margarine in wrappers.[45]

Margarine became a product in which consumers were given a range of functional and emotional choices. While Blue Band conveyed images of 'mothercare', Becel and Flora touched on fears of heart disease, while Rama was a premium taste brand conveying feelings of pleasure. During the 1980s there was further segmentation as Unilever launched 'butter-like' brands, such as Krona in Britain, and responded to increasing health consciousness by introducing new low-fat spreads. The 'healthy lifestyle' platform formed the basis of advertising for these products, beginning with Lätta launched first in Sweden. Similar products were launched in Belgium (Effi) and Germany (Du darfst). The 'brand personality' of Du darfst was described in 1989 as 'Attractive, light, high spirited, natural and modern—a "friend" upon whom the confident modern feminine woman, who has found herself and her lifestyle, can rely. Du Darfst means joy of life and eating pleasure and not effort and renunciation.' The main target group was higher-income, working women aged

29 The launch of the *Du Darfst* brand of low fat spreads in Germany in 1975.

25–50 living in cities who were 'self confident and figure conscious' and 'interested in fashion, cosmetics and beauty'.[46]

The opening up of new market segments, or products launched in response to such segments, occurred across Unilever's product range. Rexona—sold as Sure in Britain and South Africa and Reward in Turkey and New Zealand—was Unilever's main brand of deodorants which by the end of the 1970s was available in fifteen European and thirteen Overseas markets. It was advertised on the basis of its functional effectiveness in combating bodily odour. It was used only under the arm and did not contain high levels of fragrance. The brand image—'Rexona won't let you down'—stressed how the product would prevent its user from being socially stigmatized. The brand was constantly renewed with technical improvements. By the early 1980s it was positioned as a high-efficiency, family, value for money brand.[47]

Impulse was a different concept. This perfumed deodorant was first launched in 1971 by the innovative South African personal products company. In 1965 this company had launched a deodorant under the Shield brand name borrowed from the United States, and two years later had launched Shield for Sportsmen, Unilever's first venture into male deodorants inspired by the combination of South Africa's sporting culture and the cultural preference for a high degree of cleanliness. In South Africa, Unilever's largest competitor was Bristol-Myers, which sold the Mum deodorant. In 1970 Bristol-Myers invented the perfume deodorant concept and launched it, initially in Scandinavia, as Mum 21, in a package rather than the traditional can. It was the distinctive packaging which initially caught the attention of Unilever in South Africa, and Impulse was launched before Mum 21 could be established. It was designed as a more suggestive and sexier product aimed at young women, and supported by an inspirational advertising campaign developed by a local South African agency, which depicted a scene where a young man was compelled to act irrationally in response to the perfume he detects on a passing stranger—the 'Impulse girl'.[48] By 1985 Impulse was sold in thirty countries. Advertising remained based on the original South African concept. The strong romantic overtones were the essence of the brand's appeal to young women, with consistent advertising and frequent introduction of new variants being used to maintain the brand.[49]

During the early 1980s the perceived growth in the demand for a specific male brand of deodorant led to the launch of Axe body spray in France. Unilever was far from being the pioneer of 'male' products. Estée Lauder in the United States had introduced the Aramis range of men's prestige toiletries in the late 1960s,[50] and over the following decade many other male fragrances appeared on the American market such as Shulton's Old Spice and Fabergé's Brut. Unilever had not built on the initial excursion into this market in South Africa, but during the mid-1970s it began to approach it again with the Denim range of male toiletries, including a fragrance in Britain and a disposable razor in France. The Denim male deodorant was marketed for the man 'who doesn't have to try too hard', but sales were small.[51] A major assault on the male market began with the Axe deodorant, launched in France in 1983, and called Lynx in Britain. By 1990 Axe/Lynx's sales of £120 million exceeded those of both Rexona and Impulse.

In ice cream, new brands opened up major new segments of the market. Cornetto ice cream was based on serving ice cream in an edible cone or wafer. This practice was firmly established by the 1950s, but the concept suffered from the technical difficulty of preventing the cone from becoming soggy. This problem was overcome by the Italian firm Spica that was acquired by Unilever in 1962.[52] Unilever had

ΛXE

Origins Following the success of Impulse in the 1970s and early 1980s, Unilever further segmented the body spray market by developing a perfumed deodorant spray aimed at young men. Axe was first launched in France in 1983 where it quickly established itself as a popular brand.

Growth By 1985 Axe (or Lynx as it is known in the UK, Ireland, Australia, New Zealand, and Ego in South Africa) was available in Germany and the UK, and its sales doubled in 1986 as it was extended to four more European countries. By 1987 Axe was available in most western European markets, and had also been introduced to a number of Overseas countries. From the outset, Axe had been available in a range of variants. New varieties were introduced every year, and individual lines were withdrawn when demand fell. As early as 1986 Axe aftershave was available, and the brand name was soon extended to a range of shower gels. The 1990s saw Axe further extend its reach to shaving products, razors, styling mousses, and various other grooming products. It became the largest male toiletries brand worldwide, accounting for 7.5 per cent of world deodorant sales, and available in fifty-three countries. It is dominant in Europe, South America, and Australia, and was launched in the United States in 2002.

Brand Identity The brand name was selected from a variety of options (which also included Ego, Rogue, Aura, and Torq). Axe was eventually selected because it was suitable for international extension and because it had no specific meaning in most countries, enabling advertisers to add values to it. In English-speaking markets, Lynx was preferred, as this suggested masculinity and also gracefulness. As a perfumed body spray aimed at young men in the 15-24 age bracket, Axe/Lynx has sought to appeal to a highly media-aware target audience through innovative and imaginative advertising. A 1990s commercial, in which a young woman found herself receiving seductive looks from various other females after mistakenly applying her boyfriend's Axe body spray, won several advertising awards including the silver prize at Cannes.

made little effort to find a way of producing a hand-held ice cream cone before discovering that they had acquired one when they bought Spica, but after the acquisition there was a rapid perception of the potential of a branded ice cream cone. In 1963 Cornetto began to be launched in Europe as the first packaged and branded ice cream cone. The fact that the ice cream went to the bottom of the cone, and that the inside of the cone was coated with a mixture of coconut oil and chocolate, helped generate the image of a luxury product sold at an affordable price, and in a number of European countries it was a success.

A test launch of Cornetto in Britain in 1964, in contrast, proved a complete failure. The main problem was the issue of the crispness of the cone, for while in Italy the turnover rate for ice cream was very high, in Britain stocks were held for much longer, and they became 'soggy'. Cornetto had to be withdrawn from the British market. The successful relaunch in Britain in 1976 demonstrated the combination of functional and emotional benefits needed for a successful brand. Unilever had progressively improved the production processes and storage methods to reduce the problems of soggy cones, and the British product was also initially sourced from the successful Belgian company. However, after the previous problems it was essential that a favourable brand image was created, and the Wall's advertising campaign became a classic. After the association of Italy with luxury ice cream in the minds of British consumers was identified in market research, an advertising campaign was devised in which Cornetto was seen being eaten in a number of immediately recognizable 'picture postcard' Italian settings, such as the Colosseum, St Mark's Square, the Leaning Tower of Pisa, and the Rialto Bridge.[53]

The final element introduced into the British advertising commercial was a song. To the tune of the Italian love song 'O Sole Mio' the lyric was invented:

> Just one Cornetto
> Give it to me.
> Delicious ice cream
> of Italy.
> A nut
> And chocolate dream.
> Give me Cornetto
> From Wall's Ice Cream.

Subsequent research into the effectiveness of the Cornetto commercials found that the song was 'a crucial and fundamental element of the campaign'.[54] This advertising for Cornetto was not, however, easily transferred elsewhere where the British stereotype image of Italy was not recognized. The most commonly used Cornetto advertisements elsewhere were based on the Italian 'Cuore di Panna' ('Heart of Cream') commercials based on a series of vignettes which showed Cornetto being consumed by young people in a variety of situations. The emphasis was on generating an emotional appeal to the brand by associating it closely with an idealized youthful lifestyle.[55]

In the case of Magnum, Unilever was more the follower than the creator of a new market segment. While Cornetto opened up a new market sector which was bigger than had originally been thought, Magnum was aimed at a market sector that was already known to exist. A strong premium adult ice cream market had emerged after the launch of the Dove Bar in the United States in 1984. The greying of Western populations gave the ice cream manufacturers a major incentive to develop such adult brands. In 1986 Mars purchased the producer of the Dove Bar, and began almost immediately to build a large new factory in Germany to begin an assault on the European ice cream market.

Unilever had been actively researching means to develop a large adult market for ice cream from at least the late 1970s. In 1985 Wall's in Britain established 'Project Renaissance' to re-examine the market for impulse ice cream using extensive interviews with consumer panels. The research concluded that the problem for ice cream was its association with children, and childhood memories of messy and sticky experiences. The way forward was seen in terms of developing a product which could offer adult excitement and indulgence. The ideal hand-held ice cream was envisaged not just as a piece of ice cream in a cone to be eaten on the beach, but as something that was 'sexy'. It was to be a 'secret affair—a lover to be "used"'.[56]

The search for this 'ideal' brand proved long. The name Magnum had been first used in ice cream for a vanilla-like ice cream on a stick with a strawberry coating produced by Wall's in the UK in 1958. A new Magnum was launched in Britain and Belgium in 1987, but it was a conventional ice cream that made little impact. The following year Unilever tried the more upmarket but equally unsuccessful Frac in Italy using high-quality real chocolate, dairy vanilla ice cream, and packaged in a box like the Dove and Häagen Dazs ice creams in the USA. The 'true' Magnum, launched in Germany in January 1989, was originally conceived by the marketing group there not as a new brand, but as an upmarket version of Langnese Iglo's existing Nogger brand, dating from 1960, and by the 1980s positioned as a 'tough guy' ice cream aimed at young adults.[57] The Magnum name was eventually adopted because it had associations with 'big' things, such as a magnum of champagne and a popular American television series about a private detective. The marketing director of Langnese Iglo drove the project despite the initial scepticism of Co-ordination about the proposed high price, arranging to have it manufactured in Denmark.

A key development was to find a supply of quality chocolate for the new product. Unilever could make high-quality ice cream, but it had traditionally employed imitation chocolate in its products. A contract was negotiated with the Belgium firm Callebaut, which also supplied Häagen Dazs, to manufacture chocolate for Unilever's exclusive use. Most real chocolate could not be frozen, but Callebaut had managed to develop high-quality chocolate which could be stored at temperatures as low as −40 °C.[58]

Once launched, Unilever's formidable marketing capabilities were able to make Magnum a rapid success, despite its selling at over DM2. Unilever's distribution network and influence over small retail outlets were exploited to the full. The Magnum brand was developed with all of the characteristics of the ideal hand-held ice cream

covering part of fixed costs, but there was also a desire to restrict the growth of competitors. The recommended strategy was not to encourage the emergence of a private label market, but if a retailer was determined to pursue this strategy, then Unilever companies would undertake third party manufacture. However, they were instructed never to offer better quality to retailers than Unilever's own brands.[88] In contrast, Detergents and Personal Products Co-ordinations had firm policies against supplying retailer brands.

'We are brand producers', Unilever's Board was reminded in 1982, 'and brands are under pressure.'[89] The overall impact of private labels on Unilever's business from the 1960s was to edge the company towards higher-margin brands. The success of this strategy meant that a loss of market share was often not translated into a loss of profits, though the strategic options of Unilever narrowed. The growth of private labels limited its ability to regain the initiative by means of retail price cuts and special promotions—both of which retailers could quickly match—or by seeking alternative distribution channels.

Global Brands

By the 1960s Unilever had thousands of different brands and product lines. These brands had strong national identities built up over the years, and occupied discrete and long-defined positions in national markets. A welter of national rules and regulations about everything from packaging to advertising reinforced national differences. The fact that names sounded differently, and had different associations, in different languages, also resulted in many different brand names being used. Manufacturers often considered different brands in different countries as a protection against 'grey' trade between countries where the price levels differed.

Unilever's kaleidoscope of numerous national brands was not unusual. The use of different formulations and packaging for different countries was the norm, and reflected the realities of markets, habits, and tastes that had developed in different ways. This diversity remained enormous even within western Europe, let alone in North America and the Overseas countries. Habits of washing clothes, the temperatures at which clothes were washed, and the type of machine used all varied greatly. Although toothpaste was almost universally used in developed countries, there were significant national differences in usage. In Switzerland average annual consumption was 497 grams per annum in the early 1980s, but in neighbouring France it was only 287.[90] Around the same time Unilever research indicated that while 90 per cent of British women and 67 per cent of British men used deodorants, only 61 per cent of French women and 25 per cent of French men used such a product.[91]

This diversity was at its greatest in foods consumption. The use of oils and dairy products for spreading and cooking differed greatly. They happened also to be products whose manufacture offered limited economies of scale. Preferences in meals and meal components remained extremely local even between neighbouring European countries. When Unilever supplied tomato soup to Belgium from a Dutch factory, it had to make it taste different for that market.[92] A product such as ice cream was far from homogeneous. In 1977 while Germans consumed 6 litres per head of ice cream per annum, Swedes consumed 9 litres, and Australians over 19 litres.[93] National legislation on the composition of ice cream varied considerably. In Britain cheap vegetable substitutes and sugar were used instead of milk fat during the Second World War, and this usage continued thereafter. Almost all British ice cream was non-dairy, and British legislation did not require a milk fat content. In Germany 'ice cream' was required by law to contain at least 10 per cent milk fat, while the equivalent figure in France was 7 per cent. French legislation even defined the minimum levels of natural flavours which had to be used in ice cream.[94]

Unilever's portfolio of food brands reflected this diverse national heritage, as well as the pattern of growth through numerous acquisitions. There were strong local brands which were hardly sold elsewhere. In the Netherlands, Calvé had a large and successful business in peanut butter. Launched in 1948, Pindakaas was served on top of bread and margarine or butter for breakfast, and advertised on Blue Band lines as making children strong and healthy. By the 1960s it was virtually a Dutch national institution, but it was not sold elsewhere except in South Africa. Unilever's problem was how far its numerous Pindakaas-like brands could be internationalized.

By the late 1950s there was recognition within Unilever that its national approach to branding might be a problem. As trade barriers fell and economic integration in Europe made the rationalization of production facilities across countries a possibility, Unilever's multiple brands were a potential major obstacle to such rationalization. American firms seemed to perceive such opportunities earlier than their European counterparts. 'In fields varying from Coca Cola to motor cars', one marketing manager in Unilever observed in 1958, 'Europe is gradually getting more and more continental brands.' These in turn, he continued, offered the possibilities of achieving economies of scale in advertising, as well as in research, manufacturing, and packaging. The problem was that Unilever had 'very few brands which are truly European and our activities even in the super brand class are much more on a national basis'. Unilever's brands, he continued, 'tend to be better tailored to their individual markets and our advertising campaigns better suited to the national mood and taste. With greater standardisation throughout Europe . . . these advantages will decline and become an expensive luxury.'[95]

Ik vind het gewoon lekker.

Calvé PINDAKAAS

32 The highly successful *Pindakaas* peanut butter, sold in the Netherlands from 1948 (*taken in 1984*).

The problems of Unilever's excessive number of brands, the limited number of international brands, and a lack of brand harmonization were to be discussed for the next three decades. In the heady days of the World Co-ordinators in the early 1960s there was a considerable momentum for the identification and growth of international brand names, although it was recognized that it was not practical to use one formulation all over the world. By 1964 Detergents Co-ordination had a strategy for 'International Brand Intentions' and an International Pack Design designed to identify the elements in a brand's 'make-up which it is the aim of Unilever policy to make the common property of that brand on a world-wide basis'.[96] Foods 2 Co-ordination, which controlled a collection of local foods brands, also devised an International Brand and Pack Policy. Wherever canned soups were marketed, this Co-ordination instructed in 1963, the Unox name had to be used together with a standard packaging design 'for all soup varieties and all sizes of can'.[97]

The momentum behind the development of strong international branding policies was lost during the subsequent extended debates on the authority of Co-ordinators. Even after Co-ordinators were given executive powers in European countries in 1966, companies remained highly protective of local brand names and brand positioning that had been built up over the years through advertising and promotions. There was no lack of analysis of the costs of this situation. A study for Personal Products Co-ordination in 1978 made the point both that 'large brands do seem to be more profitable', and that 'small and declining brands' needed to be eliminated not only because of low profitability, but also because of 'hidden costs'

33 The variety of brand names and packaging used in Europe for Unilever's liquid abrasive cleaner *(taken in 1984)*.

such as absorbing a disproportionate amount of management time and requiring frequent price and stock adjustments.[98] However, the plethora of local brands and variations in their contents persisted.

The comparison with P & G was stark. In 1975 Unilever supported 665 detergents brands in the forty-two countries in which it operated, while P & G had 186 brands in the twenty-one countries in which it operated.[99] Unilever not only had more brands in each particular market than its major competitors, but its brands varied from one market to the next. Unilever's strongest European detergents brand in the 1970s was Persil, but this could only be sold in a handful of European countries. The proportion of total sales accounted for by the leading brands of P & G and Unilever (Ariel and Persil respectively) differed greatly. While Ariel accounted for around half of P & G's fabrics sales in Europe, Persil made up less than a quarter of Unilever's sales. Unilever had Omo in the Netherlands, Germany, and elsewhere, and Bio Presto in Italy.

The main focus of Co-ordinators in the 1970s was to attempt to build coherent international brand positioning for Unilever products rather than brand names. There were a clutch of 'international' brands whose coherence Co-ordinations oversaw with 'brand positioning' statements which included target consumer group, functional and emotional benefits, pricing policy, packaging, and promotional policy.[100] These brands were protected, such as Lux soap and Sunsilk shampoo, and only

Origins The Omo brand name was first registered in the UK in 1908, and almost immediately developed into an international brand. Within a year the brand name had been registered in Canada, Austria, and France. After a short-lived attempt to sell Omo as a bleaching powder, the brand quickly established itself as a soap-based washing powder for white fabrics. By the 1920s Omo had become a perborate soap powder. Early Omo advertising featured the face of an owl and used the phrase *Old Mother Owl* (with the two eyes forming the 'O's and the beak making an 'M'). The owl was presumably meant to imply that Omo was a wise choice for a mother to make. It is unclear whether the owl imagery inspired the Omo name or vice versa. The underlying emphasis in the marketing was clear enough from the outset: the earliest known slogan was 'Omo makes whites brighter.'

Growth By the 1960s Omo was among the world's leading washing powders, and Unilever's most profitable detergents brand. Though Omo has remained unchanged in terms of its name and its image, the product itself has undergone continual developments. In the 1950s Omo was relaunched as a synthetic detergent in European markets. The late 1960s saw it relaunched in the Netherlands, Belgium, and Switzerland with a formulation containing enzymes. From the late 1970s Unilever's new medium-temperature bleach (TAED) was added to the Omo formula.

Brand Identity Omo has long been one of Unilever's most trusted fabrics wash brands, with a reputation for efficiency and reliability. Its precise market positioning varied between countries, but the brand is primarily associated with consistency and versatility. It can be used for the whole wash, on all fibres and at all temperatures.

the most powerful operating company could dare to interfere with the overall brand identity. It was specified that the Sunsilk brand was to be used for women's hair preparations only, and that it should be marketed under the house name of 'Elida'.

The rapid international transfer of Close-Up toothpaste from the United States was achieved with a strong international brand focus based on the claim that it improved the appearance of teeth and the freshness of breath.[101] However, often the diffusion of brands and concepts around the world was not rapid. Dove soap provides one example. After its initial enormous success as a premium toilet soap in the United States, the brand was launched successfully in Canada. By the mid-1960s it was being test marketed in Europe and the research laboratory at Vlaardingen was well advanced with a European formulation for the product.[102] Thereafter, and following the unfortunate brand extension into dishwashing liquid, the impetus for the transfer of Dove soap waned. It became established folklore within Unilever that the formulation was too expensive to sell in Europe, though a more underlying problem may have been the deep distrust about anything coming from Lever Brothers during these years.[103] It was not until 1989 that Dove was first launched in Europe, beginning with Italy where there was a proven willingness to buy premium products for skin care. By then other companies had launched premium soap bars which were priced well above Lux.[104]

The full harmonization of brand image, formulation, and packaging remained rare even when strong international brand positioning statements existed. In the mid-1970s the small Lux soap tablet was produced in Europe in eight different weights, and the Rexona tablet in four. Mentadent toothpaste, although a new brand, developed with an assortment of local variations. Although everywhere it was a gum health product, Mentadent tasted different in different countries, with a very medicinal taste being used in some countries to reinforce the brand position- ing. While most countries used a pink paste to highlight its difference from standard toothpastes, in Austria and Italy a green gel was used, and in Sweden a white one. Although the majority of Mentadent packs were white with a black logo with red and black lettering and a red stripe, in Austria, Italy, Spain, and Greece the stripe was in green with green and black lettering. While the Austrians and Swiss promoted Mentadent with doctors, the Italians and South Africans made the biting of a crisp, green apple the prominent feature of the TV advertising.[105]

In foods the situation remained more extreme. Food was a very 'local' business, and all the large international companies had a mix of local, regional, and interna- tional brands. Formulations usually also varied between countries. Nestlé had some hundred blends worldwide for its Nescafé coffee in the 1980s.[106] All companies faced a struggle to maintain internationally consistent brand identities and positioning. CPC's Knorr brand, which had been closely protected during the 1950s and first half of the 1960s, subsequently fragmented in Europe and elsewhere as local marketing teams produced their own campaigns, a trend which only began to be reversed in the late 1980s.[107] The distinguishing feature of Unilever was that, within the spectrum of local adaptation in foods, it was usually the company which adapted more. Its European base and its tradition of decentralization led to a culture in which differ- ences rather than similarities were especially stressed. The mirror image of the com- petitive advantage of 'knowing' their markets was the proliferation of brand names and the enormous difficulty in rationalizing them.

Even strong international brands on closer examination turned out to be anything but harmonized. Becel appeared a well-harmonized brand sold in—by the end of the 1980s—seven European countries as well as Australia and Canada using an identical name and a similar logo. The basic positioning of a beneficial effect on blood choles- terol levels was also common. However, there were major differences in strategic positioning. A quasi-medicinal role in some markets, such as Germany, contrasted with a more popular general heart health position in others, such as the Netherlands and Belgium. The specialist position limited the volume of sales, but allowed Becel a high price premium, close to butter in Germany, while the other position sold more at a lower premium. German Becel had a price premium of 67 per cent over the Dutch version of the brand. Advertising expressions and pack graphics varied partly as a result of positioning differences, as well as local legal restraints around the cholesterol claim area. Becel formulations also varied widely within Europe. The most expensive product had one of the more nutritionally mundane fatty acid compositions.[108] This situation was an obstacle to manufacturing rationalization. Moreover as opinion formers about health and diet became more internationalized, so different positioning for the Becel brand became more uncomfortable.

There were similar problems with Lipton Tea. Co-ordination regularly issued guidelines to local companies to prevent fragmentation in its use, and in 1984 an international logo was designed.[109] Nevertheless the packaging and presentation and logos on Lipton teas remained diverse. In some countries—such as Italy and the Far East—leaf tea was positioned as young and informal, while in others—such as Norway and Portugal—it was sold as an 'old' product. In others, such as Greece, it was presented as a drink for all the family. In such major tea-drinking countries as Britain, New Zealand, and South Africa the Lipton name was not used at all, and tea was sold under an array of local brands such as PG Tips, Choicest, and Bushells. Other local brands such as Elephant and Morning Star competed with Lipton in some countries.[110] Meanwhile, Lipton jams, mayonnaise, soups and other products featured 'shields in every conceivable colour, a wide variety of logo's [sic], an extreme of visual diversity'.[111]

From the mid-1980s there was a renewed momentum to achieve brand harmonization. This was a period when the value of brands began to receive new attention, and in Britain a number of large firms took controversial steps to capitalize the value of their brands on their balance sheets.[112] Personal Products and Detergents Co-ordinations began to push harder for concentrating resources on fewer brands and achieving greater brand harmonization.[113] However the real push within Unilever at the time was to improve financial performance, and to achieve restructuring through acquisitions and disposals. The strong commitment to local decision-making continued to handicap radical brand rationalization, especially as there was a real danger of demotivating managers long accustomed to selecting which product lines and brands they would sell in their own markets.

By 1990 Unilever still had around 1,500 brands. Well over half were in foods, and at least 170 personal products and 320 detergents brands were marketed. There were few large, truly international and consistently positioned brands. Lipton Tea's sales of £600 million made it Unilever's largest single brand and the most international, but it was dwarfed by Nescafé's sales of £2.9 billion, Kraft's £2.5 billion,

Maggi's £2 billion, and Knorr's £700 million. The prices and marketing positioning of Unilever's other foods brands continued to differ widely. The Cup-A-Soup product was sold at the end of the 1980s in fifteen different countries using seven brand names and nine varieties of sub-brands, including minute soup, soup-a-snack, and lämmin kuppi.[114] Calvé was used for dressings and cold sauces in around eight European countries, but the brand was used on instant desserts in Belgium, instant soups in Turkey, and low-calorie peanut butter in the Netherlands.[115]

In detergents and personal care it was a similar story. Omo's sales of £280 million made it Unilever's largest detergents brand at the beginning of the 1990s, but P & G's Ariel and Tide were both three times as large. Sunsilk was Unilever's largest personal products brand with sales of £190 million, but P & G's five largest brands of Max Factor, Crest, Pert/Wash + Go, CoverGirl, and Oil of Ulay all sold more. Max Factor sold around £450 million in that year. In toothpaste, Unilever's largest brands in terms of annual sales were Close-Up (£130 million), Signal (£100 million), Pepsodent (£90 million), and Mentadent (£80 million), while P & G's Crest alone sold £250 million.

During the first half of the century Unilever had transformed numerous regional brands in many countries into national brands, but the creation of international brands proved more complex. The problems caused by an excessive number of brand names, few of which were large international brands, were identified within the company, but its culture and organization constrained a solution. Unilever's wide geographical span of operation obviously meant that brand names and positioning, formulations, and packaging would vary, and often need to vary, but Unilever's managers proved far more alert to national differences than to cross-border similarities. This local focus was a feature of every aspect of Unilever rather than a unique marketing characteristic. The result was that Unilever's competitors moved more quickly to build international 'power brands' which could be marketed more forcefully than Unilever's portfolio of local and regional brands.

Marketing and Unilever's Renewal

Unilever's vast expenditure on marketing reflected its position as one of the world's largest consumer products companies. As Fig. 5.1 shows, although Unilever spent considerably more on marketing than on research and development, from the mid-1960s there was a steady decline in the relative size of Unilever's spending on marketing as a proportion of sales, partly because of the increasing diversification beyond branded consumer goods, but partly also because of the need to curb costs. There were significant variations within this overall pattern. Total marketing

Soap, which was not subject to government price controls, became the main profit earner in India. Unilever held a particularly strong position in branded premium soaps. It was a paradox that although government policies were increasingly restrictive towards foreign firms—helping to deter companies such as P & G from entry—the high level of protection also made India a profitable market for the firms which did manufacture there. However, government controls over foreign exchange, and a lack of local alkalis, meant that Unilever was unable to begin manufacture of synthetic detergents until the 1970s. In 1943 a factory had also been opened in Calcutta to manufacture such personal products as talcum powder and shaving soap, but this did not prove a growth area for a long time. Unilever found itself squeezed between local manufacturers of products such as hair oils and competition from Colgate, which held a strong market position in toothpaste. It was largely because of profits on soap that Hindustan Lever was able to remit dividends amounting to £7.8 million to its parents between 1956 and 1969, despite adverse political and economic conditions which included a war with Pakistan, droughts, and a major devaluation.[66]

By 1967 Hindustan Lever was ranked in the top five private sector firms in India in terms of sales. It had 7,000 employees and six factories. It had already diversified in several directions. An interest in the potential for convenience foods, especially producing and marketing dehydrated peas and dried milk curd, led Unilever into organizing its own supplies. The largest project involved building a new factory for milk products at Etah in Uttar Pradesh which would be surrounded by milk-collecting stations and milking centres. Hindustan Lever would make contracts with local farmers to bring their cattle to the milking centres, and would then transfer the milk to collecting centres and on to the central factory for processing. The Etah plant produced dairy products including skim milk powder and baby foods.[67] Overall sales of convenience foods proved disappointing. The dehydrated peas, which because of India's hot and humid climate needed expensive packaging, were too expensive for middle-class consumers, while the rich had servants who could buy fresh peas and shell them. A report in 1968 noted that Hindustan Lever had a larger business distributing and selling condoms on behalf of the government than in convenience food products.[68]

The regulatory and political environment for foreign companies deteriorated during the 1970s. The initial problems were related to the serious impact of price controls, which by early in the decade had rendered the vanaspati business completely unprofitable. While some local firms were able to use unorthodox methods to avoid price controls, this option was not open to Unilever.[69] Between 1972 and 1974 Unilever held extensive negotiations with the Indian government for relief from the effects of price control over soap, which was eventually removed provided the large manufacturers introduced a poor man's toilet soap at a controlled price.

A critical part of the arrangement was that Hindustan Lever persuaded the government that it could make soap by using non-edible oils like castor oil and rice bran oil instead of imported tallow, permitting the government to use the foreign exchange it had allocated for the import of tallow to import badly needed fertilizers instead. In 1975 price control was also removed from vanaspati, which enabled Hindustan Lever to begin to re-establish the Dalda brand.[70] There was a marked improvement in profits from the mid-1970s, and by the end of the decade Unilever executives were notably impressed with the flexibility and success of the Indian company.[71]

A second major problem faced by Unilever in India was the enactment of the FERA legislation under which all companies not engaged in 'core' or non-technology industries had to bring their shareholding down to 40 per cent from 1974. IBM and Coca Cola were among the multinationals that divested from India rather than accept the dilution of management control.[72] Unilever, however, opted to negotiate rather than divest. A strategy was followed of resisting the reduction of the Unilever shareholding down to 40 per cent, and seeking instead to retain the 74 per cent shareholding permitted for firms in the high-technology or core sectors. After long and complex negotiations, an agreement was reached with the government under which a foreign company was permitted to hold 51 per cent of the equity, provided that 60 per cent of its turnover was in the core or high-technology sectors, and that it exported 10 per cent of its production.

The next challenge for Hindustan Lever was to satisfy the government that it met these criteria. Hindustan Lever became one of the five recognized Export Houses in India and exported a wide range of products, including a mandatory 10 per cent of its total exports from the small-scale sector. Not only company products were exported, but also carpets, shoes, garments, marine goods, and other products processed under company supervision and specification. By the early 1980s Hindustan Lever had become India's second largest private sector exporter. An attempt was also made to persuade the government that it was a high-technology manufacturer. Unilever began to develop a major research facility in India in the 1950s, and it was able to highlight the technologies developed for using non-edible oils in soap manufacture, and new chemical processes for relying on Indian turpentine and Indian lemon grass oil for perfume.

For a number of years Unilever's majority control hung in the balance. A new government elected in 1977 issued an order requiring Unilever to go down to a 40 per cent shareholding within two years. Unilever responded with delaying tactics on the grounds that the shareholding should be reduced in two stages. The first step to 51 per cent was implemented in 1978, but a subsequent change of government provided an opportunity to delay the second stage. In 1981 Unilever was permitted to retain a majority shareholding. Unilever became one of a relatively small number of foreign companies which successfully bargained with the Indian state to maintain their majority shareholding.[73] Given the wide dispersion of ownership of the shares held by the public, this left Unilever more or less in control of the company.

Unilever's bargaining position was facilitated by the goodwill felt towards the company in official Indian circles. The R & D programme was widely seen as enhancing the company's reputation with the government and the professional classes.[74] Hindustan Lever also won praise for being willing to invest beyond consumer goods, notably in chemicals with a project to manufacture sodium tripolyphosphate, culminating in a plant at Haldia which went into operation in 1979.

The Etah project won plaudits also. The factory had run into severe losses by the early 1970s, and Unilever even tried to give it away to the local government for nothing.[75] It was eventually realized that success depended on increasing the milk availability in the Etah district. An integrated development programme was launched in 1976 aimed at providing the Etah farmers with guidance and knowledge of animal husbandry. Managers from the company were placed in residence in the villages, and Hindustan Lever intervened with the banks and the tax authorities to improve the procedures for farmers to get loans. A medical scheme was introduced for spreading health and hygiene in the villages. A programme was commenced for the reclamation of uncultivable land, which represented over 5 per cent of the Etah district. By 1978 the Etah dairy project had become profitable, but more important was both the goodwill it generated and the practice of sending managers into rural areas. It became accepted practice that every management trainee began her or his career spending a couple of months in a rural village, learning to connect with their consumers.

During the 1980s there was a significant restructuring of Unilever's Indian business. There were acute financial difficulties and labour unrest at Lipton India Ltd, the tea company acquired by Unilever with the acquisition of the Lipton International in 1971.[76] It had a 60 per cent outside shareholding under the FERA legislation. Although divestment was an option, Unilever felt constrained both by a feeling of moral commitment to the outside shareholders as well as by the need to protect the Lipton brand name.[77] Unilever transferred management staff from Hindustan Lever and made an attempt to turn the business around, but no radical changes could be made because of the complexities of getting the agreement of the outside shareholders for structural change or refinancing.[78] It was against this context that in 1984 Hindustan Lever's business in vanaspati was transferred to Lipton, which rescued that firm from its narrow product base in tea and underutilized sales force. As a 40 per cent foreign-owned company, Lipton was free of FERA constraints and could expand as it wished. On the other hand, the reduction of Hindustan Lever's turnover alleviated the problems of meeting the Indian government's 10 per cent export requirement, while the transfer increased the relative size of Hindustan Lever's businesses in activities such as chemicals favoured by the government.

The acquisition of Chesebrough-Pond's resulted in further restructuring. Hindustan Lever had launched a number of important personal care brands, including Clinic shampoo in 1971, Liril soap and talc in 1974, Close-Up toothpaste in 1975, and Fair & Lovely skin cream in 1978, but the overall business remained small. In 1986 it was integrated into the Indian affiliate of Chesebrough-Pond's, which was 40 per cent owned, and headed by an ex-Unilever manager. This provided the organizational basis for a strategy for faster growth in personal care.[79] In contrast, the acquisition of Brooke Bond did not result in an immediate integration with Unilever's other Indian operations. A merged company would have controlled 25 per cent of total tea consumed within India, and it was decided to postpone any restructuring until competition issues had been resolved.[80]

Unilever's challenges in India became more economic during the second half of the 1980s. Hindustan Lever faced serious competitive pressure from Nirma, a low-cost detergent manufacturer. The fabrics market had been dominated by hard soap, but Unilever's premium powder brand Surf was decimated after 1975 when Nirma launched a powder at parity with hard soaps, but with much better washing power, providing a new 'value for money' concept. Having begun with low-price products, Nirma moved upmarket with products which directly competed with Unilever's customer base and took market share from them. In response, Hindustan Lever began to launch several low-cost but quality products, including Wheel detergent powders and bars, Lifebuoy soap, and Breeze toilet soap. The Wheel brand, launched in 1987, held over one-fifth of the market by 1993.

A number of factors were important in Unilever's survival and growth in India. In addition to its long-established presence in the country, the early commitment to localization provided a strong management cadre which, in addition to business capabilities, was able to negotiate concessions within the political system. Hindustan Lever's senior management was highly respected. In 1986 Ashok Ganguly, a scientist who had become Hindustan Lever chairman six years previously, was chosen as Businessman of the Year by the magazine *Business India*. Unilever was flexible enough also to permit rural development and heavy chemicals projects which enhanced the company's image within India, while the acceptance of low levels of remittances allowed the building of the business, as well as its survival in difficult times.

Brazil: Surviving Inflation

Unilever was an early foreign investor in Brazil. Irmãos Brazil had begun by making toilet soap in 1929, and six years later toothpaste was introduced. During the

16 A supermarket demonstration for Zwan meat products in Mexico in 1987. Zwan was acquired by Unilever in 1971 as part of the acquisition of Zwanenberg NV.

17 Unox started sponsoring the Dutch Elfstedentocht during the mid-1990s, and also sponsored skating on natural ice.

19 An advertisement for Ragu pasta sauce in the United States in 1988. The Ragu brand, which dated from the 1930s, was acquired by Chesebrough-Pond's in 1969, and passed into Unilever ownership in 1986.

18 An advertising promotion for Cup-A-Soup in the United States in 1987. In 1970 T. J. Lipton pioneered the new market for instant soups in the United States when it launched Cup-A-Soup.

20 Advertisement for turkey feed sold by BOCM Silcock, Britain's largest animal feeds company, in 1987.

21 A Ben & Jerry's ice cream street vendor in Britain, shortly after the firm was acquired by Unilever in 2000.

23 Enjoying a Knorr Cubitos seasoning cube, sold in the Caribbean and Brazil, in 2004. Knorr was acquired by Unilever through the acquisition of Bestfoods four years previously. The original German business originated in the early nineteenth century.

22 Enjoying Slim-Fast on North Shore beach, O'ahu, Hawaii in November 2000.

1950s Unilever began selling the soap powder Rinso, and in 1959 introduced Omo, Brazil's first synthetic detergent. Brazil was not a large business, but at least Unilever had a base in one of the world's largest countries which was about to begin an era of fast growth. Between 1950 and 1981 Brazil was to achieve nearly a tenfold increase in industrial output. Its population reached 130 million by the latter year, with some 70 per cent of them urban.[81]

Unilever took three crucial steps to build a larger Brazilian business. The first was the acquisition in 1960 of Unilever's main detergents competitor Companhia Gessy Industrial, which was about twice Unilever's existing size in the country. This company was owned by two brothers of Italian descent who were not on speaking terms, and was managed by former P & G managers.[82] The business was offered first to P & G, but when the latter hesitated Unilever's manager in Brazil telephoned Harold Hartog, then on the Overseas Committee, who travelled to Brazil with Unilever's Finance Director, and bought Gessy.[83] It was a risky decision, as the Brazilian economy was already manifesting signs of high inflation, but it was also visionary. The new Gessy Lever, created in 1961 by merging the two companies, was excellently positioned as the Brazilian economy started to industrialize rapidly and mass urbanization took place, as the government pursued import substitution policies. Meanwhile high levels of protection shut out competitors.

The second crucial step taken in Brazil was the building of a managerial cadre. Gessy Lever was the first large Brazilian company to recruit university graduates. Initially they were recruited to form a new marketing department. The first Brazilian president of Gessy Lever, Paschoal Ricardo—appointed in 1974—was recruited as a sales manager in the 1950s and became marketing director in 1965. As in India, the recruitment and retention of high-quality local management was essential both for growing the business and for relations with the government.

The third crucial step Unilever took in Brazil was to find a means of survival in conditions of high inflation. By the 1960s inflation was already 20 per cent, and reached 60 per cent in some years. By 1980 it had reached 100 per cent per annum, and ten years later annual inflation stood at over 2,500 per cent. This high level of inflation had a number of severe consequences, including that a company might make a considerable profit in local currency, only for it to become loss making in hard currency. Inflation was not an issue for Unilever's fixed assets such as factories and other fixed capital, where an accounting system was in place for calculating depreciation on the basis of replacement values. The problem was the impact on working capital. The Brazilian business had long supply lines with lots of the raw materials for use in detergents manufacture coming from Europe; these had to be paid for in hard currency. On the other hand Unilever did not receive income until it had sold its products, which could take three weeks to reach consumers in the further parts of the country. In the context of this situation, inflation had a very distorting effect on the calculation of profits because of its impact on Unilever's stocks and debtors, mitigated by the effect on money due from creditors. Unilever's traditional accounting system based on historical values sent completely the wrong management signals.

During the 1960s the Dutch accountants Unilever sent to Brazil—as to so many other countries—developed a management reporting system appropriate to a country experiencing high inflation. The first step was to limit the problem by borrowing money, and so passing on the problem to the supplier of the funds. One member of the Brazilian Board was dedicated to dealing with the numerous banks—up to one hundred—from which money was borrowed. This left a part of the working capital 'uncovered'. An 'inflation charge' was calculated based on the inflation rate and the length of time money was at risk. Unilever's reporting system showed historical profit margins. The accountants then calculated outside the books another column which deducted the 'inflation charge' from the margins. The price was then set. Subsequently, different inflation charges were worked out for different products because the turnover of funds differed.[84]

A further layer of complexity in dealing with inflation related to the issue of price controls. Unilever needed to persuade the government to allow price rises, and also to get the right amount of increase, for there could be as much as a four-month lag before prices could be raised.[85] Unilever operated in a context where it was known that prices would be increased, but not by how much. The solution was to phase production. The company sought to produce when it could make a profit, just after the prices were increased. At that stage managers tried to get as much out to the market as possible, selling at a discount. Then over time the discount was reduced, and the company stopped selling to the trade towards the end of the period. The underlying principle was only to sell when a margin was obtainable. Although this presented a challenging business environment, the system of price controls and high inflation was arguably easier to handle for a large company such as Unilever, which could play with several different products, than for single-product companies, which were much more vulnerable.[86]

Subsequently in Brazil, and a number of other Latin American economies, Unilever encountered not simply rapid inflation, but hyperinflation. Survival in hyperinflationary conditions required more than inflation proofing accounting systems. In such situations, Unilever managers learned to operate on a cash flow basis in order to protect the substance of the business. Daily or more frequent meetings had to be held to review cash positions, sales performance, and practically everything else as conditions were constantly changing. Wages needed be paid on a weekly or sometimes even daily basis, while every attempt would be made to try to secure extended credit from suppliers. At the same time zero gearing was necessary because of the need to be protected from very high real interest rates. And while product of sustained investment and considerable nerve in the face of sometimes adverse conditions. The decision to buy Gessy was risky, but the rewards in terms of market share in detergents were high. Thereafter Unilever ploughed funds back into Brazil to grow the business, whilst developing methods of management accounting—later transferred elsewhere in the Overseas countries—which enabled managers to run their businesses profitably and effectively in conditions of high inflation.

South Africa: Profits and Ethics

Sunlight soap had been first sold in South Africa in 1891, and Lever Brothers had begun manufacturing in 1911 in Durban. The business had grown rapidly, becoming multi-plant, but remained essentially a detergents operation until the Second World War, with products such as toothpaste and toilet soaps imported from Britain. The basic reason was the peculiar nature of the market, which had a minority White population broadly equivalent in income levels to developed markets, and a larger and much poorer Black majority.

During the post-war decades Unilever's business diversified into household cleaning products, shampoos, deodorants, margarine, fats, ice cream, soups, cheeses, chemicals, and animal feeds. Apart from restrictions on the sale of margarine, Unilever was free of government constraints and expanded both through greenfield building and acquisitions. A subdued level of competition compared, say, to Australia resulted in the South African business being consistently profitable. The most important international competitor was Colgate, which held a strong position in toothpaste, and in 1964 had pre-empted Unilever with the first synthetic detergent, Fab. Leaving aside this irritant, a high level of tariff protection completed a dream scenario for Unilever. As in Brazil, in 1969 the South African business was divisionalized into eight companies—the largest of which was Lever, the detergents company—organized on product lines under the control of the wholly owned Unilever South Africa (Pty) Ltd.[95]

During the late 1960s and early 1970s sales increased quickly as the market expanded at annual rates of 7 and 8 per cent. Many capital projects were undertaken, including extensions of the cheese, detergents, and margarine factories, and the construction of a new personal products factory. Detergents provided at least two-fifths of the profits. Unilever had an entrenched position with rural consumers, and as their incomes rose they changed in increasing numbers from Sunlight soap to powders. Lever had pursued novel marketing methods to reach rural consumers, including mobile selling and demonstration units, leading to a situation when brand names such as Sunlight and Omo became generic for soap and detergents.[96]

Meanwhile Elida Gibbs came up with a series of innovations in deodorant products, including Impulse. There were few really weak parts of the South African business, although both animal feedstuffs and ice cream were sold in 1975 and 1980 respectively. The development of a packaged convenience foods business was also slow, as the White population had Black servants and less demand for convenience, while the Black population was too poor to purchase such products.[97]

By the mid-1970s South Africa's importance to Unilever was considerable, but it also looked increasingly risky. South Africa was a White-ruled state committed to policies of racial segregation towards its non-White majority population on a continent where colonial regimes had been replaced by independent African states bitterly hostile to South African policies. Change of some kind appeared inevitable.[98] As internal dissent grew in South Africa, symbolized by the major riots in the Soweto township in 1976, there seemed to be a growing risk that the change might be violent.

South Africa posed moral dilemmas for Unilever. There was strict racial segregation in its South African factories.[99] A breakdown of Unilever South Africa's 5,400 employees in 1973 showed that its 465 managers included just 1 Black African; its 1,600 monthly paid staff included 112 Africans, 96 (mixed race) Coloureds, and 97 Indians. In contrast there were no Whites among the 3,331 weekly paid employees.[100] Unilever began experiencing problems transferring expatriate managers to their South African operations because of their—or in some cases their family's—political objections to the regime. In 1970 Kenneth Durham declined Woodroofe's invitation to go to South Africa on these grounds.[101]

The essential issue for Unilever was whether it wished to act as a social pioneer to challenge the system, or whether it would act as a law-abiding corporate citizen and follow government policy. Unilever's answer was the latter, but it was more active in some respects behind the scenes than its public statements indicated. During the early 1970s it introduced a scheme for recruiting and developing Africans for management positions. Eight African graduates were taken on, but the experiment failed because of suspicion by White employees. Subsequently, it was decided to concentrate on developing basic skills of African employees, and to keep a low profile while making 'quiet progress . . . in the advancement of Africans at staff grades'.[102] In salary structure, Unilever eliminated discrimination by colour in its salary scales in the early 1970s, by which time it was already paying more to non-White employees than other international competitors and especially local firms. Unilever benchmarked itself against its competitors, and felt confident that its wage rates and promotion policy were ahead of the average, though visitors from Europe sometimes felt obliged to prod the local management to speed up the promotion of non-Whites to management positions.[103]

Unilever reacted as the South African government began to liberalize some of its more discriminatory laws in response to both international pressure and the

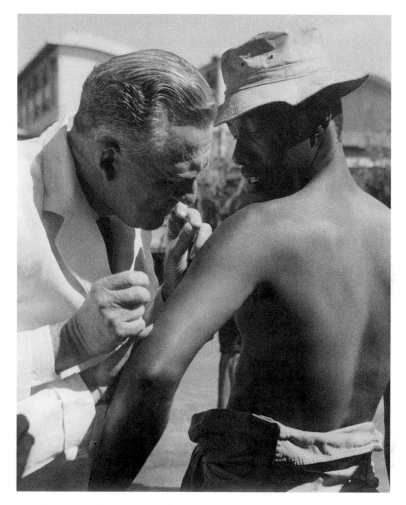

37 Innoculating an employee of Wall's ice cream in South Africa against smallpox in 1966.

growing need for skilled labour. In 1975 Unilever South Africa launched a development programme to achieve within five years 5 per cent non-Whites in their management and assistant management grades. This target was achieved in 1979, and then raised to 8 per cent. By 1980 out of 709 managers, Unilever had 18 Africans, 3 Coloureds, and 17 Indians, though there remained the context in which the business operated. 'The black manager is integrated from 8 am to 5pm but segregated from 5 pm to 8 am,' one report noted in 1980. 'During working hours he may well be responsible for white staff, who accept this relationship. But during non-working hours he has to return, possibly driving his Company car, to the black township.'[104]

During the second half of the 1970s Unilever's sales in South Africa began to stagnate in terms of constant prices as the economy slowed down, although as dividends and service fees were fully remittable South Africa continued to be a major source of funds to Unilever. There was a severe recession for some years, and simultaneous price wars in detergents against new entrant Henkel as well as long-established Colgate, and in margarine against local competitors.[105] South Africa's isolated international political situation and its impact on investor confidence was effectively dragging the economy down. However, a high gold price could still produce rising incomes and growing business.

During the 1980s Unilever's strategy in South Africa had two themes. It sought to preserve a large business which produced the largest single source of remittances of all the Overseas countries. At times there were ferocious price wars with competitors, especially in margarine.[106] Unilever continued to invest heavily in expanding capacity. In 1980 Lever Brothers acquired Quality Products, the market leader in toilet soaps, hard soaps, and household cleaners, and owner of a popular value for money skin lotion called Dawn Lotion. During the first half of the 1980s a new toilet soap production facility was constructed in Durban. The acquisition of Brooke Bond Oxo created the largest tea and coffee business in the country. Subsequently the local Chesebrough-Pond's and Elizabeth Arden businesses were added. At the same time Unilever needed to increasingly justify its investment in the country at a time when there was widespread public calls for divestment.[107]

The importance of South African remittances made the political risks of the country a matter of considerable concern. There were frequent visits to the country and assessments of the situation. During autumn 1982 Maljers visited the country specifically to assess the political situation. He was characteristically critical to the local managers, and in his subsequent report to the Board was explicit about his own views that apartheid could 'only be rejected as a system'. However he concluded also that the South African regime was not going to collapse for some time, and recommended that the most useful thing the company could do in South Africa was to help social progress, especially in education.[108]

The political risks of South Africa were a matter of discussion whenever that country was discussed, but did little to prompt Unilever to consider changing its commitment to the country. In 1984, although the South African company predicted 'increased civil disturbance and terrorist activities' and 'increased pressure for trade sanctions against South Africa by the rest of the world', corporate strategy involved 'continued heavy investment in manufacturing capacity and plant modernisation'.[109] The management sought to build contacts within the emerging new South Africa. As Unilever was headquartered in Durban in Natal province, this meant that the closest political links were developed with Chief Buthelezi, the president of the Zulu Inkatha movement. In some ways this was fortuitous as Buthelezi at that time had a more favourable view on capitalism than the African National Congress (ANC). In 1987, when Michael Angus and the chairman-designate of

Unilever South Africa met Buthelezi, he noted that Lever Bros. had always 'inspired' him, and he also rejected divestment.[110] Unilever also made contacts with a wide range of other opinion makers, including academics, and with the ANC.[111] Nelson Mandela's release from prison in 1990 symbolized the radical changes under way, but as Unilever South Africa looked into the future, it still predicted further pressures for divestment and sanctions.[112]

The likely direction of political change had its impact on marketing as Unilever sought to develop more sales among the Black population.[113] A new 125g wrapper was introduced in 1989 for Rama margarine designed to develop the Black market by increasing the frequency and quantity used.[114] Lipton hired a market research manager to help 'develop a keen understanding of Black eating needs'.[115] Market research was also undertaken by Melrose, the South African cheese company, to establish why Black consumption of processed cheese was much lower than White consumption. If the problem was found to be in lactose intolerance, it was thought that Unilever 'might have an interesting opportunity with a new product concept which would eliminate critical ingredients and therefore be specially designed for this target group'.[116] However a proposal to develop soya-based products encountered little interest from the Foods Executive back in Europe.[117]

Unilever built an extremely strong business in South Africa on the basis of an early start in the market and subsequently sustained investment. High levels of protection and the absence of most international competitors provided the basis for a profitable operation which could continue to remit dividends with little hindrance. The decision to stay in South Africa in the 1980s despite a barrage of criticism from outside and even inside the firm was another manifestation of Unilever's long-run determination to stay in markets if at all possible. Unilever's employment and marketing strategies evolved as circumstances changed. By the 1980s the company was building contacts with the opinion formers of the likely new leaders of South Africa. As elsewhere, Unilever had earned a reputation for both business competence and corporate ethics which meant that all parties, whatever their own differences, had no wish other than that Unilever stayed in South Africa.

Perspectives

The retention of the large presence in emerging markets was a singular achievement in an era of hostility to Western multinationals in many countries, economic instability including hyperinflation and the world debt crisis, and the economic decline of Africa. Unilever built and maintained businesses in countries which many of its international competitors declined to enter because of perceived risks. Its companies maintained high standards of managerial and technical competence, and sought to maintain high standards of corporate behaviour in countries where ethical standards were sometimes seriously threatened.

Unilever's formidable position in emerging markets rested on multiple factors. It was a first mover in many countries, and built businesses through decades of heavy investment in plant and marketing, with low dividend flows in return. Its overall size and scope of operations permitted such patience. The company's knowledge of many markets was cumulative and deep. Unilever often found itself well placed in domestic markets as they became protected by high tariff walls, even though it also had to contend with price and capacity controls, dividend limitations, and other government regulations. Whether through making toilet soap from palm oil, or engaged in rural development, or building their own power plants to run factories, Unilever's management was flexible enough to adjust to the environment of emerging countries. Unilever was more willing to accept the risks of emerging markets than many Western consumer goods firms, and as a reward it was spared competition from its international rivals. The almost universal recognition that Unilever was an honest business enterprise, which made and sold products which a lot of consumers wanted, meant that the company was accepted as an honest broker by quite different political regimes.

Finally, Unilever's commitment to localization of senior management was critical. In many countries Unilever identified, and promoted to the most senior positions, some of the best business leaders of their generation. This meant not only that Unilever's businesses were managed by extremely good people, but that the company was able to function as a virtual 'insider' within governmental and business networks in many countries. This strategy worked particularly well in India, and became the basis not only for Unilever's survival in the country during the 1970s, but also its subsequent spectacular growth. Unilever was thus able to marry its formidable corporate knowledge base with local capabilities and knowledge. Unilever's long history in many countries and its willingness to localize senior management positions gave it the information and the capability to respond to risks and not to seek safer havens in the developed world.

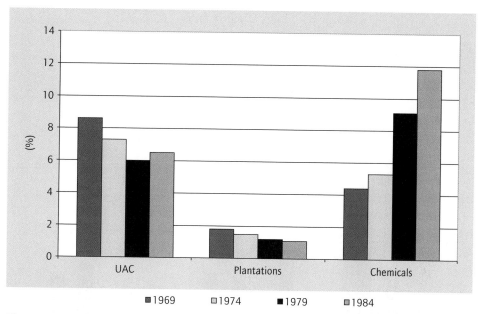

Fig. 7.3 Capital employed in UAC, Plantations, and Chemicals as a proportion of Unilever total, 1969–1984 (%).

House symbolized both this autonomy and the gap in cultures between UAC and its parent. In 1955 a separate Plantations Executive, renamed Group two years later, was formed, which reported directly to the Special Committee until 1974.[4] From 1975 Plantations Group reported via the Overseas Committee, but Plantations again gained a main board director in 1979 when T. Thomas joined the Overseas Committee and was allocated responsibility for plantations. Thomas retained responsibility for Plantations when he became Chemicals Co-ordinator in 1980, and it passed with him into the new Agribusiness Co-ordination in 1986. Chemicals got its own Co-ordination in 1965, which twenty years later became the only Co-ordination with worldwide responsibility.

The ownership of UAC and plantations first raised the issue of how to handle intra-firm trade within Unilever. Following a major collapse in commodity prices in 1921, it had been decided that the trading relationship between Lever Brothers and UAC's predecessor, the Niger Company, would be conducted on an arm's-length basis. This practice continued when UAC was formed and became wholly owned by Unilever. In the early 1930s it was agreed that Unilever would be treated as a most favoured customer of UAC, which had to offer palm oil and oilseeds to the company at prices no higher than to any other buyer, while Unilever agreed not to buy west African produce without giving UAC first option. Transfer pricing was explicitly ruled out in 1932, when it was stipulated that transactions had to be conducted at

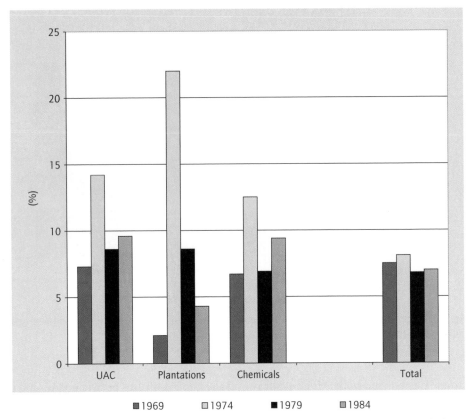

Fig. 7.4 Yields on UAC, Plantations, and Chemicals and Unilever average, 1969–1984 (%).

market prices. Under the same arrangement, Unilever was not restricted to selling its products through UAC, while UAC could sell products from other manufacturers in competition with those of Unilever.[5] By the end of the 1920s the principle was also firmly established that Unilever companies purchased the produce of Unilever plantations at market prices, so a purely commercial relationship existed between them and the companies which used their produce. From then on the ownership of plantations was justified by their ability to make profits.[6]

Post-war vertical integration resulted in a substantial growth of intra-firm trade within Unilever. During the 1960s and 1970s it represented around 9 per cent of total sales, and included the sales of chemicals, perfumes and flavours, oils for margarine, and packaging materials, as well as transport and distribution, advertising, and market research services. As in the cases of UAC and plantations, by the 1960s the general principle was established that 'the normal relationship between Unilever suppliers and Unilever users should be one of free bargaining. Users should have free access to buy from, and suppliers should be free to supply, the outside market'.[7] This policy encouraged Unilever firms in chemicals, as well as in packaging, transport, and other services, to go in search of third party markets, but it also highlighted the issue of whether their ownership by Unilever was either necessary or desirable.

Overall, the inclusion of trading, plantations, and chemicals within the boundaries of Unilever raised fundamental questions about both the nature of the company and its competencies. The following sections consider the nature and performance of Unilever's investments in these activities before returning to an assessment of their overall contribution to Unilever.

The United Africa Company

The presence of UAC within Unilever, let alone its size and importance, was extraordinary. By the 1960s the withdrawal from commodity trading and general importing was largely completed. Many of the residual merchanting activities were transferred to a Manchester-based affiliate, G. B. Ollivant, which had been rescued from near-bankruptcy and acquired by UAC in 1933, but which remained almost entirely autonomous—even possessing its own Board and accounts—and even in competition with UAC until the end of the 1970s.[8] UAC's new strategy involved investing in manufacturing and other value-adding activities such as automobile distribution in west Africa and elsewhere. As almost all African countries imposed heavy tariff barriers to encourage industrialization, this strategy provided a potentially viable route to rebuilding and growing the business.

UAC's former structure of broadly similar and often competing companies was reorganized into specialist product divisions concerned with automobiles, chemist shops, cold storage and refrigerated foodstuffs, hardware, and textiles, to implement this new strategy. There was no convergence between UAC and its parent. The new businesses were not based on the branding and distribution of consumer goods, but on knowledge about, and contacts in, west Africa. By the end of the 1960s UAC was a mini-conglomerate. It had over one-third of its capital invested in specialist trading, slightly over one-quarter in general trading, and just over one-fifth in manufacturing. The remainder was in diverse activities including oceanic and river transport, property, insurance, and construction.

Alternative scenarios to UAC's diversification in Africa and 'redeployment' in Europe were not considered, even though the UAC's existence within Unilever was not universally applauded. Members of the Special Committee such as Ernest Woodroofe, let alone the NV chairmen, considered UAC as rather out of place in a modern business enterprise, but UAC was a powerful vested interest. It had been highly profitable in the past, and it had also produced a number of exceptionally able managers. These included Cole himself, who kept a protective hand over the company. As the late 1960s were a time when British and Dutch tensions over Co-ordination were considerable, the British directors had no interest in diminishing one of the pillars of the British 'side' of the company, while the Dutch directors respected UAC as not in their sphere of influence.[9]

Nor was the alternative strategy considered of trying to meld UAC closer to other Unilever companies in Africa. UAC was excluded from manufacturing Unilever's products, which for historical reasons were the responsibility of other parts of the organization. During the 1920s UAC's predecessor company had controlled a pioneering soap manufacturing company in Nigeria, but on the formation of Unilever this was placed under the control of the Overseas Committee.[10] Thereafter UAC and the Overseas Committee retained quite separate businesses. UAC's A. J. Seward companies in Nigeria, Ghana, Sierra Leone, and Ivory Coast manufactured and sold ethnic skin and hair products and proprietary medicines, which paralleled and even duplicated the businesses managed by the Overseas Committee. When UAC invested in manufacturing, it did so in a variety of joint ventures—itself a rare phenomenon within Unilever—with European and US manufacturers who contributed the industry knowledge it lacked.

UAC's most profitable joint ventures for long periods were in brewing. The post-war origins of this venture lay in the threat by another company to start brewing in Nigeria, which threatened UAC's large import market, much of it supplied by Heineken. The upshot was the formation of Nigerian Breweries Ltd., owned one-third each by UAC and Heineken, and the remainder by other beer importers. Production began in 1949. In 1958 UAC and Heineken also built a brewery in Ghana. The low-cost lager, chilled for tropical consumption, proved popular.[11] By 1970 UAC had also established a partnership with Heineken in Sierra Leone and Chad. During the mid-1960s UAC contemplated using the Heineken alliance to develop brewing interests worldwide. Discussions took place on possible collaboration in many countries, including South Africa, Indonesia, Malaya, Greece, Italy, and Canada, but from the late 1960s relations between the two partners cooled, especially following Unilever's abortive merger negotiations with Allied Breweries, as well as conflicts of interest caused by UAC's joint ventures with Guinness.[12]

In 1961 UAC entered a joint venture with Guinness to brew stout in Nigeria, which had become Guinness's largest overseas market. UAC had initially suggested a marketing joint venture with Guinness, but the brewer opted instead to go straight away into bottling. This became its first overseas brewing business. The initial shareholding was Guinness 57 per cent and UAC 33 per cent, and a Nigerian local government the remainder. Guinness stout was marketed in Nigeria as a cure for various diseases, as well as a means to increase male sexual potentency. A high level of profitability persisted even after price controls began to be imposed during the 1970s.[13]

Overall by the early 1980s UAC had accumulated investments in thirteen African breweries, including eight in Nigeria—four each with Heineken and Guinness—two each in Ghana and Chad, one in Sierra Leone, and a minority shareholding in a Kronenbourg brewery in the Congo.

UAC also invested in west African textiles. During the Second World War UAC had proposed the establishment of cotton mills in Nigeria, but the colonial authorities had not responded enthusiastically, both because of a desire to protect Nigeria's hand-spinning industry, and because textile imports were a major source of government revenue. UAC finally opened a textile factory in Nigeria in 1965, rather late in the day, only to have it wrecked during the civil war. UAC was far more successful in the former French colony of Ivory Coast. In 1970 UAC opened a factory to print wax-block textile, a venture which emerged out of the large west African trade in Dutch wax prints, a product of the old batik prints trade between the Netherlands and the Dutch East Indies which had passed by the west coast of Africa. Uniwax, a joint venture with the Dutch wax printing firm Gamma in which UAC held over 40 per cent of the equity, was initially designed to protect UAC and Gamma's market for wax prints, which was potentially threatened by plans to build an integrated textile factory by a Japanese firm. Uniwax became a profitable industrial venture employing Gamma's unique technology and specialized designs, and by the mid-1970s controlled 70 per cent of wax-print production in west Africa.[14]

UAC held the large Caterpillar franchise for tractors and other equipment for Nigeria, Ghana, Sierra Leone, Kenya, Uganda, and Tanzania, and it was also an importer of General Motors trucks and cars into west Africa, and Austin cars into east Africa. The business involved the provision of extensive servicing facilities, and in the late 1950s UAC also constructed its own assembly plants in Nigeria and Ghana. Later Isuzu commercial vehicles were assembled. UAC also assembled televisions and radios in collaboration with Matsushita in Nigeria. The possession of sole importation franchises for leading brands made it the market leader for office equipment in Nigeria and Ghana. The Kodak franchise in Nigeria, Ghana, Sierra Leone, and Ivory Coast, including local processing in Nigeria, also gave UAC market leadership in photographic equipment in those countries. UAC also had its own packaging business in Nigeria which supplied all the labels and corrugated packages needed by the breweries and by the Lever Brothers business in the country. UAC had the only nationwide distribution system in Nigeria, and as a result had a large distribution business which could reach the three-quarters of the population which lived in the countryside. The Kingsway chains of department stores in the larger cities of Nigeria, Ghana, and Zaire became national symbols of advanced retailing.

Nigeria was always the largest host economy for UAC. It was Africa's largest country—by 1980 its population had reached 80 million—and for a time its economic prospects were regarded as bright, even though the civil war in the late 1960s cast doubts on the country's stability. The oil price rises after 1973 transformed the country's economic prospects. UAC's predecessors had performed a quasi-government role in the nineteenth century, and that aura remained in Nigeria, where it was the largest private sector company. In 1976 two-thirds of UAC's profits came from Nigeria, and by 1983 this figure had risen to four-fifths.

Ghana was the second most important host economy with almost one-fifth of total UAC capital employed. In Ghana, like Nigeria, UAC's position was far more akin to a national institution than a commercial firm. It made large contributions to charities, rural development, and community programmes. In 1957 it built and donated a large sports stadium in Kumasi at a cost—then very substantial—of £90,000—and afterwards donated a community centre building in Accra. UAC established and maintained a range of medical facilities and hospitals, including one at Samreboi for the workers in its timber business which by the early 1970s was providing free treatment for some 35,000 patients per annum. A wide range of company training schemes was also developed, while UAC made grants to the University of Ghana and for secondary school scholarships.[15]

The remainder of UAC's capital was widely dispersed throughout west and east Africa, the Arabian Gulf, the Canaries, Morocco, and the Solomon Islands. In the Arab world, UAC was forced to close its once-substantial Iraqi business in 1964, but from the 1950s opened a string of trading partnerships in the Gulf, beginning with Dubai in 1951 and reaching Saudi Arabia in 1969. The Gulf business originated from sale on clients' account of alcohol to ocean-going vessels, and gradually the business expanded to direct sales, concentrating on air-conditioning and alcohol, items not of interest to local merchants. During the 1970s alcohol sales provided around three-quarters of UAC's total profits. In the Solomon Islands, UAC began logging operations in 1963, selling timber to Korea and Japan. There were also UAC's numerous diversified acquisitions in Europe by this stage.[16]

During the mid-1970s UAC boomed. Reinforcing the awesome oil-induced prosperity in Nigeria and the Gulf, there were booms in other commodity prices, especially cocoa and sugar. The most pressing managerial challenge was to ship sufficient merchandise from Europe to these markets, and to cope with often inadequate port facilities. An article in *Unilever Magazine* at the end of the 1970s noted that UAC had 'grown into one of the most exciting businesses in the Concern'.[17]

UAC seemed able to succeed even when countries were afflicted by civil wars, and despite government restrictions. In many countries compulsory 'localization' involved the sale of shares at prices which were below what Unilever considered their fair value. The most serious blow came in Nigeria in 1972 when the Nigerian Enterprises Promotion Decree forced UAC to sell 40 per cent of its shareholding to Nigerian shareholders. In 1977 UAC was required to sell a further 20 per cent of its shareholding to Nigerian shareholders. In Ghana UAC had to sell a 40 per cent stake in its operations. UAC's shareholdings in the brewery joint ventures with Guinness and Heineken were reduced to fewer than 15 per cent. Yet the demand for beer was so enormous that UAC received excellent returns even with its reduced equity. It was easy to overlook the longer-term implications stemming from the loss of full owner-ship, including the threat to future flows of dividends and profits, and the fact that it was becoming more difficult to control the affiliates, including their standards of corporate conduct. UAC also lost its freedom to sell them easily, given the complex web of governments and individuals that became stakeholders.

In retrospect, it can be seen that the high profitability of the UAC business resulted in misjudgements concerning the nature of its capabilities. This was most evident in the attempts to build businesses in Europe. UAC's managers knew about doing business in Africa, especially west Africa. UAC possessed region-specific rather than product-specific competencies. It knew about distribution channels, and the legal system, and it knew about the business community in Africa. This knowledge was not transferable to Europe. Even within Africa UAC's franchise was a diminish-ing asset. Its profitable businesses rested on joint ventures or franchises with other firms who sought to benefit from UAC's knowledge of African markets. These inter-firm collaborations were essential to the repositioning of UAC away from commod-ity and general trading, but they also made UAC dependent on the continuation of good relationships with these firms, while any hope of extending its business beyond Africa depended on their co-operation. UAC's joint venture partners were first-class companies in their industries, and consequently the joint ventures were considerable business successes, but UAC's contribution remained its region-specific knowledge and distribution expertise. When UAC attempted to persuade its part-ners to go into ventures with it elsewhere, they showed little interest, while over time they also accumulated their own understanding of west African markets.[18] Timber was one of the few ventures where the skills and expertise were internalized with UAC. It became a recognized leader in dealing with tropical hardwoods, with operations in the Solomon Islands and Indonesia as well aswest Africa.

The profits from the oil boom disguised such problems. Even the most unlikely parts of UAC boomed, including the shipping affiliate Palm Line, which provided a fast liner service between west Africa and Europe. In the late 1960s the Palm Line's ageing fleet appeared to have no future in a context where nationally owned ship-ping lines looked set to dominate west African shipping, and in 1974 UAC decided to withdraw from shipping. However, growing profits thereafter led to a reversal of this decision, especially as the company collected freights in hard currency and had no remittance problems. The fleet was expanded again. Second-hand ships were acquired, and new ships ordered, taking the fleet to seven vessels in 1982.

The collapse of the Nigerian oil boom, coinciding with the recession in Europe which all but finished off most of UAC's putative diversifications, revealed the fragile underlying nature of the UAC business. Nigerian government oil revenues had soared from $1.4 billion in 1973 to reach over $23 billion in 1980. Oil exports provided over 95 per cent of Nigerian foreign exchange earnings and almost as large a share of the government's total income. After 1980 output fell sharply, initially with OPEC's reduction in production, and then with general oversupply as the industrialized world went into recession. Government oil revenues fell even further because of a rapid depreciation of the Nigerian naira against the dollar. By 1983 government oil revenues had fallen to $10 billion, and the level of reserves was hardly sufficient to pay for a few months of imports. Nigerian purchasing power fell even more sharply because of the cost of servicing an external debt which had grown phenomenally.[19]

While UAC may have had little future in a Unilever which was searching for its 'core' competencies, the near-collapse of Nigeria sealed its fate sooner rather than later. The subsequent rundown of the business was quite fast. By the end of 1989 UAC's business, which had employed 71,000 people at the beginning of the decade, was reduced to three activities—Textiles, Power Applications, and Breweries—employing around 17,000 people.[20] Divestment proved a long process. Unilever was locked in by fear of a political backlash to withdrawal, and acute problems in disposing of the remaining businesses, especially because they were not wholly owned, and because the right price could not be obtained because of exchange control regulations. There were also

39 One of the Palm Line's ships, Kumasi Palm, (*taken in 1963*).

problems with joint venture partners and franchisers. Unilever's franchises in Britain and west Africa represented Caterpillar's largest worldwide franchise, and Caterpillar was known to oppose their sale to any existing franchisees.[21]

UAC was a large, if curious, component of Unilever. The original reasons for its presence having entirely disappeared, it 'reinvented' itself as a profitable business. UAC's strong franchise in west Africa rested on first mover advantages combined with flexible strategies. It faced no significant international competition in most of its businesses. Local-based competition was sometimes more serious, in part because of the willingness of some local firms to engage in corruption of officials and others, but UAC's ethical standards brought their own benefits in the shape of reputation. The problem for UAC was that its knowledge and competencies were non-transferable, and a diminishing asset even within Africa, while its main host region was afflicted by long-term political, institutional, and economic problems. While the reallocation of capital and management to the rest of Unilever would have been logical, this ran in the face of strong sentimental attachment to UAC and differences in corporate culture which meant that UAC managers were all but untransferable elsewhere in Unilever.

From a different perspective, UAC functioned as a 'cash cow' which gave its parent the time and resources to restructure its businesses in Europe and to regain control of its US business. During the 1970s a sharp reduction of new entrants produced a steadily rising age profile. By 1984 the average age of all UAC managers was 47 with average length of service of over twenty-three years.[22] In a deteriorating economic and political environment—despite the Nigerian oil boom—these ageing managers sustained large and profitable brewing, batik, tractor distribution, and other businesses, while maintaining ethical standards in a region in which corruption was becoming endemic.

Plantations

After initial investments in plantations before the First World War, Lever Brothers and later Unilever's plantation investments continued to expand. In 1929 other plantations were added in the British Cameroons and Nigeria. In 1947 a small palm oil estate was acquired in Johore in Malaya, and in 1960 a palm oil plantation was started from jungle in Sabah, now part of East Malaysia.

Unilever's extensive plantation interests spanned Africa, Asia, and the Pacific. However, over half the acreage was in the Belgian Congo (Zaire), followed (by 1980) by Malaysia (15 per cent) and Cameroon (12 per cent), with smaller acreages in

Nigeria, Ghana, and the Solomon Islands. Over two-thirds of the total acreage was devoted to palm oil. Unilever's large involvement in African palm oil reflected its early involvement in the industry, for by the 1960s the former domination of the worldwide industry by Nigeria, the Belgian Congo, and Indonesia had been successfully challenged by Malaysia following the introduction of the Tenera variety of palm oil, found until the 1930s only in the wilds of west Africa. By 1982 Malaysia accounted for 56 per cent of world production, and 85 per cent of world exports of palm oil.[23] A further 16 per cent of Unilever's plantation acreage in 1980 was devoted to rubber, with a smaller amount of cocoa under cultivation, and a tiny amount of tea, despite Unilever's importance in the world tea business.[24]

While the UAC occupied a sacrosanct position within Unilever, there was no special aura around the ownership of plantations. As palm and other oils were sold to Unilever companies on a strictly arm's-length basis, it was not surprising that the point of owning plantations came under question. During the early 1970s the Corporate Development director proposed at least partial divestment, and a potential buyer to whom at least the rubber plantations could be sold.[25] However this was not an era when radical divestments were made in a hurry. When the Special Committee, in the following year, discussed selling the Congo plantations with the management groups involved in that country—Plantations, Overseas Committee, and UAC—it reached the conclusion that if Unilever 'gave up the plantations, there could be repercussions for our other businesses in the country'.[26] Unilever plantations were high-profile ventures and large employers, and their disposal was no easy matter.

The discussions on divestment at this time, and subsequently, were influenced by variations in the profitability of this highly cyclical industry. In constant money terms, agricultural raw material prices declined over the post-war decades. The price of crude palm oil fell in constant US$ money terms by around 2.5 per cent per annum between 1950 and 1990, and that of tea by 3.4 per cent per annum. However, there were large fluctuations within these trends. The price volatility of oil and fats was higher than for most primary commodities. Palm oil prices surged in both the mid-1970s and the mid-1980s. Fig. 7.5 shows the movements in profits of the Plantations Group over time, adjusted in 1990 prices.

During the second half of the 1960s profits were flat and modest, and there was little enthusiasm for developing the business further. Yields averaged fewer than 3 per cent between 1966 and 1969, but in the early 1970s they rose to over 8 per cent as a result of high commodity prices. Sceptics maintained that Plantations were a commodity-type business which tended to reduce yields over time.[27] However, high yields reduced any sense of urgency about divestment. The counter-argument for staying, then and later, was that Plantations represented only a small part of Unilever's total capital employed, whose returns if low could do little overall

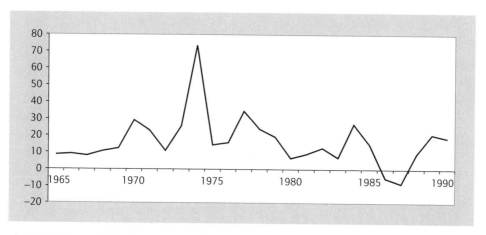

Fig. 7.5 Unilever Plantations group profits 1965–1990 (constant 1990 £ million)*.
*The profits from the plantations acquired with Brooke Bond in 1984 are excluded until they were integrated with Plantations Group in 1989.

damage, while on occasion they could be high. In a small way, Plantations could even be regarded as something of a hedge, for their good years coincided with high raw materials prices for Unilever's major businesses.

The future of Plantations Group was the subject of a report commissioned by the Special Committee in 1974. It suggested that Unilever's plantations interests should focus on those crops and countries which were profitable, and of greatest relevance to the business as a whole. This was interpreted as concentrating largely on palm oil, coconuts, and 'tropical products'. It was argued that Unilever should 'in principle' divest itself of rubber plantations 'since there is no synergy with the rest of the business', and that the cocoa and tea plantations should also be sold. Total divestment from the Congo was recommended.[28] In practice, the plantations were retained in their entirety. By 1976 there were plans for possible new investments in Ecuador, Colombia, Brazil, and Indonesia.[29] Within two years the Special Committee were converted to the case 'for extending our direct involvement in primary products'.[30]

The new enthusiasm for plantations reflected not only high yields caused by rising commodity prices in these years, but also evidence of a moderation in the hostility of host governments towards foreign-owned plantations. During the 1960s the foreign ownership of land had started to become sensitive. In 1971 Unilever had handed its Bindo plantation to the Gabonese government without payment.[31] Unilever's plantation operations in the Congo were nationalized in 1975. The plantations were returned to Unilever in the following year, though with the government retaining a 40 per cent stake. Unilever's operations became closely linked with a World Bank scheme for agricultural development in the Congo.[32] It remained hard

40 Harvesting coconuts on a Unilever plantation in the Philippines in 1963.

to transfer remittances out of the country, but by the early 1980s Unilever found the government 'taking a more sensible attitude toward agriculture'.[33]

Elsewhere, the wave of anti-foreign sentiments on plantation ownership receded. In Malaysia the government had achieved the localization of the plantation businesses of many of the large British-owned groups at this time, including Sime Darby and Harrisons & Crosfield, and by the 1980s around two-thirds of the palm oil industry was government controlled. Unilever was able to deploy its negotiation skills and contacts to retain its ownership of plantations, though it did not seek to expand further as it did not want to risk enforced dilution of its equity. In Africa pressure mounted to retain plantations, rather than to sell them. During 1976 Unilever agreed with the government in Ghana to set up a new palm oil plantation from virgin bush in return for being allowed to remit earnings from its other businesses in the country.[34] In 1979 a decision to sell off the rubber plantations in Nigeria was reversed on political grounds.[35] By then the state of Nigerian agriculture had become critical—the country was even importing palm oil which had once been its principal export—and a Unilever divestment was politically unacceptable. There remained problems remitting profits from the African plantations back to Europe, but even in this respect there was a slight improvement during the final years of the 1970s.[36]

Unilever began to consider expanding its plantation interests. While palm and coconut oil retained their status as key crops, by the early 1980s cocoa and rubber were also seen as of interest for expansion, not least so as to widen the portfolio of risk.[37] Concerns about political risk in Africa stimulated a search for geographical diversification, as did the much greater profitability achievable elsewhere. During the early 1980s Unilever's estates in Malaysia produced over 80,000 tons of palm oil with 3,000 workers, while those in the Congo produced 67,000 tons with 23,000 workers. It was calculated that in the event of the rather optimistic scenario of all Unilever plantations being located in Malaysia, the profits from plantations would soar nearly fourfold.[38]

During 1978 Unilever acquired three plantations in Indonesia.[39] In 1981 a new development was commenced in the Llanos (plains) of Colombia; in 1982 the purchase of the Blohorn business brought with it two plantations in the Ivory Coast, and in 1983 Unilever purchased a 51 per cent shareholding in a privately owned palm oil plantation business in Thailand. This group had been responsible for introducing palm oil into the Krabi province in the south of the country during the 1970s, and Unilever's Thai business had been their largest customer. By 1985 Indonesia had become the favoured site for new plantation investment, and long, but ultimately unsuccessful, negotiations were held to acquire a large rubber estate in Sumatra—which would over time be converted to palm oil—owned by the US tyre company Uniroyal.[40]

The acquisition of Brooke Bond resulted in a major expansion of Unilever plantations, giving Unilever large tea plantations for the first time. Brooke Bond's plantations, located in both India and east Africa, accounted for the production of around 2 per cent of the world's tea in 1984. In 1980 the Kenyan business also diversified into flower cultivation, and by the time of Unilever's acquisition this had become the largest single carnation and rose project in the world. The case for the ownership of the tea plantations was tangential, except perhaps for some experimental purposes.[41] There was no intra-firm trade within Brooke Bond, and the tea from its plantations was sold in open auctions in London, India, and Africa. Unilever continued after 1984 to buy the bulk of its tea at auction.

There was also a downside to the ownership of the plantations, for they increased the risks of Unilever being criticized for exploiting cheap labour in poor countries.[42] The relative importance of wages in the overall cost structure of plantations meant that if costs were to be kept competitive, there was little opportunity for increasing wages. Yet for Unilever to be seen to pay tens of thousands of plantation workers what in European terms were very low wages was detrimental to its corporate image of being a benevolent employer, not least at a time when there was considerable criticism in the Netherlands and elsewhere about its investment in South Africa. The major means of increasing wages for plantation workers was to increase productivity on the estates, but that option also presented difficulties, as any reduction of employment in India or Africa was a sensitive matter.[43]

By the middle of the 1980s, as the Special Committee began to focus on core business, the role of plantations—labour intensive, cyclical, unpredictable, based on raw materials, and located in tropical countries—came under renewed scrutiny. However, the fact that commodity prices were again high, and profits from plantations expanding, facilitated the acceptance of Plantations as a 'core business'. They were at the centre of the new Agribusiness Co-ordination formed in 1986, which also included aquaculture—of which the Scottish salmon farming company Marine Harvest was the largest component—a nascent seeds venture, and the animal feeds company BOCMS.[44] A sudden collapse in palm oil prices below $200 per ton, or their lowest levels for forty years, soon afterwards led to a revaluation of the plantations strategy. Plantations Group made their first ever losses in 1986 and 1987.[45] The new emphasis was on countries with a low cost base or a protected market.[46] In Zaire, Unilever concentrated its plantations in the north of the country where returns were more favourable, and had sold all the plantations in the south by the end of the decade. The rubber plantations in Nigeria were sold also.[47]

A central concern as the 1980s progressed was to obtain more benefits from Unilever's considerable scientific knowledge on plantations. Historically, Unilever had been involved in many important innovations in the world palm oil industry. During the 1950s Unilever's Congo subsidiary had developed new processing technology tailored to the characteristics of the Tenera palm. This was transferred

41 The British Prime Minister Margaret Thatcher receiving a cloned palm at Colworth in November 1981.

subsequently to its subsidiary in Malaya. During the early 1960s Unilever in Nigeria bred oil palms with resistance to a chronic disease known as Vascular Wilt, enabling a great increase in the yields from palm oils, while two decades later a significant breakthrough was achieved in insect pollination after Unilever introduced the *Elaeidobius* beetle to Malaysia from Cameroon in 1981. This had a spectacular effect on yields. In Sabah, the proportion of palm kernel oil yielded went up from 4.8 per cent in 1978 to 6.1 per cent in 1982.[48]

Tissue culture research attracted particular interest. During the late 1960s fundamental research began at Colworth House on cell culture with a view to cloning oil palm, which proved a complex and time-consuming task.[49] In 1980 Unilever entered a joint venture known as Unifield with Harrisons & Crosfield for oil palm cloning, with activities in Britain and Malaysia.[50] By 1983 the joint venture was showing real signs of progress, and the first fruit began to be derived from experimental clones. A likely 30 per cent improvement in yields was anticipated, and early projections were that by 1987 all of the new palms planted in its worldwide planting programmes would be cloned.[51] However, the application of the new technologies proved more complex than had been imagined. The cloned plants failed to develop a proper sexual identity.[52] Experimental research into cloning continued, but with diminished expectations, and responsibility passed to the recently acquired Plant Breeding Institute in Cambridge.

In 1990 Unilever remained one of the world's largest plantation groups. The Malaysian oil palm plantations, and the tea plantations in Kenya, Tanzania, and India were of notably high quality. Palm oil, coconuts, and tea were identified as 'strategic' crops at the heart of the business, but an element of opportunism remained also. The former Brooke Bond flower business was notably profitable—with a yield of over 15 per cent in 1988—and although flowers were hardly a core Unilever business, there was no great enthusiasm for divesting it either.

Unilever's assessment of its plantations business passed through several stages. During the late 1960s and early 1970s low yields and the logical implications of the arm's-length relationship of plantations to the rest of the business had led to consideration of divestment. However, as profits grew with the commodity booms of the mid-1970s, there was a new enthusiasm which led to further expansion. The acquisition of Brooke Bond in 1984 increased the acreage further. During the mid-1980s plantations were accepted as a 'core business'. The justification for Unilever's plantations business was its profitability rather than any benefits from vertical integration. There was hardly any supplier/buyer connection because almost all plantation products were sold through auctions or agents into world markets. They were useful, however, in creating goodwill for Unilever as foreign exchange earners and major employers, though these very factors served to lock Unilever into their ownership.[53]

Chemicals

During the post-war decades Unilever's small chemicals business gradually expanded, although it remained largely confined to Britain, and only comprised 3 per cent of Unilever's total sales and profits in 1965. Unilever's involvement in chemicals caused more unease then, and later, than some other investments, despite the fact that there was a direct linkage with Unilever's detergents and foods businesses. The industry was capital and technology intensive, and required substantial investment in plant, personnel, and research. As a result, many sectors were dominated by large, internationally active firms. It was a moot point whether Unilever had the capabilities to move from manufacturing chemicals sold in-house to building a larger business selling to third parties.[54]

Against this background, Unilever gave more consideration to its future strategy in chemicals than some other instances of diversification. A 'Study Group' on the future of chemicals was established in the mid-1960s.[55] The subsequent report formed the basis of Unilever's chemicals strategy for well over a decade. It recommended the slow development of third party sales, the avoidance of large acquisitions in favour of well-managed smaller companies, and the avoidance of the commodity end of chemicals in preference for speciality chemicals, sold for specific performance and often to serve a unique purpose. These appeared to offer the prospect of higher margins and profits without the necessity of massive capital investment in fixed assets. The distinction between commodity and speciality chemicals, later a commonplace, was a notably early one, certainly in Europe.[56]

In 1966 a new Chemicals Co-ordination began to implement this strategy. In the following year a Divisional Structure was introduced for the Fatty Acids Division—later named Unichema—and for the resins and emulsions—later named Urachem, the other chemical companies remaining as profit centres. However, building a viable chemicals business proved a tough challenge. Between 1969 and 1974 overall yields averaged nearly 8 per cent, and they reached over 12 per cent in 1974, but they plummeted during the second half of the decade, though—as Table 7.1 shows—there were variations between different parts of the Co-ordination.

The different components of Chemicals Co-ordination—which did not assume responsibility for the small chemicals businesses in Overseas countries—varied greatly in their products, and relative sizes. At the end of the 1970s Unichema accounted for just over 30 per cent of total sales, and Urachem for a further quarter. Unilever Emery was smaller, accounting for around 13 per cent of sales. Crosfield and PPL accounted for around 10 per cent of total sales each, and FID for 5 per cent. While Urachem and Crosfield sold largely or entirely to third parties by the end of the 1970s, Unichema and PPL remained heavily dependent on sales to other Unilever companies.

Table 7.1 Unilever Chemicals business, 1966–1980

Company	Main product areas	Third party sales 1979 (%)	Yield 1976–1980 (%)
Unichema[a] (Fatty Acids Division)	Oleochemicals and derivatives; glycerine; hydrogenation catalysts	15	3.5
Unilever-Emery[a]	Oleochemicals and derivatives		
Urachem	Thermosetting polymers; PVA emulsions; powder paints	100	1.0
Crosfield	Sodium silicate; silicas; cracking analysts	87	6.0
Food Industries Division (FID)	Flavours, emulsifiers, vitamins, colours	74	2.0
Proprietary Perfumes Limited (PPL)	Perfumes	21	17.0
South Africa	Silicates; fatty acids		
Australia	Fatty acids		
Canada	Chemicals for paper and textiles		
India	Diversified		

[a] The data is for Unichema and Unilever Emery combined.
Source: Chemicals Co-ordination, Strategy for Chemicals Business of Unilever (Dec. 1980), UAL.

The strategy to develop a speciality chemicals business faced a number of constraints. Unilever was chronically handicapped by a lack of management expertise in speciality chemicals.[57] The new Co-ordination inherited a disparate collection of companies with historically contingent structural problems. In the mid-1960s around three-quarters of Unilever's chemicals sales were made in Britain, and fifteen years later the proportion of sales was still 45 per cent, and two-thirds of profits.[58] This was unfortunate given the problems of British manufacturing at this time. Unilever was accustomed to protecting strongly the knowledge within its boundaries, and this caused additional constraints. Although Chemicals Co-ordinators were anxious to develop third party sales, much of Unilever's chemicals business supplied other parts of the company. This caused unease because of the possibility of the 'leakage' of knowledge to competitors. The result was an extreme reluctance to supply foods chemicals to food manufacturers other than Unilever.[59]

Among the various companies at the time, Unilever Emery was unusual in being partly owned. It was formed in 1960 as a 50/50 joint venture between Unilever and Emery Industries of the USA, which wanted to expand to Europe. The American company had strengths in ozonization, polymerization of unsaturated fatty acids, and separations systems which made possible the manufacture of specialized chemicals for a variety of end-uses. The joint venture was launched by the acquisition of Gouda-Apollo, a Dutch oleochemicals business, and the construction on their site of ozonization and polymerization plants which could make use of oleochemical feedstock. With know-how and marketing expertise from Emery, and good management inherited from Gouda-Apollo, Unilever-Emery developed as among the better performing parts of the Unilever chemicals business. The main difficulty was a deteriorating relationship between the two partners. While Unilever wanted to secure full ownership of the venture, and join the Gouda factory to Unichema, the family-owned company declined to sell its shareholding.

Unichema—or the Fatty Acids Division until 1973—manufactured fatty acids, glycerine, and oleochemicals. As Unilever was one of the world's largest traders in and users of oils and fats, Unichema's position was quite strong. Intra-firm sales to Unilever edible fats and detergents companies accounted for around 85 per cent of total sales. Overall Unichema accounted for around 30 per cent of the total European market for fatty acids and glycerine. However, as these were basically commodities, with no brand loyalty, this market share was too low. The main production sites were Bromborough in Britain, and Emmerich and Bergedorf (Hamburg) in Germany. Both the British and German plants lagged far behind that in Gouda in terms of efficiency. They had no research or chemical engineering expertise, and little marketing capability. The British plant was set up with a large capacity to service export markets which subsequently disappeared, while the German business was marginalized in a market dominated by Henkel. The Co-ordination spent years trying to raise the standards of the British and German factories to the Gouda level, with the ultimate aim of merging them, if it could ever acquire full control of the joint venture.

Urachem was not only large in terms of Unilever's chemicals businesses, it was also notably unsuccessful. This group was put together by acquisitions of resins and emulsions firms in Britain, Germany, Sweden, Italy, and France during the second half of the 1960s and the 1970s. The business originated as a plan to break out of the narrow product range within Unilever's current chemicals portfolio. The market for thermosetting polymers appeared to have a good growth rate, and the industry was fragmented. It was believed that by acquiring medium-sized national companies—many of whom held know-how agreements with large US firms—and welding them together, it would be possible to create an effective Europe-wide business. Another attraction was that the diversity of raw materials meant that manufacturing methods were by 'batch' rather than continuous methods of production, so economies of scale were not so dominating as in petrochemicals or heavy chemicals. The problem was that Unilever lacked the management resource either internally, or from the acquired companies, to bring the acquired companies together, to exchange know-how, and to create a unified marketing organization, without which it was impractical to develop a serious research effort. As the European economies went into recession in the mid-1970s, Urachem's performance rapidly deteriorated, while the increase in crude oil prices transformed adversely the cost structure of the industry. Sales, which were totally third party, entered a serious decline. Yields fell away, in part reflecting a drift of the business from the speciality to the commodity sector.[60]

The one exception to this picture was Vinyl Products, which was the largest producer of polymer emulsions in Britain when it was acquired in 1969. Unlike the rest of Urachem, it was primarily involved in water rather than oil soluble products—and was thus not exposed to rising oil prices—and it also had a strong research tradition. Vinyl Products became a pioneer in the development, by means of polymerization under pressure, of ethylene vinyl acetate, a key advance in polymer technology, in which—by coincidence—National Starch had also become interested at the same time.

In 1964 the soaps and chemicals businesses of Crosfield had been separated, and all Unilever's chemicals businesses in the north-west of England had been combined under the firm.[61] Crosfield's continued to specialize in the manufacture of sodium silicates, a product in which it shared the British market with ICI, and it had a wide customer base beyond Unilever, including textiles and paints companies, and the construction industry. It also exported around 40 per cent of its production. During the second half of the 1970s Crosfield was the only part of Chemicals Coordination which increased its sales, but its plant was old, and to some extent the firm was living on borrowed time.

Among the smaller chemicals businesses, PPL was to evolve as one of the more successful. Based in Ashford in Kent, this originated as the Perfumery Department of Lever Brothers. When Del Mar became Co-ordinator in the mid-1960s, he was highly sceptical of a business which made only 5 per cent of its sales outside Unilever.[62] The perfume used in Lux alone represented 15 per cent of PPL's sales. However, the firm, which had both a creative management and a good record of innovation, proved able both to expand third party sales, and to retain almost all its Unilever business against outside competition.

Unilever's major competitors in perfumes also manufactured food additives, as the two sectors shared the same basic chemistry, but in Unilever Food Industries Division (FID) was kept separate from PPL. This had been formed in 1965 when Advita was merged with two established British flavour houses, and was used to provide ingredients and flavours for Batchelors and the other food companies. It was initially a weak and fragmented venture—ruling out any early merger with PPL—and a considerable effort was required to provide a new factory—on Merseyside—to replace the factories of the small flavour businesses previously acquired, and to establish a consolidated marketing operation. A further problem was that the Unilever food companies often had their own flavour development and manufacturing units.

An important stage in the development of FID was the acquisition of the goodwill of Unilever-Emery's food emulsifier business on the Continent in the early

42 Unichema's factory at Gouda in the Netherlands in 1984.

1970s. This business had been built up by Unilever-Emery, but given the importance of food emulsifiers in the manufacture of margarine, ice cream, and other key products, Unilever was concerned about the leakage of know-how into a company in which it had only partial control. This led Unilever to force through, against the opposition of its American partners, the sale of the goodwill of the business. A plant for the manufacture of the range of products was built at Zwijndrecht and was run on behalf of the FID, which took over responsibility for the business. This event, together with the installation of a flavour mixing plant at Maarssen, gave FID a position in continental Europe. By the end of the 1970s FID marketed more than 1,000 flavours, emulsifiers, natural colouring agents, vitamin blends, and other additives worldwide, becoming especially noted for its savoury flavours used in canned meat products, soups, and curries and its sweet flavours for convenience foods.[63]

The impact of the mid-1970s recession in Europe was severe on chemicals companies which, for the most part, had only a modest share of their markets. The structural problems were acute, though a strategic review in 1980 concluded that, despite 'the almost unplanned growth of Unilever chemical interests', Unilever should remain in an industry which 'still offered the possibility of good growth and profits'. Using the then fashionable Boston Consulting Group matrix, this review classed PPL and FID as 'stars', Unichema and Crosfield as 'cash cows', and Urachem as a 'dog'.[64] By then the surging oil prices of the second oil shock were exacerbating problems even further, virtually the entire chemical business became loss making, and the Special Committee was prepared at most to agree to further slow organic growth.[65] As financial pressures mounted, and consequent concerns to do something about underperforming businesses, the Chemicals Co-ordinator felt obliged to use the National Starch acquisition to defend the position of the entire business. Having just made a large acquisition in the industry, he reminded fellow directors in 1981, 'it would look strange to get out of the field'.[66]

During the first half of the 1980s Unilever's chemicals business in Europe was substantially reorganized. The aim was to focus resources on the segments of markets in which Unilever had proven capabilities. In 1980 Unilever finally purchased the shareholding of its American partner in Unilever Emery after relations had deteriorated so badly that Emery Industries had threatened litigation. Unichema's old factory at Bromborough was radically modernized. During 1982 virtually all of Urachem was sold except Vinyl Products. In the same year PPL and FID were merged finally into one company, PPF, which also included the small and

43 Testing fragrances at PPF in Paris, in 1984.

persistently loss-making Bertrand Frères business, which manufactured processed oils for upmarket perfumery in France. Investment was made also in developing a research base in the industry.[67] As the European economies recovered from the recession, the profitability of the chemicals business rose sharply, reaching a yield of 9 per cent in 1984.

There was little product overlap between Unilever's European business and National Starch. Beginning as a glue and adhesives manufacturer, during the 1930s the US company had vertically integrated into corn starch milling so it could create a range of adhesives for the packaging industry. Its main wet milling plant in Indianapolis produced starch which was chemically modified for use to thicken and enhance taste in sauces, salad dressings, desserts, and other food products. This was a high-margin business whose market was rapidly expanding alongside the consumption of convenience foods. National Starch was also a leader in the use of different types of starches in the paper industry. Corn milling produced a range of valuable by-products, including corn oil and animal feeds products. National Starch also manufactured polyvinyl acetate for use in adhesives, widening its customer base to industries such as automobiles, electronics, and petroleum.[68]

The twin pillars of National Starch's business were customer service and research, as well as close relations between sales, marketing, and technical 'know-how'. The consumers for National Starch's products were other manufacturers who—in contrast to the consumer markets most familiar to Unilever—were concerned with technical quality and service more than price or brand image. National Starch's relationships with its customers were often built up over long periods. The most important meetings in the company were not those of the Board, but the compulsory Research Meeting. This contrasted considerably with Unilever, few of whose senior management in chemicals were technically qualified, and whose technical staff was largely confined to the laboratories. National Starch sold a package which included both the product and the know-how to use that product most effectively. It was this service that came to comprise a large portion of the selling price.

While Unilever was traditionally concerned to prevent knowledge 'leakage', National Starch supplied speciality starches to all the leading firms in the food and other consumer products industries. National Starch created systems which protected customer confidentiality, so ensuring that they could sell to competitors. This protection of customers' proprietorial interests was the bedrock of the National Starch business, and contrasted with Unilever's more inward-looking culture, which found it hard to work with other companies, and was reluctant to learn from them.[69]

The case for all Unilever's chemicals business to be globally integrated was strong, given that markets had become international in this industry, but the problem was how to achieve global integration while preserving 'the drive, intensity and entrepreneurial flair of the NSC organisation'.[70] Unilever's eventual conclusion was that

8

Human Resources

Unilever's 'Most Important Asset'

'Our employees', Unilever's Annual Report for 1990 observed, 'are our most important asset.' Before the Second World War, Unilever already employed around 100,000 people, but the post-war decades saw the number of employees expand dramatically, to reach around 350,000 in 1974. As Fig. 8.1 shows, Unilever employment then fell until the acquisition of Brooke Bond in 1984, with its large number of plantation workers, led to a surge in numbers again. Thereafter disposals and further rationalization reduced numbers to 300,000 by 1990.

Over time, there was a shift in the location of Unilever's workforce. In 1965 around 200,000 or nearly three-quarters of Unilever employees were in Europe, of whom 90,000 worked in Britain. Germany and the Netherlands accounted for a further 70,000 employees. In that year, Unilever also employed 40,000 in the UAC and over 34,000 in Plantations, though these plantation workers accounted for only just over 1 per cent of Unilever's total remuneration costs. By 1990 European employment had shrunk to fewer than 110,000. Employment in Britain had fallen to 35,000, whilst that in the Netherlands and Germany had halved compared to twenty-five years previously. Over one-half of Unilever's employees by then worked outside Europe or North America, with nearly one-quarter of them—over 70,000—in Africa, and a further 30,000 in India.

The size and complexity of Unilever's business posed enormous challenges. The company needed to find the optimal way to manage such a varied, changing, cosmopolitan business spread geographically over virtually the whole world, and

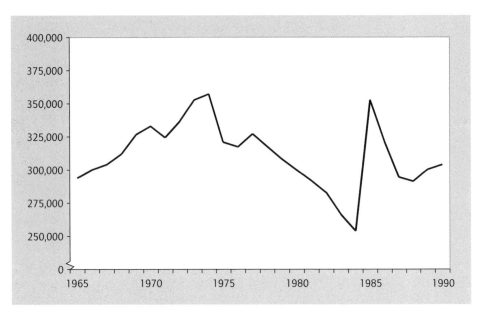

Fig. 8.1 Total employment in Unilever, 1965–1990.

spanning quite diverse industries and activities. This task involved seeking to recruit, train, develop, motivate, and retain the right people as managers who could maintain competitiveness, and carry the company forward to future generations. In order to be competitive and innovative, and to function as a 'knowledge organization', Unilever needed not only to recruit talented people, but also to unlock their potential. None of Unilever's international competitors had such a large—and diverse—workforce. Nestlé came closest—it employed 200,000 in 1990—but the workforces of the US-owned firms, even P & G, were always far smaller.

The following sections explore the key issues and challenges Unilever faced in its human resource management from the 1960s. We begin with a brief account of how this function was organized. This is followed by studies of management recruitment, development, and training. The chapter then goes on to discuss Unilever's relationships with trade unions and its policies towards industrial democracy and industrial disputes.

The Management of Human Resources

In the 1960s Unilever's Personnel Management—the term human resource management was coined much later—was fragmented. Unilever had a multiplicity of personnel units. At the apex, a 'Personnel Policy Committee', consisting of heads of the Personnel Divisions and directors from the Continental European Group, the UK Committee, the Overseas Committee, and the UAC, had been formed in 1958. The committee sought to establish standard personnel procedures and met every month, with the full committee meeting the Special Committee every year to review the placement of more senior managers.

Beneath that committee, there were three bodies providing centralized personnel services. A Personnel Division in London provided services to the UK Committee and the Overseas Committee, and controlled management development, job evaluation, and employee relations. A Personnel Department in the UAC functioned as a self-contained unit which recruited managers and supervised their subsequent career development and training. Finally, the Personnel Department in Rotterdam provided services to the Continental European Group on management development and job evaluation, although it did not recruit management trainees or deal with employee relations. Some central personnel services—principally training, but sometimes recruiting—were undertaken also by other departments, including the Finance, Marketing, and Research Divisions. There was virtually no contact between the two sides of the North Sea in recruitment, training, or management development.[1]

Below the central Personnel Divisions, there were a number of layers of responsibility for personnel matters. In continental Europe, national managements were responsible for graduate recruiting and training, employee relations, and training. In Britain, company managements took most decisions on placement and management development. The UK Committee handled transfers between companies, and used the London-based Personnel Division as its own local Personnel Department. The larger national managements reporting to the Overseas Committee and the UAC, such as South Africa, Australia, and Nigeria, also retained full-scale Personnel Departments. Lever and Lipton in the United States functioned wholly autonomously. Beneath the national managements, most operating companies handled personnel matters, dealing with staff below the level of middle management.

This structure was a major obstacle to the professionalization of management sought by Hartog and Woodroofe. In 1967 the Special Committee commissioned the US management consultants Booz Allen and Hamilton to examine the issue. Their report recommended the creation of a single Personnel Division headed by one director, and 'manned with acknowledged professionals able to provide leadership in specialised fields of personnel'.[2] This policy was implemented in 1968 when the Dutch director Eltje Smit was appointed Unilever's first unified Personnel Director, resident in London, and with offices in both head offices. In 1971 he was replaced by Han Goudswaard, who remained in post until 1983, combining the position with the vice-chairmanship of NV after 1974. He was assisted by two British and Dutch deputies.[3]

A central initial concern of the new Personnel Division was to unify the separate London and Rotterdam personnel systems.[4] Thereafter Personnel Division's focus was on the creation of a policy to identify and develop the careers of future senior managers of Unilever. National managements continued to have responsibility for graduate recruitment and the initial identification of young managers of high potential. National managements and operating companies also continued to manage other personnel matters, such as pension funds and the implementation of health and safety regulations, and deal with non-management employees. The subsequent major organizational change came in the mid-1980s when some tasks were delegated from national management to operating companies, including the initial training of management trainees. National personnel management continued to play an important role subsequently in the recruitment and career planning of trainees and high-potential managers; industrial relations policies and practices; and ensuring the smooth and consistent implementation of overall Unilever personnel policies.

Both the UAC, until its demise in the mid-1980s, and the United States remained outside the remit of the Personnel Division. UAC continued to recruit itself, and there were few transfers to or from other parts of Unilever. The United States was a law unto itself. Even during the 1980s there was little integration in human resource management across the Atlantic.

In Unilever, therefore, while most aspects of human resource management were local affairs, the identification and development of people identified as future corporate leaders was regarded as a matter of great importance and placed in the hands of the centralized Personnel Division, which reported directly to the Special Committee and Board. Personnel ranked alongside Research and Finance as one of the three functions Unilever sought to manage at this level of the company.

Management Recruitment

Around 15,000 of Unilever employees were managers in the middle of the 1960s. This number had reached 20,000 by 1976, and then stayed almost constant. Leaving aside the special cases of the United States and the UAC, by the 1960s Unilever's managers typically joined the company after graduation from universities in their early to middle twenties in schemes which promised a wide scope of career development. Although recruited for the most part by national managements, in most cases they were recruited to a prospect of a Unilever career rather than to a career in one company or product group. There was an assumption that, if they were effective, it was more than likely that they would work for Unilever for their entire careers, and—if they held British or Dutch passports—that they had the opportunity to reach the highest level of the company. Unilever only rarely recruited mid-career executives before the 1980s, and most of those it did recruit entered Unilever through acquired companies.

National recruitment systems had strong common features. By the 1960s recruiting was usually confined to graduates, reflecting the fact that Unilever had been among the first European companies to use graduates as a source of potential senior managers. In many countries Unilever maintained close and regular contact with universities, with procedures in place—such as talks or courses for final-year students—designed to keep the company name well in front of student minds as they contemplated career choices. Virtually everywhere the appointment process involved selection by application form, testing, and individual and group interviews with senior line managers acting as selectors.

In Britain and Ireland, the most common route for graduate entrants was the Unilever Companies Management Development Scheme (UCMDS), established in 1952 with the intention of providing a systematic approach to the recruitment of future managers. By the mid-1960s between sixty and one hundred new recruits entered the UCMDS scheme each year in a highly selective process. It was assumed that such recruits would have the potential to reach at least upper-middle management by their mid-thirties. After the Second World War a 'Junior Training Scheme' had been created for people who had left school at 18 with 'A' levels, and who if they did well then entered UCMDS, but in 1968 this was abandoned, leaving non-graduate recruitment to management a matter only for operating companies. A second route of entry for graduates in Britain was the Unilever Engineering Management Training Scheme (UEMTS), introduced in 1971 in order to attract more engineers. Finally there was direct entry into the companies themselves. This was a less common means of entry than the formal training schemes, but for certain candidates it was considered more suitable.

Management recruitment was a serious matter. Every senior manager in Britain, including company chairmen and main board directors, was required to take part in at least one recruitment selection panel a year. Recruitment was a rare thing that Unilever did *as Unilever* rather than through the operating companies. Paradoxically, this meant that the Unilever recruitment process was better known to final-year students than the nature of Unilever's business itself.[5] Unilever expended considerable efforts on maintaining links with the career advisory services found within British universities, and its recruitment strategies became increasingly proactive as competition for the best graduates intensified. By the 1980s there were around 1,400 companies competing in the British graduate recruitment market, with US firms led by P & G and Arthur Andersen dispatching teams of people, often headed by young high-flying managers, to British campuses in pursuit of the most promising students.

Oxford and Cambridge provided more recruits to Unilever management in Britain than any other institution between 1965 and 1990, followed by the universities of London, Birmingham, and Manchester. There were also significant numbers from other 'well-respected' universities, such as Durham, Bristol, Edinburgh, and Southampton. However, there were few academic institutions which did not provide at least one Unilever graduate trainee. The 493 UCMDS recruits between 1965 and 1973 came from 59 institutions, even though 17 per cent were from Oxford, 14 per cent from Cambridge, and 12 per cent from London. Of the 1,069 UCMDS/UEMTS Board passes between 1980 and 1988, Oxford contributed 14.5 per cent, Cambridge 13 per cent, and London 10 per cent. Birmingham was next with 5 per cent. However 16 different polytechnics (later renamed 'new' universities) were represented among the graduate trainees in the 1980s, while the engineering recruits taken into the UEMTS scheme came from a wide spread of institutions. The 22 students that got through that selection process in 1987 came from 19 different universities.[6]

The diverse educational background of Unilever's managers was reflected at the top of the company. Unlike many 'blue chip' British companies of this era, the most

44 Michael Perry, Chairman of PLC 1992–1996 (*taken in 1990*).

The central concern of Personnel Division was to ensure that sufficient high-quality people were recruited to meet the requirements of Unilever's senior management over the following decades. Other organizational changes at the time seemed to run counter to this ambition. The introduction of executive Co-ordinations in 1966, which led to recruitment numbers being much more focused on the immediate requirements of companies, followed by the deteriorating financial conditions of the early 1970s, led many companies to cease recruiting altogether. In 1973 Personnel Division responded to this unwanted situation by setting targets.[15] However, some countries, including the Netherlands and Germany in the 1970s, did not meet such targets. The problem was that companies were under constant pressure from Co-ordinations to cut costs, and sometimes found it hard to justify recruiting young managers at a time when they were making other employees redundant.[16] In 1979 Personnel Division predicted that within five years 50 per cent of Unilever's senior managers in Europe would be over 50 years old.[17] This dire prediction did not come to pass, except in the technical function where career progression was slow. In marketing, less than one-fifth of Unilever managers in Britain and the Netherlands were over 50 in 1988, though in Germany the proportion was almost two-fifths.[18]

The difficulty was more acute because Unilever had problems retaining management recruits. During the 1980s Unilever lost 70 per cent of its management recruits in Europe and the major Overseas countries within eight years.[19] Unilever tended to be philosophic about the high turnover, partly because it represented the departure of people who could not make the grade, and partly because it was the cost of recruiting high-quality people, and then providing them with an excellent training. Unilever 'functioned as a training school' for other firms.[20] However, the rate of resignations was at times high. A study of the fates of marketing trainees recruited between 1973 and 1975 showed that around three-quarters of them had left the company by 1982 in Britain, the Netherlands, Germany, and Italy.[21] The loss rates in the 1980s in Britain, France, and Germany were considerable, and put extra strain on attempts to recruit high-calibre graduates. Despite high levels of recruitment, by the end of the decade Unilever found that the high turnover rate was leaving it short of very good people for more senior posts.[22]

The recruitment and retention of managers in the Netherlands posed a particular problem. In 1981 Personnel Division warned the Special Committee that the recruitment rate 'could not even support the requirements in the Netherlands let alone contribute at the international level'.[23] The latter point was an important one. Unilever did not have problems recruiting in the Netherlands, and its retention rate was good, but there were heavy demands on Dutch managers. It was considered essential in retaining Unilever's Dutch identity that Dutch managers would hold many expatriate posts, and—together with the British—fill almost all the most senior positions. As a result there was within Unilever, at least until the 1990s, 'a non-written rule. You have to make sure enough Dutchmen come in.'[24]

This 'unwritten rule' faced a structural problem given that the Netherlands only had—in the 1980s—a population of 15 million people, and an extremely well-developed business sector vying to recruit good-quality managers. Moreover, as Unilever's size in the Netherlands was not especially large and falling over time, there was a logistical problem recruiting a management cadre who might want to start, and finish, their careers in their own country. Although managers worked for about five years in the Netherlands and then began to be sent abroad to gain foreign experience, there was an unwritten expectation that when it was desirable—with children going to school or retirement approaching—a job would be made available for them in the Netherlands. The development of Dutch management potential was thus constrained by the problem of getting them back to the Netherlands again.[25] During the late 1980s Unilever put in place a number of proactive policies which involved a considerable degree of central influence on filling posts in the Netherlands. These included paying special attention to the early development of Dutch managers, and using the limited number of middle management posts in the Netherlands almost exclusively for the development of high-potential young managers.[26]

During the 1980s Unilever's overall recruitment policies everywhere began to be modified. Concerns about growing volatility in the labour market began to encourage a more positive interest in mid-career appointments.[27] Unilever's distinctive networked corporate culture, in which knowing the right people was the key to doing things, did not make this easy, and turnover rates were initially high. Building relationships and knowing the right people was a cumulative process which those who had entered the company as management trainees had begun in the early twenties.[28]

There was a growing interest in recruiting female managers also. In the post-war decades the proportion of women entering Unilever management positions was minimal. In Britain until the early 1960s advertisements for UCMDS specified that vacancies were for men. This policy was subsequently modified, but only 9 per cent of UCMDS entrants were female between 1965 and 1973.[29] The women applying to UCMDS often encountered problems at the placement stage of the process. The belief among certain senior (male) executives at the top of Unilever that more women managers might be beneficial proved hard to translate into reality because of more traditional attitudes at lower levels of the hierarchy.[30]

In the Netherlands, there were fewer female recruits to management than in Britain. In 1973 a mere 31 of Unilever's 1,324 Dutch managers were women, and one of the 201 Dutch senior managers.[31] As early as 1957 Unilever established a discussion group in the Netherlands to consider the question of 'the position of women in Unilever'. This concluded that 'the woman's place is more generally considered to be in the home'.[32] A new examination of the issue in 1973 noted that 'almost nothing has been done since 1957 to improve the situation'.[33] It remained unusual for Dutch women in general to work after marriage, and when they did work, they had part-time jobs. Unilever reflected, as usual, its host society, and until the 1980s its recruitment campaigns for managers in the Netherlands were male oriented, both in language and in visual images. For the most part, women were regarded primarily as potential secretaries rather than as managers, and while in Britain a tradition of graduate secretaries raised at least the possibility of a transfer into management—though this rarely happened in Unilever—in the Netherlands a secretarial post was basically regarded as a transitional stage between leaving education and getting married and starting a family.[34]

Unilever was not unusual with regard to the gender imbalance in recruitment compared to other large European companies, or indeed those in the United States. The Harvard Business School did not admit women into its regular MBA programme until 1963, and even its class of 1973 was only 5 per cent female.[35] However as the market for the best students became increasingly competitive in the 1980s, and as the greater employment of female managers in the United States became observed, the recruitment of more women became a priority.[36] By 1989 over half the intake to UCMDS in Britain were female, with the commercial and personnel functions exceeding 50 per cent. In Japan, where Unilever's inability to hire good-quality managers had constrained its business, the situation started to be dramatically improved by the recruitment of large numbers of female graduates. Unilever soon learned that it was easier to hire women managers than to retain them, especially when they reached their late twenties and early thirties. Hardly any of the women recruited to management training schemes in the 1980s in Britain remained in Unilever for as long as ten years.[37]

The management recruitment patterns of the UAC and the companies in the United States diverged considerably from those described above. The UAC had a large number of managers—over 2,700 in 1970, of whom 2,000 were Europeans, largely British, and the remainder Africans. UAC recruited its own management trainees until the early 1980s, when it began to use UCMDS. As late as 1984 only 15 per cent of UAC's senior managers possessed a degree. A further 9 per cent had an accountancy qualification and 2 per cent had engineering qualifications. Historically UAC were eager recruiters of graduates from poorer backgrounds, and also sought a number of more socially refined entrants as counterparts for government officials.[38] Although there was significant French management in UAC, it does not appear to have recruited any Dutch managers. In the United States, Lever and Lipton followed the local practice of mid-career recruiting, as well as appointing many MBAs.

Unilever, then, was able to recruit some of the best young graduates for its management in many countries. It was a prestigious and attractive employer, which could afford to select the best, and which invested a great deal of resource in that selection process. The academic backgrounds of its managers showed a wide diversity, in contrast to the widespread recruitment of MBAs by most US corporations. Despite such diversity, Unilever's highly structured and centralized recruitment process selected a certain type of personality—intelligent, articulate, sociable, 'nice', and male. They fitted, and were designed to fit, in a company whose style of management—as one study in 1982 noted—'required a high level of information and consultation before decisions were taken'.[39] There remained limited avenues for people with alternative perspectives or backgrounds to reach the higher ranks of the company.

Career Development

Virtually everyone who worked for Unilever was assigned a job class (JC) somewhere between one and thirty-six. Management positions were those of JC 20 and above, while senior management posts were those of JC 27 and above. Job class 36 was that just below the level of main board director. Unilever's management trainees were expected to reach a management position (JC 20) within two to three years of joining. It was assumed that they would have the potential to reach JC 24–6 by their mid-thirties, and it was hoped that they would then go on to fill senior management roles for the remaining twenty or so years of their careers.

The principal concern of Personnel Division was with these high-flying managers. 'There are about 200 men', Heyworth observed in 1949, 'who take on themselves the decisions which make or mar the success of the business as a whole. The biggest job of top management is to ensure the quality of this 200. To do so it is necessary to know something of the quality of about three times that number in order to be able to make the best selection when vacancies arise.'[40] At the heart of Unilever's system of career development designed to shape these '200 men' was a series of lists, known as the A, B, C, and D lists, the definitions of which are given in Fig. 8.2.

A young manager hoping for a successful career within Unilever needed to get onto the D list. His or her company and the national management were responsible for the D list, and for ensuring that promising young managers placed on it could broaden their experience. If successful, they could expect to be elevated to the C list, where Personnel Division followed the progress of the individuals, and 'watched to make sure that they were not too long without a move'.[41] It was once on the C list that the opportunities for postings overseas or in different Co-ordinations became available. The selection of candidates from the C list for a vacancy was a

A List All senior managers in JC 30+.

A.1 Those who have the potential to advance to substantially more senior jobs.

A.2 Those who are operating at or near potential, including some who could be considered for moves to positions of comparable authority.

A.3 Those whose retirement within the next five years is being considered. In those countries where retirement at 60 is now available, the A.3 list is likely to include nearly all senior managers in JC 30 and above who are aged 57/58 and over.

B List Senior Managers who have reached JC 27/29 and who are considered to have the potential to fill positions at JC 30 and above within five years.

C List Managers who are considered to have the potential to fill positions at JC 27 and above within five years.

D List Managers other than C listers, who are in JC 20/23, and who are considered to have the potential to fill positions in JC 24/26 within five years.

Source: Based on 'Management Development – Development Lists, November 1982, AHK 2272, UAR.

Fig. 8.2 Definitions of categories on Unilever's Management Lists.

collaborative effort. A shortlist of candidates would be drawn up based on skills and experience, and while this was designed as an objective process, the final selection of a candidate might well be influenced by informal contacts within the Unilever network.

The higher up the hierarchy a manager progressed, the more important it was that he or she had a sense of identity as a Unilever manager, rather than a company one. To have worked in more than one company, probably in more than one product group, and in more than one country, was regarded as essential for career advancement.[42] Unilever's stress on international experience and mobility contrasted with most US-based multinationals, where employment outside the United States for any length of time was routinely regarded as the death knell of a successful career, although total mobility within the United States was often expected.

Within Rotterdam, there was always a concern for the interests of Dutch managers when a vacancy occurred. 'The Dutch tried to promote the Dutch,' it was later recalled, 'suggesting Dutchmen when vacancies appeared.'[43] This worked in a typically informal Unilever fashion to protect the Anglo-Dutch balance within the company, despite the greater numbers of British managers. The chairmen of NV were said to carry a list of the best Dutchmen in their pockets for when vacancies arrived, at both Board and less senior levels. There appears to have been no equivalent behaviour on the British side, perhaps because they felt less under pressure because of larger numbers, or perhaps because they were simply less organized.[44] For one reason or another, studies after 1977 showed that Dutch management recruits into Unilever progressed faster up the managerial hierarchy than their counterparts in Britain and Germany.

The progress of managers through the more senior ranks of Unilever was overseen not just by Personnel Division; an active interest was taken by the Special Committee itself. The Special Committee had a say in all appointments to posts of JC 32 and above and from 1985 its approval was also necessary for all appointments from JC 30 upwards.[45] Every year the Personnel Division met with the Special Committee to discuss the A list of the top 200 to 250 managers in Unilever.[46]

There was no predictable route to the ultimate apex of a Unilever career, a seat on the Board. Personnel Division identified potential 'stars' early on, while those marked for directorships were selected by the late thirties and early forties. No one joined the Board after the age of 50. However, the qualities needed actually to be appointed to a directorship were indefinable. It was important quite early in a career to be successful at running something, and to get noticed for it, while avoiding making a major error of judgement. This was partly a question of being in the right place at the right time, which in turn meant deciding which opportunities to accept. It was unwise to be sent to a company in a thoroughly hopeless situation, although this was one way to get noticed if a manager could improve matters. Significantly, at least two NV chairmen had difficult assignments—one in Colombia, and the other in Unilever's Spanish detergents company—early in their careers, enabling them to show their mettle.[47]

Given the size of Unilever and its networked nature, it was usually helpful to have a patron or 'mentor' to support career development and, ultimately, the case for a place on the Board.[48] Career development within Unilever was a meritocratic system, but one in which networks facilitated progress. Progress up to Board level involved drawing a careful balance between appearing strong and distinctive, yet avoiding giving too much offence to those higher up the hierarchy. British and Dutch managers also had to be careful not to sufficiently annoy 'the other side' that they might seek to 'veto' their appointment to the Board, and, even more, to the Special Committee.

An important aspect of management development was the appraisal system. Unilever's first appraisal policy document was issued in 1969.[49] The policy was designed to meet both the needs of individual managers and the business plans of the companies where they worked. It was based on the then fashionable model of 'management by objectives' which involved the mutual agreement of objectives and then working towards them. Each manager's immediate superior conducted the task of appraisal, and the whole appraisal process was conceived as taking place on a one-to-one basis. The idea was that the manager and their boss should first of all draw up a work plan, with clearly defined objectives, covering a period of at least six months. As this period drew towards its close the appraiser was meant to draw up an 'appraisal record', which would form the agenda of an appraisal interview. In the interview, the manager was able to compare their individual performance with their work plan; it also provided the opportunity for them to discuss any problems, future career plans, and pay—as well as any amendments to future work plans or job descriptions. During its first decade of operation the appraisal system had problems differentiating the quality of managers. Most managers were graded 'good'.[50] A McKinsey report as early as 1970 suggested that, instead of appraising managers individually, they should be judged in comparison with others in their 'peer group' who performed a similar role.[51] However, it was not until the 1980s that such suggestions began to be seriously considered.

By the 1980s the appraisal system came under increasing pressure as it became linked to the subject of performance-related pay. Unilever's traditional management salary policy was rooted in the belief that managers would remain within Unilever for the whole of their career. Salaries reflected a manager's level of seniority, length of service, and job class, rather than being used as an incentive to encourage outstanding managers to stay. In the 1960s each job class was assigned a 'job value', which was then increased at intervals by a fixed amount. Managers, it was expected, would be paid approximately two-thirds of job value on their appointment to a new job class, and the rate at which they progressed towards the maximum job value depended on their performance.[52] Priority was given to ensuring that the pay of Unilever's managers compared favourably with that of other companies, but the salary differentials between Unilever managers themselves were seldom given serious consideration.[53]

The highly structured system of job classes was not designed to provide great incentives to dynamic individuals, but it was rooted in Unilever practices and defied attempts by the Special Committee among others to make it more flexible.[54] However, in 1983 more incentives for managers began to be introduced with the implementation of Annual Cash Awards in most European countries. These were bonuses paid to senior managers who exceeded their targets, but managers at a lower level did not benefit in the same way if they exceeded personal performance targets. It was Overseas companies, especially those in Brazil and South Africa, which took the lead in introducing bonus systems for a wider spectrum of managers.[55] The percentage of Unilever managers receiving bonuses rose from 16 per cent in 1984 to 39 per cent in 1988.[56] In 1988 the system was extended again with a scheme available to all senior managers, based on the principle of achieving targets, not surpassing them. The targets themselves were 'expected to be demanding'.[57] In all of these initiatives Unilever typically followed rather than led the general trend among large European companies.

This was also the case with the implementation of stock options. By 1980 the UK national management wanted to follow the growing practice of British companies and introduce a share or stock option scheme, provided on a 'save as you earn' basis to all employees.[58] But it was not until 1985 that a scheme restricted to a small group of senior British managers above JC 31 was introduced, based on performance achievements. This followed changes in British legislation which provided attractive tax terms for approved stock option schemes, and which more or less obliged British companies to introduce such schemes. Although there was no equivalent Dutch legislation and the tax situation also differed, a similar scheme was introduced for around thirty of the most senior NV managers.[59] The response of the Special Committee to a Personnel Division plan in 1990 to extend a stock options scheme to managers outside the Netherlands and Britain contained the revealing comment that 'although times were changing they were not convinced of any need for deviation from this basic policy. We do not wish to be pioneers in remuneration strategy.'[60]

Unilever was more of a pioneer in developing an international management cadre. During the post-war decades a few 'foreign' managers were able to work their way through the ranks to senior levels, but it was only British and Dutch managers whose careers were specifically planned and monitored with eventual elevation to the Board in mind. It was accepted as early as 1960 that managers from outside the UK or the Netherlands might reach the Board. In that year plans to appoint a German fell through after he took a senior appointment in Germany. Subsequently plans to appoint a Frenchman were also frustrated by his unexpected death.[61] Consequently, it was Oscar Strugstad, a Norwegian, who became the first foreign director in 1973. Over the following two decades an Australian, an Indian, an American, and two Germans followed.

A report proposing the establishment of a Unilever traineeship in Europe in 1962 argued that 'the international character of Unilever calls for an international type of manager'.[62] From the late 1970s more non-British/Dutch managers began to appear on the management development lists.[63] During these years the progression of managers from continental Europe onto the A and B lists became more widely accepted. These continentals, especially Germans, were to some extent regarded as 'honorary Dutchmen', in the same way as Irish or Indian nationals became 'honorary British', when Board appointments were considered. While most of the Board appointments of non-British or Dutch nationals arose in particular circumstances, Personnel Division identified the two Germans who reached the Board, Hans Eggerstedt and Okko Mueller, for Board appointments quite early in their careers, and as a result they were both given international experience outside Germany.[64] Nonetheless, it remained throughout the 1980s the general assumption that Unilever's top level of management should naturally be made up of Dutch and British, together with a limited number of other different nationalities. Each 'side' needed to give up one of 'their' seats on the Board if an 'outsider' was brought in.

'Foreigners' were arguably not the only outsiders in the Unilever system of career development. During the 1960s the greater professionalization of Unilever management, seen in the creation of Co-ordinations and a unified Personnel Division, began to highlight the differences between the successful and high-flying managers, and the many other thousands of managers, for whom organizational developments such as the introduction of Co-ordination, and the emerging pressures to become more efficient and control costs, posed more threats than opportunities. Their status, which had once seemed far superior to that of ordinary workers, began to be eroded. The chasm between the managerial elite of Unilever, who moved between companies and product groups, and aspired to progress through the lists to the higher reaches of the company, and the rest of the management, became ever more apparent. The mass of middle managers remained, doing their duty, leading working lives in which lunch might often be the most exciting event, hoping to be given a modest annual increase in salary and holiday entitlement, and feeling increasingly disconcerted.

It was in the Netherlands that the concerns of middle managers were first felt. A forerunner of these concerns was a letter written in October 1965 by a group of young commercial managers from several of the operating companies in the Netherlands to the directors of NV and the boards of Dutch operating companies. The Noordwijk letter, as it became known from the town where the young managers had met to discuss their grievances, complained about inadequate scope for their development, paternalism, and faulty communications within Unilever. They were especially concerned that their work seemed to carry only very limited responsibilities.[65] Two months later, on 6 December, the signers of the Noordwijk letter met senior members of Dutch Personnel Management to discuss their concerns in a mammoth five-hour meeting. Specific concerns about promotions and advancement were discussed, but the changing shape of the Unilever organization was also raised, especially growing bureaucracy and inadequate flows of information.[66]

The Noordwijk young managers received considerable attention. Their complaints were listened to, and discussed, with the overall conclusion that the letter was 'a healthy phenomenon establishing communication' by young people who assumed 'that they will be listened to'.[67] The shock of receiving such complaints was considerable, however, and even four years later NV's directors were still recalling 'the Noordwijk meeting of a large number of young managers'.[68] By then managerial complaints had started to take another form, towards which the Dutch Personnel Department was less sympathetic.

During the second half of the 1960s Unilever's Dutch managers began to become unionized. This was a period when both trade unions and the government were increasingly concerned to reduce wage inequalities, both between different regions within the country, and between different types of employees.[69] Although trade unions did not achieve their goal of a single collective wage agreement for all employees within the Netherlands, they did succeed in creating one collective wage agreement for workers and those performing lower white-collar jobs, namely assistant managers. Assistant managers became part of Unilever's ARU (Arbeidsreglement Unilever) personnel.

As assistant managers joined with other employees, and as job insecurities grew, middle managers felt increasingly vulnerable. In 1965 an organization for 'Higher Personnel' was established in Van den Bergh en Jurgens. By renaming this organization and changing the articles of association, the VHUP (Vereniging voor Hoger Unilever Personeel) emerged in 1969. Its purpose was to 'fight' for managers' rights.[70] The same development occurred around the same time at Philips, KLM, the National Railways, and other large Dutch business enterprises. There was no parallel in Britain.

The formation of the VHUP was in part in reaction to the growth of influence of the trade unions among the other employees, for middle managers feared being excluded from policy-making. The middle managers also sought protection against moves to level incomes. During the 1970s trade unions tried to get Unilever to apply its remuneration system for so-called ARU-personnel—the personnel falling under collective wage agreements—to assistant managers. Unilever objected, continuing to rely on the appraisal system to set individual managers' salaries, and used the VHUP to back its policies.

The VHUP occupied an awkward position within Unilever. Feeling 'different' from regular employees, who were treated collectively, the middle managers were accustomed to individual treatment and organized themselves into representational bodies only reluctantly. They believed that in the past they had had the right of open communication lines with directors, and could negotiate their own employment personally. The formation of the VHUP illustrated growing distrust amongst middle management towards upper echelons, even though VHUP repeatedly stressed that it was not a trade union, and merely wanted to improve communication with the top and to look after middle managers in an increasingly complex world.[71] In some respects, the VHUP suffered from an identity crisis, for although it did not want to be a trade union, it did want to represent the concerns of middle managers.

In the decades after its formation, the VHUP found itself uncomfortably positioned between senior management and the trade unions. It did not want to integrate into existing employees' organizations, which it saw as concerned primarily with workers' interests and supportive of the policy of levelling income differentials, as well as connected to political parties. The Dutch umbrella organization for 'Higher Personnel', the NCHP (Nederlandse Centrale voor Hoger Personeel), wanted to be recognized as an equal partner in discussions between employers and employees in the Netherlands. It tried to gain an employee-seat on the Sociaal Economische Raad (SER), established in 1950 to advise the government with regard to economic and social policy. This was not welcomed by the trade unions, which considered that organizations like the VHUP would voice the interests of employers. They regarded the recognition of such organizations as a weakening of parity between employees and employers within the SER. The senior management of Unilever also had little initial regard for the VHUP, which was seen as an unwelcome pressure group.[72]

The VHUP tried to represent the interests of middle management in numerous ways. It often made the case that increases in the remuneration of middle managers appeared to lag behind lower echelons of the company, and supported managers threatened with redundancy.[73] As time went by, VHUP settled down to an uncontroversial existence, intervening to represent its members in many practical matters, such as the allocation of car parking spaces outside offices.

Unilever had a problem with middle management during these years. Middle managers were regarded as a 'silent majority'—in the words of one report in 1970—which lacked mobility, were primarily interested in job security, and had the potential to obstruct the development of younger and more able managers.[74] The organizational evolution of Unilever left it with too many middle managers, or at least more than its competitors, especially in Europe. Unilever companies had one more hierarchical level than their competitors between the bottom of the structure—workers in the factories or salespersons—and the company chairman. This additional level stemmed from traditions of narrower spans of control, and the employment of more managers in supervisory roles. Unilever companies had a higher proportion of managers in support and specialist functions, such as planning and analysis, than its competitors, and fewer managers in such line functions as buying, production, and selling.[75] Middle managers, once the bedrock of Unilever, were thus progressively seen as obstacles to the 'streamlining' of the business.[76]

Unilever developed a well-organized and centralized system for management development, whose ultimate aim was to make sure that the 'top 200 to 250 people' in the company were of optimal ability who had a wide range of experience, and who had been suitably tested over the years. The preoccupation with getting the top management right may have led to underinvestment in middle management. Yet the system produced, by common consent, a managerial cadre which was highly regarded in the world business community. Management development within

Unilever was, for all the importance of networks, meritocratic, even if a variety of glass ceilings—for non-British and Dutch nationals and for women—inevitably meant that potential talent was not fully exploited.

Management Training

Unilever devoted considerable resources to training. In 1979 it was estimated that the company spent £14 million on training in Europe, and £7 million in the rest of the world. In Europe 25,000 employees—or around a sixth of the total—had received training at an average cost of £550 per head. In the Overseas countries, 13,000 employees had been trained at an average cost of £140 each.[77]

All Unilever managers attended training courses at some stage in their career. The type of courses they participated in depended on a number of factors, including management level, potential for further promotion, and business function. Of these factors, the most important was management seniority. The most senior managers did not generally receive formal training in-house. They were kept abreast of the latest developments in their area by attending external courses, usually provided by the leading American business schools led by Harvard, MIT, Columbia, and Stanford. The general management courses inside Unilever stopped about JC 26/27, leaving the 'upper crust'—as they were described in 1976—catered for by outside establishments on an individual participant basis.[78]

These courses were expensive and often quite lengthy. The Advanced Management Programme (AMP) at Harvard Business School lasted thirteen weeks and had high fees. Unilever did not usually send managers to the United States for such courses unless they were well established in senior positions, and the courses they attended were often intended to further their existing knowledge and expertise, rather than prepare them for a higher level of responsibility. Harvard's AMP focused widely on a range of areas including marketing and financial management, organizational behaviour, as well as wider issues such as business and society. The Program for Management Development at Harvard, which was aimed at 'really outstanding' younger managers, was broken down into the following component parts: '25% functional management, 25% quantitative controls and systems, 25% human resources, 12.5% environment and 12.5% business policy.'[79]

The value of these courses was not just their content, but the opportunity they provided for Unilever's European managers to spend a prolonged period in the company of American managers, and to gain some experience of the nature of American business culture and practices. Unilever regarded the faculty at the US business schools as better than in the European business schools, but it also wanted its managers to gain US experience. Even an International Senior Managers' Programme, sponsored by Harvard Business School but run in Switzerland, was not regarded by Unilever in quite the same light as other Harvard courses. Personnel Division considered that 'from a Unilever viewpoint the programme suffers only in the sense that it is a European environment and has a largely European membership. It is therefore not a complete alternative to the US programme.'[80]

Unilever also sent senior managers, or those expected to fill senior positions within a short time, on a range of courses within Europe. The Senior Executive Programme at the London Business School, the General Management Course at the Administrative Staff College, Henley, and the International Programme for Senior Executives at the IMI in Geneva (a predecessor to IMD in Lausanne) dealt with general issues, while others such as the Advanced Management Programme at INSEAD, the Executive Programme at London Business School, and the Senior Managers' Development Programme at the Oxford Management Centre were more focused on specific subjects such as finance, accounting, or political/economic analysis and planning.

For the majority of managers training was provided internally. The main training facility was the Four Acres site near Kingston-upon-Thames, eleven miles south-west of central London, although many training courses were also provided on a national level. Built as a family home in the late 1920s, Four Acres was requisitioned in 1940 for the use of the exiled Dutch government. It was acquired by Unilever in 1954, and opened as a residential training facility in 1955. It received further extensions and refurbishments in 1962 and 1990. Tuition was often provided by American business school professors.

At the highest level, the Senior Business Managers' Programme was aimed at chairmen and very senior managers. For those at a slightly earlier stage in their career—usually aged between 30 and 43—there was the General Management Course which was intended to help managers prepare for, and cope with, the qualitative shift from departmental to general management. Below the level of senior management, the main training programme was the two-week International Management Seminar, which was held seven times a year and accommodated up to thirty-two managers at a time. Participants came from all parts of the business (international and multifunctional), and their responsibilities usually lay at a departmental level (mostly in job classes 22–4), though it was expected that they had the potential to be promoted by at least two job classes within five years.

The purpose behind Unilever's managerial training programmes changed over time. During the 1960s they were seen as largely supplementing the learning

46 The Four Acres Training Centre, at Kingston-upon-Thames in Surrey, England, in 1977.

experiences obtainable from actual management experience. It was assumed that young managers would gain practical experience within the workplace, while training courses would help them see their role in a broader context.[81] In the same decade a more functional philosophy took hold. It was felt that managers needed to learn relevant information, and the provision of training courses began to be closely aligned with broader corporate objectives. Co-ordinations drew up their own training programmes for managers.[82] Other training programmes focused on specific issues such as buying, sales, marketing, research management, and organizational development.[83] Towards the end of the 1970s the emphasis changed again with recognition that the needs of individual managers also had to be considered alongside corporate requirements.[84] Policy became firmly aimed at developing the potential of individual managers, including an understanding of the environment in which they lived, with the aim of stimulating an ability to respond to change.[85] The shift was linked to growing concerns about retention. It was seen as increasingly important for Unilever to be able to attract, keep, and quickly promote the most promising graduates and young managers.

Unilever, then, devoted considerable resources to training, and especially to the training of its managers. Its high-flyers were offered the best executive education in the United States, while all its managers were provided with a range of courses at

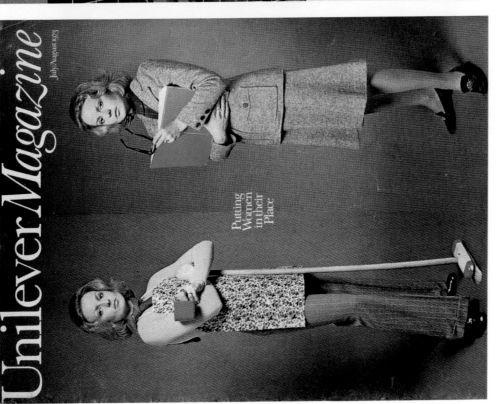

Unilever Magazine
July/August 1973

Putting Women in their Place

Meer fleur in de kleur... meer wit in 't wit met Wetenschappelijk Omo.

Gekleurd goed en witgoed kunnen even vuil zijn...

Toch wast u ze afzonderlijk (kleur bij 60°, wit bij 95°) en ze moeten allebei even proper uit de was komen!

Als eenzelfde poeder dat kan, dan spreekt het vanzelf dat het iets speciaals moet hebben.

Omo heeft dat. Want Omo heeft een wetenschappelijke formule waarin veilige kleurwaskracht en grondige witwaskracht wetenschappelijk verenigd zijn.

60° 95°

Wetenschappelijk Omo - voor kleur en wit, altijd de properste was ter wereld.

Omo is een LEVER waspoeder.

24 The front cover of *Unilever Magazine* in 1973. The issue included a feature on women in management.

25 Advertisement for Omo brand in Belgium in 1974. This brand had originated as a bleaching powder in Britain in 1908, and was relaunched as soap powder in the following year. By the 1970s it was widely used as an international brand.

26 An advertisement for Persil in Britain in the 1970s, when it held around 40 per cent of the market.

27 Clothes washing with Breeze detergent in Thailand in 1983.

Is your favorite brand packaged for generations to come?

We're looking towards the future.

The environment is part of the future our children will inherit for years to come. And as the makers of Wisk,* Surf,* all,* Snuggle,* Final Touch,* and Sunlight,* we at Lever are taking steps so the plastic in our bottles can be used over and over again.

Now you can enjoy the benefits and convenience of our plastic bottles knowing they can find new life far from landfills.

We're using recycled plastic.

New recycling technology now allows us to include 25% to 35% recycled plastic in many of our bottles of Wisk and "all."

laundry detergents, as well as Snuggle and Final Touch fabric softeners. Through this effort, we will save the equivalent of 50 million plastic bottles a year from going into landfills.

We need your help.

Turning used plastic into new plastic bottles makes a whole lot of sense and a lot less waste. So that all our bottles can help, we've coded them for easy identification and sorting.

But we need more recycled plastic. That's why we've printed an important message on our bottles asking you to support recycling in your community. Because the more plastic collected, the higher levels of recycled plastic we'll be able to use. And that's plastic that won't go to waste.

Together, we can help reshape the future.

LEVER

Shared World,
Shared Responsibility.

© 1990 Lever Brothers Company

28 Advertisement stressing Lever's environmental record in repackaging in the United States in 1990.

Comfort '83 Shaping up, staying loose

83's no year for sagging sadly. Your clothes have got to hang right, stay in shape. Use new richer, creamier Comfort in the final rinse and they will. Woollens will be deep down soft, synthetics won't cling, cottons and polycottons will shed creases more easily. Everything will stay smarter, longer. You'll look good, feel great.

New richer, creamier Comfort.

29 Advertisement for Comfort fabric conditioner in Britain in 1983. In that year it was relaunched as with improved softness benefits on synthetics and a richer creamer appearance.

30 Advertisement for Rin washing powder in India in the early 1990s.

Let National's polymer emulsions set an international standard for your nonwovens.

Wherever you call home, you'll find that National's binder emulsions deliver the performance you need in nonwoven products. They deliver wet and dry strength, softness, absorbency and solvent resistance in a wide range of applications.

Thanks to National's worldwide production capabilities, we can deliver the same polymer emulsion from plants local to each of your producing locations. As a result, you can standardize your nonwoven's performance and quality around the globe.

Whether your applications are in medical, industrial or consumer nonwovens, let National help you set a new standard for quality and value... worldwide. Write or call National Starch and Chemical Corporation, Finderne Avenue, Bridgewater, NJ 08807. (201) 685-5425.

National Starch and Chemical Corporation
RESINS & SPECIALTY CHEMICALS

31 Advertisement for National Starch in 1988.

various levels. The relationships forged at Four Acres and elsewhere provided one of the webs that held the Unilever organization together.

Industrial Relations, Trade Unions, and Co-determination

Unilever was aware that growing information flows and economic integration were beginning to impinge on employee matters. International confederations of labour unions began to be formed, including the ICFTU, which was social democratic in outlook and whose affiliates included the British Trades Union Congress and the Deutsche Gewerkschaftsbund. The ICFTU, whose affiliated unions had 50 million members in the 1970s, was particularly well organized on a European level, and was well represented in Brussels. Another related development was the formation of 'International Trade Secretariats', which were confederations of national trade unions organized on an industry-wide basis, which sought to match the international spread of firms. By 1972 the International Federation of Chemical and General Workers Unions (ICF) and the International Union of Food and Allied Workers (IUF) had started to collaborate together to hold discussions with firms spanning both industries, including sharing information about Unilever companies.[86] In June 1973, at a joint conference of the IUF and the ICF in Geneva, a Unilever World Council of Trade Unions was established, which remained in existence for several years, but its effectiveness seems to have been undermined by the difficulties of achieving co-ordinated action between the different national groups.[87]

Unilever regarded industrial relations as a matter for individual operating companies and national managements. It had no wish for wages to be compared between countries, or for workers in one country to support those elsewhere, or for unions to negotiate internationally.[88] It was a corporate priority to make sure that trade unions never felt that they could negotiate above the heads of national managements outside their own countries.[89]

Unilever companies followed the industrial labour practices prevalent in each country. Managers were rarely especially enthused by the post-war spread of concepts of industrial democracy in parts of Europe, but they were prepared to bow to the inevitable, and it was implemented if national laws required it. Unilever implemented 'co-determination' arrangements for consultation of employees when required by such laws.[90] Germany took the lead in the introduction of co-determination. Employees were granted a 50 per cent representation on the 'supervisory boards'—German corporate governance featured a dual system of supervisory and management boards—of iron, steel, and coal firms, and in 1952 this was extended to other industries, though these had only a one-third employee representation on their supervisory boards. Deutsche Unilever had a one-third employee representation on its supervisory board thereafter. In 1976 the legislation was amended to oblige all German companies employing more than 2,000 people to appoint supervisory boards that were split evenly between representatives of workers and shareholders. The chairman of the supervisory board (always a shareholder representative) could use a second (casting) vote in cases where the board was split, so the balance of power was always in the shareholders' favour, but with neither side being able to outnumber the other the emphasis clearly needed to be on co-operation.

Away from representation at board level, Germany was also the pioneer in the development of works councils. In 1952 all German companies were required to appoint works councils and, depending on the size of the company, a certain number of employees would be released from their normal duties to devote all of their time to works council matters. In companies which had several factories or employment sites, company works councils were formed. Unions tended to have a very strong influence on these works councils, but the advantage of the company council was that it provided a single body through which employees' interests could be represented. In Unilever, employees up to the level of JC 25 were represented. The German works councils operated on a number of levels. They were entitled to information on all economic matters relating to the company, and had to be consulted on broad strategic issues such as personnel planning, dismissals, production methods, and training. They also had the right of co-determination on matters of a more routine nature such as working hours, holidays, and bonuses. In 1976 a total of 905 of Unilever's German employees were elected to 180 works councils, 52 of whom were freed from all other duties.[91]

In the Netherlands, a requirement for companies to form works councils, elected by employees, had been introduced in 1950. Until the early 1970s the Dutch works councils had limited powers of communication and consultation with management on matters directly affecting the workforce. From 1971, and especially towards the end of the decade, the powers of the works councils were extended, and employers ceased to be their chairs. The works councils were given the right of veto over the appointment of members of supervisory boards, they could hold 'consultation meetings' with boards of directors six times a year, and major decisions such as mass redundancies or mergers needed their consent. In 1976 some 330 Dutch employees were members of 33 works councils, though only two of them were full-time.[92] After 1973 large companies in the Netherlands were required to have supervisory boards, but an exemption was made for international holding companies where the majority of the employees were employed outside the Netherlands. Unilever NV was given an exemption under this provision. Dutch wage negotiation was heavily institutionalized, and in this matter Unilever was recognized as the ultimate employer rather than individual operating companies. The Dutch national management negotiated on behalf of all the Dutch companies.

In most cases the presence of employee representatives on boards of directors proved to be largely symbolic, but Unilever did not wish to see co-determination laws being harmonized across Europe. There was particular concern that the German system of 50/50 representation of employees and shareholders on supervisory boards might be adopted as a European norm.[93] Unilever was especially anxious to maintain its control over who was appointed to management boards in different countries or companies, fearing that otherwise corporate coherence would disintegrate.[94] In countries where co-determination legislation did not as yet exist, Unilever was inclined to stress its limitations during public debates about its possible introduction. It followed this strategy in Britain during the mid-1970s when a government inquiry—the Bullock Commission—was established to look at the issue of co-determination. Unilever argued that employee participation needed to grow 'from the shop and office floor and that Board level representation must be the culmination of this growth, rather than vice versa', and instead called for the establishment of a widely based works council system.[95] The Commission's final report recommended employee representation on boards, provoking an angry response from the British employers' association. Sir David Orr joined representatives from ICI and Courtaulds in a meeting with the British Prime Minister to stress the 'disastrous' nature of the Bullock recommendations.[96]

The nightmare scenario for Unilever, which caused great concern throughout the second half of the 1970s, was that some form of co-determination would be extended to the Boards of PLC and NV, through pressure either from the European Commission or from national governments.[97] The problem was that maintenance of identical Boards formed a crucial component in the complex and sensitive arrangements which kept NV and PLC functioning as one company.[98] Towards the end of the decade it was felt a real likelihood that the British and Dutch governments might legislate for employee representation on the Boards of PLC and NV.[99] However, the election of the Thatcher government in Britain in 1979 resulted, rather to Unilever's surprise, in the sudden disappearance of this issue from the government's agenda. There were concerns that it might reappear as a 'matter of high priority' if a Labour government were re-elected, but as matters turned out that was not going to be for a further eighteen years.[100]

Co-determination, works councils, and other arrangements for employee consultation were important contributory factors to the slow pace of rationalization of Unilever's business seen in continental Europe. Quite apart from government pressures and expensive legal obligations if workers were made redundant, Unilever needed to consult and consult again if it wished to close plants. Although sometimes impatient with this constraint, Unilever managers did not necessarily completely object to the system, as they were after all a Dutch company which formed a core part of a business system which strongly emphasized consensus-seeking and conflict avoidance in labour relations.

It was not Unilever's preference to engage in confrontational labour relations anywhere in the world. Apart from the preference for negotiation, especially on the Dutch side of the business, there was a strong inclination towards keeping a low profile, which meant avoiding well-publicized labour disputes. However in a number of countries, including Britain, Unilever found itself involved in serious disputes with its workforce especially between the middle of the 1960s and the end of the 1970s. There were a number of historical and other reasons why Britain was particularly prone to poor labour relations, but they were certainly not helped by its pervasive social class system, which remained far more persistent than in other Western European countries.[101] This was also the country that resisted the introduction of co-determination, and where it was easiest to make workers redundant. Unilever faced special problems as it had accumulated a considerable portfolio of underperforming British businesses.

Strikes or other labour disputes came to affect virtually all Unilever's companies in Britain. The majority of disputes were settled fairly quickly, yet the regularity with which rounds of pay negotiations brought the threat of strike action or a factory 'go-slow' pointed to the confrontational nature of relations between unions and company managements at this time. Unilever's preferred strategy in Britain came to be not to attempt deliberately to provoke disputes or confrontations in order to implement desired changes, but also not to make concessions until it was clear that these were absolutely necessary. Unilever managers tended not to be combative, and they often seemed ill prepared in the face of unwanted industrial action. Moreover Unilever companies operated in markets where new competitors such as retailers were threatening their positions, and they could ill afford disrupted production.[102]

During the late 1970s Unilever experienced a series of prolonged and acrimonious disputes which affected three of its main operating companies. A strike at Batchelors, which began in July 1977, had its origins in a pay settlement reached two years previously in 1975 which had not been implemented following the introduction of income controls by the government, desperate to counter inflation rates approaching 25 per cent per annum. Under the new policy regime, voluntary collective bargaining between unions and employers continued, but the government sought to set maximum limits for pay awards. By 1977 the government had a policy to keep the increase in national average earnings to within 10 per cent. The trade unions at Batchelors believed they had a case for an award over this figure because they had been forced to forgo part of their 1975 pay award, and in July 1977 they demanded that this earlier settlement be implemented. The management at

Batchelors felt that they were obliged to keep within the government's 10 per cent guidelines.

A damaging strike followed which meant, among other things, that Batchelors missed out entirely on the annual pea season, which was extremely costly for a company whose canned peas provided a major source of profits. The bad feeling was aggravated by the fact that not all companies were as rigorous as Batchelors in sticking to the government's guidelines.[103] Eventually after nine weeks the two sides reached an agreement in the form of a productivity deal, whereby a pay increase in excess of 10 per cent could be justified provided that it was self-financing. About eighty employees were made redundant as a result. The outcome was regarded as very satisfactory by the Special Committee.[104]

The problems at Batchelors were dwarfed by events at Birds Eye. By the autumn of 1977 this company faced numerous disputes at all its plants, which were spread over Britain at Kirkby, Yarmouth, Lowestoft, Grimsby, and Eastbourne. The situation was not exactly unexpected, as Birds Eye was experiencing collapsing market share and profits by the second half of the 1970s. A programme of rationalization was begun, involving substantial redundancies, and it was not long before industrial disputes started spreading throughout the company.[105] The most serious problems were in Kirkby, in the Merseyside region of England. Merseyside's two principal claims to fame at this time were as the birthplace of the Beatles and the location of some of Britain's worst industrial relations. By the late 1970s tens of thousands of port workers and employees of Ford, British Leyland, and BAT factories in Merseyside were engaged in industrial action, and the Birds Eye factory was soon enmeshed in the same situation.

During the autumn of 1977 production at Kirkby was brought to a standstill during a month-long strike by process workers demanding a large wage increase, which the management claimed breached the government incomes guidelines. The strikers eventually returned to work in mid-October after about a month, having agreed to accept local productivity agreements. However, a new round of industrial action begun by the engineers at Kirkby evolved into one of the most serious stoppages faced by any Unilever company. After a work-to-rule, an overtime ban, and a series of one-day stoppages, a fully-fledged strike was called at the end of November. The action was taken by around one hundred skilled craftsmen represented by the engineering union AEUW, but it resulted in a total of 1,200 workers being laid off. Managers were the only persons to cross picket lines and continue working at the site during the dispute.

The dispute was linked once more to the government's pay guidelines. The Birds Eye management insisted that workers were being offered the absolute maximum allowed under the government pay guidelines. The union was neither interested in the government's pay guidelines nor would it accept a productivity deal.[106] The strike took place against an escalating conflict between workers of all grades and the senior management of Birds Eye. There were sympathy strikes at the other factories in support of Kirkby, and the dispute moved in directions which Unilever strongly disliked. A member of the strike committee announced their intention for a wider coalition of unions 'aimed eventually at a united trade union body for all Unilever companies'.[107]

Both unions and management exhibited a high degree of intransigence. There was a chasm of mutual incomprehension between the concerns of workers in Kirkby and managers at Birds Eye's head office in the pleasant and comfortable southern English town of Walton-on-Thames. In December 1977 Birds Eye announced that it had put its £6.5 million investment programme in the Kirkby plant on hold. A similar threat at Yarmouth helped to hasten the arrival of an agreement there, but in Kirkby it served to make matters a good deal worse. The local Member of Parliament denounced Birds Eye's threat to cut off investment as 'a totally inappropriate and high-handed move calculated only to make matters worse', which was tantamount to 'blackmail'.[108] However, such political concerns did nothing to soften Birds Eye's tactics. During March 1978 the company issued dismissal notices to all 1,200 hourly paid workers at the factory, and announced that because of the strike there would be no chance of any redundancy pay.[109]

Within days of the dismissal notices going out, an agreement had been reached within the 10 per cent government guidelines. The redundancy notices were then withdrawn, but 450 people lost their jobs at Kirkby in the aftermath of the strike. Birds Eye estimated that the five-month strike cost the company £3 million.[110] However this did not mark the end of industrial relations problems in the Merseyside area. Within a year the Van den Bergh's plant at Bromborough became involved in a dispute over shift allowances, leading to a six-week halt to production in the spring of 1979.[111]

Unilever's serious labour problems in Britain receded rapidly following the election of the Thatcher government in 1979. There was a sharp increase in unemployment as a result of the new government's macro-economic policies, which saw both interest rates and the British exchange rate rise rapidly. The subsequent mass unemployment and social disruption undermined the ability of unions to secure support for industrial action, while legislative changes made it more difficult for unions legally to use strike action as a means of protest. In 1989, when Birds Eye Wall's closed its Kirkby factory as 'costs remained too high and productivity too low', there was little that the unions could do about it. As it happened Mrs Thatcher was visiting Liverpool on the day of the announcement. Unilever had briefed her beforehand, and found her 'supportive'.[112] Without making any significant policy changes of its own, Unilever found itself virtually free of industrial relations problems in Britain in the 1980s.

Unilever was unable to escape the harsh industrial relations climate prevailing in Britain during the 1970s. Strikes took a formidable amount of management time, and underlay the poor profitability of some of the British-based businesses. Unilever often preferred to move more slowly in making redundancies if this enabled it to avoid bad publicity. Most of its managers were uncomfortable in aggressive labour relations disputes, yet when forced into situations they also proved willing to take tough negotiating positions.

Perspectives

By 1990 Unilever was even more convinced than in the past about the importance of its human resource capabilities. 'Human resource and particularly management quality in depth', the Personnel Director at that time told his fellow directors, 'will become the determining factor for our future growth, either as an opportunity or a constraint.' Unilever was still losing 70 per cent of its management recruits within eight years of recruitment. There was still a perceived need to reduce the 'dominance' of the British and the Dutch at senior levels, 'both for practical reasons and as a signal to high flyers from other regions'; there was still a need 'to increase the productivity of management by training and also by ensuring that there are never unnecessary layers'.[113] Unilever still had, although this was not mentioned, no woman within striking distance of the main board.

Managing Unilever posed an enormous challenge, not only because of its size, but also because of its industrial and geographical spread. The complexity was increased by the need to confront major cross-cultural challenges, beginning with the British and Dutch relationship within the firm. Unilever recruited and developed a very able managerial cadre to meet these challenges. Human resource management was regarded as extremely important, more so than in many other large companies, and its achievements were considerable. The Unilever system identified talented managers early in their careers, and then guided the development of those careers. An elaborate system of management training enhanced skill levels, and also helped build a corporate identity. The aims of this training programme were modified over time as expectations and labour markets evolved. The management development system functioned in a fair and rational fashion, and was inherently meritocratic. It was implemented in ways which helped to keep the British and Dutch influences within the company in balance, while by the 1980s Unilever was also slowly seeking ways to incorporate other nationalities into its senior positions. In 1990 the top management of P & G and Nestlé remained overwhelmingly American and Swiss respectively. The eighteen Unilever directors in that year included two Germans, one Irish, one American, and one Indian. While Unilever had hardly become a 'nationless corporation' by that date, it was among the most international and cosmopolitan of the world's largest corporations.

By the end of the 1980s Unilever was still exploring ways to unlock the full potential of its managers. Resources were highly concentrated on 'high flyers' rather than the mass of managers, who were often considered more of a cost than a resource. The extensive process of consultation meant that even its 'top 200' managers spent much of their time in committees and debates rather than in getting things done quickly in the market place. If Unilever was to flourish as a dynamic competitive force and a 'knowledge organization', all levels of management and the workforce had to be engaged and motivated.

9
Corporate Culture

During the early 1980s there was a sudden spate of studies, mostly written by McKinsey partners or consultants, on the corporate culture of firms. Peters and Waterman's *In Search of Excellence*, published in 1982, became a major international best-seller. It was followed by numerous studies which maintained that corporate culture was one of the key determinants in corporate performance.[1] A firm's 'culture' resides in the shared values and assumptions which evolve over time, and which are typically taken for granted.[2] This 'culture' is at once hard to define, as it is not written down in any document or set of rules, yet pervasive, shaping the choices that managers make, and how decisions are implemented.

This chapter begins by describing Unilever's 'culture'. The following sections consider first the national dimensions of Unilever's culture, and then its coexistence with multiple subcultures. Finally, the gender implications of Unilever's culture are discussed.

A Networked Organization

There were many strands to Unilever's corporate culture, but three values stand out as what one writer has called 'pivotal', or central to the company's functioning.[3] These were the beliefs in the importance of integrity, local autonomy, and human relationships. These values provided the core tenets whereby Unilever was managed.

Unilever considered itself a company of integrity. The managers who oversaw the early growth of Unilever after the merger in 1929—men such as Francis D'Arcy Cooper, Paul Rijkens, and Lord Heyworth—were bywords for honesty and fairness. From its origins, Unilever was a culture in which dishonest actions were not options. However fierce the rivalries might be with competitors, Unilever managers would not 'bend the rules' to achieve victory.

The concept of integrity was wider than honesty. 'Making money' per se was not seen as the exclusive goal within Unilever, either for individuals or for the company. Lord Leverhulme became a rich man, and was an acquisitive one, but his ferocious work ethic even during his last years appears to have been driven not by the urge to get ever richer, but rather from a sense of responsibility to others.[4] Working for Unilever was never the way to get very rich. Unilever managers were, or were expected to be, motivated as much by their work as by their salaries. Nor was this a culture which saw profit maximization, at least in a narrow sense, as morally acceptable as an exclusive corporate goal. The influence of the 'enlightened paternalism' of Leverhulme, most vividly evidenced at the factory and community at Port Sunlight, remained strong in the post-war decades.[5]

After the war the concept of 'corporate social responsibility' was added to this strand of the corporate culture. This idea had first originated at the beginning of the twentieth century in the United States, initiated by wealthy businessmen such as the steel magnate Andrew Carnegie who believed that firms should be concerned with more than profit-making. Commitment to the concept waned during the subsequent troubled economic and political conditions between the 1920s and the 1940s, but in the 1950s there was renewed interest.[6] Rijkens was a prominent exponent of the philosophy, maintaining that within the context of being a profit-making business which sought to earn appropriate returns for its shareholders, a firm such as Unilever had responsibilities to other stakeholders including employees, consumers, and the environments in which it operated.

In 1948 Rijkens recruited the like-minded Pieter Kuin into Unilever as Economic Adviser from the Dutch civil service. He worked directly under Rijkens, and became a main board director in 1961. Both men encouraged Unilever to assume a more public role in line with its responsibilities to society, and they also emphasized the implications for the behaviour of Unilever's employees.[7] 'A businessman who confines himself strictly to his legal and contractual obligations', Kuin wrote after his retirement in the house magazine, *Unilever Magazine*, 'will probably be one of two types—a mean little man or a hard-headed bully. . . . Making money is important', he continued, 'but the ultimate satisfaction is in doing a meaningful job, and doing it well'.[8]

The belief that Unilever should be, and was, concerned with more than profits was widespread. In 1959 an article in the then house magazine *Progress* maintained that the company was 'a citizen of many lands, and it owes in varying degrees the obligations of citizenship towards many communities. Such an organisation can be a powerful force for good in the world.'[9] The belief that Unilever should be a 'force for good' was not a cynical public image. A survey of managers' opinions in 1972 revealed a strongly held view that Unilever was a company where integrity was an integral part of its actions.[10] Unilever people, rather than rules per se, were seen as the ultimate guarantors of this integrity.[11] It was not entirely without reason that Unilever was sometimes described as a 'church'.[12] At least in the more senior management levels, the level of commitment expected was almost akin to a religion. The religious imagery was reinforced by the fact that the chief executive was three persons who spoke as one.

The second pivotal value within Unilever was the importance of local autonomy. It was a core assumption that the key to competitive success was local knowledge and responsiveness to local markets. Unilever managers preferred to provide choices rather than to offer standardization. P & G was also a highly marketing-oriented company, but it differed from Unilever in placing more emphasis on technology-based solutions to consumer requirements, and being more inclined to see similarities between markets and cultures.

It was believed within Unilever that the commitment to local autonomy made it a unique kind of multinational, which set it apart from US firms such as P & G. An internal report in 1984 summarized the widespread view about that company within Unilever:

Procter have a particularly strong corporate culture. There is a marked sense of corporate identity, reinforced by apocryphal stories from their history. There are Procter 'ways of doing things'. . . . Procter's staff departments exert particularly strong control, in ensuring that Procter approaches are followed round the world. . . . Outside the USA, Procter are a very American company: they are seen as a prime disseminator of US business ethics and practice, with strong identification with US foreign policy.[13]

P & G's ability to use 'strong control' to achieve faster transfer of technologies and brands around the world was on occasion grudgingly admired, but Unilever had no wish to operate in such a fashion. It was proud of its local identity. There was no wish to be identified with anyone's 'foreign policy'.

The third pivotal cultural value at Unilever was the belief in the importance of human relationships in managing the company. Unilever, one former director remarked, 'is characterized by indefinable relationships'.[14] Unilever executives constantly stressed that it was the strength of relationships—and not formal bureaucratic rules—which held its management together. The 'belief in the importance of maintaining direct human relationships as part of the everyday job of management', another former director observed, 'ran throughout the business. The ethos of Unilever was cohesion and therein lay its strength.'[15]

The importance of relationships within Unilever was emphasized in one study published in *Harvard Business Review* in 1996. The authors identified four types of corporate culture according to their degree of 'sociability'—the 'degree of sincere friendliness among members of a community'—and 'solidarity'—a 'community's ability to pursue shared objectives quickly and effectively, regardless of personal ties'. Mercenary cultures featured high solidarity and low sociability; communal cultures had high solidarity and high sociability; fragmented cultures had low solidarity and low sociability; and, finally, networked cultures had low solidarity and high sociability. Each type of culture could generate competitive advantage, but it needed to match the existing business environment. Unilever was highlighted as a classic example of a networked organization. It was described as a company which recruited people from similar backgrounds, and then passed them through a series of rituals and shared experiences creating 'widespread fellowship and goodwill'.[16]

Unilever's corporate culture during the immediate post-war decades might be better described as fragmented rather than networked given the chasm between London and Rotterdam. However, as that chasm narrowed, the level of 'sociability' increased, and was sustained through several mechanisms. Managers from many countries and product areas met on courses at Four Acres. The networking consequences of the training courses were explicitly recognized. 'A "hidden" objective', one Personnel Division memorandum on the training courses in 1978 observed, 'is the "Unileverisation" factor which is an important part of our culture—the building of understanding, supportive, helping and trusting relationships within the Concern.'[17] The effect of attending courses at Four Acres was to create 'an informal network of equals', Maljers wrote in an article in *Harvard Business Review* published in 1992, 'who know one another well and usually continue to meet and exchange experiences'.[18]

An important part of the building of relationships was the use of major conferences of senior managers as a means of policy-making, and also policy dissemination. Each year the two chairmen, in London and Rotterdam, addressed a meeting of up to 500 senior managers from all over the world. These events originated before the Second World War, when they were normally held in the boardroom in London. It was known as the 'Chairman's Review' until around 1952, when the term OBJ (Oh! Be Joyful)—taken from Psalm 100—was coined. After the annual OBJ at the head offices, chairmen of operating companies received copies of the main points, and presented similar reviews to their own middle management. Information and policy was thus cascaded downwards throughout the organization. The OBJ, Maljers told one such gathering in The Hague, 'is of more than routine importance . . . The OBJ is an important binding element in Unilever, a tradition which we all highly value.'[19]

Unilever's rotation of its 'high-flying' managers through various jobs in different product groups and countries was important in building webs of personal contacts. It was the strength of relationships which permitted the decentralized nature of the company to function as a collective whole, and which underpinned its flexible and pragmatic approach. Despite the appearance of a bureaucratic organization with formal rules and procedures to cover every eventuality, important decisions were taken on the basis of relationships and 'know-who'. Success in securing resources depended on the ability to mobilize support and allies behind the idea.

Although there was always much discussion within Unilever, the important decisions rarely took place at formal meetings. There was minimal debate at Board meetings as outcomes were agreed before anything reached the Board for decision. Nor was decision-making transparent. The Special Committee was the only body which had a holistic view of the whole company, and its deliberations were secret. It was through personal networks that news of new product and brands would spread around the company. Managers often heard of new developments from chance encounters, or from meeting people at Four Acres.[20] There were many such chance encounters within Unilever, as the company was 'relentlessly social'.[21]

The emphasis on relationships at Unilever had a number of implications. The *Harvard Business Review* study in 1996 suggested that one downside of networked organizations such as Unilever was 'low solidarity'. This was a situation in which 'employees may be so busy being friends that they lose sight of the reason they are at work in the first place'. In such a culture, there was a tendency to tolerate poor performance and a slow response to competitive threats, and often a lack of strategic focus. It was hard to enforce central direction.[22] It is not evident that Unilever's managers were always 'friendly' with each other, but undoubtedly things had to be done by persuasion rather than coercion. London and Rotterdam controlled capital expenditure levels and enforced ethical codes, but in most matters discussion and compromise was the norm. Frequently discussions continued after final decisions had apparently been made. Change was possible, but most likely to be achieved when the argument went 'with the grain' of the culture and the majority opinion, rather than running counter to it.[23]

In the culture of relationships, open dissent was frowned upon, and also dangerous because each manager or director needed allies when he or she had a case to make. Distrust was often masked behind apparent consensus. A lack of 'trust' may have been a feature of the Anglo-Dutch heritage, because people were forever seeking the 'hidden agenda' of the 'other side'.[24] As a result, although there were constant discussions and meetings, different functional areas within the company— such as marketing and research—often did not work well with one another. Unilever had a networked culture in which teamwork was weak. In some respects it was one of the least cohesive businesses among large international firms.

The fact that decisions were reached through relationships rather than through coercion meant that decision-making was often slow. Unilever was a company in which, at its apex, three men from different countries had to agree if they wanted to do something. Except in extraordinary circumstances, votes were not taken, and the members of the Special Committee talked until they agreed. This kind of situation was replicated in the decision-making process throughout the organization. A report on Unilever's management culture in 1982, accepted by the Special Committee, observed that there 'was too much emphasis on information and consultation', and that managers were 'too concerned with discussion and evaluation of all options to the detriment of the entrepreneurial spirit'.[25] The lower reaches of Unilever's management appeared full of people who attended numerous meetings, and knew how to talk in 'committee speak' and to lobby for their own particular interests, but who were ineffective in making things happen in the real world. One former director identified Unilever's 'lack of ability to act' as one of its main weaknesses.[26]

Unilever was often described as being conservative or risk-averse, but this does not capture the essence of the situation. Unilever took large risks as a business enterprise. The building of the European frozen foods and ice cream businesses involved large capital investments from which no immediate financial return was likely. Unilever was not, however, receptive to more individual styles of risk-taking entrepreneurship. Every survey of employee attitudes concluded that Unilever was not the place for 'entrepreneurs'. 'I would think that anyone who is a bit adventurous, or extremely independent', one such survey showed in 1972, 'would hate to consider it.'[27] In 1980 a Marketing Division report on product innovation, or rather the apparent lack of it, noted an absence of entrepreneurial types who would act as champions for 'high-risk, very unfamiliar or complex projects'.[28] 'There are no weird entrepreneurs', a mid-career recruit to Unilever was reported as saying in 1989.[29] A company which depended on relationships could not afford to hire many disruptive individuals.

The emphasis on relationships was reflected in descriptions of Unilever's culture as 'clubby' or 'cosy'. A much-cited quotation was that 'Unilever was a gentlemanly occupation'.[30] During the post-war decades there was a strong feeling of 'family' characteristic of the notion of the 'Organization Man' which was then widespread. In return for loyalty and identifying their goals with their organizations, individuals were offered job security and long-term careers. By the 1980s socio-economic changes had greatly changed such relationships between organizations and individuals, but in Unilever such values remained evident. A report on mid-career recruits found the 'club' atmosphere strong at the end of the 1980s. Unilever, it was observed, 'has many of the characteristics of a gentlemen's club or a boys' boarding school. We also heard it likened to the army, the church, a police state, a foreign country, and the British Empire, all of which have deeply embedded value systems which originated in the mists of time.'[31]

The 'club' was the product of history. 'After 65 years of careful selection and training of managers, we now have a cadre of truly international managers', Sir Michael Perry told an audience at Yale University in 1995. 'It is those managers who over generations have steadily evolved the culture of this company—a common culture, which some call a "club".'[32] This was a 'club' where the rituals and rites were so understated as to be hardly apparent. Yet if Unilever was a 'club', Perry observed, 'it's the most competitive club I know, because membership is a privilege that may be joked about but is fiercely guarded'.[33]

During the post-war decades the culture included toleration of poorly performing businesses and managers. The senior management of Unilever were well aware that some parts of it underperformed, but did not regard it as acceptable to sell them. P & G had a culture where non-performing managers quickly left the company.[34] Unilever had a culture where they rarely left the company.[35] Poorly performing managers would not progress—Personnel Division was far too competent for such a thing to happen—but they would be found a role which did not do actual harm to Unilever, and enabled them to keep their self-respect. Although poor performance was tolerated, Unilever managers were expected to be committed. 'You've got to put the company first,' Cole maintained in 1963.[36] The mid-career recruits into Unilever in 1989 found such attitudes alive and well. Unilever, it was reported, 'comes first and family comes second and personal interests come third. If there were ever a clash between a Unilever meeting and a school governors' meeting, for instance, the Unilever meeting would automatically have priority.'[37]

It was not an easy matter to introduce strategic or organizational changes which challenged the pivotal values of Unilever's culture. In theory, the most effective means to encourage change in a company was a major external threat. The investments of P & G in post-war Europe represented such a threat, but Unilever's response was initially muted. This was partly because only the detergents side of the business was affected, but also because Unilever's overall size tended to make it slower to react to such threats. The 'Concern', as the company was universally referred to internally, was a vast organization. Unilever had an image of itself as a world leader and trendsetter in business. The result was an inward-looking orientation which did not, until the 1980s, benchmark itself on a worldwide basis, however much the shares held in individual markets were considered.[38]

During the post-war decades most large corporations were inclined to the view that the only things that mattered were inside their own boundaries. However, Unilever may have been peculiarly inclined towards the 'not invented here' and 'we know best' approach. One report in 1970 perceived 'an inward-looking philosophy that causes others to accuse us of arrogance'.[39] This philosophy made Unilever less interested in collaborating with other firms than, say, Nestlé, which made noticeably more use of alliances and minority holdings.

If a decision was particularly difficult or complex, and especially if it appeared to challenge a pivotal value such as local autonomy, managers supporting change typically resorted to hiring external consultants to break the deadlock by 'legitimizing' a certain course of action. The use of McKinsey to settle finally the twenty-year debate about Co-ordination in 1970 was a classic example. By the end of the 1980s Unilever spent some £15–17 million per year on hundreds of outside consulting projects.[40] In many cases—though Unilever was not unusual in this respect—the desired answers were known before the project was commissioned.

Although the pivotal Unilever values were strong and persistent, they were redefined over time. Hartog and Woodroofe began the process of redefining the meaning of local autonomy, and making Unilever less of a 'gentlemanly occupation'. 'Three years ago the Company was seen as slow moving and paternalistic but it will never be seen that way again,' one manager was reported as saying in 1972. 'Financial difficulties led to wide scale management redundancies at all levels. A job with Unilever will never be viewed in the same way again.'[41]

During the 1980s the Special Committee broke down barriers to change on a larger scale. The most radical change was the diminished tolerance for poorly performing businesses, and the willingness to disrupt long-standing relationships and traditions by selling historic parts of the business. The culture shock experienced within the company was considerable, and it was meant to be considerable. In 1985 a meeting between the Special Committee and the Personnel Division noted the degree of 'uncertainty' within Unilever as a result of 'the evolution of Unilever culture, from a sleeping giant to a quick-acting company. People who had known five years ago exactly what the culture was were now feeling somewhat bemused. Everybody agreed that a culture shock had been necessary. They realised that we were now achievement oriented.'[42]

This 'achievement-oriented' culture was more aware of external threats than previously, and had a new recognition that achievement involved an increased willingness for individual managers to take risks. This theme was pursued in particular by a younger generation of senior managers. 'We must be prepared to take risks', Niall FitzGerald told a meeting of German managers in 1987 shortly before he joined the Board. 'And we must accept in taking risks that things will go wrong. That is the essence of risk-taking. Things do go wrong. . . . if our sole purpose in life is to avoid mistakes we take no decisions and there is no progress and there is no growth. We have to grow or decline.'[43]

Unilever's corporate culture enabled a diverse business to operate effectively, and to high standards of professional management and integrity. It was often said that

Unilever executives could recognize each other at airports even when they had never met.[44] Although obviously an exaggeration, there was an element of truth, at least for senior management. Unilever managers were, more often than not, honest and transparent rather than conniving or deceitful, liberal but not radical, more motivated by job satisfaction than material gain, hard-working with a touch of being true believers in the good they were doing. They were inclined to be low profile. A tolerance for underperformance and tendency towards being inward looking diminished over time, but undoubtedly it was a culture in which individualistic risk-taking was not the norm.

Unilever and National Cultures

Despite much talk about 'stateless' firms or 'global' corporations, most large multinational companies continued even in the first decade of the twenty-first century to reflect the cultural values of the country from which they emerged. In most cases the boards of such companies remained dominated by nationals of those countries.[45] Within such a context, Unilever seemed a cosmopolitan firm. This was often one of the first characteristics of the company noticed by people who joined it from more conventional 'national' firms.

This did not mean that Unilever was culturally 'stateless'. The London and Rotterdam head offices were adorned with paintings of the British and Dutch monarchy. Different elements of Unilever's corporate culture could be traced to stereotypical views of either British or Dutch management. The preference for meetings in which there was a search for consensus was a typical feature of Dutch management. The tendency to fix outcomes in corridors and rest rooms was a noted characteristic of British managers. Both national cultures emphasized high standards of honesty, and both had long traditions of the Protestant work ethic.

Yet Unilever was not interested in turning the many other nationalities who worked for the company into British or Dutch men or women. The 'Unilever way of doing things', Woodroofe told an audience at the Harvard Business School in 1968, was not an 'Anglo-Dutch philosophy but one to which all nationalities have contributed'. He went on to question whether large American corporations did not 'lose something of the variety of ideas which might otherwise have been brought to their businesses by nationals of other countries whom they employ(ed), because those nationals have been Americanised'.[46] Unilever recognized the benefits of cultural diversity decades before the subject started to enter management textbooks.

The Anglo-Dutch relationship within Unilever was of enduring interest inside the company, and the object of curiosity outside it. The relationship was complex, but not incomprehensible. Unilever had been formed in specific historical circumstances between firms in the same industry with common interests. The basic organizational arrangements made at the time—the Equalization Agreement—provided a sound basis for the merger. Thereafter, and with various ups and downs, the British and Dutch components of the company learned to work together.

The relationship between the British and Dutch was undoubtedly assisted by cultural compatibilities. The two countries were geographical neighbours on either side of the North Sea which shared a common mercantile, seafaring, and colonial heritage. According to the most authoritative study of national cultural values ever undertaken, by the Dutch sociologist Geert Hofstede, many British and Dutch cultural values were quite similar. In contrast, his study showed the values of Dutch and Belgians, or British and French, as almost diametrically opposed to each other.[47]

There was, therefore, a sufficient basis to permit a functioning relationship built on compromise and pragmatism. The willingness of the Dutch to speak and write English was essential, even if over the years there were quite a number of British managers and directors who learned Dutch. Virtually all internal Unilever correspondence was written in English, except when it involved exclusively Dutch matters. Although the Dutch had a tradition of learning the languages of neighbouring countries, the fact that business was conducted in a foreign language was not easy. Many members of the post-war generation were more at ease in German or French than English. In the 1960s and 1970s, Dutch directors attending Board meetings would sometimes 'feel like second class citizens'.[48] They were prepared to accept this situation as the pragmatic solution. The language issue was not seen as threatening their cultural identity, or the readiness to protect what were seen as Dutch interests. The Dutch were as proud of their culture as the next European, perhaps more so, but Unilever could function bi-nationally because such pride was expressed in a pragmatic fashion.

There were compromises on the British side also. Many British clung tenaciously to an exaggerated view of the importance of their country and its ways of doing things. This sense of superiority, combined with a parochial view on the world, helped fuel Britain's troubled relationship with the European Union. However, feelings of superiority were typically expressed in a pragmatic fashion, and combined with an appreciation of commercial realities. The British within Unilever were thus willing to concede that their Dutch colleagues had strengths which they lacked, especially knowledge of 'the Continent', and fluency in the languages spoken there. Over time, the British managers in Unilever made an evolution from the 'culture of Empire'—reflected in the situation where all Board meetings were held in London and preceded by British business—towards a more European outlook. They were ahead of most of their counterparts working in purely British businesses.

Cross-cultural tensions between the British and the Dutch within Unilever were more like those within a family rather than major issues of contention. The two cultures had different styles of discussion and negotiation. 'The English', as Harold Hartog put it, 'have a far more charming and indirect way of expressing themselves and the Dutch are blunt and abrupt.'[49] The more abrupt of the Dutch were advised privately on occasion that their British colleagues required more 'charming' ways of saying the same thing.[50] Within the corporate decision-making process, it was sometimes possible to take advantage of cultural differences to reach optimal outcomes. In London, the British typically tried to reach a consensus on a matter before a meeting through informal discussions in corridors and elsewhere. This process was known as 'soaking the issue'. Decisions reached in London were 'pre-cooked', but then tended to work. In Rotterdam, there was a more direct system of open discussion, but it was often necessary to manage outcomes. There was a case for using London to make 'difficult' decisions, and Rotterdam to make 'unpopular' decisions.[51]

British and Dutch directors and managers had sufficient common purpose and compatibility to work with each other when necessary. When there were conflicts at the level of the Special Committee, it was far more a matter of conflicting personalities than cultures. Each side gave sufficient space to the other to maintain their own spheres of influence. Foods, and especially Edible Fats, remained a strongly 'Dutch' sphere, whilst Detergents, and especially Personal Products, was a strongly 'British' one. UAC's management was almost entirely British. Even in the Overseas countries, there was some division. Unilever often sent British managers to India and South Africa, while Dutch managers were often found in Brazil and Turkey.

While in the 1960s Unilever's senior management was overwhelmingly British and Dutch, twenty years later the appointments to Board level of other nationalities had resulted in a more cosmopolitan mix. Yet Unilever remained a 'European' and not an 'international firm'. Values such as the belief in the importance of relationships rather than formal rules, the role of social networks, the acceptance of cultural homogeneity, and the tendency to see the differences between markets rather than the similarities, were widely shared within European companies, and set them apart from their US counterparts. Unilever remained no more 'stateless' than any multinational, but considerably more cosmopolitan than almost any other.

Subcultures

Unilever's culture was sometimes seen as less 'strong' than that of some competitors such as P & G or Johnson & Johnson, both known for their high levels of commitment to corporate goals and cultures where almost all managers shared a consistent set of values and methods. It was often maintained that such 'strong' cultures delivered significant advantages, although only if the culture was strategically appropriate. One leading American study of corporate cultures in the United States between 1976 and 1986 identified P & G as having almost the strongest culture of any large US corporation. Both Colgate and CPC were seen as having much less 'strong' cultures. However, the same study also observed that such a strong culture was not necessarily an advantage. 'The highly analytical, methodical and risk-averse behaviour in Procter & Gamble's culture', it was noted, 'has been criticised both by outsiders and by some of its own management.' In terms of average return on invested capital between 1977 and 1988, P & G appeared well down the rankings of US firms, behind 'weak' culture firms such as CPC.[52]

Unilever's tradition of strong local autonomy often led to the assumption that the firm had a 'weak' corporate culture, but such a view misunderstands the nature of Unilever. The corporate culture reviewed above was 'strong' in that it bound together the senior management which was the central concern of the Personnel Department. 'The key to preserving the unity of Unilever', it was observed in 1989, 'was to maintain a common culture and commercial language and a common policy for the recruitment, development and remuneration of managers.'[53] This 'strong' corporate culture coexisted with, rather than was weakened by, numerous subcultures found in the operating companies. Unilever's distinctive competitive advantage was created by the presence and interaction of these different layers of culture within the organization.[54]

Unilever was a company built through the acquisition of many other firms, all of which retained their distinctive ways of doing business which reflected their own histories, their countries, and the industry in which they were concerned. Unilever had as many corporate subcultures as it had operating companies. Co-ordinators were constantly engaged in the interface between Unilever's corporate culture and the subcultures of the operating companies, and they often had to pursue quite different working relations with different operating companies.

The differences between operating companies were often profound. In the 1960s Unilever had two frozen products companies in Britain—Wall's which sold ice cream, and Birds Eye which sold frozen products—which had very different cultures. This reflected different histories, and different types of business. While Wall's sold impulse products to confectioners and newspaper shops, Birds Eye sold functional products to large supermarkets. An attempt to merge them during the mid-1960s failed largely because 'the psychological approach of the two companies to business was very different . . . as different as chalk and cheese'.[55] They were eventually merged in 1980, and then only with considerable difficulties.

The different subcultures had a considerable impact on recruitment and training. In Britain, Lever Brothers and Elida Gibbs prided themselves on the intellectual capacity of their managers. They were known to treat new management trainees well, regarding them as gifted individuals who should be allowed flexibility to make their contribution. In the foods companies Birds Eye and Batchelors Foods, confidence, toughness, and an ability to deal fairly but firmly with those around them were valued as much as intellectual ability. New recruits at those two companies were expected to be able to get on with their job in a busy and competitive environment.[56] BOCMS was noted for giving responsibility to managers at a younger age than in many Unilever companies. It served as a 'nursery' for many of Unilever's senior British executives.

UAC's subculture was radically different from that of the rest of Unilever. This reflected the huge difference between selling branded consumer goods and trading in Africa. This made it difficult to transfer managers between UAC and the rest of Unilever, or even to build a relationship between UAC and other Unilever affiliates on the ground in West Africa. UAC managers were unique within Unilever for being recruited solely for service outside their home country. While Unilever managers were oriented towards marketing and brands, their UAC equivalents bore more than a passing resemblance to colonial administrators, yet in other respects it was the most 'entrepreneurial' component of Unilever. In the UAC—as in most trading companies—managerial responsibility came early. Administrative arrangements were often more 'flexible' than in Unilever. During the 1960s, for example, while the Overseas Committee mandated that its managers travelled first class, both for health reasons and so they could work 'the moment one arrived', in the UAC managers could downgrade the ticket and keep the difference, a practice which the Overseas Committee regarded as 'anathema'.[57]

The subcultures of operating companies reflected industry differences, and this characteristic may have increased in relative importance from the 1960s alongside the new Co-ordination structures. The Co-ordinations created new networks between managers in different countries, whilst creating barriers between them and other Unilever managers in the same country but a different product category. There was little if any interaction between detergents or foods companies within Unilever. Within the Foods category, the structure of the Co-ordinations resulted in weak links also between edibles, frozen foods, and sundry foods.

The culture of each of the product categories reflected the type of product they sold. The managers in Detergents worked in an industry characterized by strong competition between large firms. Unilever companies in particular competed against P & G, and this shaped the culture of the detergents companies. There was great rivalry and no love lost between the two firms. Managers in detergents had a strong *esprit de corps* derived from this competition. They believed they were fighting the toughest competitors, and for many years that competition almost defined the culture of Detergents Co-ordination.[58]

Unilever's detergents companies prided themselves on their professional management and competence. They believed that detergents were at the cutting edge of marketing. The London-based Detergents Co-ordination firmly believed that the British operating company Lever Brothers produced the best marketing managers in the business. Lever Brothers had a strong corporate ethos which manifested itself in a great deal of solidarity within the company. Their managers were always on the look out for each other, and if there was an opening somewhere they would try to get one of their people appointed.[59] At times this was a culture which bordered on arrogance. During the 1980s it encouraged the bold, but unrealistic, strategies of making large inroads on both the Japanese and US markets.

There was a different subculture in Edible Fats. Companies such as UDL in Germany held massive market share in margarine. As successful companies, they could attract and reward talented managers.[60] The large European edible fats companies had track records of being successful businesses at the forefront of modern marketing methods, with up-to-date factories, and lots of cash to spend on equipment and new initiatives. They faced no major international competitor. They were freer to develop longer-term and imaginative brand segmentation strategies. Given their competitive strength and the fact that food tastes remained local, the edible companies were much more inclined to stress the continuing importance of national differences. It was characteristic that it was the detergent side of the business which pushed for the creation of Europe-wide companies during the second half of the 1980s. At that time Edible Fats Co-ordination remained committed to the view that—referring to the famous Sony product—there would never be an equivalent to an 'Edibles Walkman'.[61]

Unilever's competitive position in the market place rested on the strengths—or otherwise—of its operating companies. This point was often lost on outside observers of Unilever. In 1985 Durham responded, in a characteristically robust fashion, during an interview for a US business magazine, which had introduced the company as having 'long been considered solid but slow-moving—it has been likened to the British civil service'. Durham argued that 'The people who say that we don't respond quickly enough have no idea that, for example, we have a company in Malaysia that looks after the Malaysian detergents business, and can react to market developments the morning they happen. The CEO doesn't have to phone up and say, "How should I react?" He reacts. If he doesn't react, then we lose money, and he gets his backside tanned. So, in many areas, the speed of reaction is that of a small, well-organised company.'[62]

The most problematic feature of the coexistence of Unilever's corporate culture, in which a pivotal value was a belief in local autonomy, and numerous individual subcultures was an unwillingness to intervene if one of the subcultures became non-performing. This was at the heart of the problem with Lever Brothers in the United States between the 1950s and the 1970s. After the traumas of the late 1940s, Lever Brothers developed a 'culture of decline'. Its managers did not believe they could compete with P & G, nor were they prepared to make any bold moves in other directions, such as a major acquisition in the personal care sector. At the same time poor performance bred insecurity and produced a culture which resisted assistance from its European parents.

Unilever's competitive success rested on its combination of a strong corporate culture which retained its internal coherence and numerous subcultures which permitted it to generate varied responses to the varied environments operating companies faced worldwide. The existence of numerous subcultures was not without costs. It made the tasks of merging or rationalizing the businesses of individual firms more complex, while Unilever was not well equipped to respond to subcultures which became poorly performing. However, the subcultures were also a source of both creativity and flexibility.

Culture and Gender

It was curious for a company many of whose customers were women that the corporate culture of Unilever was often described as 'male'. Yet the origins of the company lay in manufacturing large batches of soap and margarine out of fats, which might be regarded, at the risk of stereotyping, as more of a 'male' than a 'female' industry. Unilever's personal care business remained small until the 1980s, and for one woman manager during the post-war decades gender may have been an element in this situation. 'The whole idea of being linked with up-market beauty products and fragrances', she later observed, 'rather embarrassed the tough business executives who operated in Unilever House.'[63]

While the proportion of female recruits to management rose over time, the problems of retention meant that the number of female managers did not rise significantly. Between 1973 and 1984 the number of female managers within Unilever increased from 415 to 601. This increased the proportion of female managers in the worldwide total from 3 to 5 per cent, although with national variations. In 1974 over 10 per cent of the 231 managers at Lever Brothers in New York were female.[64] In Scandinavian countries the proportion of female managers reached 15 per cent by 1984, but at that date less than 3 per cent of Unilever's managers in the Netherlands were female. This latter figure had reached 8 per cent in 1990. In 1985 an article in *Unilever Magazine*—appropriately entitled 'Women in Management: The

Revolution that Never Happens'—argued that at least 'women in the business are no longer treated as performing animals'.[65]

At the top of Unilever, a handful of women might have been potential candidates for Board positions, but there was insufficient support to get them to this final stage. The experience of one woman, who might have been one such candidate in the 1960s, showed that the problems faced by women in Unilever were more complex than outright gender discrimination. Eleanor MacDonald was recruited by the personal products company Atkinsons as a manager in 1947, having worked previously for the London retailer Selfridges. Although asked at her interview if she was 'going to get married', MacDonald was hired for her 'knowledge of women' and her 'capacity for communications'. She found Unilever 'very much a male orientated company', but her success in developing a new range of cosmetics brands nonetheless led to her appointment to Atkinsons' Board.

After twelve years at Atkinsons, MacDonald was headhunted in 1959 to become 'Women's Adviser to the UAC', charged with building up trade with African women. This was a high-profile senior management position, which took her around thousands of miles in West Africa working with African women to explore their needs as consumers. The appointment of a senior female executive to explore the marketing opportunities offered by African women consumers was radical for the time. MacDonald focused initially on improving the provision for African women in the Kingsway retail stores. Then, after complaining about restricted responsibilities, she was given a major public relations role also. Finally she retired early from Unilever in 1970 to found her own management training consultancy for women. As she noted in her subsequent autobiography, she left on good terms with Unilever—'whose ethos [she] admired greatly'—but also with a sense of underfulfilment:

as I came to think back on the whole experience later, the climate for women's progress was not then positive enough to allow of their full development. It was too dependent on perceptive senior managers. I had happily had several of those, but also unimaginative ones who, without wishing me ill, did not know how to create a feminine scenario.[66]

MacDonald was an independent and ambitious woman who might well have advanced further if she had been male. The same probably went for at least two of the women in senior positions in the 1970s. Dorothy Wedderburn was originally a research scientist who rose to head the Information Division, liaising at the highest levels with governments. Eileen Cole became head of Research International, the market research company. Both were considered by some of their contemporaries as suitable for directorships.[67] Neither of them had sufficiently strong support from male patrons higher in the Unilever hierarchy to be considered for Board-level appointments. In some instances, women became too useful in their jobs, and so senior executives may not have nominated them for promotion 'because they were too good to lose'.[68]

In Unilever people rose to the top through 'patrons', and there were a number of 'perceptive senior managers' who supported female candidates. During the 1970s Edgar Graham, one of the main board directors and chairman of the Overseas Committee, was one of the most important. Graham was instrumental in MacDonald's move to the UAC.[69] This was part of a wider commitment to promoting women which included championing his secretary to get a managerial appointment.[70] However the number of such 'perceptive' male managers willing to go to great lengths to promote women was never great.

There was a continuing 'maleness' about Unilever's culture which was apparent to many women. The female mid-career recruits to Unilever management examined in the 1989 consultancy report commented on 'the chauvinism and bias against women' within Unilever.[71] An examination conducted in 1990 of a small sample of British women managers who had left Unilever to pursue careers elsewhere found that 'all left for career reasons, all felt their companies had not engaged with them and had let them drift away. . . . in the Unilever companies they felt they were placed according to the needs of the business without effective consultation.'[72] A conference on 'Retention' in Unilever held in 1990, observing the high rates of female resignations, noted that 'too often, women managers encounter male chauvinistic attitudes that are deeply rooted'.[73] Unilever appeared to have 'some sort of barrier (or very fine filter) which inhibits [women's] progress much beyond JC 24'.[74]

The end of the 1980s saw initiatives designed to improve the practical components of the 'fine filter'. In 1988 British personnel management set up a group to study 'Women in Management'.[75] The recommendations eventually led to the introduction of the Maternity Package allowing mothers-to-be to take eighteen paid weeks off before birth and twenty-two weeks after the birth, fully compensated with a lump sum payment, and the Career Break Scheme which facilitated leaving the business for five years and then returning. During the late 1980s, a British women managers' network was also established, periodically publishing news about policies and legal changes.[76]

It was more difficult to change aspects of the culture itself. There was a hardworking 'macho culture', which was not so much anti-female as such, but rather made no allowances for women unless their lives were identical to those of men. One woman in London head office, having given birth on a Saturday, was asked to report for work on the following Monday, having been informed that 'pregnancy is not an illness'.[77] As one former Unilever manager put it, 'jobs in the higher ranks of Unilever cannot be done part time'.[78] Women found that they had to avoid discussing their personal lives openly, because their career was likely to be adversely affected should they be labelled 'potential mother'. In most companies there was an implicit double standard that a married male manager was seen as an asset with a stable support network at home, while a married female manager was likely to be seen as a liability who could not give undivided attention to her work. In the hard-working Unilever culture, this may have been a specific issue. The majority of women considering maternity, it was concluded in 1990, 'feel that maternity and a Unilever career is more difficult than that option would be in other companies'.[79]

The most serious obstacles for career advancement for women in Unilever lay in the pivotal importance placed on networks and mobility. Social networks were sometimes built around young male managers playing sports together and going drinking after-wards. In 1990 consultants concluded that the 'template' of a successful manager at Unilever was perceived to be: 'a successful sportsman'; 'a member of the bar culture'; 'fast moving, but not emotionally involved'; 'firm, decent but not connected'; and 'competitive, articulate, go getting'.[80] It offered a new level of complexity for young males, who were already competitive with each other in the office and in the sports field, to face young female colleagues in social situations. Another problem was that senior male managers may have felt more uncertain how to offer young female man-agers the 'mentoring' which facilitated the careers of their male counterparts. There were few senior female managers to be mentors, or to serve as role models.

The heavy emphasis on job mobility and international experience, usually begin-ning in the late twenties, favoured either single people or people with partners will-ing to be flexible around their spouse's career. This imposed special strains on the personal lives of women, given that only a few male spouses were as yet prepared—or in most cases able—to follow their spouses, especially to a foreign country. It was only during the 1980s that Unilever began to address the problem of 'dual careers' even for Unilever male managers married to women with careers.

The gender basis of Unilever's culture manifested itself in the issue of 'dual careers', which in most instances—for the above reasons—involved Unilever male managers and the complications caused by wives with their own careers. The prob-lem was that international mobility played havoc with the lives of such couples. The assumption was that the wives of Unilever managers would look full-time after their families, and they were given appropriate assistance to enable this if their husband moved to a foreign country. Couples were sent sometimes on five-day courses at the Centre for International Briefing at Farnham Castle in Britain for cross-cultural training. An article in *Unilever Magazine* in 1986 on 'what it's like to be married to a Unilever executive' noted that 'women repeatedly commented on the interesting people they met. . . [and that] the chance to learn more about a country, its culture, business and politics, enhanced their lives and those of their children'.[81]

By that date the opportunity cost to such wives was also becoming recognized. The same article noted the 'cruel paradox' that 'the unemployment of many of these women is the result of their husbands' successful employment'. At the same time there was a recognition that the spouses of Unilever executives also increasingly wanted to pursue their own professional careers.[82] If Unilever wished to retain its talented male managers, and to keep their relationships intact, it was recognized by the end of the decade that the dual career issue had to be addressed. Finding a solution was another matter, for it was frequently extremely difficult to arrange a win-win outcome for both partners.[83]

In 1990 Unilever had fewer very senior women managers than a generation previously, and still lacked a woman on the main board. From the 1980s an extensive literature on the topic testified to the scale of the problem in general, and also the complexity of resolving it, at least without a completely radical transformation of how societies worked.[84] It was only in 1998 that Unilever appointed its first woman as an Advisory Director.[85] This was not atypical for a European company. Nestlé also lacked a female director in 1990, although the large US consumer goods firms including P & G, Colgate Palmolive, and CPC all had at least one female director by that date. In Britain, even in 2002 only 2 per cent of FTSE 100 directors were woman, and over forty of the biggest 100 companies had all-male boards.[86]

Perspectives

Unilever's distinctive corporate culture, based on the pivotal values of integrity, relationships, and the importance of local decision-making, provided the sinews which held Unilever together, despite its geographical spread and its product diversity. This culture was renewed and refreshed by rotating managers around the business, and all manner of meetings and courses. Knowledge circulated around the 'Unilever world' through countless webs of personal networks. This 'core' corporate culture coexisted with numerous subcultures in the operating companies, enabling Unilever to function across so many product groups and countries.

The main drawback of Unilever's culture was its proclivity against rapid change. The requirement for constant negotiation and compromise, the dependence on relationships rather than coercion, the unwillingness to challenge local autonomy, the need to manage numerous subcultures all worked in this direction. Consequently it took a long time to make things happen, whether it was culling the number of brands, or incorporating women into senior management. Unilever's sheer size and its dominant position in many markets reinforced the slow pace of change, as it permitted a kind of insularity and a focus on internal political disputes.

In 1990 Unilever's corporate culture was recognizably similar to that prevailing in the 1960s. The commitment to integrity and local autonomy remained. Unilever remained a networked company in which relationships were extremely important. However, there had been significant redefinitions of how these values were expressed. Gentlemen had given way to professionals. Few employees felt entirely confident of a job for life. Cosiness had begun to give way to calls for greater risk-taking, and a recognition that Unilever either had 'to grow or decline'.

10

Innovation

In Search of Profitable Innovation

Unilever was among the largest corporate spenders on research in the world consumer packaged goods industries. By 1980 over 7,000 people were employed in the company's research laboratories spread worldwide.[1] Yet there was a persistent concern that Unilever was not realizing its full potential in innovation. In 1972 a McKinsey report on 'Achieving Profitable Innovation' concluded that, despite a level of spending which matched its competitors, Unilever was 'not a consistent leader in significant innovation'.[2] Eighteen years later another McKinsey report concluded that Unilever appeared 'to lag' in 'pioneering major new businesses', in part because its 'excellent scientific base' was 'not being fully exploited'.[3]

These observations seem curious at first sight. During the second half of the twentieth century Unilever has been responsible for scientific and technical innovation across a wide range of product areas. The problem, as illustrated in Table 10.1 based on evidence in the McKinsey report in 1972, appeared to be that Unilever was too often a follower rather than a leader. To make matters worse, it was often the case that Unilever had generated similar ideas at an earlier stage, and had also often held talks with potential suppliers of novel raw materials, but had been slow to realize market potential. This became a perennial refrain. 'History showed us to be always very slow at getting results', the Special Committee noted a decade after the McKinsey report, 'and we must develop some mechanism for reaching objectives as fast as possible.'[4]

Unilever's difficulties in 'achieving profitable innovation' proved easier to identify than to remedy. Corporate innovation is a complex process in which the contribution

Table 10.1 Unilever's position in new product development, 1950–1972

Product	Company introducing	Date	Unilever entry
Butter-flavour margarine	Unilever	1950s/1960s	1950s
Pufa margarine	Unilever/Various US	1950s/1960s	1959
Yoghurts	Various	1940s	1968
Spreads	Various	Early 1960s	1969
Instant tea	Nestlé	1950s	1960s
Early synthetic detergents	IG Farben, P & G, Colgate	1940s	1950
Enzyme washers	P & G	1960s	1968
Anti-caries toothpaste	P & G	1956	1958
Head and shoulders shampoo	Van der Vilt, Olin, P & G	1961	1968
Aerosol antiperspirant	Various	1950s	1960
Bath additives	Various	1950s	1968

Sources: McKinsey & Co., *Achieving Profitable Innovation* (Aug. 1972); W. J. Beek, *History of Research and Engineering in Unilever 1911–1986* (Rotterdam: Unilever, 1996), 8.14, 8.15.

of scientists 'inventing' something forms only one component. Innovation involves at least four identifiable stages—research, development, production, and marketing. Unilever invested in research with the ultimate goal of gaining competitive advantage through developing new or improved products which consumers wanted to buy. Successful, or profitable, innovation required getting all the stages in the process working coherently as a package. Unilever was far from alone among large corporations in finding new product development and new business creation very challenging. Many studies have identified the technological and resource lock-ins, and routine and cultural rigidities, which hinder successful innovation. One estimate is that only about one in ten research and development projects turned out to be a commercial success, and that no profitable application emerged from about half of all industrial R&D.[5]

This chapter begins by considering the overall evolution of Unilever's strategies for research. This is followed by a closer examination of the work of Unilever's central research laboratories. There are then case studies of selected successes and failures in innovation which provide a fuller understanding of the organizational and cultural factors involved in the innovation process.

The Evolution of Research Strategy

An independent Research Department had been created in 1946, which became the Research Division in 1961. The identification of research as requiring a dedicated organizational structure symbolized the extensive interest within Unilever, enthusiastically supported by Heyworth, in the potential of science for business. This enthusiasm was widely shared in post-war business. In Britain, overall corporate funding of research grew at a spectacular pace, increasing seven-fold between 1950 and 1961, and many times the rate of growth of manufacturing output.[6]

Before 1945 research and development had been conducted by Unilever's numerous operating companies. The amount of spending was considerable—Unilever was in the top twenty corporate spenders on research in Britain in 1945[7]—but one disadvantage was a considerable amount of duplication. The Research Department and later Division began a process of trying to co-ordinate the work of different laboratories, a process that over time evolved into a more directive strategy, including an interest in longer-term basic research. The rationale for making Research a central division of Unilever rested on the argument that the science and technical bases of many of its product groups were common. Between 1955 and 1960 spending on Research—essentially at the three large European laboratories at Port Sunlight, Colworth, and Vlaardingen, and excluding the 'in-house' expenditure in operating companies and research spending in the United States—grew from £2.5 million to £7 million. The number of staff employed at the three laboratories increased from 900 to 1,800.[8]

Unilever research, therefore, came to be organized in two main components. The Research Division controlled central laboratories and was funded by a percentage levy on sales of companies. There were also a large number of 'in-house' facilities including factories, workshops, and small 'application-oriented' laboratories located within the operating companies. These were primarily concerned with 'development', but some of the larger laboratories undertook some basic research. Between the 1960s and the 1980s these two different components accounted for about one-half each of the total spending on research and development.

The function of research was seen initially as providing 'knowledge'. It was not believed that Unilever should shape too closely the direction in which research was heading, but that it should have access to the latest scientific knowledge. The Research Division allocated researchers to particular areas, initially with only limited consultation of the companies. Scientists were not subject to strict controls, and were allowed to get on with the kinds of research they considered to be worthwhile.

The remoteness of much research from the market place differed widely from the practices in contemporary US corporate laboratories, yet there were considerable achievements, including the development of pufa margarines, and continuous advances in flavour research, and refining and processing of fats. Unilever's growing understanding of the raw materials and processes involved in margarine manufacture was exploited by both the improvement of existing brands and the introduction of new products. These years also saw significant improvements in crop raw material production and in vegetable processing, which underpinned the growth of the frozen foods business.

During his tenure as Research Director after 1955, and subsequently after joining the Special Committee in 1961, Woodroofe exercised a major influence over innovation strategy. He encouraged the geographical dispersion of research, including the opening of an Indian research laboratory.[9] He sought to promote a 'team culture' in research.[10] He was also an enthusiast for greater linkages between Unilever and universities, in part because of a desire to improve the quality of the company's own researchers.[11]

Woodroofe was anxious to improve certain aspects of the innovation process. The science base of the company, like much else, was badly fragmented, with considerable rivalries between Port Sunlight and the Dutch laboratory at Vlaardingen. Vlaardingen was focused on pure research, and inclined to look down on the more applications-oriented laboratory at Port Sunlight. Woodroofe began a process of trying to build a closer relationship between the British and Dutch laboratories. He would also have liked to build a closer relationship with Unilever's laboratory in Edgewater, New Jersey, but although he made fairly regular visits there, the autonomy of Lever Brothers meant that there was no question of Research Division taking responsibility for the laboratory.[12]

Woodroofe was also concerned that Unilever research was excessively defensive, with—he estimated in 1959—no more than 10 per cent of research spending allocated to new product development. It seemed hard to develop radical innovations because operating companies were usually not interested in developing and marketing concepts far beyond their existing businesses.[13] They were especially not interested in technologies which might undermine their existing brands and products.

The general belief that Unilever would be able to build completely new business streams through scientific innovation rested on the contemporary view that large corporations had the capacity to extend their boundaries almost without limit. In fact, there were managerial limits to such growth, which Unilever was to discover, while it turned out that large corporations faced organizational and cultural constraints to their range of innovation. Later research on corporate innovation was to identify it as a path-dependent and cumulative process, in which 'a firm that is already successful in a given activity is a particularly good candidate for being successful with a new capacity of the same sort'.[14] In other words, while it was legitimate to expect Unilever to be at the forefront of innovation in edible fats and detergents, building businesses on the basis of innovation in entirely new products categories was likely to be fraught with difficulty.

The formation of new organizational entities within Unilever to handle new innovations provided one possible strategy. The research laboratories produced numerous novel product ideas—for instance Port Sunlight researchers in the late

1950s produced a detergent which left washed cotton shirts crease-resistant—which were not followed up as they were too small or marginal for Unilever, but which could have been pursued by smaller, more entrepreneurial units. Woodroofe in 1959 suggested the creation of a 'cradle company' whose sole job it would be to foster new products. This was an idea well ahead of its time, and Woodroofe concluded that there would have been too much resistance to such a radical proposal for it to be implemented.[15]

Woodroofe was most concerned about the gap between researchers and the 'market place'. While Research was responsible for knowledge innovation, the development and marketing of products using that knowledge rested with the operating companies. There was no institutionalized mechanism for transferring concepts from Research to the companies, and the process was haphazard, with companies looking round for ideas, but under no obligation to pursue them. The authority of Research did not extend beyond the laboratories to the development laboratories. Woodroofe's preference would have been for the teams of scientists who came up with a new product concept to continue working on its development in the companies, but it was not possible to overcome the organizational chasm at the time.[16] Instead, the research laboratories were given a market research budget so they could do their own market research, while the consultants Urwick Orr provided courses to teach researchers about the business environment.

Unilever had some deep-seated problems in its innovation process at this time arising from the fragmentation of knowledge and capabilities within the organization. The lack of communication or even trust between different parts of the company was a major constraint. As the author of one paper on Unilever's lack of an 'outstanding record for new product innovation' observed in 1973, 'even within management groups, communication of new ideas may be delayed or inhibited by inter-company rivalry. Between management groups, new product concepts may become secret weapons in demarcation disputes with consequent duplication of effort.'[17] Financial arrangements did not help matters. The budget for central research was calculated as a percentage of sales in a specific area, so research in the largest product groups of edibles and detergents received the lion's share of resources. This rather worked against the creation of a forward-looking research culture.[18]

During the 1960s the era of expansion in research spending continued. Smaller laboratories were opened in Saint-Denis in France, Welwyn in Britain, Duiven in the Netherlands, and Hamburg in Germany. Major building programmes were launched at Port Sunlight and Vlaardingen. There was a continuing search for a closer integration of research within the company, though basic research was still assumed to be vital for sustaining competitiveness. In 1970 the Central Research Fund (CRF) was created, and allocated 10 per cent of the total annual research budget of the

Co-ordinations in order to finance such basic research to be conducted in the central research laboratories. The identification of projects to be supported was intended to be undertaken by the Research Director and the Special Committee.

By 1970 the size of the Research Division reached 4,600 staff, reflecting a fivefold increase from 1955, while the budget had reached £32 million by 1970, or almost £220 million in 1990 pounds. Total worldwide research spending was probably double that figure.[19] However, during the late 1960s financial pressures began to mount as Unilever's overall performance faltered. In 1968 the smaller research laboratories began slowly to be integrated into the larger ones: Duiven, for example, was merged with Vlaardingen. In 1971 budget cuts resulted in a 10 per cent reduction in the Research Division's workforce. By 1975 Unilever spending on Research in constant prices had fallen sharply, again mirroring wider trends, which saw the level of corporate funding of research in Britain fall away in constant prices, and as a proportion of manufacturing output, in these years.[20] At Unilever, tighter budgets were accompanied by expectations that research should not merely generate 'knowledge', but culminate in products which could actually be sold.

This was the major thrust of McKinsey's report on *Achieving Profitable Innovation* in 1972. The consultants stressed the need for Co-ordinations to develop formal business strategies which could, in turn, be used as the basis to develop research strategies and priorities, which could be converted by Research Division into specific laboratory programmes. The larger companies also needed to identify more clearly consumer needs and the opportunities for new products. McKinsey also recommended organizational changes so that Research and the rest of the business could communicate better, including the appointments of R&D managers in Co-ordinations, and product area managers in Research Division.

Although many of the McKinsey recommendations were implemented, the following years saw considerable tensions between Research and Co-ordinations, who favoured research projects with shorter time horizons which could deliver 'value for money'. Contributions to the basic research funded by the CRF were especially resented given that often there was no identifiable product as a result. In 1974 a Research Planning Group, involving the Research and Corporate Development directors, and the heads of the three largest European laboratories, was formed to try to secure tighter research 'planning' and the more effective creation of new business opportunities. More formalized and detailed reporting procedures were introduced, but it proved complex—and possibly counter-productive—to fit the work of Research Division into standardized Unilever reporting procedures. In 1976 it was first proposed that the Research Division produce a long-term plan which would combine in one document 'the objectives of the business and the strategies of research to meet them'.[21] However it was only in 1979 that the first such plan appeared.

In 1976 the CRF underwent reorganization into two areas. The first was basic or background research structured around 'themes'. These usually encompassed a broadly defined science area—cellular behaviour and biopolymer cells were identified in 1976, and biosciences, physical sciences, and engineering by 1979.[22] The second area, entitled Corporate Development, encompassed areas which might lead to major future growth, including the ill-fated Hyacinth project discussed later. This reform contributed to an improved relationship between Research and Coordinations, which included willingness by the latter to give longer commitments to research projects.[23]

Despite the growing efforts to translate new science into products, discontent at Unilever's performance in innovation grew.[24] This was part of a general corporate disillusionment, widely discernible amongst US firms also, with the commercial results of heavy spending on university-style corporate laboratories.[25] In 1978 Durham had conducted a critical internal review of Unilever's innovation performance, which he considered was hindered by 'structural and social constraints'. He recommended that European research should be concentrated at Port Sunlight, Colworth, and Vlaardingen.[26] Over the following three years the smaller European laboratories were closed. In 1978 a 10 per cent cut in real expenditure on Research Division imposed for two years highlighted the dissatisfaction felt about innovation performance. Unilever's total expenditure on research and development worldwide rose from £133 million in 1978 to £219 million in 1983, but in constant prices this meant no increase whatsoever. It is unlikely that this cost-cutting and search for efficiency gains did much to stimulate risk-taking innovation of the kind Unilever most needed. By 1987 spending had risen to £330 million, which did represent a real increase, but this level was still below Unilever's estimated research spending in 1970.

During the 1970s there was a problem with Unilever's innovation performance. In the fabrics wash sector of detergents Unilever accumulated a poor track record. The lag in synthetics in the 1940s and 1950s proved only the beginning of a syndrome where Unilever always seemed to be a follower rather than a leader. Unilever was slow to introduce enzymes in detergents. Unilever researchers had identified the potential benefits which enzymes could provide—the removal of protein stains—long before the first enzymatic product, Biotex, was launched by Kortman & Schulte in the Netherlands. There were rumours that Unilever abandoned research on an enzymatic product at the behest of marketing people who felt there was no demand for such a good. However, the primary concern was the effect of an enzymatic detergent on existing products. Unilever eventually responded with Luvil and Biological All, which were successfully launched in Europe, yet during the 1970s research on enzyme products was cut for financial reasons.

Tetra-Acetyl Ethylene Diamene (TAED) was the major scientific innovation in detergents made by Unilever in these years. Medium-temperature bleaching based on TAED was the most significant technical advance in fabric washing since enzymes were introduced. Its development took place in the context of a shift in European washing practice, especially from the early 1970s, from boiling at 95°C to washing at much lower temperatures. This was partly in response to a fall in the proportion of white cotton clothes in the wash with the growing use of coloured cottons and synthetics—which needed to be washed at 60°C or less—and partly because higher energy costs added to the cost of washing in automatic machines at high temperatures. TAED was a bleach activator which reacted with the primary oxygen bleach in a detergent to provide cleaning at lower temperatures. In the

47 Advertisement for *All* detergent in the Netherlands in 1980, highlighting the benefits of TAED.

United States, most detergents used different bleach from in Europe—hypochlorite rather than persalt—which made the use of a TAED molecule more difficult.[27]

Development work began on TAED as early as the mid-1960s, but it was subsequently suspended and not restarted until 1974. By 1978 Unilever still had not successfully marketed a product containing the compound, by which time the main patent was nearing its expiry date, and its 'major protection' against competitors beating the firm onto the market rested on an exclusive supply contract with Hoechst, who were well placed to charge Unilever a high price.[28] Concerns prevalent in Europe about the environment and energy consumption may not have been properly appreciated by the British-based Co-ordination, perhaps because average wash cycles were shorter in Britain than elsewhere in Europe. Generally the location of much detergents research at Port Sunlight may have been a problem since Britain was not a dynamic market for new trends in consumer appliances, nor was it noted for taking a lead in environmental matters.[29] By the 1980s TAED was being used by all the major detergents companies in Europe.

The slowness in detergent innovation especially during the 1970s was a major problem. Various organizational initiatives were launched to try to improve matters. New product development involved Research, Co-ordination, and designated European 'lead' companies, selected on the basis of their size, market positioning, and country of operation, who were regarded as the initial exploiters of important new products. In detergents, the designated 'lead countries' were Britain, France, Germany, and Italy. In theory, Research worked on new properties, and as these neared application it interacted with the lead companies to establish ways to apply the properties in the market. After the McKinsey report in 1972 'product area managers' were introduced to interact between Research and European operating companies, but with disappointing results. In 1975 the Research and Development Application Unit was established at Vlaardingen specifically charged with transferring and applying fully developed product and process technology to European operating companies. The RDAU included managers with company development experience, and development managers from the companies were seconded to work at Vlaardingen. A few years later the Overseas Research Application Centre was set up at Port Sunlight to help provide specialized resources for Overseas markets.

A recurring pattern at Unilever seemed to be that, having developed a technology, it was assumed that there was a ready consumer market for products based on it. Unilever seemed locked into the assumption that consumers would want to buy things in which it had innovated, and hardly felt the need to seek their views. This assumption was increasingly erroneous as memories of past scarcities faded and consumers became more diverse and selective. The cases of long-life yoghurt and the Hyacinth feminine hygiene project, discussed below, were indicative of this problem.

During the 1980s there was a new determination to improve the innovation record, although there were different emphases. The Special Committee was primarily concerned to make Research more selective in its use of resource. In 1985 they asked for 'doubtful cases' to be brought to them, as they 'did not want to start diversifying again in a multitude of directions'.[30] The Special Committee wanted to get more commercially successful products in the 'core' businesses out in the market place quicker than in the past.

A different emphasis was found among a number of directors who believed that Unilever's science base represented enormous potential which needed to be exploited more effectively. They wanted faster innovation of marketable products, and also believed that Unilever had the capacity to use existing resources to build new business streams through innovation. These directors included Sir Geoffrey Allen, a chemical engineer with a background in universities and government, whom Orr had recruited as Research Director in 1980, Wally Grubman, the chairman of National Starch, and T. Thomas, a chemical engineer by training and former chairman of Hindustan Lever, whom Orr had appointed to the main board as Chemicals Co-ordinator in 1980.

Allen had a long-standing experience of the interface between science and business, and he was firmly convinced that research needed to be matched to the needs of business, and that this was wholly compatible with maintaining the highest calibre of science. He felt that engineering played a vital role in turning bright ideas into actual products, and in 1983 Research Division was renamed the Research and Engineering Division, while the CRF became the CREF. Allen oversaw a shift in emphasis in research from seeking to develop new products to trying to focus on the explicit needs of the business. He sought to work closely with Co-ordinations to improve their links with research, actively fostering closer links between Chemicals Co-ordination and National Starch in research matters, as well as encouraging technical relationships with T. J. Lipton.[31] He supported the efforts of the Detergents Co-ordination to set up a central development unit to try to secure a faster pace of innovation—Co-ordination reckoned at that date that it was taking Unilever seven years to get new ideas from the bench to the market place, far slower than competitors—though this encountered scepticism from the foods side concerned to maintain Unilever's contact with local markets.[32]

There remained considerable difficulty defining an overall research strategy even at the end of the 1980s.[33] Although the profitability and importance for Unilever of ice cream was growing from the mid-1980s, for example, research still consisted of a diverse range of many small local company-supported projects focused on the short term, and with little regard for an overall corporate strategy. A major ice cream research project—'Voyager'—was initially launched in 1989 with five scientific teams of technical staff costing £750,000 per annum—supported by one junior marketeer. It was not until the following decade that real attempts began to be made to put resources behind more focused international projects.

at both Port Sunlight and Edgewater in the 1950s designed to find a product which did not leave 'scum' after washing. The research at Port Sunlight was abandoned after the chemical used produced an adverse dermatological reaction. However, a different chemical was investigated at Edgewater which did not have this problem. Eventually it was found that a stable detergents bar could be made if stearic acid was added. Once the Lever marketing people learned that stearic acid was the same ingredient as used in cold creams, they rapidly conceived of the new product as something that 'creams as its cleans'. This became the basis of the immensely attractive brand, far removed from the original conception of an 'anti-scum' product.[46]

Edgewater's subsequent dwindling innovation performance reflected the overall problems of Lever Brothers. Lever's presidents were drawn from finance or marketing, and had less interest in long-term product development. Following a McKinsey report on improving the profitability of Lever Brothers in 1973, it was decided to cancel projects that would not impact on the company's profits within five years, and around thirty research staff were dismissed. This period also saw new laws on environmental and other matters which left the depleted research staff scrambling to respond. Ingredients such as hexachlorophene and chloroform, which had been used in toothpastes, were banned, forcing research to focus on finding substitutes. Whatever the reasons, the diminishing innovation performance at Edgewater contributed to Lever Brothers' weakened competitiveness, and—given that the United States was so important a source of innovation in many products—to overall problems for Unilever. Detergents Co-ordination firmly believed that Unilever's continued reliance on Europe rather than the United States as its main centre of innovation was a considerable disadvantage.[47]

The radical steps taken by Unilever to renew its business in the United States from the late 1970s included a great expansion of the Edgewater facility. Staff were transferred from Europe, and within a five-year period Lever research staff almost doubled. The period was fortuitous in the sense that the second oil shock led many large US companies such as Exxon to make a lot of staff redundant. Staff were recruited before the new buildings were ready, and then sent on secondment to Europe for a year during which they not only received training, but also became more aware of developments elsewhere in Unilever. In 1980 the laboratory was also placed under the control of Unilever Research.

The basic research undertaken at Unilever's laboratories led to the development of many new products, and enabled the constant improvements and reformulation which kept existing brands contemporary and competitive. The geographical spread of Unilever's central research facilities, which might be regarded as a dispersion of research resource, had the benefit of enabling Unilever to recruit scientists and link to academic networks in several different countries.

Innovation Failures: Yoghurt, Apollo Fabrics Wash, and Hyacinth

Yoghurt

Unilever's entry into the European yoghurt market illustrated some of the problems of the innovation process within the firm. While yoghurt was already eaten in a number of European countries including the Netherlands before the 1960s, that decade saw a major expansion in yoghurt consumption in other countries such as Britain and Italy, where yoghurt had hardly been consumed previously. This growth was particularly associated with the introduction of fruit and flavoured varieties. In contrast, in the Netherlands most yoghurt was eaten plain and delivered by the milk-man. Unilever was early to identify a business opportunity. Apart from a number of larger firms such as Gervais Danone and Chambourcy, the yoghurt sector was still dominated by a multitude of small firms—often dairies—in the late 1960s, yet it appeared susceptible to mass branding techniques.[48]

Unilever's best hope in yoghurt might have been the acquisition of one of the larger companies, but when Gervais Danone did come up for sale in the early 1970s, the proposal to buy it was blocked by the Special Committee.[49] This effectively sig-nalled that it was not intended that Unilever would become a major participant in the industry. Instead a series of smaller companies were purchased, especially in France, which brought little expertise or market share, but which occupied consider-able management time. Meanwhile considerable research spending was allocated to developing an appropriate product.

The decision to place yoghurt under the auspices of the Edible Fats Co-ordination rather than one of the other foods Co-ordinations had serious implications. The dairy business managed by the Co-ordination was an odd collection of small and medium-sized firms, some of which had been acquired as part of ice cream companies, and some set up in the large margarine operating companies, whose managements tended to see them as little more than a nuisance. The business was never allowed to grow to a size where economies of scale in production and distribution could be achieved. Within this Co-ordination, yoghurt was deemed to be important not because of the inherent qualities of the product or its consumers, but because it was usually located next to margarine in the 'cool cabinet' of supermarkets. It was seen as essential to dominate the area where the highly profitable margarine was sold. This drove the research effort, which was focused on developing a 'long-life' product which could be sold in the 'cool cabinet', and in turn shaped how the product was conceptualized. A member of the Co-ordination advised companies seeking to enter the yoghurt market not to attempt to cater for 'existing yoghurt eaters . . . whose habits include half an hour of inversed perpendicular meditation before meals', but rather to appeal to traditional consumers of Unilever's 'tasty, fruity desserts and snack foods'.[50]

This strategy rested on a misunderstanding of the importance of health and freshness as factors in the growing consumption of yoghurt. Not only were long-life products the opposite of the popular image of yoghurt as fresh and natural, but Unilever knew this to be the case. In 1969 it was noted that 'we would never sell or advertise our products as keepable, even though they are and we like them to be because this permits more economic production and distribution. The consumer suspects a keepable fresh dairy product, and the trade might keep it in reserve stock for when the non-keepable private label is sold out.'[51] In other words, Unilever's strategy from the start was directed towards the development of a product whose principal characteristic had to be kept quiet from consumers.

Germany was chosen as the entry market, in part because Unilever had owned a processed cheese business in that country since the 1930s. Germany, like Britain, was also a market where the taste/shelf-life combination was more likely to be accepted than in France or the Netherlands. After test marketing, the Elite brand of yoghurt was launched nationally in 1969 available in seven fruit varieties, marketed by the

48 Preparing for the national launch of *Elite* yoghurt in Germany in 1968.

margarine company UDL. In Britain Unilever launched a new brand, Dessert Farm. However by the mid-1970s the yoghurt business was losing over £10 million annually, mainly in Germany and Britain.[52] By the end of the decade Unilever had almost entirely withdrawn from the business.

The failure in yoghurt had a number of causes. Longer-life products were expensive because of the post-pasteurization of yoghurt, while the more elaborate production process slowed down the ability to introduce new flavours and varieties. Yet the real problems stemmed from the focus on the cool cabinet strategy and the technical ability to produce longer-life products rather than observing what consumers wanted and exploring ways it could be satisfied. Unilever Research delivered a series of innovations which extended the shelf life of fresh dairy products. Continuous improvements were achieved by in-line pasteurization and sterilization, aseptic filling, and optimized cultures for long keepable live yoghurt. But the whole innovation process was technology driven rather than market or consumer led.

Apollo

The failure of Apollo in Germany suggested a similar lesson that product innovations introduced with little awareness for the market were unlikely to succeed. Apollo was a new fabric wash brand launched in Germany in a test market in February 1977; it was the first Unilever detergents product to contain TAED. By time it was introduced Unilever were a distant third in the German detergents market behind Henkel and P & G. Apollo lay at the heart of Unilever's plans for improving this position.[53] However, the test market for Apollo failed, and by the end of 1978 the brand had been abandoned.

Apollo's failure was not the result of faulty background research or technical development. Although it took Unilever a long time to recognize the commercial opportunity offered by TAED, the research and development stages of the product process ran smoothly. Indeed there was a widespread conviction that Unilever had an important technological innovation. Even though the brand performed poorly in test marketing, perhaps because it had an unpleasant smell, the response from those who did actually buy it was positive. Co-ordination drew the conclusion that Apollo's failure had been largely the result of poor advertising, and that it was a highly effective washing powder.[54]

The Apollo episode illustrated weaknesses across the range of the innovation process. It was launched into a mature market which meant not only that it faced stiff competition from major competitors, but that it was less than enthusiastically welcomed by the trade. Retailers had no need to encourage newcomers into a market already swollen with strong brands.[55] The supermarkets were reluctant either to display Apollo in the most prominent positions, or else to sell it at a discounted price.

It had been envisaged that Apollo would become a leading brand that could be sold at a premium price, yet by the summer of 1977 it was recognized that Apollo's price needed to be cut. However, price-cutting seemed to result in consumers purchasing the product in bulk for one time, rather than serving any sampling role.[56]

There was a lack of connection between technical accomplishment and marketing. It proved hard to explain to consumers why TAED was important enough for them to switch brands.[57] To launch an entirely new brand on the basis of TAED alone placed a huge amount of expectation on a single technical innovation, especially in a market where competitor brands were so firmly established. The marketing of the brand was not facilitated by the fact that Lever Sunlicht could not spend heavily on advertising—it had to reduce sharply its media spending during the mid-1970s—and it already had the Omo, Sunil, and Korall brands in the German fabrics market. Matters were further complicated by a difference of emphasis between the German company and Co-ordination. The former wanted to establish a clear brand identity in the German market by emphasizing Apollo's ability to remove stains in low-temperature washes. Detergents Co-ordination, with an eye on developing a new European-wide brand which could match P & G's Ariel, considered Apollo should aim to become a big-volume seller on the basis of wider claims as a solution to main wash problems.[58] In Britain, environmental concerns were less pronounced than in Germany, and this may have led Detergents Co-ordination to see a low-temperature wash as a narrowly 'specialist' position.[59]

Apollo provided a clear demonstration that a technical innovation was no guarantee of a successful new brand. The innovation needed to be communicated to consumers who had to be convinced that it satisfied a need. After the failure of Apollo, Unilever changed its strategy, and introduced TAED into existing brands. The most significant outcome of the Apollo episode was to sound the death knell for any hopes of developing a successful new European or international fabrics wash brand.

Hyacinth

The Hyacinth project to develop disposables, especially in feminine hygiene, was Unilever's most costly innovation failure in the 1970s. From the late 1960s Unilever had been interested in the disposables market. After the failed attempt to acquire Smith & Nephew in 1968, Unilever continued to search for another acquisition or partner given that it had no expertise in this product category, but the search resulted in no suitable candidates.[60] Smith & Nephew—codenamed 'Hyacinth'–remained of interest, but Unilever was no nearer to an acquisition.[61] However, during 1973 a research group at Colworth—recently strengthened by the recruitment of distinguished academics from Edinburgh University—developed a novel polysaccharide-based superabsorbent termed 'Lyogel', which appeared to offer cost and other advantages over existing materials used for sanitary protection.[62] The technology involved complex chemistry, but the upshot was that Lyogel could absorb up to forty times its own weight in water, or twenty times its own weight in body fluids such as urine or blood. At the end of 1973, the Special Committee concluded that while 'every effort' needed to be made to find a partner with 'some experience', it would be 'worth going ahead' with product development based on Unilever's own innovation.[63]

By the mid-1970s research on Project Hyacinth—which took the name over from the proposed acquisition—was costing around £1 million a year. The Special Committee, which never considered Unilever had much chance of succeeding alone, watched with growing scepticism.[64] During the spring of 1975 Personal Products Co-ordination was instructed by the Special Committee to find an appropriate partner, or else abandon the project, and meanwhile to cut the expenditure on Hyacinth research by a half.[65] The budget cut was accomplished by abandoning research into nappies, not least because it emerged that the new gel absorbed the urine from babies at a slow pace, and did not spread it evenly. Unilever was unable to use a sponge in conjunction with its gel to speed up the absorption process because P & G already had a patent for this. Thereafter the Hyacinth research focused on sanitary towels and tampons. These were difficult markets as there were strong incumbents. Tampax held dominant positions in many countries—holding 80 per cent of the British tampon market in the mid-1970s—while Smith & Nephew held 70 per cent of the British sanitary towel market. Women were cautious and conservative consumers of such intimate products, which meant that Unilever had no chance of successful entry without a major advantage.

No partner was found, but nor was the project discontinued. The case for continuing was that so much time and money had been spent establishing a technological advantage that Unilever should persist with trying to get a commercial product.[66] During 1976 Co-ordination secured permission for Elida Gibbs to launch products in Britain, but there were technical delays and difficulties manufacturing the gel. Although the Special Committee had authorized a small pilot plant to make the gel, this did not prove feasible, and for reasons of economies of scale Co-ordination went ahead with building new plant inside a personal products factory in Brussels—chosen because effluent regulations were lower than elsewhere at the time—to manufacture the gel, and supply it to factories in Britain and Germany which were to make the sanitary towels. The Special Committee was 'surprised to find that the project seemed to have expanded considerably'.[67] In fact, if Unilever was to have made a serious entry into the market, a much larger capital investment would have been required.

During 1977 the Finesse brand of sanitary towels was test marketed in three British towns in preparation for a national launch in 1980, and in 1978 Cosmea was launched nationally in Austria, which was intended as a test market for Germany. By then other superabsorbent towels were already in the market, although Unilever gained a 10 per cent market share in Austria within six months. However Cosmea ran into problems when it was launched in Germany two years later, as the market leader in sanitary towels took legal action claiming Unilever advertising was untrue.

During 1980 the Hyacinth project reached its nemesis. The planned national launch in Britain was delayed for a year with continuing supply problems.[68] P & G's Rely tampon, a superabsorbent product which had been the result of a large research effort and was intended by the US company as its next blockbuster product, became the centre of a major controversy after it was linked to several deaths in the United States through 'toxic shock syndrome'. Unilever watched the Rely episode unfold with alarm, but it was its own accumulating production and launch problems which finally ended the Hyacinth project. There were supply problems as sales increased, and then a decision was taken to close the Belgian factory where the Lyogel was made. It was regarded as too expensive to build another plant elsewhere. Co-ordination decided to replace Lyogel with an alternative superabsorbent material called Permasorb made by National Starch. The Special Committee declared itself 'very disturbed' that 'the fact that we were now going to use a material which was equally available to any of the competition meant that we no longer had any technical advantage whatsoever'. The decision was taken to close the business.[69]

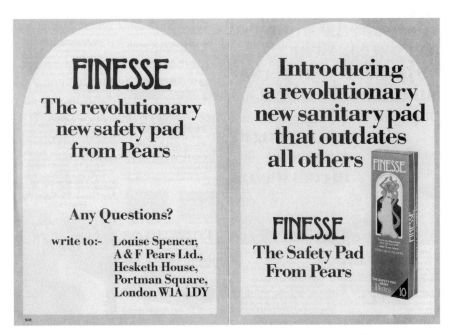

49 Unilever's *Finesse* sanitary pad, soon after its launch in Britain in 1977.

The total financial cost of research, capital expenditure, and marketing for the Hyacinth project seems to have been at least £15 million over the course of the 1970s, in return for which Unilever failed to establish a disposables business. The episode was widely interpreted as demonstrating that hopes of achieving diversification into new product categories on the basis of research were at best exaggerated.[70] This led to a strengthening of resistance to research-led innovation in areas that lay outside Unilever's mainstream markets, and a strengthening of critics calling for major reforms in the speed and control of Unilever research. The project could also be interpreted as showing Unilever as being slow in bringing innovations to the market and, when it did, reluctant to make very big investments supporting them. The Hyacinth case in particular revealed that one major problem in Unilever's processes was that the Special Committee exerted its authority far too late, after substantial funds had been spent. They were kept informed of Hyacinth, but lacked either the willingness or ability to cancel it, despite constantly expressing the view that Unilever did not have the resources to make a success of this product category by itself.

The above cases of unsuccessful innovation do not demonstrate deficiencies in scientific research. Researchers delivered a 'keepable' yoghurt, TAED was an important innovation in fabric wash, and Lyogel was a considerable scientific achievement. The problems arose because this research was not integrated into an innovation process. The commercial exploitation of technical innovations was pursued with little regard to the market place. Consumers did not want longer-life yoghurts, especially if they did not taste as good as fresh ones. Nor did German consumers want another detergents brand whose novelty was hard to explain. Female consumers might have responded to a much more efficient form of sanitary protection, but the market already had tried and trusted brands, and by the time Unilever got any products on sale similar technologies were available and already coming under question. While the Special Committee's ability to influence a project's outcome was greatest at the earliest stage of development, at Unilever they tended to become involved only later in the project, when it was heading for trouble.

Innovation Success: Cif/Jif, Viennetta, and Clearblue

Cif/Jif

The interaction between technological innovation, marketing, and consumer demand which made for a successful innovation can be seen in the development of

collaborative links were also formed with Birmingham University that led, in 1978, to the launch of the Immunostics range of antibody products. Immunodiagnostic research continued at Colworth, and the science that underpinned Immunostics was applied in the development of a number of systems, including, most notably, the 'dipstick' concept—a simple, one-step assay system whose basic principles were subsequently employed in Clearblue.[84]

Meanwhile Colworth had also built on the discovery by Cambridge scientists in 1975 of monoclonal antibodies—molecules that recognize only one type of antigen and therefore can be used to target a defined antigen—and in 1980 filed the Paired Monoclonal Antibody (PMA) patent, which protected the groundbreaking technique of using two monoclonals of narrow and different specificity to bind different sites of an antigen. This science had a number of possible uses, and by the early 1980s the Colworth researchers were already considering its use in pregnancy testing.[85]

By 1980 Unilever was at the forefront of the science of immunochemistry, but the achievement seemed fated to join the catalogue of unfulfilled potential seen elsewhere. There were increasing doubts about the competence of UAC to pursue a medical business, and its proposed acquisitions in this field in the United States were blocked by the Special Committee. The Sensititre business was eventually sold to its American distributor after Unilever had failed to exploit its early lead.[86] The decision to close down the Animal Feeds Co-ordination in 1982 also led to a decline in funding for immunological research.[87]

However Unilever's immunological research had impressed both the Research Director and Chemicals Co-ordination.[88] In 1982 a decision was made to take the medical diagnostics business out of UAC, and placed it under a new Medical Products Group within the Chemicals Co-ordination. Given that the established formula of using CRF funds to undertake basic research which would then be taken over by the relevant Co-ordination was not applicable, it was decided to provide funds from central Unilever sources. The Special Committee acknowledged that, from its inception, Medical Products Group would be making losses for three to four years while building up 'necessary' knowledge.[89] This structure provided Medical Products Group with direct access to the higher levels of Unilever and secure financial support. Meanwhile new managers were recruited from other firms, including Beechams and Glaxo, and a small new R & D group was set up in a converted warehouse in Bedfordshire near Colworth. UAC's Seward's laboratory was incorporated into the new Bedford laboratory, and the medical diagnostics business relaunched as a new company, Unipath, formed in 1983.[90]

By 1984 the strategy was 'to build a reputation as an advanced technology group with quality products'.[91] Research was pursued in a number of directions jointly with leading universities and medical institutes, with great interest in the application of monoclonal antibodies in the treatment of cancer. However it was soon decided that the business needed one major commercial product within a year, or otherwise it 'would become our research boutique unless we related ourselves to the marketplace'.[92] In the belief that there would be a future shift in the diagnostics market to consumer homes, research was refocused on products designed for the Over the Counter (OTC) consumer market. Pregnancy testing became the focus of attention at Unipath.

A concerted research and marketing effort led in June 1985 to the launch of a new pregnancy testing kit Clearblue through pharmaceutical outlets in Britain. OTC pregnancy tests existed prior to Clearblue's launch, and the research was focused on developing a product that offered distinct advantages over the competition. Home use dictated a need for easy to use systems which were sensitive, fast, and reliable. After consumer research identified the 'particular distaste' of consumers for taking a urine sample,[93] a unique 'bucket' collection system was devised that was hygienic and non-invasive. A test result was obtained within thirty minutes. Expertise from Unilever's food packaging businesses was employed to improve the packaging and attain a shelf life of six months.

The Unipath marketing team comprised a sales team of specially recruited science graduates, which remained separate from Unilever marketing generally. This provided the basis for a close technical/marketing interface.[94] Clearblue was carefully positioned in order to create a 'niche market'; it was strategically targeted towards the modern independent woman in control of her life and the 'discovery' of pregnancy. Advertising often pictured a woman—in soft focus and in a private space—usually the bathroom—consulting the test outcome alone. A strong brand image was also developed: the launch 'involved extensive product support' which, for example, included the creation of a distinctive 'Fan Device' trademark which sought to convey reassurance and suggest femininity. The product was launched rapidly elsewhere in Europe and in the United States mainly through third party distributors.

The success of Clearblue led to a range of OTC kits. During 1988 Clearblue One Step—or Clearblue Easy was it was known in the United States—was launched as the first pregnancy test kit to use PMA technology, which incorporated a porous nitro-cellulose membrane built into a 'one-pot' system which eradicated the 'wash and wait' stages of previous kits. The Clearblue One Step test gave a result within three minutes. The product rapidly gained 50 per cent of the British market, and became a world leader following its introduction elsewhere in Europe and the United States. PMA and the dipstick system provided the basis for several other products, including Clearplan, a home ovulation test launched in 1989.

By 1990 medical products was a profitable, but very small, product category, with a mere 0.3 per cent of Unilever's total sales. However, the way Clearblue had been

50 *Clearblue One Step* in 1989.

developed outside the conventional Unilever structures was instructive. The patron-age of several directors was essential to fostering this research area, but there was more to its success. Unipath also developed a highly innovative culture, with a strong emphasis on clear and open channels of communication, which differed sharply from the culture found so often elsewhere in Unilever. There was a higher level of risk acceptance, and a willingness to tolerate and recover from failure. A research programme on fertility monitoring—'Project Frog'—undertaken with Elida Gibbs was abandoned after it appeared the technology and the market were not ready, but without any of the concern for sunk costs and recriminations seen in Project Hyacinth. There was also a striking interaction between the technology and the market, enabling Unilever to translate research into a brand that found success in the market place, and build a wholly new business in the process.[95]

In the cases of Cif/Jif, Viennetta, and Clearblue the interfaces between research, development, production, and marketing in the innovation process were smooth. In the example of Cif/Jif, Unilever's French company took up the basic research devel-oped at Port Sunlight, and developed a formulation and image close to the market. Viennetta was developed within one operating company that got the concept right, and discovered an attractive product. While Clearblue was based on a basic research, the branded product was developed by the new Unipath company which escaped the friction between functions so often seen within Unilever. It served as the kind of 'cradle company' that Woodroofe had contemplated in the late 1950s.

All three cases were examples of innovations in 'concepts'. Jif/Cif was both an abrasive cleaner and a 'liquid cleaner'. Viennetta was both an ice cream and a dessert. Clearblue was an efficient pregnancy test product, but the underlying concept was of giving women more control over their lives. As consumers became more affluent and discerning, and faced a growing range of choices, opportunities for successful innovation were found more often in new concepts than in inventing new products narrowly defined. The problem for Unilever was that the discovery of such new concepts was likely to emerge from a holistic understanding both of the possibilities of scientific and technological research and of the nature of the marketplace.

Perspectives

Unilever possessed an impressive science base. Almost certainly no other large company in the world conducted over a twenty-five-year period such a wide spread of research spanning not only detergents, household cleaners, toothpaste, deodorants, and all kinds of foodstuffs, but also chemicals, palm oil cloning, animal vaccines, sanitary towels, and pregnancy tests. Unilever research developed an international reputation for excellence.

The problem was that this research too often did not deliver commercial results commensurate with the scale of resource devoted to it. It seemed to take a long time to turn a scientific innovation into a commercial product. The contribution of scientific research to renewing and building the margarine business was a major exception, but in detergents and foods, industries with strong international competitors, Unilever too often moved more slowly. Unilever's problems in new product and process development were not unique amongst large corporations, but there was a long-term dissatisfaction among executives that its performance was weaker than its major international competitors.

From the 1950s Unilever sought to leverage its research capabilities by providing more central direction. This was rational in such a decentralized organization where the strategic exploitation of science might otherwise have been undermined by duplication of effort. However the central direction of research led Unilever into unsuccessful innovations, such as long-life yoghurt and feminine hygiene, where too little attention was given to the needs of the market. The view that if Unilever had a good scientific or technological innovation, it had the capability to translate it into success in the marketplace, lingered, even though consumers increasingly had more choices and a higher level of sophistication in making them. It was significant that successful innovations such as Jif/Cif and Viennetta were characterized by being developed and refined close to one market. They also began on a small scale. It was not Unilever's approach to make huge P & G-style investments in new innovations which might radically change consumer demand.

The innovation process had to steer a course through the Research Division, the research laboratories, Co-ordinations, operating companies, and the Special Committee. There were structural constraints on successful innovation in the ways that Unilever was organized both horizontally—between Co-ordinations and Research—and vertically—between Research and operating companies. This constellation acted as a 'closed system' given the distrust of collaborative ventures with other firms, which meant little effort was made to tap into outside sources of technology available from, for instance, larger suppliers. The identification of priorities was complex in such a diversified firm, but became hazardous given the lack of communication between research, development, manufacturing, and marketing. The Special Committee intervened too late in the whole process, after problems had arisen, rather than at the crucial starting point of projects.

There was a wider issue of corporate culture. One authority on 'innovative firms' lists the norms which appear to assist the development and commercialization of new products and processes. These include 'the autonomy to try and fail; the right of employees to challenge the status quo; open communication to customers, to external sources of technology and within the firm itself. With respect to commercialisation or implementation, teamwork, flexibility, trust and hard work.'[96] Unilever's culture did not closely fit these characteristics. The 'solution' to the 'innovation problem' involved confronting the cultural and organizational legacy of the company. It was easier to build a small innovative entity such as Unipath relatively isolated from the mainstream organization than to transform the entire company. Unilever began the 1990s still searching for solutions to the perceived deficiencies in its innovative capabilities.

11

Acquisitions and Divestments

Buying and Selling Firms

Unilever pursued two alternative routes to expanding and enhancing the competitiveness of its business. It sought to grow organically through innovation and capital investment, and it bought—and sometimes sold—companies. From the late 1950s the pace of acquisition quickened, recalling the heady days after the First World War when Unilever's predecessors had acquired numerous firms.[1]

Between 1965 and 1990 Unilever acquired around 540 companies, usually some ten to twenty each year until the mid-1980s, when the numbers increased to over fifty companies in some years. Unilever spent £6,600 million buying these companies, equivalent to £9,618 million in 1990 prices. In constant prices, the cost of acquisitions did not fluctuate greatly until the second half of the 1980s, when there was a huge surge in the amount of money spent on buying other firms. Annual peaks in expenditure coincided with the four large acquisitions: National Starch in 1978 (£252 million), Brooke Bond in 1984 (£390 million), Chesebrough-Pond's in 1986 (£1,993 million), and Fabergé / Elizabeth Arden (£996 million) in 1989. Unilever was primarily a buyer rather than a seller of companies. It was only in 1985, for the first time in Unilever's history, that the money received from disposals exceeded the cost of acquisitions. This was not to happen again until 1992, and most spectacularly 1997, when speciality chemicals were divested.[2]

The typical Unilever acquisition was of a small or medium-sized firm. A study of the 197 acquisitions made by Unilever between 1983 and the first quarter of 1990 defined 145 of them as 'small', costing less than £10 million. The average cost was only £2.6 million, and the firms involved were overwhelmingly confined to one product group and one country. A further forty-five acquisitions between 1984 and 1990 were 'medium-sized'—valued at between £10 million and £100 million—and included Shedd (1984) in the United States, the meats company Revilla in Spain (1986), and the Brazilian and Mexican operations of Anderson Clayton (1986). Finally these years saw seven acquisitions of over £100 million. In addition to Chesebrough-Pond's, Fabergé/Elizabeth Arden, and Brooke Bond, these included Naarden (1986), Durkee (1988), Calvin Klein (1989), and Boursin (1990).[3]

The majority of acquisitions were in Europe. Between 1965 and 1990 Unilever acquired almost 340 companies in Europe, but only 75 in North America and 120 elsewhere. US acquisitions were expensive, and as a result the impact of the large purchases made in that country meant that two-thirds of the total acquisitions expenditure over the twenty-five-year period was in the United States, compared to just over a quarter in Europe. The Overseas acquisitions—of which Latin America and Asia accounted for nearly forty companies each—were cheaper, and they amounted to barely 10 per cent of the total acquisition costs.

Foods accounted for the largest number of acquisitions—over 130 companies—between 1965 and 1990. There were also 78 Chemicals acquisitions—all but 12 dating from after the acquisition of National Starch—and over 60 acquisitions in Edible Fats. In contrast only 22 Detergents and 13 Personal Products companies were acquired. There were also a considerable number of acquisitions—over 60 acquisitions between 1965 and 1969—which fell into the category of 'Other', reflecting the efforts at diversification. Their number had fallen to zero by the 1990s.

In terms of cost, almost one-half of Unilever's total acquisitions expenditure—amounting to £3,255 million—was on personal products, of which over 99 per cent occurred after 1986. Foods provided the second largest category—some £1,340 million—with the Brooke Bond acquisition providing almost one-third of the total amount. The third largest product category was chemicals, on which £740 million was spent, all but 0.5 per cent after 1978. A modest £117 million spent on detergents represented less than 2 per cent of the total amount spent on acquisitions.

This chapter begins with a review of corporate acquisition strategies and capabilities. This is followed by an analysis of the policies towards the integration of acquired companies. An overall assessment of Unilever's performance in acquisitions is followed, finally, by an examination of the role of divestments.

Acquisitions and Strategy

Unilever was a company which originated as a merger and grew through acquisitions. The use of acquisitions as part of strategy was, as a result, a long-established tradition by the 1960s. In foods, including ice cream, the purchase of small and medium-sized firms was a major means of growth. Unilever was always interested in modest acquisition opportunities which could incrementally expand its main businesses. A characteristic purchase was that of Croklaan in 1970. This Dutch company, which produced speciality vegetable oils and fats for the food industry, was one of two European competitors to Unilever in the field of speciality fractionated fats. Unilever was also prepared to buy itself into new product categories, as seen in UAC's 'redeployment' into Europe.

In the highly concentrated detergents and soap industry, there was little Unilever could acquire except in particular markets. In 1964 the acquisition of De Fenix, although relatively small—costing £2.5 million (or around £22.5 million in 1990 prices)—gave Unilever important local brands in the Netherlands, notably Robijn, a washing conditioner, and Glorix, a bleaching product. The great prize would have been Henkel, with whom Unilever shared the ownership of the Persil brand, but although there were meetings at the highest level with Henkel about the possibility of an acquisition, this privately owned company never became available for purchase.[4] There were occasional acquisition opportunities in Overseas markets, such as Gessy in Brazil.[5]

The broad outlines of Unilever's policies towards acquisitions were long established. The matter was regarded as of sufficient importance for Special Committee approval to be required for all acquisitions or disposals of business, irrespective of the size or form of the deal. Firms often approached Unilever rather than the other way round. Unilever always preferred to take at least a majority shareholding in any company, and sought to make all acquisitions on an agreed basis. From the mid-1950s the phenomenon of the 'hostile' takeover bid, made against the wishes of incumbent directors, spread in Britain, and it became an established feature of the British and US business systems, but remained rare in the Netherlands and most other continental countries.[6] Unilever contemplated hostile bids at various times, including against Rowntree in 1973, but its first successful one was Brooke Bond.

Unilever developed guidelines for acquisition procedures from quite early. In the middle of the Second World War, the Special Committee had approved a document giving 'guidance on the acquisition of new businesses'. This focused on providing 'checklists' for the valuation of a firm and its future prospects.[7] A similar checklist twenty years later was broadly similar. It required extensive information about the management, marketing, production facilities, financial, and legal situation of a business to be acquired. In practice, it was acknowledged that there was often not time for such a detailed investigation, and it prioritized a number of issues including an evaluation of the present management 'and whether and in what way it should be strengthened', market position, suitability of the production facilities, and financial performance.[8]

In practice, acquisitions remained an instinctive and subjective affair. In many countries standards of corporate disclosure were such that there were uncertainties about the real nature of firms being purchased. The accounting practices followed by many family firms in southern Europe was often a troublesome issue. The acquisition of Frigo in 1973 was illustrative of some problems faced. Initially a price of £8 million was proposed, but this was later increased to £11 million. Unilever considered this to be too high, but it was argued that a premium needed to be paid to secure growth opportunities in the Spanish ice cream market.[9] Once the acquisition had been completed, it was discovered that many of Frigo's assets were all but valueless, though there had been suspicions that there were problems even while the negotiations were under way.[10] A legacy of poor financial controls included the maintenance of a separate and secret set of accounts in order to avoid taxation.[11] It took years to unravel this system, and to install Unilever financial systems. As Unilever lacked sufficient managerial resources in Spain, expatriates had to be drafted into Frigo several years after the acquisition. Frigo remained loss making throughout the 1970s, with the non-ice cream parts of it especially weak.[12] The Special Committee's verdict, looking back in 1981, was that Frigo had been 'bought on the minimum of information and had very nearly proved a disaster. Had the Special Committee known the full details when considering the acquisition proposal they would never have agreed to it.'[13]

Unilever's acquisitions procedures and skills were initially ad hoc. The Allied Breweries and Smith & Nephew episodes left Unilever as a bystander in the boom in British merger activity between 1968 and 1973, when over one-fifth of that country's largest 200 quoted firms were acquired.[14] The most serious legacy was a loss of nerve, and a reluctance to risk a major acquisition for fear of another misfortune.[15] During the early 1970s concerns about the cash flow position, and a conservative view of the appropriate level of gearing on the balance sheet, reinforced this caution.

Subsequently Unilever's acquisitions skills began to be carefully honed. Cob Stenham, his counterpart the secretary of NV, Arie Haak, and the Corporate Development directors worked to raise the level of professionalism in acquisitions, and introduce greater coherence in their execution.[16] There was a new insistence that acquisitions needed to be justified by reference to the overall strategy of Co-ordinations, and an explicit statement was made that acquisitions 'within our own or related fields of activity . . . ought to have priority over those in entirely new fields of activity'.[17] Further guidelines were issued asking for financial data on proposed acquisitions, along with clearer statements of the strategy behind them.[18] The repeated circulation of such guidelines suggested that standard procedures continued not to be routinely followed, while the idea that acquisitions needed to be undertaken as part of a coherent corporate strategy also seemed slow to take hold.[19]

Unilever was unusual among large corporations in undertaking most acquisitions itself rather than relying on investment bankers, who were employed not to search for possible targets, but rather to make the deals Unilever wanted to happen. Their advice was also important whenever regulatory issues arose, especially in the United States. In London, Lazard Brothers acted for Unilever. The small associated house of Lazard Frères was appointed to act for Unilever in New York in 1972, apparently because of its 'demonstrated skill in getting deals done'.[20]

Unilever's preference was for acquiring modestly sized firms. The largest acquisition between 1972 and 1978 was that of Lipton International, for which £12 million was paid. Many of the 'larger' acquisitions—for amounts over £5 million—were for firms beyond Unilever's core consumer goods businesses, including UAC's acquisitions of the British car leasing firm Ford & Slater (1973) and the builders' merchant Kennedys (1974), and the £8 million acquisition in 1975—half the total acquisitions expenditure in that year—of Nairn Williamson, the British home decorating company.

The Nairn Williamson acquisition was characteristic. Unilever's involvement in the British plastics industry had begun in 1964 when it had paid £4.6 million for half of the equity of Commercial Plastics, which manufactured vinyl film and sheeting, including a decorative covering material called 'Fablon'. A banker working with the founder of the business, an émigré Russian entrepreneur, was a friend of the then Finance Director and persuaded him to make the investment to finance further growth, despite the lack of any relationship to Unilever businesses. Unilever money was used to build a new factory and to move the head office into exclusive offices in London's Mayfair before, in 1967, Unilever acquired the remainder of the equity of the loss-making concern.[21] As the performance of Commercial Plastics improved, it began to seek acquisitions. Nairn Williamson, which specialized in floor coverings, was seen as attractive.

The actual acquisition originated in Nairn Williamson's approach to Unilever. Negotiations proceeded slowly until news broke that another company was interested in purchasing it. Unilever then moved quickly to make the acquisition, which was widely seen in the press as being in response to the rival bid.[22] A subsequent unpublished study of the takeover began by advising readers that if they were 'expecting a business school case history of corporate planning, full of soundly based market projections, investment decisions and industrial logic', they should 'read no further'.[23] In fact, the Nairn Williamson case illustrated that Unilever's skills in acquiring companies had improved. The problem was that

32 Advertisement for Legend Beer in the early 1990s. Nigerian Breweries had originated as a joint venture between UAC and Heineken, and Unilever retained a 15 per equity stake until 1996.

33 UAC textile manufacture in the Ivory Coast in 1985.

34 Unilever inherited from Brooke Bond not only tea plantations, but large investments in tropical flowers. The photograph shows carnations in Kenya in 1990.

35 Advertisement for Lux cream bar in the Netherlands in 1975, featuring the film star Brigitte Bardot.

36 Advertisement for Lifebuoy Soap in Britain in the 1980s. Lifebuoy toilet soap had been launched in Britain in 1933.

37 The packaging for the Dove cream bar in the United States in the 1990s emphasised the brand image of gentleness and simplicity. The original Dove synthetic soap bar was launched in 1957. Forty years later it had become one of Unilever's biggest global brands.

39 Advertisement for Close-Up toothpaste in South Africa in 1979.

38 Belgian advertisement for Signal toothpaste in 1988. The striped toothpaste had orig-

the overall strategy of expanding into the British floor coverings market made so little sense for Unilever.

The long search for a major acquisition in the United States was the central theme of the 1970s. It was characterized both by the sustained determination to make such an investment, and by the degree of openness with regard to the sector in which it was made. By 1973 a set of Acquisition Criteria for the United States were agreed. These included that companies were in Unilever's 'own or adjacent fields of activity preferably within an acquisition price range of about $50m to $250 million'; that the price–earnings ratio of the acquired company should be in a range of about 10:25; that the acquisition did not create anti-trust problems; that the company had 'a good management and will not require a big new management injection'; that 'the tender offer will not be contested'; and that the 'prospective company does not have a significant part of its operations—that could not readily be sold to a third party—which are operating in a field unrelated to Unilever's own or adjacent areas of activity'. Corporate Development's stated list of acquisition priorities was, in order of priority, personal products and possibly cosmetics companies; frozen foods and ice cream; sundry foods, preferably in new product areas such as baby foods; chemical companies, in polymers and fatty acids and flavours; packaging companies and specialized transport companies. As if this was not broad enough, 'adjacent fields' such as 'contract catering, floor polishes, disinfectants, disposables etc' were also to be considered.[24]

There were many reasons why no large acquisition was made in the United States during the mid-1970s. The Special Committee did not want to spend a great deal of money, remained paranoid about anti-trust, and determined that any acquisition should be agreed. Lever Brothers and T. J. Lipton either could not afford, or did not want, to make a large acquisition. The fact that geography rather than product drove Unilever's acquisition strategy also made for a wide search. When the Corporate Development director Henk Meij was sent to the United States in 1976 to begin a more active search for a possible acquisition, he launched a systematic procedure which involved looking first at a wide range of industries, and then at firms. After possibilities were discussed with the management groups, it was concluded that the industries 'in the priority bracket' were areas of chemicals and food and drinks, plus personal products and industrial detergents, with 'some doubt' whether UAC, animal feeds, and paper and packaging should be allowed a major US acquisition.[25]

Starting from the industries identified as of interest, Unilever and Lazard Frères looked at all companies above $100 million in sales, including private companies and major divisions of large groups. This produced a list of 700 companies which by January 1977 had been reduced to eighteen, giving priority to 'stronger and more sizeable companies up to the level of $1 billion'.[26] The eighteen candidates included a roll call of leading names in US business, including Chesebrough-Pond's, Del Monte, Gillette, Heinz, Mars, Quaker Oats, Tampax, and Wrigley. The candidates were scored Low, Medium, and High according to four criteria: industrial attractiveness, financial risk, legal risk (i.e. anti-trust), and likely resistance. Unilever's central concern was to avoid a contested takeover or an anti-trust referral, while it needed a company with good management because it self-evidently did not have an oversupply of good managers knowledgeable about the United States.[27]

In due course a short list of three candidates was discussed. Gerber, the baby food manufacturer, and CPC were eventually ruled out, and National Starch was selected as the desired 'third leg'. Unilever ranked the company as having 'medium' industrial attractiveness and financial risk, a low danger of anti-trust referral, and a medium to high risk of resistance to an acquisition. The company's management, which had resisted merger proposals from other firms, was well regarded, but the key factor became its availability. By October 1977 National Starch had indicated its willingness to consider a deal, provided the price was right and also that a tax-free arrangement could be made for large stockholders, who were primarily senior executives or former executives of advanced age.[28] The largest shareholder, who owned 15 per cent of the common stock, was willing to sell provided the company kept its autonomy, and as a result considerable guarantees on that matter had to be given during the acquisition process. During December Van den Hoven and Orr crossed to New York to negotiate directly with National Starch. The personal involvement by the chairmen was both critical in getting the deal finalized, and indicated the importance with which it was regarded.[29]

Whatever the strategic logic of acquiring a speciality chemicals company, National Starch represented a turning point for Unilever's acquisition strategy. It showed that the company could make a large acquisition and one, moreover, in the United States. Yet it was a further six years before the next large acquisition was made. The Special Committee continued to be cautious, turning down a series of acquisition proposals of US firms from Personal Products Co-ordination, often on the grounds of apparent weak management.[30] When a search began in earnest for a major new acquisition in the early 1980s, the industry criterion remained as broad as in the 1970s, as did the strong preference for agreed takeovers.[31]

The acquisitions search in the early 1980s was thorough, but cautious. By 1982 Richardson Vicks was among the most preferred candidates.[32] By the summer of 1983 the Special Committee had come to the conclusion that Richardson Vicks was the 'only company of real interest' on the acquisition list,[33] but by the end of the same year it had been decided not to proceed as the price 'was considered too high'.[34] There were particular concerns that a takeover could only be made in a hostile fashion, and because so much of the firm's profit was derived from Europe, while Unilever wanted dollar-generating income.[35] A subsequent meeting of directors heard voices maintaining that Unilever was 'over-cautious' in the context of the 'dynamic acquisition environment' of the United States.[36]

Unilever's next major acquisition was not in the United States at all, but Brooke Bond. The idea of acquiring this firm went back to at least 1972 when, following the acquisition of Lipton International, Unilever had sought to enter the large British tea market. After attempts to buy Tetley and the much smaller Twinings had come to naught,[37] Brooke Bond was considered, but ultimately it was decided not to bid for the company, in part because of its unwanted ownership of plantations.[38] However, the firm's substantial share of the British tea market remained attractive, while its overall performance by the early 1980s suggested a poorly managed business which Unilever might improve. In particular diversifications into high street butchers and South American ranching turned out less than successful.[39]

Despite a decade of looking at Brooke Bond, however, the initiative for making a takeover bid finally came from Lazards rather than Unilever. During March 1983 Unilever was alerted by its merchant bank that a 'mystery bidder' for Brooke Bond was in the market. Although that bidder subsequently lost interest, Lazards expressed their feeling 'that somebody else was interested, probably an American company'.[40] It was the Finance Director who pushed forward the idea of Brooke Bond as a good acquisition in order 'to become the world-wide leaders in tea'.[41] The Special Committee itself was initially more interested as a means to strengthen its British foods business, as Brooke Bond included some prominent foods brands, including Oxo cubes and Fray Bentos corned beef.[42]

Once agreement had been reached within Unilever, planning for a hostile acquisition went fast. By mid-July there was a plan for the post-acquisition of Brooke Bond, the basis of which was rapid absorption into existing businesses and the immediate sale of the unwanted butchers and timber merchant businesses.[43] Events conspired to make the acquisition less clean than envisaged. An initial strategy to acquire close to 5 per cent of the shares and then launch a 'dawn raid' to get as close as possible to 15 per cent was pre-empted by a sudden bid from the British sugar company Tate & Lyle. Unilever responded with its own bid on 2 September. Uncharacteristically for Unilever, Brooke Bond's chairman heard about the acquisition on the BBC news on Sunday evening. By lunchtime the following day Unilever had bought half the shares.[44]

The Brooke Bond acquisition was Unilever's first successful hostile acquisition, and it contributed to a new assertiveness. The Special Committee's meeting at Marlow in May 1984 had already decided to take another look at Richardson Vicks.[45] Over the following months interest in Richardson Vicks continued to grow as Personal Products Co-ordination sought to make a large acquisition in the United States. At the time the health care sector was seen as particularly attractive. During the spring of 1985 Co-ordination initiated discussions with Richardson Vicks regarding a possible joint venture.[46] The Special Committee actively considered a range of options, including a bid, for Richardson Vicks, but had by June again concluded that the price was too high.[47]

The catalyst for subsequent action was rumours during August of a takeover bid for the company. Unilever's name was mentioned, and the US company was contacted to deny the rumours.[48] Within a month Unilever heard further market rumours that Richardson Vicks had reached a lockout deal with another US firm. A decision was taken to force the issue. The chief executive of Richardson Vicks was telephoned to ask for a meeting about a merger. When the US company replied negatively, Unilever began to plan a hostile takeover bid. In mid-September Unilever made a tender offer, which was unique in having a two-tier price. It offered $56 a share if the board co-operated, and $48 if they did not.[49] This valued the company at £1 billion, or $1.3 billion, or around 50 per cent higher than the market price before acquisition rumours had led to the share price moving upwards. Richardson Vicks not only rejected the offer, but also went in search of White Knights, including Pfizer and P & G, which both came forward with higher offers.

The initial decision to go hostile caused ill will. Unilever had never done a hostile acquisition in the United States, and executives underestimated the degree of 'hostility' that could arise. It also considered itself not well served by some of its US financial advisers.[50] The Richardson family took a considerable dislike to Unilever. Relations deteriorated further after a 78-year-old family member who had been on the board for twenty-five years had a fatal heart attack during discussions on the bid.[51] Immediately after the Unilever offer, the Richardson family started buying shares in the market, and they had already introduced in 1984 a stipulation that any merger had to have two-thirds shareholder approval.[52] Unilever filed suit in Federal court aimed at stopping the company or the Richardson family buying company shares or voting any shares purchased since 6 September, and won a temporary restraining order. On 26 September Unilever raised its offer to $60 per share if the Board agreed, but within a week P & G had secured the company. A hostile bid had been pursued in such a fashion that Unilever's major US competitor was left to acquire the business. It was apparent that if Unilever was to launch hostile takeover bids, the possible consequences of failure needed to be thought through more carefully at an early stage in the process.

Within a few weeks other US acquisition candidates, and especially Chesebrough-Pond's, were being discussed. This company had been on Unilever's list of potential acquisitions since the 1970s given its portfolio of successful mass market brands. It also seemed to be potentially 'in play' as Unilever had heard of takeover rumours concerning Chesebrough-Pond's during the previous year.[53] At that stage the US firm was only one of several candidates under serious discussion, including Germany's Beiersdorf, Beecham, and Gillette.[54] After the Richardson Vicks episode,

Unilever was even more convinced that it only wanted an acquisition as a 'White Knight'. In the case of Chesebrough-Pond's there were doubts concerning the quality of the firm's management and its diversified portfolio. Co-ordination believed the firm was poorly managed, and there was alarm about how much of it would have to be resold after an acquisition, especially the unwanted Stauffer Chemicals business.[55] Co-ordination recommended finally against making an acquisition in December, though it remained interested in buying individual pieces if it was broken up.[56]

A new search began, aimed at making another large US acquisition. The Special Committee by this stage envisaged a US acquisition costing no more than $2 billion. Given Unilever's modest position in the US foods industry, both CPC (by then known as Bestfoods) and Pillsbury were studied closely.[57] However, by the autumn personal products had re-emerged as 'No 1 by a long way', with medical products and 'all other consumer packaged goods core businesses' as joint No. 2 in the list of priorities. By November Unilever's shortlist of desirable targets included, once more, Chesebrough-Pond's.[58]

It was an initiative from another company which finally prompted the acquisition of Chesebrough. In October Unilever heard that there was increased activity in its shares, and it was decided it 'would be worthwhile to proceed immediately to do more work so that we would be prepared if needs be'.[59] During one Wednesday in November Tabaksblat and the new Finance Director, Niall FitzGerald, had concluded during a lunch that Chesebrough-Pond's would be a perfect fit for Unilever. On the following Tuesday it was heard that American Brands planned to make an offer for the company.

Unilever moved with a speed and decisiveness which amazed observers which regarded the company as incapable of either fast or radical decisions. FitzGerald and Tabaksblat flew to Rotterdam to meet the Special Committee, and it was decided to reach out to Chesebrough-Pond's as a White Knight.[60] The two men then flew to New York, and worked through the case with bankers and lawyers over the three days of the Thanksgiving Holiday, before making a case for an acquisition to the Special Committee. When they ran the numbers, it was calculated that Unilever would get $1 billion for disposals of unwanted assets, and on this basis an offer price was calculated. Maljers and Angus then flew over to the United States to finalize the deal.[61] An offer for the shares of $72.50 per share in cash was made, valuing the company at around $3.1 billion. Later it was learned that it was the extra 50 cents that finally swung the balance in favour of the Unilever offer.[62] By January 1987 the agreed acquisition was completed.

By this time Unilever was an accomplished acquirer of companies. In foods Unilever almost routinely acquired one firm after another—many of them family owned—in Europe. The purchase of Les Nutons in Belgium in 1984 was typical of many such acquisitions. Co-ordination wanted to expand its pâté business, which required strong 'artisanal' knowledge in both manufacturing and recipe formulation. It seemed better to acquire an established firm, and then transfer its knowledge within Unilever, than to try to develop its own capabilities. There were two leading Belgian pâté suppliers, but Unilever preferred Les Nutons as it was believed to be more marketing oriented, while the owner was in his fifties and willing to sell. An approach was made to the company.

The actual acquisition involved months of negotiation. The owner wanted to remain for one year after the acquisition, and it was agreed that key senior management would remain with the business for at least three years. The introduction of Unilever systems was to be 'gradual and pragmatic'.[63] An original offer of £2.6 million was made before the 1984 results were completed and when profit expectations were revised downwards—as Belgian pâté exports were hit by the so-called African 'pig plague'—so the price went downwards and was eventually agreed at £1.6 million, though not before another contender had briefly appeared on the scene.[64]

During the late 1980s Unilever also pursued a strategy of acquiring olive oil companies in the Mediterranean. In Spain, the Costablanca Group was acquired, while Fima—Unilever's Portuguese joint venture owned with Jeronimo Martins—acquired Victor Guedes. The largest acquisition was in Italy, where Unilever already owned the firm of Dante. San Giorgio was acquired for over £25 million from the family owners in 1989, with the intention to combine it with Dante to give Unilever market leadership in the Italian branded olive oil market at around 15 per cent.[65] The company had bought refined oil for its Pure product at a cheaper price than Unilever paid for its own refined olive oil, but it emerged over time that the bought oil was being adulterated. Unilever had to move to in-house refining. It also had to abandon a planned advertising expenditure designed to build up the consumer image of the brand, a necessary step as Unilever had lacked market research data before the acquisition and had not realized that San Giorgio's strength was trade rather than consumer based.[66] As a result, San Giorgio seriously failed to meet the targets of market share and sales in the original acquisition proposal.

The San Giorgio episode demonstrated once again the pitfalls of acquiring some family businesses in southern Europe. It was not the only example. After purchasing Revilla in Spain in 1986, it was discovered that its meat products were sold through a system of discounts to retailers which Unilever could not countenance. The business was eventually sold again.

The 1980s also finally saw an increase in the number and size of acquisitions in 'the rest of the world'. Previously, the Overseas Committee had not made extensive use of acquisitions as a tool of strategy. This was not only because Unilever's resources were focused on trying to make a large US acquisition, but also because buying companies in many countries involved complicated and time-consuming negotiations with fam-

51 A truck carrying *Revilla* meats products in Spain in 1987. The firm had been acquired by Unilever in the previous year.

52 The acquisition of *San Giorgio* in 1989 helped give Unilever ten per cent of the Mediterranean olive oil market within a few years.

ily owners, as well as many political sensitivities. From the early 1980s there was a new willingness to acquire, however. Significant acquisitions were made in Asia—in Taiwan and Korea—and in Africa, where in 1982 £29 million was paid for an 80 per cent share of the diversified Blohorn business in Ivory Coast.[67] In Latin America, acquisitions included Anderson Clayton and Conasupo and Visa in Mexico.

Despite the large expenditure on acquisitions during the second half of the 1980s, Unilever remained a cash-rich business, reflecting both its position in mature products, and a proactive Treasury policy which included vigorous trimming of Unilever's asset base by selling off some its vast amount of property, including office buildings. Although Unilever's gross gearing moved upwards, it was only with the Fabergé acquisition that Unilever's debt rose from an average of £300 million to £3 billion. In 1990 the company had still not issued any equity since 1950. Unilever retained its traditional image with the financial markets as a 'conservative' company—it held a triple A credit rating—with low borrowings, and an ability to fund organic growth without any increase in borrowings.

Despite the large amount spent on acquisitions during the second half of the 1980s, Unilever never became a transactions-driven company on the lines of the British conglomerates of the era such as Hanson Trust or BTR, or US leveraged buyout firms such as Kohlberg Kravis Roberts. There was a long-term business strategy behind Unilever's acquisitions rather than a concern to maximize short-term financial gains from acquiring and breaking-up underperforming or undervalued companies. 'This is a culture where people buy businesses they know how to run,' Stenham told a British accountancy journal in 1986; 'they buy businesses to keep them rather than to turn them over'.[68]

Unileverization

By the 1980s acquisitions seemed almost a routine matter, but Unilever executives knew from experience both that in practice no acquisition was ever wholly routine, and that each carried its own risks even for the most experienced manager. 'Acquisitions are competitive, dangerous and expensive,' FitzGerald, by then Edible Fats Co-ordinator, reminded his colleagues in 1989. 'Success or failure will depend on the speed and effectiveness of post acquisition integration. Very particular experience and skills are required.'[69]

The initial phase of integration of an acquired company was known within the company as 'Unileverization', just as an acquisition by P & G was described within that company as 'Procterization'. 'Unileverization' involved at its most basic the introduction of Unilever's accounting systems, as well as—where necessary—its

Outcomes

The view that acquisitions were 'dangerous and expensive' was not idiosyncratic to Unilever. The pioneering management literature of the 1950s on the growth of firms was at pains to stress that making acquisitions and successfully integrating them required considerable managerial capabilities as 'mistakes may be costly and not always reparable'.[85] By the 1980s there was formidable academic evidence that many acquisitions failed. One major US study in 1987 estimated that around one-third of all acquisitions made by US firms in the 1960s and early 1970s were subsequently sold following poor performance.[86] Foreign acquisitions in the United States, which increased greatly in the 1980s, often seemed to disappoint their new owners, in part because foreign companies tended on aggregate to acquire US firms with below average profitability.[87]

In aggregate, it became widely accepted that only around half of all corporate acquisitions overall turned out 'successful'. Any value that was added often appeared to go mainly to the shareholders of acquired firms. The reasons for this situation ranged across a spectrum, from the excessive bid premiums often used to buy firms, to the unexpected costs and difficulties of integrating acquired businesses. Many mergers and acquisitions seemed to be conducted by managers seeking to maximize their own utility instead of shareholder value.

Unilever was acutely aware that some acquisitions turned out better than others did. By the 1970s management groups were expected to provide post-acquisition statements, though few did so. On occasion, the Special Committee would ask for a formal 'post-mortem' designed to provide evidence some years after the acquisition on actual performance compared to the original proposal. A prime purpose was 'to learn from past experience, in order to improve future decisions on acquisitions'. In 1980 the procedures were tightened, with a requirement for management groups to notify the Special Committee soon after an acquisition if there were significant variations from the facts shown in original proposals. Full 'post-mortems' were mandatory only at the behest of the Special Committee.[88]

During the late 1970s Unilever began investigating the 'success' rate of its acquisitions in general. This was a difficult, and subjective, exercise given that so much depended on the time period and the criteria employed. An initial study in 1978 of fourteen of the sixteen acquisitions costing over £5 million made since 1970 concluded that three—Frigo, Zwanenberg, and Kennedys—were decidedly 'unsuccessful', while three others—Lipton, Nairn Williamson, and Glenton & Mitchell in South Africa—were 'highly successful'. The measure was financial performance. Subsequently Corporate Development sought to place this research in the context of what was known about the performance of corporate acquisitions in general. The conclusion was that Unilever's performance was 'about average', but that Unilever's experience confirmed the 'high risk of the acquisition route'.[89]

The 'risks' of acquisitions, especially in non-related industries, became progressively apparent within Unilever. In 1983 an internal study of Unilever acquisitions since 1970—restricted to forty-three cases costing more than £2 million in 1982 values, but excluding National Starch—analysed them by geography, whether they were industrial or consumer, and 'type'—horizontal, vertical, or new activity. The most striking conclusion was that, while only a quarter of the twenty-five horizontal acquisitions were considered a failure, over two-thirds of the sixteen new activity acquisitions were placed into that category. It also emerged that larger acquisitions seemed to work much better than smaller ones.[90]

The problems of both 'new activity' and 'small' acquisitions were demonstrated by UAC's 'redeployment' to Europe. The whole logic of UAC's diversification made little strategic sense, but the approach to acquisitions exacerbated the problems. The acquisitions were undertaken by each division of the UAC rather than the company as a whole, encouraging the proclivity to acquire a large number of small companies, in industries as varied as automobile distribution, office equipment, builders' merchants, garden centres, and many others. These small companies were time consuming to manage, yet did not serve as the basis for growth. Moreover UAC did not have the managerial resources to manage many of the firms which were acquired, because its managers knew a great deal more about marketing in West Africa than they did about builders' merchants or office equipment manufacturers in Britain. There were also often acute clashes of corporate culture. The small entrepreneurial firms which were acquired suddenly had the heavy hand of Unilever bureaucracy and reporting systems imposed on them, destroying their dynamism and causing key staff to leave.

The drawbacks in acquiring multiple small companies were well illustrated also in the case of T. J. Lipton. Its acquisitions between the 1960s and the 1980s all followed the same broad strategy of identifying a promising regional brand in the United States that was believed to have the potential to sell in the national market. In almost every instance it proved impossible to expand the brand beyond its regional area. This pattern became established with Good Humor ice cream, and was then repeated over the following three decades. Usen Products, acquired in 1969, became one of the most serious failures. Its Tabby canned cat food business began to lose market share immediately after the acquisition, and in the mid-1970s was stranded with less than 3 per cent of the national market for gourmet cat food. Following the regular Lipton pattern, this was a regional business in an industry where the largest firms were already national.[91]

The acquisition of Lawry's Foods Inc. in 1979 was virtually Lipton's only success story. Lawry's saw volume growth of nearly 7 per cent per annum between 1979 and

1984.[92] This was a medium-sized but innovative West Coast foods business, whose main product was Seasoned Salt. Lawry's had originated in a family restaurant, and it retained a strong brand image. At the time of the acquisition, Unilever gave a structured undertaking that it would leave the Lawry business entirely separate for three years, with a strong concern on retaining the innovative nature of the business, and integration proceeded slowly.[93]

By the early 1980s the Special Committee began to express growing scepticism at Lipton's record in small acquisitions, and started to veto suggestions.[94] Yet a series of similar acquisitions continued to be made, in snacks, soft drinks, and Mexican foods. The case for each acquisition always seemed convincing. T. J. Lipton's president made a personal appearance before the Special Committee to argue the case for the snacks acquisition. 'The American obsession about nutrition and health', he advised, meant that 'snacks that offered health benefits must be a fast growing area'.[95] While Americans may indeed have been interested in 'healthy snacks', a lack of consumer tests or retail surveys before the acquisition, combined with a failure to identify defects in product quality, contributed to another failure.[96] After a review of another unsuccessful acquisition, the Special Committee concluded that the lesson was that Lipton had some difficulty in absorbing small, not very well-run businesses.[97]

It is evident from Unilever's experience that the degree of success in acquisitions was usually closely related to the degree of knowledge it had of the product and the geography of the acquiree. Brooke Bond was a prime example of this rule, as were—in a negative sense—the UAC acquisitions in Europe. National Starch stands as an outlier in this respect, though less so if it was to be seen as more of a trade investment than an acquisition in the conventional sense.

Overall, the impact of acquisitions on Unilever's business needs to be kept in perspective. During the 1960s and the 1970s the cost of acquisitions averaged around 10 per cent of Unilever's capital investment. While the National Starch acquisition was the largest ever made by a foreign company in the United States, it added only 2 per cent to Unilever's total sales. Unilever also had its appropriate share of disappointments. Yet the Special Committee was probably right in its judgement that the company's performance in this regard was above average.

Divestments

Unilever's disposals of companies were few in number and size until the mid-1980s. Three-quarters of the total company disposals made by Unilever between 1965 and 1990 occurred between 1985 and 1990. Unilever mainly sold businesses in Europe, strikingly so as the size of divestments grew in the mid-1980s. Companies in 'core' consumer goods businesses were rarely sold, and divestments were largely limited to 'Other' industries. This only changed slightly from the mid-1980s, with the divestments out of oil milling and some unwanted elements of acquired companies.

In the 1960s Unilever had virtually no experience of selling companies, and rarely considered such a step unless there were exceptional circumstances. UAC's heavily loss-making joint venture to brew beer in Burgos, Spain, qualified as one such exceptional circumstance.[98] Paradoxically, it was barely one month after joining Unilever that Stenham was dispatched to Spain to try to sell the company. Almost by accident he met someone from the Spanish brewing company San Miguel in a bar, and eventually a sale was made. As he later recalled, he was 'the sort of person who would meet people in a bar, while Unilever was full of people who wouldn't'.[99]

During the late 1960s and early 1970s Unilever disposed of unwanted textile and other assets in Germany, mostly acquired during the diversification of the 1930s. In 1971 Unilever sold its German textile company Odermark, which had about 4,500 employees, for almost £4 million. The largest sale was the retailer Frowein & Nolden, which operated more than sixty supermarkets and self-service shops in the Düsseldorf area of Germany, in 1973. Unilever had been eager to sell this rather unprofitable company for years, not least because it put Unilever in the difficult position of competing with other retailers who were its customers. However it was 'locked in' both because German labour laws required a high level of compensation to the 1,500 employees if it was closed, and because most of the shops were rented on long-term contracts which could not be easily broken. A further complication was that just under a tenth of the equity was owned by the founding family.[100] Unilever finally extracted itself by merging its company with another, and then selling its own shareholding. The sale raised £8 million and was Unilever's largest divestment for many years. The Unilever manager of Frowein & Nolden stayed working part-time with the merged company for six months to secure a smooth transition.[101]

There were only a handful of disposals during the 1970s. There was a striking contrast with corporate America where the decade saw a huge number of divestments as well as acquisitions.[102] The main 'disposals' took the form of the forced sale of some of the equity in companies such as Hindustan Lever and UAC Nigeria. The Special Committee was as reluctant to sell on a large scale as it was to acquire. In the late 1970s the manager of the BOCMS proposed that either Unilever should acquire their largest competitor in British animal feeds in order to achieve a critical mass, or else the business should be sold. The Special Committee declined either course.[103] There were almost no disposals of poorly performing businesses, despite Unilever's considerable difficulties in Europe and the United States. It was only in 1981 that

T. J. Lipton finally sold its highly unsuccessful businesses in Tabby cat food and Morton House canned meat products.

In much of Europe, labour legislation made selling or closing companies difficult and costly. This was not the case in Britain, but there remained the same reluctance to sell a business. The one significant sale was of the retailer MacFisheries, which had attempted to diversify from selling fresh fish into more general food retailing, but which again placed Unilever in the difficult position of competing with its own grocery customers. In 1979 Unilever swapped its shops for a 25 per cent shareholding in another retail chain—which was sold a few years later—but Unilever retained its fish processing business until 1985.

A sea change in attitudes began as the second recession of the early 1980s began to bite. In 1982 Urachem was sold, and the cull soon moved beyond chemicals. Even before the 'core business' strategy was fully worked out, lists of 'poor performers' were being used to draw up candidates for disposals.[104] The subsequent wave of disposals during the mid-1980s rid Unilever of a swathe of its accumulated low-margin businesses. Initially the idea of selling a business was traumatic, both for Unilever's senior management and for the workforce. The employees of companies which believed themselves to be on the 'disposal list' naturally felt insecure. In 1985 the Special Committee was obliged to clarify that presence on the disposal list was not primarily connected with profitability, but rather 'whether or not it fitted the Unilever strategy'.[105] Once the process started, it began to become easier, and over time routine. Unilever was rewarded by growing favourable comment from investment analysts.[106]

By 1984 Unilever had produced its first 'policy guide' to selling a business. It was established that one executive should take responsibility, and in the case of major disposals this would be a main board director. Procedures to maintain confidentiality had to be established and include provisions for the involvement in due course of trade unions, works councils, anti-trust authorities, and so on. There was a particular problem of prospective conflicts of loyalties of staff during the course of sale. The preferred procedures were that staff from the companies concerned should be involved as little as possible in the fact-finding and negotiations, and that the employment futures of key individuals should be clarified as early as possible. It was desirable that a responsible commercial manager who would be staying with Unilever after the sale continued to work in the business during the course of the sale. It was considered preferable that there should be a 'clean break' with 'no residual shareholding, Unilever representation on the board or bank guarantees'.

Personnel considerations weighed heavily. National personnel departments were to be consulted as soon as possible, especially to establish how the 'rationale' for the disposal would be put to employees, continuity of employment, and redundancy arrangements. Central Pensions Department was also to be involved from the outset. Employees transferred with the business had to leave the scheme, though pensioners normally remained with the business.[107]

Unilever was always concerned about the human consequences of divestments. It tried to find reputable buyers for the companies it sold, who could be expected to carry on the business and treat employees well.[108] During the sale of the oil mills at Europoort in the Netherlands and Spyck in Germany—which employed around 500 people—Unilever had extensive negotiations with the trade unions and works councils, who were naturally concerned about their futures given that the oil mills sold some 30 per cent of their oils to Unilever companies. Unilever sold the business for almost £100 million to the prominent and reputable US firm Archer Daniels Midland.[109] However, the US company subsequently closed the mills in a short period of time.

Unilever was also sympathetic to management buyouts. Firms sold to their managements included the Carryfast parcel service, the Brooke Bond timber business Mallinson Denny, UAC's Autogem auto parts and motor distributorship, and the Cofna animal feeds business in France. One of the most successful buyouts was that of Tibbett & Britten. Unilever's SPD had taken a shareholding in this British firm, which specialized in the transportation of garments on hangers, in 1969, and it expanded rapidly, especially after securing a contract with Marks & Spencer in 1973. The manager who had been responsible for the original investment in 1969 was by 1984 chairman of SPD, and he led a management buyout of Tibbett & Britten when the decision was taken to divest it. Subsequently the company grew to be one of the world's largest international logistics companies, retaining most of Unilever's 'management disciplines and control systems' until its acquisition by Exel in 2004.[110]

Perspectives

In one widely read business strategy text, a prominent British management writer concludes that, 'taken as a whole, merger activity adds very little value'.[111] This negative view of mergers was not borne out by Unilever's experience. Poor individual acquisitions were made. Unilever made successful acquisitions in pursuit of wrong-headed strategies. Generally Unilever's conservative approach to acquisitions resulted in few irretrievable disasters. The opportunity cost was, especially in the 1970s, the failure to build large personal care and foods businesses through acquisition. The parallel reluctance to divest meant that low-margin businesses were retained.

Unilever developed as a formidable acquirer of firms. Especially from the 1970s effective procedures to acquire and absorb other firms were developed. Post-acquisition strategies became increasingly systematic, and were well judged and flexible enough to take account of individual circumstances. The result was that Unilever was able from the late 1970s to build major businesses in personal products and speciality chemicals through acquiring other firms and integrating them. Likewise, the post-war decline of Unilever's US business was reversed by acquisitions. Arguably, Unilever became more successful at acquiring and absorbing other companies than at organic growth through innovation.

12

Corporate Image and Voice

Unilever in a Changing World

By the 1960s a large corporation such as Unilever could no longer function as an enclosed world which existed solely to sell its goods and services in the market place. As the era of wartime austerity gave way to rising incomes, governments, consumers, and others began to take a more critical look at the strategies of big business. Governments passed an increasing number of laws and regulations which affected the way firms could operate. US-style anti-trust laws began to find their way into the legislation of European countries. The impact of multinational firms operating across borders became an object of growing concern, and also of criticism, especially as many people in former colonial countries sought reasons for their poverty compared to the industrialized West. As the structure of corporate shareholding moved from individuals to institutions, the financial community also began to demand more information about the strategy of firms.

Unilever, like all business enterprises, found itself both scrutinized and influenced by the policies and concerns of regulators, international agencies, consumer groups, and institutional investors. This attention, and the need to respond to it, was not a comfortable situation for a company which preferred to maintain a low profile. Unilever barely had a corporate image. It was known by its brands. This chapter considers Unilever's evolving policies towards the external world, as it sought to define a corporate image, and to make its 'voice' known to policy-makers, pressure groups, and investors whose policies increasingly shaped the regulatory, political, and ideological environment in which it conducted its business.

From Grocers to Social Responsibility

In the United States, large corporations during the 1930s and 1940s had begun to develop powerful public relations departments which sought to project positive images for their firms—to provide them, as one writer put it, with 'souls'—stressing their moral legitimacy and civic responsibility.[1] Few large European companies at that time showed a similar desire to bare their corporate 'souls' in public, and certainly Unilever was not one of them. Unilever's size and span of activities made it cautious about attracting public attention to the parent company rather than its operating companies and their brands. The fact that the name 'Unilever' was never used in brands, that the products it sold were useful but innocuous, and that its chief executive was not a single business leader but a 'Special Committee', added to this low profile.

Nevertheless, both during and immediately after the Second World War there was recognition of a need to communicate beyond Unilever's borders. In the Netherlands, Unilever had been criticized since the 1930s for its 'monopolistic' influence, while in Britain the election of a Labour government in 1945 raised the fear that 'monopolistic' companies might be nationalized. The result was a feeling that Unilever needed to counter ill-informed criticism.[2] There was a new openness to outside scrutiny. In 1954 Unilever commissioned and published—in English and Dutch—a two-volume *History of Unilever*, written by a young Cambridge historian, Charles Wilson. This was one of the first instances when a European company had commissioned such an objective study of its history.

There was no enthusiasm for a US-style assertive public relations campaign designed to capture the hearts and minds of millions. Heyworth disliked the term 'public relations', arguing that it was the responsibility of each employee of Unilever to promote their company and its values. However Rijkens constantly emphasized the benefits not of a high profile, but of openness. In 1952 Unilever NV appointed a public relations officer, while an experienced journalist became its first press officer.[3] 'Courage, openness and frankness', Rijkens maintained when some Unilever directors had hesitated about the publication of Wilson's *History*, 'had paid us well in the past few years'.[4] Rijkens, and other like-minded exponents of corporate social responsibility, moved in wider circles than the edible fats and detergents business. He argued that Unilever needed connections, and a voice, in the world of farming and other interest groups. Under their influence, the 1950s can be seen as the beginning of the evolution of Unilever's image 'from a company of grocers to an enlightened firm with social responsibility and concern for public affairs'.[5]

The 'concern for public affairs' included a willingness to engage with the outside world. During the mid-1950s public relations became part of the External Relations Department in Rotterdam and an Information Division in London.[6] National

323

managements remained primarily responsible for public relations, but by the mid-1960s a Chief External Relations Officer based in Rotterdam oversaw public relations policies in countries placed under Co-ordination. Pieter Kuin established an Economics Department in Rotterdam in 1962, which began building connections with the European Union, and he also took charge of NV's external relations during that decade.

Unilever sought to present itself as a powerful, but modest, corporation, which was a force for progress in the world. 'The picture we are trying to project', a public relations manager explained to the Special Committee in 1962, 'is of a business which is efficient but liberal and humane.'[7] An important dimension of being 'liberal and humane' was charitable giving. By the 1960s large US and European companies were often active in charitable giving, especially to the arts and education, reflecting both a sense of responsibility to the communities in which they operated, and also the wish to enhance corporate images in the outside world.[8] Unilever had a long record of charitable giving, which went back to the days of benevolent paternalism at Port Sunlight, although it never gave to political, religious, or military causes. In the Netherlands, Unilever contributed around 900,000 Dutch guilders annually over the 1970s. There was a heavy emphasis on supporting education, especially related to business, and from the mid-1970s NV also made annual donations to the English School in The Hague and the American International School in Rotterdam.[9] In Britain, charitable donations were around three times as large, reaching around £630,000 in 1980, and £2 million by 1990. In Britain there was also a heavy emphasis on education, which usually received around one-third of charitable grants made by Ltd/PLC. Unilever donated some £870,000 to a range of British universities between 1965 and 1980.[10]

Unilever gave to 'good' rather than 'high-profile' causes. There was at the time no support for sport, and little for the arts, apart from some support for the Rotterdam Philharmonic Orchestra and a number of local Rotterdam museums, although during the mid-1980s NV also contributed half a million guilders to the renovation of the Concertgebouw in Amsterdam. Unilever's largest support for charity delivered few public relations benefits. When Viscount Leverhulme died in 1925, he endowed a charitable trust, the Leverhulme Trust, with a large number of Lever Brothers shares. The upshot was that 18 per cent of Ltd/PLC's capital was held by the Leverhulme Trust—5 per cent after a variation in terms of the Trust in 1983—which became one of Britain's largest private charities. The Trust's annual income was derived entirely from its Unilever shares, and was used to support scholarly research projects. Although successive Ltd/PLC chairmen served as chairmen of the Board of Trustees after they retired from Unilever, the Trust functioned entirely separately from Unilever.[11]

Unilever was not concerned to promote its corporate name and image. In 1967 a firm of consultants was commissioned to design a new logo which would express 'certain attributes of the Unilever character; internationally minded, forward-looking, dynamic and one jump ahead of most other people'. The consultants suggested six possible logos, and Unilever selected the one least favoured by them. The Unilever U symbolized the union of the two British and Dutch companies which had formed Unilever. Research at the end of the 1980s showed that at least 80 per cent of people had no idea what the corporate symbol represented.[12] Unilever's image as portrayed in its Annual Reports was dour. It was not until 1969 that it finally followed the long-established practice of competitors such as Nestlé, Colgate, and CPC of including illustrations of people and brands.

The mid-1960s saw the first formal attempts to define the company's 'identity'. A document written in 1966 described Unilever as:

an international enterprise of Dutch/British origin which combines the abilities of men and women of many nationalities. It specialises in the production, continuous development and mass marketing of non-durable goods for daily use, taking into account and anticipating the demands of the modern independent household.[13]

This image hardly permeated into the public consciousness, however, as everywhere people knew only of the brands and the operating companies. However, although studies showed that Unilever's corporate image was 'weak' everywhere, it differed between countries. In Britain Unilever was, according to surveys in the 1970s, 'rather faceless even to "opinion formers" '. In the Netherlands it was better known, had a good reputation for its advertising expertise, and was 'rather attractive as an employer'. In France it was known as 'predominately foreign orientated'; in Germany as 'concerned about co-determination'; in Italy as 'very customer oriented'; in Finland as 'adverse to agricultural interests'; and in Belgium for 'not willingly coming out in the open'.[14] In the United States, consumers and others were aware of Lever Brothers and T. J. Lipton, but their mutual ownership by a distant foreign parent called 'Unilever' was all but unknown. In West Africa, UAC had a strong corporate image, though its ownership by Unilever was widely known. A survey of Nigerian public opinion in 1970 found that the company was widely praised for its good management and for the training it offered, but was also regarded as 'too dominant' and commanding 'too great a share of Nigerian trade'.[15]

Rijkens's successors—Tempel, Hartog, and Klijnstra—were more interested in business performance than issues of openness and social responsibility. Cole's interest in external affairs was limited also, although in 1960 he retained a London School of Economics professor, Peter Bauer, as his 'personal consultant'.[16] Bauer was a conservative, free marketer, economist who made his reputation as virtually a lone voice arguing that foreign aid to developing countries would not alleviate poverty, and that guaranteed property rights and market forces were all that were needed.[17]

Dynamics and Routines

During the early 1970s the issue of Unilever's external relations rose again in corporate priorities. There was growing suspicion of 'multinational' companies because of their alleged threats to national sovereignty and practices, such as the avoidance of taxes through 'transfer pricing' (the prices charged for intra-firm trade). Western multinationals became symbolic of the differences between the rich and poor nations of the world.[18] The categorization of Unilever as a 'multinational', and by definition capable of wrongdoing, was a shock to a company whose culture stressed its integrity. 'One bright morning in the early 1960s I woke up to discover that I was the director of a Multinational Enterprise,' Woodroofe told an audience in San Francisco in 1973. 'It seemed as though somebody had invented this strange new concept overnight. Yet my company, innocently and unknowingly, had been a multinational enterprise since the turn of the century. . . . I awoke to find that the multinational corporation was a stereotyped enterprise, big, bad and irresponsible.'[19]

Unilever was attacked by several hostile pressure groups. In Britain, one such organization was called Counter Information Services, whose persistent criticisms of Unilever's 'activities in South Africa, additives and injurious ingredients in products, pricing policy, vivisection, etc' were taken seriously enough to be discussed by the Board in 1973.[20] The CIS produced a hundred-page report on 'Unilever's World' which critically examined the business of 'the ninth biggest company in the world'. The 'invisible giant', as the report termed the company, 'confronts the world as an organised force . . . its centralised administration, its computerised planning, its vertical integration, its monopolistic muscle, its huge capital base, is one army, with one goal, profit'.[21] In 1975 this Anti-Report was issued just hours before Unilever's Report and Accounts were published. It was a commentary on Unilever's low profile that several British newspapers were quick to observe that the description of Unilever's size and 'muscle' probably boosted its reputation with shareholders rather than the opposite. One newspaper described it as 'a red-hot share tip for Unilever'.[22]

Unilever's response was a new determination to create a more positive corporate image.[23] Woodroofe assumed a personal role in confronting the growing hostility to multinationals. He set up a new department in London under one of Unilever's more senior female managers, Dorothy Wedderburn—a scientist who had formerly worked in Research—to create 'a databank of information about Unilever, not only facts and figures, but policies and philosophies which could be used whenever anyone in a senior position wanted to communicate with the outside world'.[24] A similar databank was established in Rotterdam. Woodroofe also launched an initiative to bring the chairmen of other British large companies and government officials together to discuss the growing criticism of multinationals. It was agreed that each company would deal with public opinion in its own way, but they would co-operate informally.[25] Unilever laid great stress on the individuality of multinationals, in part because it did not want to be put into the same category as the oil and mining companies which were at that time the objects of great hostility in developing countries.[26]

At the international level, the United Nations emerged as the leading forum for critics of multinational firms. In 1974 the 'Group of 77', a caucus group of developing nations formed a decade previously at the United Nations Conference on Trade and Development (UNCTAD), secured a UN General Assembly resolution calling for the creation of a New International Economic Order. The agenda included criticism of multinational firms for inhibiting economic development in the Third World. Unilever took these developments seriously. In 1973 Woodroofe and Klijnstra broke with precedent, and gave evidence in person before the United Nations Commission on Multinationals in a public session in Geneva. This consisted of a 'Group of Eminent Persons' from both developed and developing countries, who were asked to examine the impact of multinational corporations on world development and international relations.

A long written statement by Unilever to the United Nations Commission, signed by the two chairmen, systematically disputed the main criticisms of multinationals. They denied that Unilever posed any threat to national sovereignty, observing that it had always obeyed the law, while listing the pressures it came under from governments which imposed arbitrary taxes, restricted dividends, interfered with prices, and forced the sale of equity at below market prices. Unilever's localization of management was emphasized, together with its extensive training programmes, and commitment to technology transfer. In his oral testimony, Woodroofe agreed with the need for multinational corporations to be more open and accepted the case for voluntary codes of behaviour, but also warned of the dangers of excessive regulations. 'It would be a tragedy', he warned 'for world economic progress to be held back by the limitations of world political progress.'[27] Subsequently, Unilever had 10,000 copies of the chairmen's evidence and speeches printed for the use of staff.[28]

The primary result of the Report of the Group of Eminent Persons was the establishment of new UN bodies—the Commission on Transnational Corporations and the Centre on Transnational Corporations—designed to deal specifically with multinational firms. The highest priority of the new Commission was given to the formulation of a code for multinational behaviour. There had been a series of attempts to formulate such an international regulatory framework for international investment and business. In 1948 the Havana Charter for the formation of an 'International Trade Organization' had included specific codes of conduct for multinational firms, but the United States declined to ratify it, and the plan for the ITO was abandoned, leaving cross-border investment to bilateral agreements between countries. There was no international property law to protect the assets of corporations, nor was there any agreed code of conduct that multinational firms should follow.

During the 1970s a number of quite different bodies resumed the search for 'codes of conduct' for multinational firms, and some companies—of which Royal Dutch Shell in 1976 was one of the first—adopted their own codes.[29] In 1976 the OECD produced a set of Guidelines for Multinational Enterprises, which aimed to provide a code that would both stimulate investment and set out best practice for companies on employment, environment, taxation, and other matters.[30] Unilever was quite closely involved, through various employers' and other organizations to which it belonged, in shaping the provisions of the OECD guidelines, in particular to avoid any obligation on multinationals to conduct industrial relations matters on an international level.[31] The guidelines, which thereafter were regularly revised, were voluntary. They appear to have had little impact on most multinational corporations, although it was Unilever's practice to follow them.

At the United Nations, there was pressure for a more ambitious code, and so began two decades of negotiations aimed at formulating one which was acceptable to all parties. Unilever became intimately involved in the process. In 1977 the Personnel Director and NV's vice-chairman, Han Goudswaard, was chosen as one of sixteen outside experts, initially known as the 'Group of Profound Persons', involved in drawing up the Code. Over the following years Goudswaard attended numerous meetings in New York and elsewhere, always in an individual capacity rather than as a representative of Unilever.[32] The atmosphere of the UN meetings was often tense. There was still no agreed definition of a 'transnational', let alone a Code, when Goudswaard attended his last meeting in the autumn of 1982. He estimated that United Nations affairs had occupied 10–15 per cent of his time over the previous five years, but Unilever regarded his participation as important in, for example, helping to circumvent efforts to secure a greater role for international trade unions in the various codes.[33] A draft for a voluntary code was only finally submitted in 1990, and this was abandoned altogether in 1992.[34]

Unilever's more open public stance during the 1970s was never translated into direct involvement in politics. The company had a long-standing policy to avoid trying to expand its influence by making contributions to political parties. In 1965 the Unilever Board had formally resolved that Unilever would never make donations to political parties in any country. This policy was reaffirmed in the mid-1970s in the context of a left-leaning Labour government in Britain which appeared distinctly 'anti-capitalist'. Although there was some discussion of supporting the opposition Conservative Party, the Special Committee ruled in favour of 'the Unilever policy of political neutrality'.[35] Among many factors behind this decision, Unilever was often under pressure to make political contributions in developing countries, and it was regarded as essential to have a strict overall corporate policy of making no political contributions.[36]

Orr and Van den Hoven became actively involved with Unilever's external image. They were prepared to engage with critics of Unilever, and capitalism more generally, and anxious to make the case for the beneficial effects of multinational corporations. In 1979, when nineteen members of the Dutch Upper House visited the Rotterdam head office—apparently the first time such a delegation had visited a company—Van den Hoven led a group of Unilever managers making short talks and answering questions.[37] The chairmen were also active at the European level. Van den Hoven was a member of the small Groupe des Présidents—comprising a number of the chief executives of the largest EU-based multinationals—which met regularly as an 'informal forum' to exchange views and formulate common policy positions.[38]

In the face of external criticism, Unilever felt that it needed to define more clearly its 'corporate identity'. Over the years the Board, the Special Committee, and others had made pronouncements on issues, but they were neither assembled in one place nor related to one another. During 1975 the Information Division was asked to make a compendium of corporate policies designed 'to provide managers with factual information to help build confidence in the Company and to enable them to talk authoritatively about Unilever both within and outside the business'.[39] It took until 1978 before a final draft was agreed.

The Compendium began with a statement of Corporate Principles built around the theme of mutual responsibility. Unilever acknowledged its obligation to act 'as good employers and citizens of the countries where we operate, respecting international and local laws, regulations and customs'. This was combined with a recognition that Unilever had 'a role to play in promoting economic growth as well as in contributing to the solution of the social problems that arise from a changing environment'. In respect of relations to governments, it was asserted that 'Unilever respects the national sovereignty of each country in which it operates', and that its policy was 'to co-operate with the Government of the day in each country'. Irregular payments to politicians or officials were never permissible, while transfer pricing was to be based on market prices.

Many of the other principles in the Compendium closely followed the OECD voluntary code. Unilever accepted the right of collective bargaining, had a positive attitude towards making consultation more effective, and was not opposed in principle to employee representation at supervisory board level, though it 'would not voluntarily seek such arrangements'. On consumer protection, it was Unilever policy to take 'great care to ensure that its products are of the highest quality and have undergone rigorous evaluation in relation to health and safety'. Unilever was committed to making sure that all its 'existing activities are environmentally acceptable, and that new or modified manufacturing processes are only introduced after evaluating their environmental effects and ensuring that these are of an acceptable level'.[40]

A curious feature of the Compendium was that, although it confirmed Unilever's status as a firm committed to acting with the highest ethical principles, the contents was not shared with Unilever's staff, let alone made public. 'Although there was nothing actually secret in the compendium,' the Special Committee decided, 'its circulation should be pretty well restricted.'[41] The fifty-seven numbered copies of the Compendium were distributed to Unilever directors, national managers in Europe, the Overseas Committee, and the Board of UAC.[42] Various elements of the Compendium were filtered into various publications, including the chairmen's speeches at the Annual General Meetings, but the restricted way the Compendium was handled showed that it was primarily conceived as a defensive document—to inform senior managers so that they could respond to hostile criticism—rather than a positive assertion of corporate image and values which could motivate staff.

There remained a tension between a desire to assert a positive corporate image, and an appreciation of the benefits of retaining a low profile. Unilever never became the target of a major international campaign of criticism similar to that faced by Nestlé, whose sales of powdered milk products led to it being blamed for contributing to infant malnutrition in poor countries by undermining attempts to encourage breast feeding. As the Special Committee noted in 1983, 'the fact that we were seen as dull and unexciting could be a considerable advantage to us'.[43] The benefits of 'dullness' were seen in 1987 when a whole issue of the radical magazine *New Internationalist* was devoted to an attack on 'Unilever's Sticky Fingers'. The issue had to begin by explaining what Unilever did. 'From our cradles to our graves Unilever sells to most of us', it was observed, 'yet it is virtually invisible.' The editor admitted that 'the things about Unilever that make me passionately angry leave other people in this office colder than a Unilever frozen fish finger'.[44] There was a dull worthiness about Unilever which made it a hopeless subject for crusading journalism.

By the early 1980s the debates about the alleged failings and dangers of multinationals were waning worldwide. Multinationals began to be perceived not as menaces, but much-needed providers of jobs, exports, and technologies.[45] Criticism of large multinationals shifted from developing countries and international bodies to consumer, environmental, and political groups in rich countries, but it would take another twenty years before 'anti-globalization' protesters would become visible forces on the world political stage. In the new climate of opinion, Unilever again felt more comfortable about its traditional low profile. The Marlow meeting in 1984 resolved 'to lower the Concern profile and de-focus outside attacks upon Unilever'.[46] In 1986 the Compendium was discontinued on the grounds that it had become out of date.[47]

The most difficult issue to maintain a low profile on was South Africa. By 1986 this was regarded as 'the only really important issue at present' in Unilever's external relations.[48] Unilever's position became more exposed as leading US multinationals and some European companies divested in response in particular to pressures from US investors. Among Unilever's competitors, CPC sold both its company and the rights to its brands, while Henkel sold its business to Colgate in 1985 after Unilever declined it.[49] Unilever found itself under considerable pressure from a number of directions, including the Dutch churches, and from its own staff. From at least the late 1970s Swedish and Finnish employees in Unilever factories were holding sympathy strikes to protest against Unilever's refusal to recognize the Black trade union, the Sweet, Food and Allied Workers' Union.[50] There were also instances of managers in Rotterdam refusing to supply information to the South African affiliates on 'political grounds'.[51]

Unilever never wavered in its determination to stay in South Africa. Senior managers believed that the company's actions had no chance of influencing the South African government, and that if it divested it would simply 'cause widespread unemployment and hardship amongst the very people that the policy is designed to help'.[52] This was the same line that the company took with external critics of its policy.[53] It was noted that Unilever abided by the EEC 'Code of Conduct for Companies with Interests in South Africa', and reported annually to the British and Dutch governments as required by that Code. However, silence remained the preferred corporate option.[54]

In 1990 Unilever's corporate image remained low profile, and this was generally what was desired. The low profile—along with high standards of corporate conduct—enabled Unilever to pass through an era of widespread criticism of multinational firms with no major blemish on its corporate reputation. There was much to be said in favour of such a large company, whose brands formed the staples of many people's daily lives, maintaining a modest corporate image. It was less clear that the accompanying image of dullness was entirely beneficial, for it carried implications for the kind of person who might seek a career within it, and for investors.

Unilever and the European Union

Unilever was an enthusiast for European economic integration. Rijkens had played a major role in the early Bilderberg conferences, chaired by Prince Bernhard of the Netherlands, which included leading European and American business leaders and policy-makers, which discussed the early stages of integration. Through their work in the European Movement, he and the like-minded Kuin laid the basis of a network of personal contacts that proved valuable as Unilever sought to make its voice heard in the making of Europe-wide policies. In 1963 Cole described Unilever as a 'child of Europe . . . We were in Europe before we started the Common Market. . . . We hardly notice the Channel.'[55]

Initially the Common Market, comprising Belgium, France, Germany, Italy, Luxembourg, and the Netherlands, was primarily a customs union, albeit one with political and legal institutions which indicated the long-term intent to move towards ever more extensive economic, monetary, and ultimately political union. The reduction of barriers to trade and capital flows was potentially advantageous to a firm such as Unilever with its Europe-wide operations, even though the organizational and cultural legacy of strong national-based companies suggested that it might take a considerable effort to realize that potential. Unilever was an enthusiast for the successive drives to deepen and extend the European Union. Although Unilever did not finance political parties, it was prepared to contribute towards pro-entry campaigns in countries seeking entry to the Union.

However as the Common Market widened (Denmark, Britain, and the Republic of Ireland joined in 1973, Greece in 1981, Spain and Portugal in 1986, and Sweden, Finland, and Austria in 1995) and deepened (as indicated by successive changes of name from the Common Market to European Economic Community to European Union), so its political and legal institutions exercised an ever greater influence on Unilever's business. European policies were shaped by many influences, of which the concerns of large firms such as Unilever were just one. Europe functioned through constant consultation, discussion, and compromise between interest groups. In this respect, influencing decision-making was similar to lobbying in Washington, DC, but the situation was more complicated because of the different layers of decision-making and jurisdiction. The influence of national governments remained very strong. At the European level, while the European Commission took the initiative in proposing and designing policies, the European Parliament had a growing influence on policy, especially after the introduction of direct elections in 1979. The decision-making process provided the business community with many ways of making its voice heard in Brussels, but the process of translating that voice into policies was complicated and unpredictable.

Unilever's 'voice' on European policy-making was exercised at multiple levels. Unilever possessed influential contacts with national governments. In the Netherlands, it was among the small group of large firms which shaped the collective views of the business community, and transmitted those views to the government. It was one of the four companies in an organization known as ABUP—meaning Akzo, Bataafse Olie Maatschappij (i.e. Shell), Unilever, and Philips—established before the Second World War, in which the largest Dutch companies shared information, agreed policy positions, and organized meetings between managers. ABUP committees agreed the policies of Dutch business towards European legislation, and transmitted those views to the Dutch government.[56] In the post-war Dutch 'polder model', public policy was made after long consultations between civil servants, business, trade unions, and others. At monthly meetings of the heads of the main industrial associations, civil servants gave briefings about policy developments, including at the European level, while Dutch officials would seek industry briefings before presenting cases in Brussels. In the Dutch system, no one element could dominate the making of public policy, but Unilever's voice was influential.

In Britain, Unilever's voice was less pre-eminent. Britain did not have a Dutch-style consensus decision-making process, and Unilever's relations with the government were openly critical at times, especially during Labour governments. During the Labour government of 1964–70 Unilever was subjected to two Monopolies Commission investigations—one on the Allied Breweries merger and the other on dominant market positions in household detergents.[57] During the 1974–79 Labour government the frozen foodstuffs business was investigated. While Birds Eye was cleared of making 'excessive' profits, it was obliged to give undertakings—only rescinded in 2000—not to grant discounts to retailers for reserving space in freezer cabinets for frozen foodstuffs.[58] Finally in 1979 the Monopolies Commission investigated the British ice cream market, though in this instance Unilever was permitted to maintain the practice of 'cabinet exclusivity'.[59]

At the European level, Unilever's preference in influencing policy was to lobby indirectly, through influence on national governments, and through associations, third parties, and networking. While the major US multinationals such as Procter & Gamble established representative offices in Brussels, Unilever did not take this step until the 1990s. Nevertheless European matters were seen as of considerable significance. Beginning in 1974, Unilever's chairmen made periodic visits to Brussels to meet European Commissioners.[60] Unilever was the only company during the 1970s and early 1980s which had such regular meetings with the Commission.[61] Former European officials and Commissioners were also appointed as Advisory Directors, including in 1985 F.-X. Ortoli, President of the European Commission 1973–6 and Vice-President for Economic and Monetary Affairs 1977–84.

Unilever also sought to have its voice heard in the European Parliament. This involved developing contacts with many different political groups, as Unilever's interests did not coincide with any single political party. In agricultural issues, such as protection for farmers and taxes on oils and fats, Unilever generally found itself in agreement with the view of the Socialists and the British Conservatives, rather than Christian Democrats, who were more sympathetic to European farmers. However, on issues such as social affairs and company law, Unilever's views were closer to those of Europe's centre right political parties. Unilever took the European Parliament seriously, and sought to have its views known. In 1980 Unilever was the only company to accept the Parliament's invitation to appear at a hearing on Europe's responsibilities to fight hunger.[62]

Dynamics and Routines

Unilever, like most European-based companies, preferred to operate through trade associations, both product and industry. The European Commission sought to deal with Community-wide associations only, and from the late 1950s there was a proliferation of European federations of professional associations which included IMACE (margarine), EUROGLACE (ice cream), FEDIOL (oil crushers and refiners), and FEFAC (animal feedstuffs). These European associations were often part of international associations. IMACE, for example, was closely linked to the International Federation of Margarine Associations (IFMA), whose membership included non-EU European countries. Similarly there was a confederation of European employers' associations (UNICE). All these organizations were engaged in a constant dialogue with the European Commission as legislation and policies were formulated and promulgated. Unilever held a strong position in many of these European associations. Fig. 12.1 illustrates the various routes by which Unilever could make its voice heard, using the starting point of the Netherlands and the margarine industry.

Van den Bergh Foods, the Dutch edible fats company, belonged to—and was the most important component of—the Dutch association of margarine manufacturers, BNMF. This in turn belonged to IMACE, in which Unilever's other European edible fats companies were also represented through their own national associations. Meanwhile Unilever NV belonged both to the Dutch food and drink industry association (VAI) and to the Dutch employers' federations (VNO/NCW). Unilever

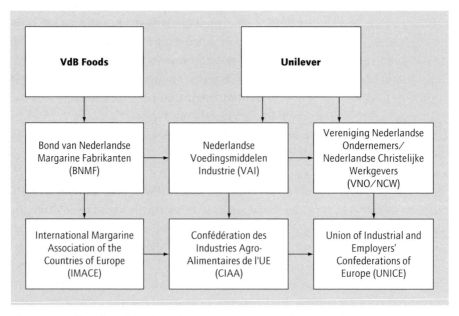

Fig. 12.1 Unilever's position in national and European trade associations.

53 Two young girls walking over the Dell Bridge with the Port Sunlight factory in the background, 1962.

in Britain (and everywhere else) belonged to their equivalents in the form of the Food and Drink Federation and the Confederation of British Industry. VAI and VNO/NCW were members of their corresponding European associations, the confederation of European food and drink industries (CIAA) and UNICE. Vertical associations, such as IMACE, were not formal members of CIAA, but they maintained close working relations.

Unilever was prominent in both the vertical and horizontal European associations. UNICE established many committees on which Unilever directors and managers were often found. In the industry associations, Unilever's influence varied according to the industry in question. In margarine, Unilever's voice was strong. Unilever managers regularly held the presidency of IMACE, while most company chairmen played leading roles in their local associations. In the European detergents association, the AIS, the voice of P&G was at least as influential. Consequently Unilever's concern had to be both to influence the association towards its views, and to counter the influence of Procter.[63]

The most important long-term European policy issue for Unilever concerned the import and taxation of oils and fats. Unilever's position as Europe's largest manufacturer of oils and fats, and the largest consumer of vegetable oils, gave it a vital interest in the EU's trade policy and the Common Agricultural Policy (CAP). The CAP was based on the system of common prices, set annually at a level which aimed to ensure farmers a fair income, while achieving market equilibrium.[64] For milk and dairy products, a 'target price' was fixed annually. This target price reflected a high consumer price for butter which was upheld by unlimited intervention buying. Imports of dairy products were subject to variable levies, whilst exports to beyond the EU were heavily subsidized.

Oils and fats regulation was an exception to this regime. In contrast to dairy products, Europe's oils and fats requirements were largely covered by imports because—with the exception of olive oil—Europe had a low self-sufficiency in oil-bearing produce. As a result, the EU had zero duties on seeds, cakes, and crude marine oils, and low duties on crude vegetable oils. Europe's growers of rapeseed, sunflower seed and also olives were supported not through high consumer prices, but through a system of deficiency payments. This policy regime was important for Unilever, as it meant that its raw materials entered the EU at world market prices, permitting a relatively low consumer price for margarine, and a favourable price relationship between it and butter.

Unilever never felt confident that this liberal policy regime towards oils and fats would be retained. There were provisions in European regulations to protect European producers of oilseeds against exceptional imports in the event of 'market disruption', when the products covered by the regulation might be subject to 'compensatory levies'. There was also a latent danger of a tax on margarine and vegetable fats. In 1964 when the Council of Ministers initially agreed on the principles governing the oils and fats regulation, they adopted a resolution stipulating that deficiency payments on EU-grown oilseeds were to be financed from a tax on margarine, but this was never implemented. In 1976 another formal proposal on such a tax was made, justified by the need to promote butter fat consumption. Unilever consistently sought to influence debates on European oils and fats legislation, through national associations, and within IMACE and UNICE, which were in constant dialogue with the Commission and the European Parliament about oils and fats legislation.

Unilever's concerns over the direction of European trade and agricultural policy grew over time. CAP subsidies to dairy farmers resulted in growing surpluses of butter—the so-called 'butter mountain'—which posed a potential threat to margarine sales. In 1978 EU launched a 'Christmas Butter' scheme whereby a certain amount of butter began to be sold at discounted prices at Christmas time. Unilever's view was that the EU's subsidy of butter prices was a waste of public money, and that it was preferable to secure a reform of CAP which would lower consumer prices. However, this position was somewhat clouded by the fact that Unilever had a stake in the existing system, because a reform could be expected to lower the price of butter. Moreover it was the CAP regime which also permitted imports of vegetable oils and fats.[65] Nor did Unilever desire any public confrontation with European farmers.[66] Meanwhile the prospect of the accession of the olive oil producing countries of Greece, Portugal, and Spain into the EU raised the new danger of taxes and levies on vegetable oils and proteins.

During the 1980s the subject came up on several occasions. In 1983 the European Commission announced a formal proposal to introduce a tax on the consumption of oils and fats other than butter, which was seen as a convenient means to solve budgetary problems. Unilever's reaction was fast, drawing on its worldwide presence to facilitate lobbying against the proposal, especially by large oil exporting countries such as Malaysia and the Ivory Coast.[67]

While the 1983 proposal was not activated, by 1985 a new challenge had arisen as the European Commission began to propagate the concept of 'rebalancing'. This involved the institution of tariffs and levies on imports of oilseeds and cereal substitutes while reducing import levies on cereals. The aim was to reduce liberal loopholes in the CAP regime, and to increase the price level of imported oilseeds, enabling a lowering of subsidies for EU-grown oilseeds and the burden on the EU budget, whilst allowing for production to increase further. This proposal threatened to increase prices to Unilever, but the greater risk was that it might lead the EU to change the tariff structure for oils and fats completely, and so undermine Unilever's access to raw material markets outside Europe.[68] Unilever ended the decade as it began it, on alert that its cost structure could be damaged by a significant change in European legislation.

There were a number of other areas of European legislation which had, or threatened to have, a major influence on Unilever's business. Among these, the harmonization of foods legislation was important. After the formation of the EU, the slow process began of eliminating obstacles to free trade in food by 'harmonizing' the legislation of member states. There were two types of harmonization. Horizontal directives affected all food products and included subjects such as labelling, unit prices, and various classes of additives. Vertical directives dealt with a particular commodity, and only applied to that product. Unilever established a Rotterdam Harmonisation Committee, composed of lawyers, researchers, and marketing people, to co-ordinate the company's activities on the Continent during the 1960s towards harmonization legislation, and to establish common Unilever positions. Although the preference was for voluntary systems of control, Unilever recognized the growing influence of the EU's drive towards harmonization as a fact of life, and sought ways to influence policy.[69] The choices for the company were not always clear-cut, however, for although it theoretically had much to gain from facilitating cross-border trade, the same development could also open up its markets to new competitors.

The impact of EU competition policy was not felt for some time, although the Treaty of Rome contained the legal basis for that policy. Article 85 condemned restrictive agreements unless exempted, while Article 86 condemned the abuse of a dominant position. By the mid-1960s Unilever was already aware that it might run into difficulties because of its size and 'dominant position', especially in margarine and detergents, where it had around 60 and 40 per cent respectively of the EU market. There was also a potential danger that acquisitions and mergers might begin to be affected by European competition law. Indeed from the early 1970s it was recognized that when a merger or acquisition led to a strengthening of an existing dominant position, then the European Commission could invoke its powers under Article 86 and even prevent a merger, though by the end of the 1980s it still had not begun to intervene to prevent mergers that created dominant positions.[70]

It was at that time that there was the first sign that Unilever would run into problems with European competition authorities with its ice cream business. The problem lay with the widespread industry use of 'exclusivity' contracts, both for 'outlets' and for 'cabinet freezers'. By 1988 Unilever had come to the view that although cabinet exclusivity was not believed to be objectionable under EU rules, shop exclusivity was 'very likely not allowed', and it began to redesign contracts to comply with what was believed to be the law.[71] However, the issue was made more pressing by the actions of Mars, which argued that its entry into the European ice cream market was hindered by exclusivity arrangements. During 1989 Mars complained to Unilever that Wall's salesmen had threatened to cease supplying shops in Britain if they stocked Mars ice cream, and that this amounted 'to an abuse of Wall's dominant position contrary to Article 86'.[72] Two years later Mars made a formal complaint to the European Commission about outlet exclusivity contracts.[73]

A final area of European legislation which concerned Unilever involved employee rights. In 1980 Unilever was alarmed to hear of a new directive originating from the Social Affairs Commissioner, Henk Vredeling, which sought to impose statutory obligations of communication and information disclosure on companies with more than 1,000 employees in the EU. The most worrying proposals were that employee representatives of each individual subsidiary inside the EU would have to be provided with quarterly information on many topics regarding all other subsidiaries individually, including outside the EU, and that, secondly, if consultation between management and employee representatives of a subsidiary did not produce an agreement, the employees could consult directly with the parent company. This was completely contrary to Unilever's practice of decentralized collective bargaining.[74]

As usual, Unilever sought to exercise influence against these proposals through UNICE. Unilever also contacted the OECD to alert them about the proposals, whilst national managers in France, Germany, and elsewhere were instructed to brief national governments.[75] As the Vredeling proposals proceeded through the

European Commission and Parliament, Unilever became increasingly concerned, placing growing hopes that the Conservative government in Britain would veto the proposals ultimately.[76] Lobbying had some effect. By the end of 1982 significant amendments had been made to the original proposal by the European Parliament.[77] By 1985 Unilever concluded that it would be a 'very long time' before any actual legislation ever appeared from it.[78]

However, the issue of European legislation to support worker participation would not go away. During the late 1980s there was a new momentum for a social dimension to the creation of a single market in 1992. There was a renewed prospect that in time consultation, information, and co-determination would be taken out of the national context and placed on a European level. In 1987 the European Parliament passed a resolution on the rights of workers in multinational companies with a huge majority, calling for directives on collective bargaining at parent company level. The European Commission began also to draft directives obliging parent firms to consult with employees.[79]

The European Union became a progressively more important influence on Unilever from the 1960s. Unilever opted to make its voice known largely through participation in trade associations, though it also engaged directly at times in discussions with European politicians and civil servants. It was an accomplished and well-networked lobbyist, though it was never able—or even wished—to dictate policy on any matter.

Greening Unilever

Before the 1960s Unilever, in common with companies and governments worldwide, did not conceptualize the 'environment' as an issue for corporate strategy. This did not mean that it operated with total disregard for environmental matters. Lever's building of the Port Sunlight Village was based on a desire to create a clean and hygienic environment for his workers. Unilever companies had a vested interest in avoiding selling products which might damage the health of their customers. However, the impact on the natural environment of factory production or the raw materials used was largely not considered by mainstream opinion during the post-war decades. In Europe and the United States some environmental degradation was often regarded as the price of economic progress, an attitude which was to persist for longer still in many emerging markets.

From the 1960s Unilever became aware of growing concerns about the environment, and more especially about the impact on it of big business. An early cause of public concern was the impact of food additives and ingredients which came into contact with the skin. Unilever had always sought to have the best possible standards of food safety and hygiene, and during the 1950s there was considerable spending on microbiological food safety research, culminating in the opening of a state of the art building for that research at Colworth in 1959. Yet at the beginning of the 1960s Unilever faced a major crisis in the Netherlands when a new emulsifying agent used in its Planta margarine appeared to give large numbers of the Dutch population an unpleasant skin rash. Unilever acted swiftly to withdraw the brand—which never reappeared in the Netherlands—and although no liability was admitted, the company paid £125,000 (or £1.25 million in 1990 prices) to some 8,000 sufferers. A court case against Unilever was eventually dismissed after five years.[80]

In the wake of the Planta affair, Unilever established in 1960 a formal 'clearance' procedure to be followed for all new additives to human foods and for new products in detergents and personal products. Companies were requested, whenever they were contemplating the introduction of new raw materials or ingredients about which there was 'the slightest doubt' as to their safety, to work in close collaboration with the Director of Research.[81] The clearance procedures were restated several times over the following years although, as so often in Unilever, local practice diverged considerably from central rules. A study in 1976 established that only a few companies followed the procedures completely, a few more used them 'irregularly', and 'the rest was not following it at all'.[82] By then the whole issue of food additives, and the processed food industry in general, had become controversial thanks to consumer activists such as Ralph Nader in the United States.

The introduction of new raw materials or ingredients affected not only consumer welfare but also that of employees. During the early 1960s Unilever began introducing enzymes—which attacked protein stains such as blood and egg—into detergents products for the first time. At Port Sunlight there was a plant which took neat enzymes from suppliers, and then granulated them into particles which could be added to powder. By 1968 it became obvious that some workers were starting to develop asthma due to allergy to enzymes. The problem was compounded when more than one enzyme was used in a product. This resulted in the introduction of stringent rules and equipment for handling enzymes which appeared to eliminate the problem.[83] Extensive testing revealed no dermatological effects.[84]

A second area of public concern was packaging. The packaging revolution from the 1950s, which saw the use of plastics, aluminium foils, and aerosols, was crucial to the fast-moving consumer goods industry. 'No packaging, no brands', the chairmen had told Unilever's shareholders in 1965. 'No brands, no business.' It was estimated that Unilever was spending £100 million annually on packaging materials.[85] Yet by then concerns about the environmental consequences of packaging had surfaced, initially in the United States, and a few years later in certain countries in Europe, especially Scandinavia and Germany. Within a few years environmental pressure groups such as Friends of the Earth were making the case throughout Europe for the recycling of waste.

By 1970 Unilever had formulated 'guidelines' concerning the environmental impact of packaging. Companies were urged to avoid 'overpackaging' and to co-ordinate with the municipal authorities responsible for waste collection. There was also a plea not to unilaterally introduce on environmental grounds packaging changes which might affect other Unilever companies.[86] However, as responsibility for packaging rested with the operating companies, it proved hard to implement a Unilever-wide policy.[87]

A third area of environmental concern was factory effluent. In the 1960s Unilever factories followed the general practice of disposing of effluents without treatment into the sewage systems, though the Engineering Division had an Effluent Section which monitored pollution from the liquid, solid, and gaseous effluent from Unilever's factories. By 1970 it was evident that this situation could not prevail.[88]

During the 1970s environmental matters rose up both the international political agenda and Unilever's corporate priorities.[89] Growing concern about the environment culminated in a United Nations Conference on the Human Environment in Stockholm in June 1972. Unilever provided facilities for the International Chamber of Commerce staff preparing for that meeting. In 1971 the Research Division appointed an Environmental Safety Officer as first contact for 'all problems of additives, enzymes, effects on skin, etc'.[90] He was supported by the multidisciplinary Environmental Safety Division at Colworth which by 1974 had a scientific staff of forty and a supporting staff of 170. Different aspects of Unilever's environmental policy were, therefore, split between the Research and Engineering Divisions. The growing corporate concern was indicated by the fact that in 1972 the Report and Accounts included a special section on 'Conservation of the Environment'. The company was publicly committed to best practice.[91]

Within Unilever the lead on environmental matters was taken by the Engineering Division Director, then Karel Veldhuis. During 1972 he gave a speech in Ohio in which he noted that 'as a world-wide organisation Unilever considers it important to adopt a responsible attitude to environmental problems'. Veldhuis estimated that Unilever would spend around $125 million on pollution abatement from effluents over the following ten to fifteen years, and far more on making sure that Unilever's products were 'absolutely safe to man and the environment', especially by the use of high-quality raw materials. He was concerned to stress the advantages of being a multinational company in this regard, for it could facilitate 'the spread of new environmental technology from one country to another'.[92] Veldhuis returned to Europe from his visit to the United States convinced that the environment was a big issue for the future which must be addressed.[93]

Dynamics and Routines

However, both the decentralized structure of Unilever, and its highly diversified nature, handicapped the development of a strong corporate-wide environmental strategy. Characteristically, Unilever sought to influence the nature of the debate within individual countries by engaging in dialogues with governments, consumer groups, and trade associations, working towards a 'position of influence'.[94] The corporate preference at this time, seen in discussions in the early 1970s concerning the merits of mandatory date marking of prepared perishable and semi-perishable foods, was for voluntary agreements rather than government legislation.[95]

A problem for Unilever in formulating an environmental policy was that, although there was a considerable amount of research on various environmental risks and threats, much also remained unknown. The urgency with which environmental concerns were addressed varied widely between different countries and different companies. Environmental concerns were much greater in Germany, the Netherlands, Switzerland, and Scandinavia than in southern Europe or Britain. By the early 1970s the German companies were already developing a central information service on packaging and investigations on the environmental impact of different packaging.[96] The 4P Group in Germany was also early in studying the issue of degradable plastics in its Hamburg research facilities.[97] However, almost everywhere during the mid-1970s the momentum which had built up within Unilever on environmental issues began to wane, in part because the attention of governments and public opinion were diverted by the oil crises and subsequent recessions.

The slowing of concern for environmental matters was seen in the case of detergents. This was an industry which attracted considerable adverse attention from environmentalists. While soap was a natural raw material which, when discharged back into nature, was rapidly biodegraded, this was not the case of detergents, and as their usage expanded, so environmental problems emerged, which the extensive advertising used by detergents manufacturers served to draw attention to. During the 1950s it became apparent that there was a problem with the 'surfactant' (or surface-active agent) used in synthetic detergents, which was tetrapropylene benzene sulphonate. There were growing reports of mountains of foam appearing in sewage treatment plants and some rivers. It appeared to be caused by this 'hard surfactant', which was only poorly biodegradable. In 1967 the European detergents industry concluded a voluntary agreement not to use such hard surfactants, which were replaced by biodegradable linear alkyl benzene sulphonate. This proved a mere prelude to decades of controversy.

The next major environmental issue arose in the 1970s and concerned the phosphate builder used in synthetic detergents, which was blamed for the eutrophication of lakes. This referred to the ageing process that gradually converted a lake to dry land, but the use of phosphates appeared to accelerate the process. In both the United States and some European countries public and political support grew behind the campaigns to 'save the lakes', although in Britain eutrophication was seen as less of a problem, as the majority of effluent discharges were into short, fast-flowing rivers rather than lakes. In the United States phosphates were banned by some states from the early 1970s. The detergents manufacturers had been obliged to launch zero-phosphate products. Lever Brothers used sodium carbonate in those states where phosphates were banned, while stating publicly that it was a less effective cleaning agent.

In Europe, the major detergents companies argued that they were not the only agencies responsible for pollution of the lakes and rivers, pointing to the pesticides used by farmers and ordinary domestic waste as major culprits. They were reluctant to put significant advertising support behind low-phosphate products without implicitly damaging the reputation of their other brands, especially as they believed the solution lay elsewhere. The preferred solution, certainly so far as Unilever was concerned, was for an improved sewage treatment system, which would prevent phosphates from reaching the affected waterways.

While the scientific evidence on the relative environmental impact of phosphates and other builders remained ambiguous, Unilever was slow to appreciate the mounting public concern on the issue. During the 1970s research into developing zero-phosphate powders was given a low priority.[98] Early attempts to develop a non-phosphate builder focused mainly on Nitrolotriacetic Acid (NTA) and zeolites. Procter & Gamble and Henkel took out patents on zeolites during the 1970s. Blocked by competitor patents from conducting any meaningful research on zero phosphates without incurring considerable extra costs,[99] Unilever concentrated most of its research on developing pyro- and orthophosphates. By using these compounds, low-phosphate formulations could be produced which achieved a level of performance regarded as 'very acceptable for many brands', and offered 'major cost savings'.[100] Even after Unilever had purchased NTA and zeolites patents in the late 1970s, it continued to focus on orthophosphates, partly because much of its other research was not compatible with non-phosphate builders. TAED—which lay at the heart of Unilever's research effort—could not be mixed with NTA.

It was not until the early 1980s that there was a recognition both that zero-phosphate legislation was a real possibility and that Unilever could not at that time make such a product. Unilever started its first zero-phosphate development programme in the Netherlands and Switzerland, though with the hope 'still to avoid zero phosphate'. In Switzerland, 'Project Green' developed a zeolite/NTA product which was launched in 1986, while a zeolite product was ready in Germany by about the same time, though even then Unilever remained attached to phosphates.[101]

During the 1980s environmental concerns grew. There were a number of reasons for this, including the discovery of the hole in the ozone layer and the increasing acceptance of the 'Greenhouse Effect' as a credible theory. Both consumer and retailer buying power began to be exercised across a range of 'green issues'. Specialist ethical retailers developed. From the mid-1980s one of the biggest British supermarkets, Sainsbury's, pursued a large-scale environmental programme, including own-brand phosphate-free detergents and CFC-free aerosols, as well as a highly successful scheme offering refunds for carrier bags returned after use.[102] There were new pressures on manufacturers from the European Commission. While the Environmental Protection Agency in the United States would, if an industry convinced it of the safety of a chemical, then help to defend it, in Europe the Commission and many governments often sided with green NGOs.[103]

Unilever regarded itself as committed to the best environmental practices, but there were critics no longer prepared to take Unilever's credentials on trust. Orr's last Annual General Meeting in London in 1982 had to be briefly suspended after interruptions from animal rights protesters.[104] Two years later the radical Animal Liberation Front placed bottles of Sunsilk contaminated with bleach in several retail stores in Britain.[105] This emotive issue became another one on which Unilever preferred to maintain a low profile, but responded to external pressures.[106] In 1989 Personal Products Co-ordination abandoned animal testing for colour cosmetics, and adopted a firm policy of reducing animal testing for product safety purposes 'to an absolute minimum' with the objective to eliminate it.[107]

The public face of Unilever in environmental matters continued to be the operating companies. When there was a crisis—and all foods and consumer goods manufacturers were at one time or another afflicted by one—Unilever as such sought to maintain a low profile. This happened again when there was a new scare in the Netherlands in 1980, when two women in the south-eastern town of Venray died from eating Iglo 'nasi goreng'. This was contaminated with nitrate, which it turned out had leaked from the cooling systems in one of the company's delivery vans. Unilever supported its affiliate in this major incident—which saw a large amount of stock destroyed and the company's turnover fall sharply—but kept a low profile itself.[108]

Unilever often appeared reactive rather than proactive on environmental issues during the 1980s. In Personal Products, which made extensive use of elaborate packaging to sell its brands, Unilever companies tended to pass from one crisis to another as they faced unexpected criticism of their products on environmental grounds. The initial response was often one of shock because Unilever managers always believed their company was doing right.[109] Detergents Co-ordination declared itself 'taken by surprise' at the criticism of Unilever products in 1990. How, it asked rhetorically, 'can anyone doubt our purity in ethical terms'?[110]

The problem was in part Unilever's traditional low profile. Its competitors were more assertive in projecting their green credentials. Henkel launched 'green' non-phosphate brands, and developed its corporate image of being 'environmentally friendly' and selling products which were 'natural' and 'renewable'. P & G also increasingly addressed the environmental concerns of consumers in advertising for products such as Ariel Ultra and Pampers, irritating Unilever who noted that 'their technology is hardly different from ours and it is certainly not superior in any scientific sense'.[111] Most large multinationals adopted formal written environmental policies. A majority claimed, like Unilever, that they went 'beyond compliance' with local laws.[112] Unilever gave little appearance of being ahead of the game. It took isolated initiatives on carton packaging for liquids in environmentally conscious countries, including Germany and the Netherlands, but P & G was more visible with its strategies of seeking to reduce packaging waste streams through light weighting of bottles, refills, and predilutables.[113] It was only at the end of the decade that Detergents Co-ordination finally became convinced that 'green issues' needed a higher priority.[114] The replacement of phosphates with zeolites was begun on a larger scale, and over the following years a builder system based on zeolite and polycarboxylic acid became predominant in many European markets, even if the scientific debate continued over whether phosphate or zeolite detergent builders had a lesser environment impact.

Unilever's decentralized organization continued to handicap the development of a corporate-wide environmental policy. In Europe, operating companies and Co-ordinations remained in the lead, despite an effort to formalize standards at the level of Unilever as a whole, notably with the formation of the Safety, Health, and the Environment Advisory Committee (SHEACO) in 1980 to 'promote Corporate policies' to improve health and safety 'where these relate to the workplace, the environment or the home'.[115] Nevertheless, each Co-ordination had its own links with Brussels through trade associations, and some operating companies also had direct links with Brussels.[116] By 1988 both Detergents and Personal Products Co-ordinations had environmental committees. The foods side of the business was rather later in formulating its environmental policies, but during 1989 Edible Fats Co-ordination began to consider a wide-ranging programme covering raw materials and ingredients, refining, packaging, and factory pollutants.[117] The decentralized organization worked most effectively on detailed issues such as product ingredients. It seemed less effective for policy formation, and lobbying, on environmental issues which spanned different Co-ordinations, including packaging, trace contaminants, and animal testing. Environmental pressure groups were not organized on the same basis as Unilever, and were not prepared to restrict their attention to one operating company or country. 'A lapse in a remote part of the world', it was noted in 1990, 'can be publicised in major market areas.'[118]

Unilever's presence in emerging markets did indeed raise many issues concerning the environment. The company was involved in such sensitive areas as plantation agriculture and tropical forests. In the former, Unilever was well respected for high standards in plantation management. From the early 1970s all development was restricted to land which had already been degraded by inefficient agriculture. In Ghana and Thailand Unilever's plantations were established in areas of secondary scrub. In Colombia, the palm oil plantation developed in the Llanos from 1981 was on grassland which had been severely degraded by cattle grazing, thus reversing the trend seen in much of the Amazon basin.

Unilever faced more potential embarrassment on the issue of logging and tropical rainforests, as concerns about global warming and the destruction of the rainforests led to a renewed bout of criticism of large multinational firms.[119] UAC was heavily involved in tropical timber in both Nigeria and the Solomon Islands. In Nigeria, African Timber and Plywood formed part of the biggest tropical timber complex in Nigeria, supporting a number of interrelated processing factories in Sapele in the Niger Delta. From the 1960s there was a growing problem of depletion of Nigerian natural forest resources caused by population growth—all the timber was used locally. The responsibility for replanting lay with the forest authorities rather than UAC, although the company did try to make more intensive use of forests for timber by using some previously uncommercial species, and also investing in processes like particleboard which utilize pieces of wood which would otherwise have been waste. In the Solomon Islands, Levers Pacific Timber had started in 1963, and had pioneered the marketing of Solomon timbers, making them the country's largest export earner by 1980. UAC had sought over time to take almost all its timber from plantations rather than the natural forest.[120]

Unilever had no wish to acquire a reputation for destroying the tropical rainforest. Its most plausible defence was that the responsibility for environmental malpractice lay with the local forestry authorities, but this could not be said publicly. UAC was left maintaining that it would co-operate in any way it could if governments asked it to do more than its traditional role of 'logging and marketing'.[121] There was a sense of corporate relief when UAC divested from Solomons timber in 1987.[122]

Unilever was also in a potentially exposed position regarding the environmental standards of its factories in emerging markets. Unilever's stance was that it followed the environmental standards set by each national government, emphasizing the threat to competitiveness if it introduced more costly, if environmentally friendly, technologies.[123] That position was some way from the optimistic assertion by Veldhuis in 1972 that multinationals could transfer best practice environmental practices to developing countries. It also became more difficult to sustain during the first half of the 1980s, especially after major incidents such as the Bhopal disaster in 1984, when gas leaked from a Union Carbide plant and killed 2,000 and injured 200,000 Indians. Governments, especially in Latin America and the Far East, became increasingly concerned about pollution, in part arising from the insistence of aid agencies on environmental audits of the major projects they financed. By 1990 Unilever was coming to the conclusion that its environmental policies worldwide had to be best practice, and if necessary tighter than local regulations required.

Unilever had identified the environment as an important issue as early as the 1960s. It did not prove especially adept at publicizing its achievements, however, and in some areas its policies were not at the forefront. It was also difficult to develop and enforce an environmental policy in such a decentralized and large concern. It was not always easy to see that best practice was followed everywhere. Moreover, Unilever faced the problem of operating in multiple legal jurisdictions and levels of economic development. If the environmental standards mandatory in a Scandinavian factory were transferred in their entirety to a country with far lower income levels, continued manufacture in that country might be rendered uneconomic. Conversely, however, the citizens of those countries had an expectation that a large company with access to best practice environmental technology and management would not pollute the environment.

Financial Community

Unlike so many companies which began as family firms, Unilever was always a managerial enterprise with a large number of shareholders. During the post-war period it had pioneered a new openness towards these shareholders. In 1947 Unilever's accounts provided a geographical breakdown of sales turnover and other information which went far beyond accounting best practice anywhere in the world, and which won widespread praise from financial journalists. *The Economist* in 1948 referred to the 'riches of information' contained in Unilever's published accounts.[124]

Yet Unilever's low profile had its consequences for relations with shareholders. The financial markets considered Unilever a worthy but dull stock, and valued it accordingly. By the late 1960s Unilever was concerned that its share prices were too low. It became a steady refrain over the years that 'the Stock Exchanges rate Unilever unreasonably low'.[125] During 1973 and 1974 there was alarm when large numbers of Unilever shares changed hands, allegedly to a Swiss-based buyer, thought to represent the Kuwait Investment Fund. Unilever's own cash and short-term liabilities were at the time considered almost enough to buy Unilever. The subject gradually receded, though as Unilever sought to make bigger acquisitions from the late 1970s, its low share price began to seem an additional handicap.

Unilever faced an unusual problem in investor relations that its shares were split between Ltd/PLC and NV. This not only caused confusion as to the size and performance of Unilever as a whole, but also meant that the company had to address two quite separate groups of shareholders. In Amsterdam, NV ranked among the five most important stocks in terms of market capitalization and turnover. The company was well known by Dutch investment analysts. By the early 1970s they met with the Secretary of NV at least twice a year. There were also numerous investment clubs in the Netherlands which managers, and occasionally directors, addressed. However the Amsterdam Stock Exchange had considerably lower price–earnings ratios than those seen in New York in the 1970s, and for this and other reasons Ltd.'s shares traditionally traded at a premium to those of NV. A great deal of NV stock was also held outside the Netherlands. Unilever held meetings with financial analysts in Zurich, and by the mid-1970s in Germany also, where about 5 per cent of NV's stock was owned.[126]

The most serious problem for NV was the United States. In 1961 NV and Ltd's shares were listed on the New York Stock Exchange, and there was a burst of enthusiasm for the former, with the share of NV's equity held by American investors rising to 25 per cent, but within a decade this had fallen to 2 per cent.[127] In 1973 Klijnstra and Orr visited analysts in the United States, but they found knowledge of Unilever 'very limited', with nobody able to understand the Equalization Agreement or a company with a three-man chief executive, which did not fit at all well with American perceptions of leadership.[128] Despite much endeavour, this situation proved hard to change.[129] A transcript of a discussion in 1978 of the investment image of Unilever by four US analysts specializing in the consumer products sector showed that they considered the Dutch/British nature of the company, its diversified business, and its accounts hard to understand. Nor were things helped by Lever Brothers.[130] The poor performance of Lever Brothers blighted any attempt to project Unilever as an attractive growth stock, especially as it was generally covered by household products analysts in New York, who paid much less attention to the better-performing T. J. Lipton.

In London, Ltd's stock was one of the blue chip investments, but the company's complexity and low profile also did little to excite the investment community. Unilever was normally followed by food sector analysts, and it did not seem as attractive as other British food stocks. The fact that so much of its earnings were made in emerging markets seemed, in the 1970s, to be a cause for concern rather than satisfaction.[131] Overall Ltd's shares traded a discount to the London market, typically of around 30 per cent. From the end of the 1960s Unilever began to address this problem. The new Finance Director, Cob Stenham, began to encourage and participate in brokers' studies, and there were also informal meetings with the largest shareholders.[132] However, the image of Unilever as a dull stock was deep seated. A favourable broker's report in 1981 noted that on any British equity comparison Ltd's shares were 'cheap', trading at seven and a half times the earnings multiple, while NV shares were 'miles too cheap' as they traded at a discount to Ltd's.[133]

nuanced. It was the reputation of its brands that Unilever wanted consumers to be concerned with, while it was the reputation of its local operating companies that was of concern to its employees. The weak corporate image made Unilever much less exposed to radical critics of large firms. There were only two stakeholder groups that were really important to Unilever as Unilever: recruits to future senior management and shareholders. As a management recruiter, Unilever was able to attract good people, if not always retain them. The main downside of the 'dull' image was with shareholders. The formidable achievement of making a business which was constantly challenging, and from the early 1980s undergoing major restructuring, seem uninteresting, led to the persistent problems of discounted share prices.

Epilogue

Unilever before 1990: Transformation and Tradition

Currently a Unilever brand can be found in one out of every two households in the world. This book has related how these brands came to form part of the everyday life of so many people as the world 'globalized' from the 1960s. It has shown how Becel originated, how Impulse began life in South Africa and spread worldwide, how Lipton tea became the world's biggest tea brand, the origins of the sensual Magnum ice cream, and how Pond's Cream became a Unilever brand.

The story behind the brands has been presented also. Dove and Sunsilk, Omo and Surf, Rama and Flora were great consumer products, but they became worldwide brands because of the capabilities of Unilever. Their success rested on the choices made on strategy and organization, on the recruitment and development of managers, on the allocation of spending between capital investment, acquisitions, and innovation, and on the negotiation of safe paths through the complexities of official regulations and government. The easiest way to understand the Unilever organization, observed an article in the US business magazine *Fortune* in 1947, was 'to think of it as the world's most difficult corporate-management job'.[1]

It was remarkable that the corporate image of a company whose brands were so well known, and whose operations were so widespread, was so indistinct. There were times between the 1960s and 1990 when Unilever appeared amorphous. It was not merely that the corporate name was not found on any brands or local companies. It was also the sheer spread of businesses it owned beyond packaged consumer products, including African trading, plantations, speciality chemicals, paper and packaging, transport, advertising, and market research companies. It was not surprising that the financial markets had problems valuing the business, which seemed at times to resemble more of a holding company or conglomerate than anything else, nor that most consumers barely knew that Unilever as such existed.

There was, in fact, coherence to Unilever which rested on at least five corporate strengths. Unilever possessed, first, strong capabilities in branding and marketing. It understood local markets, and it knew how to market to them. It was at the frontier of market segmentation strategies in packaged consumer products. It opened up new product categories in deodorants and household cleaners. Unilever's brands were not strong enough to prevent the growth of private labels in Europe, but they were sufficient to maintain Unilever's strong position in higher margin products. It was able to leverage knowledge of brands and products between countries throughout the world, matching them to income levels and changing aspirations.

Secondly, Unilever developed strengths in the acquisition of other firms, and their subsequent 'Unileverization'. After the failed merger attempts of the late 1960s, Unilever professionalized its capabilities in this respect. It was conservative, missing opportunities as a result, but also avoiding disasters. The ice cream and other foods businesses were built patiently by the acquisition of one local firm after another, and their melding into the Unilever model. Following the National Starch acquisition, larger targets were pursued. The acquisition of Brooke Bond demonstrated that Unilever could make a hostile acquisition, while the acquisition of Chesebrough-Pond's two years later showed that Unilever could move quickly and decisively if it wished. Effective procedures were put in place to absorb acquired firms, which were flexible enough to take into account individual circumstances. From the 1980s Unilever also honed skills in divesting businesses. Unilever's ability to identify acquisition targets, and to absorb the capabilities of acquired companies, became one of its principal competitive advantages.

Unilever's research base was a third strength and source of coherence. The research laboratories in Britain, the Netherlands, the United States, and India were major sources of innovation. From gum health toothpaste to household cleaners, and from insect pollination of oil palms cloning to pregnancy tests, Unilever researchers were responsible for major innovations. The science base was high quality and deep. Research on animal feeds could lead over time into a successful pregnancy test. Unilever's knowledge about edible fats and detergents was second to none in the world. This research base not only provided the foundation for the development of new products, but was also indispensable for the constant upgrading and renewal of brands. Unilever's main problem was the time it took to turn scientific knowledge into successful branded products.

Fourthly, although a low-profile corporation, Unilever was embedded in business systems and official decision-making worldwide. This was derived from the company's long-established position as a large firm in many countries, from its role as a manufacturer of everyday products for eating and cleaning, and from its employment of nationals at senior levels. The upshot, seen in the case of the EU, was that Unilever had a 'voice' in issues that concerned it, even if it was exercised discreetly through industry and other associations. In emerging markets too, Unilever was able to some extent to influence how policies were interpreted, in part because of the respect in which the company was held. The corporate reputation for integrity and competence was a major competitive advantage in this respect. A part of the reason why Unilever seemed less confident in the United States before the 1980s was that it lacked familiarity and networks within that country.

Finally, and most important, Unilever had distinctive strengths in management. Unilever invested heavily in its management. It recruited some of the best available graduates in each generation, not only from its home economies, but in many other countries also. Its early 'localization' policies opened up the most senior positions within operating companies to nationals, enabling Unilever to tap high-quality staff all over the world. Unilever managers were given extensive training, and their career development was watched over carefully. A strong corporate culture, which co-existed with numerous subcultures, helped turn Unilever's management into the central binding force of the company, preventing it from becoming a 'conglomerate' even at its most diversified. There were few 'weird' people in the higher ranks of Unilever, yet compared to most companies, Unilever was distinguished worldwide by competent and professional management.

The challenge was to translate these strengths into a competitive performance which matched its peers, and delivered appropriate levels of return to shareholders. Unilever's historical legacy provided organizational and cultural constraints on the options available. It entered the 1960s with an organization that was so decentralized as to be fragmented. The British and Dutch components coexisted only loosely with one another. There was limited central direction, resulting in an excessive number of brands and factories organized nationally in a Europe undergoing economic integration, and a virtually autonomous business in the United States. There were barriers to flows of knowledge, especially across the Atlantic, but even between European countries. Unilever managers determined to see the differences between markets, when competitors saw the similarities. It was regarded as legitimate for all components of Unilever to pursue diversification opportunities with limited consideration for overall corporate priorities or capabilities. Research projects were pursued with little dialogue with the marketing function. Although Unilever had a strongly networked senior management, the tradition of decentralized authority created in some respects one of the world's least cohesive large businesses, and one in which establishing priorities in the allocation of resources was difficult.

There was also the past legacy of vertical and horizontal integration which left Unilever owning considerable parts of the value chain. Its trawlers caught the fish which was eventually sold in its restaurant chains. Thousands of people were engaged to slaughter the animals some of whose parts ended up in Unilever's pies and sausages. Unilever made its own packaging, and transported its products on its own trucks and barges. It owned the distribution chain which delivered its frozen products to retailers. It ran its own advertising agency and market research company. These businesses were the product of past rational calculations, and some remained profitable and successful operations, but by the 1970s times had changed. Unilever found itself burdened, especially in Europe, with a high cost structure, and the task of managing businesses far removed from the manufacturing and branding of packaged consumer goods.

Much of Unilever's history from the 1960s revolved around the tension between retaining the benefits of local market knowledge and decision-making, and containing the disadvantages of excessive decentralization and fragmentation. It proved difficult to change ingrained routines and practices. Shared values and strong networks kept Unilever together, but the need for agreement and discussion before taking action meant that it was hard to move quickly on major issues. It took twenty years to implement Co-ordination in Europe. It took longer to rationalize production and brands on a Europe-wide basis. Unilever's 'hands-off' approach to the US affiliates persisted even after the decline of the detergents and margarine businesses, and the failure to grow an ice cream business, became widely discussed public knowledge. Decades of efforts went into turning scientific research into marketable products.

The managerial costs of too much decentralization, and diversification into businesses as diverse as ferries and floor coverings, became evident as the oil crisis in 1973 transformed Unilever's home market in Europe from a fast-growing 'miracle' economy into one afflicted by recession and inflation. Unilever found itself burdened by low-margin businesses. The growing strength of European retailers and private labels undermined the profitability of branded food products. International competitors eroded Unilever's market positions in detergents. The attempts to find more profitable growth opportunities through innovation, in products as diverse as fresh dairy and feminine hygiene, largely came to naught, as did attempts to buy into the fast-growing personal care business.

By the mid-1970s Unilever's sales and profits performance were flat, and it was underperforming its major competitors. Unilever was sustained by strong positions in the detergents and personal care markets of Asia, Latin America, and Africa. The advantages of decentralization were especially seen in these Overseas markets. Unilever proved flexible enough to retain them, fostered by its belief that ultimately consumers worldwide would want its products. Moreover the oil price rises resulted in an extraordinary growth of profitability of the UAC stemming from the booming economies of Nigeria and the Arab Gulf.

The Special Committee of each generation sought to minimize the gap between capabilities and performance. However, no Special Committee began with a clean sheet of paper. Indeed, they inherited such a formidable package of organizational and cultural norms, and of asset distribution, that their options for radical change appeared highly constrained.

During the years of Cole and Tempel, the key to improving performance was believed to lie in diversification. The Unilever 'fleet' sailed in a variety of directions, motivated by the underlying belief that edible fats and detergents did not provide sufficient future growth prospects. The decisions to pursue the 'third leg' in foods, to build a worldwide ice cream business, and to segment the margarine market proved critical to Unilever's future. Cole was inclined to believe that Unilever could make a success of any business that it wished. This proved to be an illusion, but it was one widely shared within the business world at the time. Diversification was the fashion of the moment, which managers were constantly under pressure to follow from consultants and opinion makers in the financial press and business schools. It was only later that the managerial diseconomies of widely diversified businesses became evident.

Hartog and Woodroofe were organizational modernizers who addressed the consequences of diversification. They drove through the concept of executive Co-ordinations against internal opposition, and encouraged a more systematic approach to cash management, acquisitions, and research strategy. Woodroofe had a remarkable perception, decades before it became the subject of numerous management books, that the basis of Unilever's unique competitive advantage lay in its knowledge base. These years saw a major search for the organizational forms that would enable this knowledge to be exploited fully.

Among the principal achievements of Klijnstra, Orr, and Van den Hoven was the correction of the Anglo-Dutch imbalance within Unilever. The British pre-eminence within the Special Committee and the Board was anachronistic, and contributed to the fragmentation of Unilever's post-war organization between Britain and the Continent. By securing that Board, and ultimately Special Committee, meetings were held in both Rotterdam and London, Unilever began to become a more balanced Anglo-Dutch enterprise which, in turn, could start to reach out towards other nationalities. During these years also Unilever's strategic thinking became more focused, with an emphasis on reconfiguring the geographical basis of its business. This was not, as yet, matched by a clear product strategy. The UAC was permitted to seek diversification opportunities beyond west Africa by buying all manner of businesses in Europe.

Van den Hoven and Orr ultimately took the decision to reassert Unilever's authority over its businesses in the United States. Unilever's weak performance in the
United States market was an unsustainable position for a firm which aspired to be a
global consumer goods player. The acquisition of National Starch demonstrated to
its own management, as much as to outsiders, that Unilever was sufficiently self-
assured to acquire a large firm in the world's largest market. However, it did not
solve the issue of Lever's underperformance, nor did the guarantee of autonomy to
National Starch's management help the case of those seeking greater influence in
the affairs of Lever and Lipton. The real turning point for the American business
came with the subsequent appointment of Angus as director responsible for North
America, and the radical moves to integrate the US subsidiaries in Unilever in strategic and operational matters, and to rebuild the detergents and margarine business.
In Europe, Unilever's organizational legacy, as well as social legislation in most of
Europe, imposed constraints on what could be achieved in the rationalization
of production facilities and brands. In some respects the most notable achievement
of the 1970s was to retain Unilever's business in emerging markets, despite the
growing political risks and low remittances from major markets such as India.

The Special Committee of Durham, Maljers, and Angus launched a major corporate turnaround. This was a visible demonstration of the impact strong leadership
could have on a firm's performance, although the circumstances were also propi-
tious for radical change at Unilever. In the wake of a second major European recession, and with the collapse of UAC's profitability in Nigeria, Unilever could not carry
on as before. Nor could Unilever's underperformance compared to its major competitors be hidden any longer from institutional investors. The strategy confirmed at
the Marlow meeting in the spring of 1984 amounted, in Unilever terms, to a revolution, which over the following six years narrowed the gap between Unilever's capabilities and its performance.

The key achievement was the identification of Unilever as being in the fast-
moving consumer goods business. By 1990 Unilever no longer fitted Cole's description of thirty years previously of being 'several different fleets . . . doing all kinds of
different things, all over the place'. Major achievements included the disposal of a
swathe of low-margin businesses and major acquisitions. The acquisition of
Chesebrough-Pond's enabled Unilever to become a world leader in personal care
just as the industry was globalizing and consolidating, as well as contributing substantially to the further renewal of Unilever's business in the United States. There
was also a culture change as Unilever shifted from a company which tolerated
underperformance to one that did not. The implementation of this culture change
and of the core business strategy was no easy matter. Entire management
groups were sold, and managers unaccustomed to radical change had to be convinced to accept the new strategic approach. By 1990 Unilever may have retained

characteristics of a 'club', but being a Unilever manager could not be fairly characterized as a 'gentlemanly occupation'.

The Special Committee system itself had both advantages and disadvantages. It was the antithesis of the charismatic chief executive increasingly favoured by large corporations.[2] It hardly contributed to a dynamic corporate image that Unilever was led by a Special Committee, and it did little to foster an entrepreneurial culture within the business. On the other hand, the system guarded against risky strategic moves, albeit not completely, as Cole's failed attempts to acquire Allied Breweries demonstrated. At its best, the Special Committee provided a mechanism for major decisions to be reached in a balanced fashion, as well as providing a basis for the British and Dutch components of Unilever to coexist with one another. Undoubtedly some Special Committees worked better than others, depending on the relationships between the individuals involved. The arrangement worked best when the two chairmen worked well together, and it was less effective when their relationship was more distant. The large and executive Board provided little check on the actions of the Special Committee. Directors executed policy rather than making it. The absence of non-executive directors, before the role of Advisory Directors was greatly strengthened in the 1990s, compounded the problem of a governance structure which provided no outside perspectives or checks on decision-making.

By 1990 Unilever was no longer an underperforming firm. Its share price still seemed low compared to its competitors, but it was not a realistic takeover target. It was also evident that the legacy of the past had not suddenly disappeared either. There were still too many brands. Innovation was still too slow. There had been major progress at cutting costs, but less in creating an atmosphere for more dynamic risk-taking. Unilever was still edging towards a thorough rationalization of its European business. The foods business was still heavily reliant on edible fats and ice cream in Europe. There was still work to be done to extract value from Unilever's capabilities.

Coming to Terms with the Global Economy

During the last decades of the twentieth century a second global economy was built, which restored and surpassed in many if not all ways the level of international integration achieved before 1914. There were extraordinary political, economic, and technological shifts in these years. Much of this change was positive, but many countries of Africa, Asia, and Latin America were left behind. The disparity between the world's richest and the poorest peoples grew.

Firms such as Unilever were the webs of this global economy. While there was a singular failure to build international or, beyond Europe, regional political institutions, large corporations operated worldwide. They transferred technologies and people between countries. By 1990 Unilever was selling its products in virtually every country of the world, and was one of the world's largest employers. It could take a South African deodorant, or a US toothpaste, or a British ice cream gateau, and spread those brands and product concepts throughout the world. Its managerial methods and systems were diffused worldwide, with networks of managers moving to implement them.

Unilever's products—ice cream and fish fingers, tea and soups, soaps and face creams, deodorants and shampoos—were not glamorous, like computers, or strategic, like petroleum, or romantic, like diamonds or sports cars, but they formed the basis of the everyday lives of tens of millions of people. Unilever undertook extensive market research, had a massive advertising budget, and formidable capabilities in brand management, and if it put its full weight behind a brand, it could exercise a considerable influence in consumer spending decisions. Unilever was instrumental in persuading young women to wear perfumed deodorants, and helped to persuade men to take more care of their personal hygiene. It was an important force behind the reconceptualization of ice cream from being a product enjoyed primarily by children to a sensual product consumed in public by adults. It persuaded millions to use toothpastes designed to maintain better gum health, and to eat margarines which might reduce the risk of heart disease. Yet despite all its resources and skills, Unilever learned that, in the last resort, it could not persuade consumers to buy a product such as long-life yoghurt, or a new brand of detergent, which they did not want. It succeeded only when it listened to consumers, and articulated what they wanted.

The global economy saw both a convergence of tastes and a growing desire by consumers to express their individuality. Unilever responded to both trends. On the one hand, it was part of the process occurring in all consumer industries whereby numerous local and national brands gave way, in part at least, to fewer international brands, which appeared to be uniform worldwide, even if their formulations differed. Unilever played a significant role in the transformation of the world's ice cream and tea industries from being highly fragmented and consisting of numerous local brands and products into much more concentrated structures in which a small number of international brands were prominent. By 1990 Unilever was on its way to producing one-fifth of all the ice cream consumed in the world. On the other hand, Unilever did not simply replace a kaleidoscope of local colour with dull corporate uniformity. In a product as ostensibly homogeneous as margarine, it gave consumers a new range of choices to suit their own lifestyles and needs. Unilever's brands gave the mass of consumers the ability to make more choices about everyday products.

In emerging markets, Unilever also sold everyday goods to consumers, whether it was vanaspati in India and Turkey, or shampoo in Brazil and Malaysia, or toothpaste in Indonesia and South Africa, or beer and batik textiles in west Africa. As incomes rose, Unilever offered consumers in these countries the choice whether to use shampoo rather than soap, or detergents rather than bar soap, or eat a margarine that might reduce the danger of heart disease. Its brands, whether Lux toilet soap or Magnum ice cream, were often aspirational. They were the rewards as people became wealthier. Unilever was not, sometimes to its frustration, able to effect rapid changes in local consumer preferences. It could not persuade Thais to eat much margarine, nor Japanese to drink much black tea.

The scale of Unilever was awesome, but the company was far from omnipotent. The power of Unilever was limited by its own ability to exercise such power. For decades Unilever executives sought to reduce the number of brands supported and develop international brands, but it proved hard to achieve this ambition. For years Unilever's head offices could not exercise effective control over their US affiliates, or secure the desired transfer of resources, technologies, and brands across the Atlantic. It took Unilever four decades to realize its ambitions to buy into the personal care industry. The company also operated in a political and societal context in Europe, which its executives fully supported, in which redundancies and divestments were constrained by social responsibility.

There were few instances either when Unilever managers were able to enjoy strong market positions without competitive threat. In detergents and personal care industries, there were always formidable international competitors. The sudden entrance of Mars into the ice cream industry showed that there was always the threat of entry even in regions and products in which Unilever's market position was strong. In Europe, the concentration in retailing and the growth of private labels shifted the balance of power from manufacturers such as Unilever to retailers. By the 1980s, low-cost producers were posing major threats to Unilever's franchises in many emerging markets.

Nor was Unilever able, even if it so wished, to challenge the sovereignty of governments. Indeed the company was constantly restricted and constrained by governments. Unilever exercised a powerful voice, and was an effective lobbyist, but for the most part its efforts were directed at stopping governments restricting its business, rather than seeking to manipulate them. Unilever operated in a world in which governments remained firmly in control.

There was little in Unilever's record to support radical critics of the impact of large Western corporations on emerging economies. While many such firms employed expatriates in their most senior positions, it was an article of faith at Unilever that nationals should be employed whenever possible. Unilever was noteworthy for its investment in training of employees. The benchmarks for performance were international, and local managers and workers gained the advantages of meeting such benchmarks. The regular recruitment of Unilever managers by other businesses and governments indicated the high level of respect with which it was regarded. Although Unilever, like most multinational companies, conducted much of its basic research in its home economies, the creation of the large research facility in India in the 1950s was a pioneering step. Unilever's local operating companies engaged in developmental research also, and they became an important part of the innovation process.

Unilever, like most if not all large multinationals, held to higher standards than many local firms in emerging countries in terms of corrupt practices, and followed more stringent internal guidelines with respect to social responsibilities, including pollution and workers' rights. This reflected a corporate culture aligned more closely with the standards prevailing in Europe, quite apart from concerns about negative publicity in its home countries if it flouted standards. As one of the world's largest plantation owners by the 1980s, Unilever had a high standard of plantation management, while its contribution to the raising of palm oil yields had a positive impact on income levels in south-east Asia and other producing countries. As the environmental consequences of modern manufacturing began to be identified, Unilever responded by changing practices. There were times when the company appeared to lag in this regard, and its decentralized organization and culture delayed the implementation of corporate-wide environmental standards. However, Unilever's corporate culture and self-image provided powerful constraints on behaviour of an unethical nature.

It was not the business of Unilever, nor did it have the capacity, to overcome the institutional, social, and other barriers to growth which rendered so much of the world's population poor. It never sought to pioneer radical social and political change in its host economies. Within this limited remit, the existence of Unilever seems to have done more good than harm. Unilever brands made the everyday lives of people more hygienic, attractive, convenient, pleasurable, and healthy than would otherwise have been the case.

Unilever since 1990

After 1990 many of the processes put in place to renew Unilever were carried to their logical conclusions. Businesses which were not considered as being fast-moving consumer goods were sold, and the 'core' expanded. Between 1991 and 1995 the divestments included 4P in Germany, most of Unilever's agribusiness, including BOCM Silcock and fish farming, the South African distribution business, market

54 Unilever NV's new head office on the Weena in Rotterdam, opened in 1992.

research and coffee companies, the A & W restaurant chain in Canada, and the Revilla meats business in Spain. In 1997 Nordsee, the German and Austrian restaurants and fish wholesale business, followed. In 1994 Unilever sold its remaining shareholding in the UACN. Two years later Unilever's 25 per cent stake in Kumasi Brewery of Ghana and its 15 per cent stake in Nigerian Breweries were sold. In 1997 the Leverton UK dealership for Caterpillar earth-moving equipment was sold.

Unilever continued to make strategic acquisitions in North America. In 1993 it acquired Breyers from Philip Morris, making Unilever the leading manufacturer of ice cream in the United States. In 1996 Unilever also acquired the greater part of the Canadian-based but worldwide Diversey business, engaged in industrial and institutional cleaning. A substantial North American hair care business was finally achieved with the acquisition of Helene Curtis in 1996. Elsewhere, the collapse of Communism led to a new wave of investment in central and eastern Europe. There was a renewed momentum of expansion in emerging markets also. Ice cream businesses were launched in south-east Asian countries including Thailand and

Indonesia. The Indian business was able to exploit new opportunities as the Indian government undertook extensive restructuring and liberalization. In 1996 it was finally possible to merge Unilever's two main subsidiaries, Hindustan Lever and Brooke Bond Lipton India, to create India's largest private sector company. During the 1990s Hindustan Lever doubled turnover every four years and profits every three.

In detergents, a global detergents strategy was put in place in 1991 which effectively extended Co-ordination into the Overseas markets. This enabled Unilever to offer a robust response when P & G attempted to enter the Indian market. However, the restructuring of the European detergents business based in Brussels took time to deliver results. Lever Europe's attempt to catch up following a slow reaction to the introduction of concentrated powders suffered a serious setback after a new washing powder range known as Power was launched with an undetected flaw in its accelerator which, acting on a particular combination of dyes, could ruin certain light fabrics. One outcome of this episode was a reconsideration of Unilever's strategy aimed at achieving co-leadership in world detergents with P & G. The previous fixation with its US competitor began to give way to a greater focus on satisfying consumers and

55 Niall FitzGerald, Chairman of PLC 1996–2004
(*taken in 1996*).

maximizing shareholder value. Meanwhile after 1990 the main strategic thrust in foods was to consolidate Unilever's leading position in margarine, tea, and ice cream. By 2000 Unilever sold ice cream in over ninety countries across six continents.

Unilever began also to address its underperformance in the commercialization of innovation. Beginning in 1992, ten 'innovation centres' were established in personal care across the world, each with its own specialization, and each in contact with the Unilever central research laboratories. This regional approach to innovation helped to address Unilever's traditional problems in innovation caused by too much decentralization, and the gap between researchers and marketing. In 1993 Organics shampoo was first launched in Thailand after joint development work by Hair Innovation Centres in Bangkok and Paris. This new product, based on the concept of nourishing hair from the roots, was rapidly rolled out as a global hair brand. By 1995 Organics was already being sold in over forty countries. From 1993 onwards Unilever adopted the 'innovation funnel' model designed to provide a clear framework for filtering new ideas and projects, so that only those most likely to succeed actually make it to the launch phase. The idea of funnels was first adopted by Chesebrough-Pond's in the United States, and then spread throughout the Personal Products Co-ordination, and formed the basis of the corporate-wide 'Innovation Process Management' which was formally adopted in 1997.

The restructuring of the mid-1980s sharply improved Unilever's performance by disposing of its many low-margin businesses. During the mid-1990s a second wave of corporate renewal began, aimed at providing a basis for dynamic new growth. Major organizational changes sought to separate strategy from operational execution, and to provide a stronger regional focus. The Special Committee was replaced by a new seven-person Executive Committee (EXCO).

In 1997 the speciality chemicals division was sold to the British chemicals company ICI for £4.9 billion. Even though speciality chemicals had developed as a successful part of Unilever, it looked out of place with the desired position of Unilever as a fast-moving consumer goods company, while it was high-technology business which would require large amounts of investment to remain competitive. The continued separate ethos and culture of National Starch was also no longer what was desired. During 1997 and 1998 smaller disposals included John West, the canned fish company, the coffee business in Australia and New Zealand, and Plant Breeding International. The cash from the chemicals sale was used in part for acquisitions of medium-sized firms, notably Amora Maille, the Dijon-based manufacturer of gourmet mustard, ketchup, sauces, and salad dressings, which was acquired in 1999, but most was returned to shareholders. In 1999 a Special Dividend of £5 billion, the largest ever in the history of Unilever, was announced.

In 2000 the new 'Path to Growth' strategy was launched. The Path to Growth consisted of a series of linked initiatives to align Unilever behind plans for accelerating

56 Antony Burgmans, Chairman of NV 1999–2005, Chairman of NV and PLC since May 2005 (*taken in 1999*).

growth and expanding margins. The principal component of the new strategy was to concentrate product innovation and brand development on a focused portfolio of 400 leading brands. During the same year £1.63 billion was paid for two US food companies, the dietary supplement manufacturer SlimFast Foods and the ice cream producer Ben & Jerry's, followed by the acquisition of Bestfoods—the name taken by CPC in 1997—for £13.4 billion. With 60 per cent of its $8.6 billion annual sales coming from outside the United States, Bestfoods both offered a solution to Unilever's long-term weakness in the US foods market and gave it a number of new truly global foods brands such as Hellmann's and Knorr. The Bestfoods acquisition was the second largest cash acquisition in world business history, and the merger involved integrating 33,000 people in 63 countries and 120 factories. Unilever's foods business was transformed from a loose federation of mainly nationally focused companies, many with local operating names, into one international identity: Unilever Bestfoods. The Path to Growth and the acquisition of Bestfoods ushered in further organizational change. In 2001 there was a reorganization involving the formation of two global divisions—one for Foods and one for Home and Personal Care.

There were further divestments also. In return for European regulatory approval for the Bestfoods acquisitions, Unilever sold a number of familiar brands, including Oxo, Royco, and Batchelors. Between 2001 and 2005 Unilever's disposals of non-core businesses also included Unipath, DiverseyLever, Elizabeth Arden, Calvin Klein, Atkinsons, and the Loders Croklaan oils and fats business.

Personal care saw the fastest growth within Unilever, vindicating the strategy pursued since the early 1950s to move Unilever into this product category. However, there was renewed growth even in parts of the business which had long been regarded as 'mature', such as margarine and spreads. In 1999 Unilever won approval from the Food and Drug Administration to launch the first cholesterol-reducing spread in the United States. Take Control was launched in Chicago in June of that year. The launch of the equivalent Flora/Becel Pro.Activ in Europe came in 2002 following regulatory approval.

The new century saw a deterioration of the benign business climate of the previous decade. Revelations about corporate governance malpractices, the terrorist

57 Patrick Cescau, Chairman of PLC 2004–2005, Group Chief Executive since May 2005 (*taken in 2004*).

Timotei. Zo mild, dat je je haar kunt wassen zo vaak als je wilt.

Timotei, een nieuwe shampoo met natuurlijke veldkruiden. Mild voor je haar en hoofdhuid. Timotei wast je haar met zorg. Je haar wordt zacht en glanzend, en krijgt de frisse geur van een bloeiende zomerweide. Timotei is zo mild, dat je je haar kunt wassen zo vaak als je wilt. **Natuurlijke mildheid. Timotei shampoo.**

Timotei heeft in wetenschappelijke proeven bewezen mild te zijn voor haar en hoofdhuid. De gif waarde van ca. is in vivavel gelijk aan die van de hoofdhuid. Bevat natuurlijke kruidenextracten.

41 An advertisement for Timotei shampoo soon after its launch in the Netherlands in the early 1980s.

40 Advertisement for Seda, Unilever's leading shampoo brand in Brazil in 1976.

DENIM
After Shave

Per l'uomo che
non deve chiedere.
Mai.

DENIM
After Shave

andrélon

Andrélon heeft **effect!**

DE NIEUWE CONDITIONERS
VAN ANDRÉLON

42 A sales brochure for Andrélon hair conditioner in 1993. The Dutch com-

43 Advertisement for Denim aftershave in Italy in 1977. The Denim brand of male

SOUTH AFRICA

Simply Elegant
The new Impulse no man can resist

Men are slaves to Impulse. So don't be surprised if a complete stranger suddenly gives you flowers. He can't help it, he's simply responding to Impulse.

Impulse is more than a body spray, it contains gentle Shield deodorant to keep you fresh all day.

And a bewitching fragrance men can't resist.

Now there's a completely new Impulse: Simply Elegant. Softly feminine and very, very romantic. Use it all over, but use it with discretion. You can never be quite sure who will respond to it!

Impulse
It's an effect a woman has on a man

FAIR LADY. OCTOBER 12, 1977.

Unilever magazine

Second Issue 1984   No 52

Gibbs discovers
the Axe man

44 Advertisement for Impulse in South Africa in 1977.

45 Front cover of *Unilever Magazine* featuring the Axe deodorant sold in France in 1984.

47 Calvin Klein's Eternity in 1993.

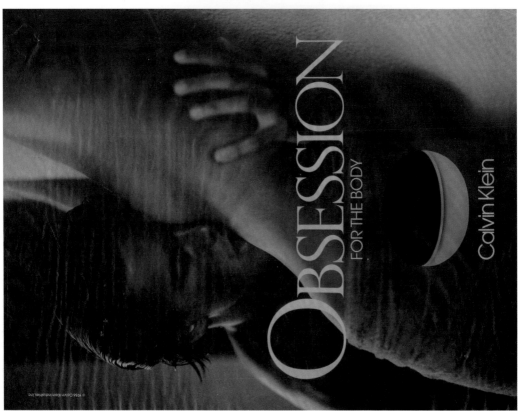

46 Calvin Klein's Obsession in 1987.

attack on the United States on 11 September 2001, and the war in Iraq in the following year showed the vulnerability of the world political and economic system. Unilever faced this changing environment as one of the world's most 'globalized' businesses. Although still recognizably a corporation which had originated in Britain and the Netherlands, Unilever was a much more 'international' business than in decades past. In 2004 the top 300 managers were drawn from thirty-three countries, with fewer than half being British or Dutch citizens. In 1998 Unilever held its first board meeting outside Britain and the Netherlands—in Shanghai, China.

There were major changes to the corporate governance of Unilever. During 2004 a single tier Board consisting of the same members was created for NV and PLC. The Advisory Directors were translated into non-executive directors, who became the majority of the Board. This restructuring involved the adoption of Anglo-Saxon governance procedures by NV as well as PLC. The following year saw further significant changes to streamline the management and leadership of Unilever. The dual chairman structure was replaced from May 2005 by a non-executive Chairman of both NV and PLC and a Group Chief Executive. Antony Burgmans and Patrick Cescau were appointed to these posts. A new executive team replaced EXCO, and the number of executive directors was reduced from seven to four.

Unilever had come a long way in its search to find the appropriate strategy, organization, and culture to gain full advantage from its formidable knowledge base. It had become a far more focused company. Its resources were no longer being spread over thousands of brands. There were no longer places to hide for underperforming businesses. However, neither the business environment nor Unilever's competitors were static. There remained no lack of new challenges.

Appendix 1 *The Special Committee and its Successors*

Dates	Chairman Ltd/PLC	Chairman NV	Third member
1956–1961	Geoffrey Heyworth	Frits Tempel	George Cole
1961–May 1966	George Cole	Frits Tempel	Ernest Woodroofe
May 1966–May 1970	George Cole	Harold Hartog	Ernest Woodroofe
May 1970–May 1971	Ernest Woodroofe	Harold Hartog	David Orr
May 1971–May 1974	Ernest Woodroofe	Gerrit Klijnstra	David Orr
May 1974–Mar 1975	David Orr	Gerrit Klijnstra	Seamus Sweetman
Mar 1975–May 1975	David Orr	Gerrit Klijnstra	Sweetman/V. d. Hoven
May 1975–Mar 1978	David Orr	Frans v. d. Hoven	Seamus Sweetman
Mar 1978–May 1978	David Orr	Frans v. d. Hoven	Sweetman/Durham
May 1978–May 1982	David Orr	Frans v. d. Hoven	Kenneth Durham
May 1982–May 1984	Kenneth Durham	Frans v. d. Hoven	Floris Maljers
May 1984–May 1986	Kenneth Durham	Floris Maljers	Michael Angus
May 1986–May 1989	Michael Angus	Floris Maljers	Johan Erbé
May 1989–May 1991	Michael Angus	Floris Maljers	Ronald Archer
May 1991–May 1992	Michael Angus	Floris Maljers	Michael Perry
May 1992–May 1994	Michael Perry	Floris Maljers	Morris Tabaksblat
May 1994–Jan. 1996	Michael Perry	Morris Tabaksblat	None
Jan. 1996–Aug. 1996	Michael Perry	Morris Tabaksblat	Niall FitzGerald

From August 1996 the Special Committee was replaced by the Executive Committee (EXCO). The Unilever chairmen since 1996 were:

	Chairman PLC	Chairman NV
Sept. 1996–May 1999	Niall FitzGerald	Morris Tabaksblat
May 1999–Sept. 2004	Niall FitzGerald	Antony Burgmans
Oct. 2004–April 2005	Patrick Cescau	Antony Burgmans

From May 2005 EXCO was replaced by a Group Chief Executive and a non-executive Chairman of PLC nd NV.

	Chairman	Group Chief Executive
May 2005–	Antony Burgmans	Patrick Cescau

Appendix 2 *Unilever and its Major International Competitors*

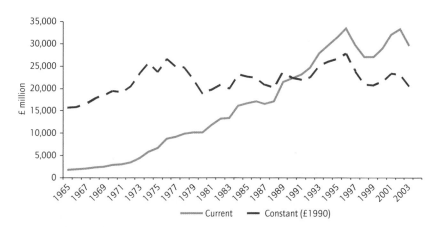

Fig. 1 Unilever sales in current and constant pounds, 1965–2003.

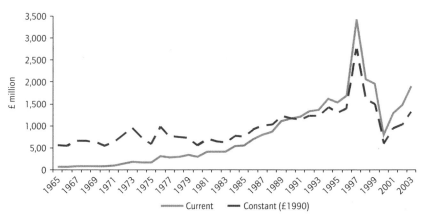

Fig. 2 Unilever net profits in current and constant pounds, 1965–2003.

Appendix 2

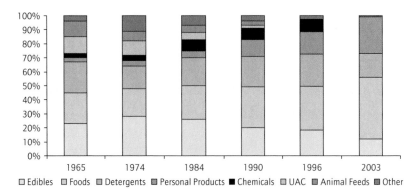

Fig. 3 Unilever sales by product category, 1965–2003 (%).

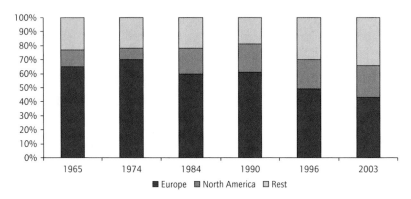

Fig. 4 Unilever sales by region, 1965–2003 (%).

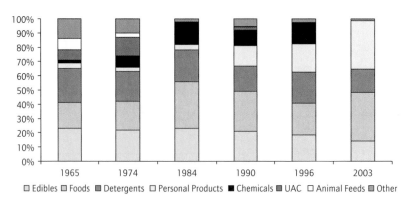

Fig. 5 Unilever profits by product category, 1965–2003 (%).

370

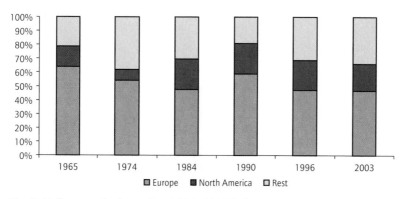

Fig. 6 Unilever profits by region, 1965–2003 (%).

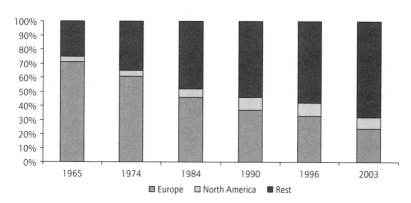

Fig. 7 Unilever employment by region, 1965–2003 (%).

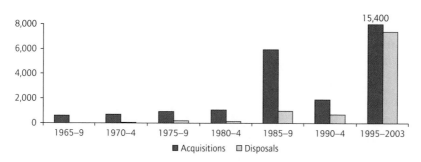

Fig. 8 Unilever spending on acquisitions and proceeds from disposals, 1965–2003 (£ 1990 million).

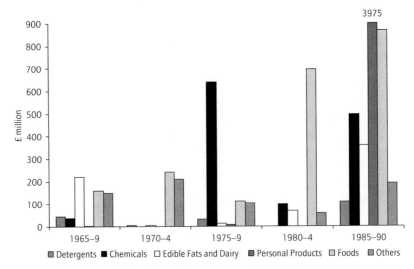

Fig. 9 Unilever acquisitions by product category, 1965–1990 (£ 1990 million).

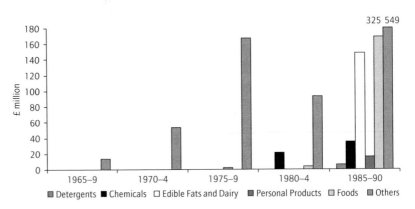

Fig. 10 Unilever divestments by product category, 1965–1990 (£ 1990 million).

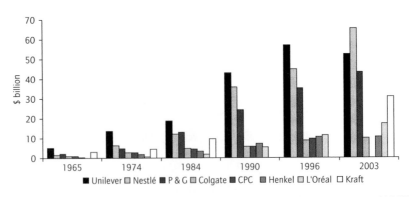

Fig. 11 Unilever and its major international competitors, sales, 1965–2003 ($ billion).

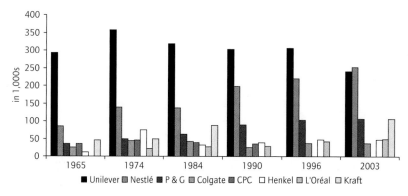

Fig. 12 Unilever and its major international competitors, employment, 1965–2003.

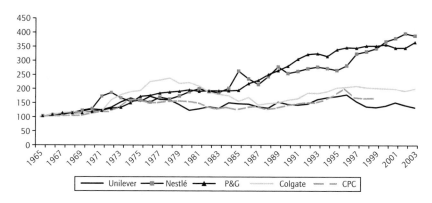

Fig. 13 Unilever and its major international competitors, 1965–2003, constant sales growth index (1965=100).

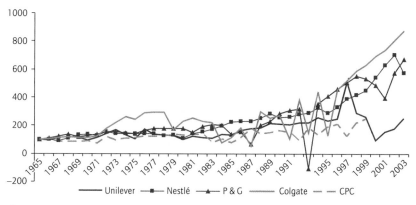

Fig. 14 Unilever and its major international competitors, 1965–2003, constant net profit growth index (1965=100).

373

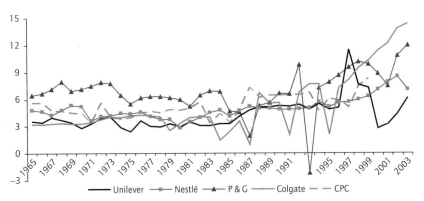

Fig. 15 Unilever and its major international competitors, return on sales, 1965–2003 (%).

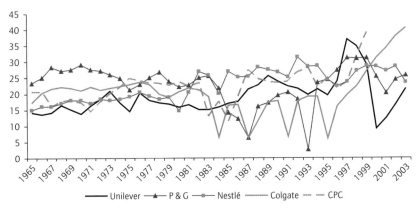

Fig. 16 Unilever and its major international competitors, pre-tax return on capital employed, 1965–2003 (%).

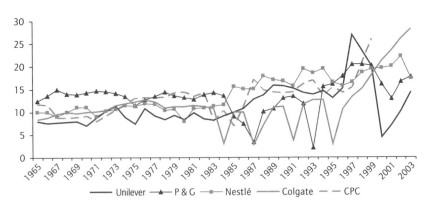

Fig. 17 Unilever and its major international competitors, post-tax return on capital employed, 1965–2003 (%).

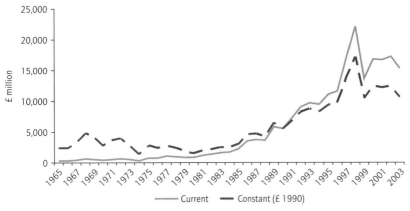

Fig. 18 Unilever Ltd/PLC current and constant market capitalization, 1965–2003 (£ million).

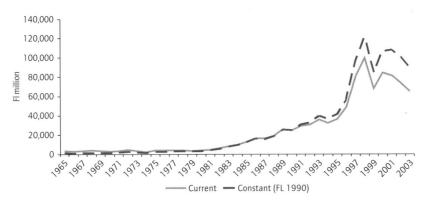

Fig. 19 Unilever NV current and constant market capitalization, 1965–2003 (FL million).

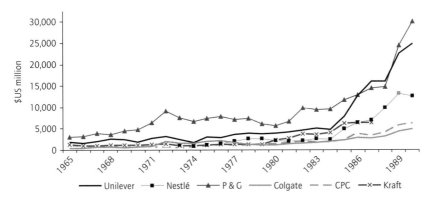

Fig. 20a Unilever (PLC and NV combined) and its major international competitors, market capitalization, 1965–1990 ($US million).

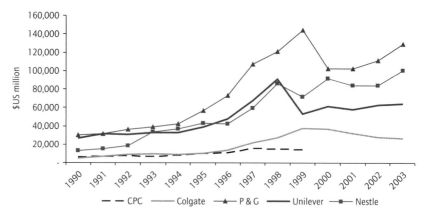

Fig. 20*b* Unilever (PLC and NV combined) and its major international competitors, market capitalization, 1990–2003 ($US million).

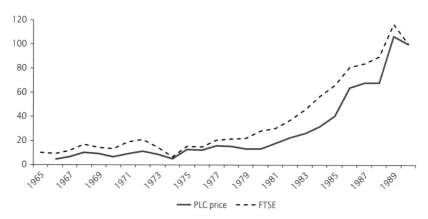

Fig. 21*a* The movement of Unilever Ltd/PLC share price and FTSE share price index, 1965–1990 (1990=100).

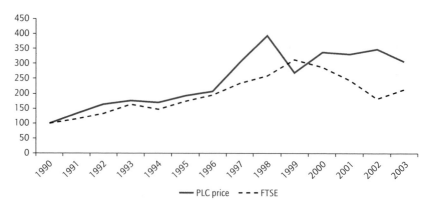

Fig. 21*b* The movement of Unilever Ltd/PLC share price and FTSE share price index, 1990–2003 (1990=100).

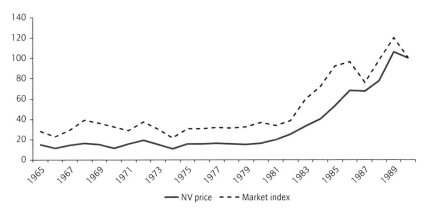

Fig. 22a The movement of Unilever NV share price and Amsterdam exchange share price index, 1965–1990 (1990=100).

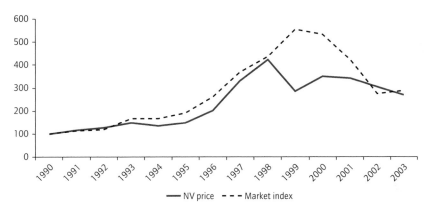

Fig. 22b The movement of Unilever NV share price and Amsterdam exchange share price index, 1990–2003 (1990=100).

Notes

Chapter 1 *Heritage and Challenges*

1. Kevin H. O'Rourke and Jeffrey G. Williamson, *Globalization and History: The Evolution of a Nineteenth Century Atlantic Economy* (Cambridge, Mass.: MIT Press, 1999); Geoffrey Jones, *Multinationals and Global Capitalism* (Oxford: Oxford University Press, 2005).

2. David Crystal, *English as a Global Language* (Cambridge: Cambridge University Press, 1997).

3. 'Corporate Strategy', Corporate Development and Economics, Jan. 1990, Report 7035, Unilever Archives Rotterdam (hereafter UAR) UAR.

4. Youssef Cassis, *Big Business: The European Experience in the Twentieth Century* (Oxford: Oxford University Press, 1997), 37.

5. Shane Hamilton, 'The Economies and Convenience of Modern-Day Living: Frozen Foods and Mass Marketing, 1945–1965', *Business History Review*, 77 (Spring 2003).

6. Charles Wilson, *The History of Unilever*, 2 vols. (London: Cassell, 1954); W. J. Reader, *Fifty Years of Unilever* (London: Heinemann, 1980); Roy Church and Christine Clark, 'Purposive Strategy or Serendipity? Development and Diversification in Three Consumer Product Companies, 1918–1939: J. & J. Colman, Reckitt & Sons, and Lever Bros./Unilever', *Business History*, 45/1 (2003), 23–59.

7. Christopher A. Bartlett and Sumantra Ghoshal, *Managing across Borders* (Boston: Harvard Business School Press, 1989), 37.

8. Detergent World Strategic Plan (1973), SD Box 9 (31/6), Unilever Archives London (hereafter UAL).

9. Davis Dyer, Frederick Dazell, and Rowena Olegario, *Rising Tide: Lessons from 165 Years of Brand Building at Procter & Gamble* (Boston: Harvard Business School Press, 2004).

10. Wilfried Feldenkirchen and Susanne Hilger, *Menschen and Marken. 125 Jahre Henkel 1876–2001* (Düsseldorf: Stürtz AG, 2001).

11. Nancy Koehn, *Brand New* (Boston: Harvard Business School Press, 2001), 142–7.

12. World Toilet Preparations Survey, 1959–1960, Report 3110, UAR.

13. Koehn, *Brand New*, ch. 5; Richard S. Tedlow, *Giants of Enterprise* (New York: Harper Collins, 2001), ch. 5. US cosmetics companies began to build international businesses during the inter-war years. See Mira Wilkins, *The Maturing of Multinational Enterprise* (Cambridge, Mass.: Harvard University Press, 1974), 83 and J. Moreno, *Yankee Don't Go Home* (Chapel Hill: University of North Carolina Press, 2003).

14. François Dalle, *L'Aventure L'Oréal* (Paris: Éditions Odille Jacob, 2001), 102–4.

15. I. Nonaka and H. Takeuchi, *The Knowledge Creating Company* (New York: Oxford University Press, 1995); Bruce Kogut and Udo Zander, 'What Do Firms Do? Co-ordination, Identity and Learning', *Organisation Science*, 7/5 (1996), 502–18.

16. 'Unilever's Role as a Multi-National Business', speech by E. G. Woodroofe and G. D. A. Klijnstra at Unilever's Annual General Meetings in London and Rotterdam, 8 May 1972, Publication 4979, 4980, UAR.

Chapter 2 **Managing Diversity 1965–1973**

1. Quoted in Charles Wilson, *Unilever 1945–1965* (London: Cassell, 1968), 3. Original interview in *The Observer*, 6, 13 Jan. 1963. Publication 5234, UAR.

2. Doreen Arnoldus, *Family, Family Firm and Strategy: Six Dutch Family Firms in the Food Industry 1880–1970* (Amsterdam: Aksant, 2002), 155.

3. Conference of Directors, 28 Feb. 1980; Board Committee on the Advisory Directors 1987, EXCO, UAL.

4. Interview with Pieter Kuin, 16 Mar. 2000.

5. Memorandum to Special Committee on 'The Future' by J. F. van Moorsel, 29 Oct. 1962, AHK 1575-01010, UAR; H. S. A. Hartog, 'After Brighton Thoughts', 10 Nov. 1965, File Corporate Relations 1997/50, UAL. Shell had a similar problem with its two head offices in London and The Hague, and at the end of the 1950s that company commissioned the consultants McKinsey to examine the issue.

6. John Kay, *Foundations of Corporate Success* (Oxford: Oxford University Press, 1993), chs. 1, 22.

7. Derek F. Channon, *The Strategy and Structure of British Enterprise* (London: Macmillan, 1973); Jan L. van Zanden, *The Economic History of the Netherlands 1914–1995* (London: Routledge, 1998), ch. 3.

8. Richard Whittington and Michael Mayer, *The European Corporation* (Oxford: Oxford University Press, 2000), 55–62.

9. See Ch. 5.

10. Davis Dyer, Frederick Dazell, and Rowena Olegario, *Rising Tide: Lessons from 165 Years of Brand Building at Procter & Gamble* (Boston: Harvard Business School Press, 2004), ch. 4.

11. F. D. Morrell, 'Heavy Duty Synthetic Detergents', 2 Dec. 1951, Special Committee Supporting Document, No. 8434, UAL.

12. Wilson, *Unilever 1945–1965*, 81–3.

13. Geoffrey Jones, 'Control, Performance and Knowledge Transfers in Large Multinationals: Unilever in the United States 1945–1980', *Business History Review*, 76 (Autumn 2002).

14. Spencer Klaw, 'The Soap Wars', *Fortune* (June 1963).

15. Economics Department, Competitive Performance in the Executive Countries, Sept. 1973, Microfiche Vtext DR 73001, UAR. On Henkel in this period, see Susanne Hilger, 'Reluctant Americanization? The Reaction of Henkel to the Influences and Competition from the United States', in Akira Kudo, Matthias Kipping, and Harm G. Schroter (eds.), *German and Japanese Business in the Boom Years: Transforming American Management and Technology Models* (London: Routledge, 2004).

16. *Procter & Gamble: The House that Ivory Built* (Lincolnwood, Ill.: NTC Business Books, 1988), 203.

17. Fabric Conditioner Review, Hamburg, 1976, UNI/CO/DT/8/2/1/5/1, UAL.

18. See Ch. 10.

19. Chairman's Review of the Year 1965, UAL.

20. Speech by E. G. Woodroofe and H. S. A. Hartog on 'The Changing Pattern of Unilever', delivered at AGM, 1971, Publication 4971, UAR; W. J. Reader, Birds Eye Foods Limited, Unilever, Jan. 1963, Publication 4084, UAR; Derek J. Oddy, *From Plain Food to Fusion Food* (Woodbridge: Boydell, 2003), 173–7.

21. Foods Study Group Report 1957–1958, Report 3109, UAR. A. W. J. Caron was the principal author.

22. Pim Reinders, *Licks, Sticks and Bricks* (Rotterdam: Unilever, 1999).

23. Paper on Unilever 1961–1971 for the Special Committee by J. P. Erbé, 30 June 1972, EXCO, UAL.

24. 'Gerrit Klijnstra: The Fair Negotiator', *Unilever Magazine* (May/June 1975).

25. Frozen Products Co-ordination, Note to the Special Committee on Nestlé, 20 Jan. 1982; Private Note of Discussion, 15 Apr. 1985; Frozen Products Co-ordination, '25 per cent Nestlé Shareholding: Key Aspects',

12 Feb. 1985; File on Nestlé Merger, CAH 2687-692 UAR.

26. Charles Wilson, *The History of Unilever* (London: Cassell, 1954), ii. 259–60 and Peter Matthias, *Retailing Revolution* (London: Longmans, 1967), 245–50; Jones, 'Control, Performance and Knowledge Transfers', 457–8.

27. Meeting of the Special Committee, 19 Aug. 1943, UAL.

28. Colin Baxter, Foods 2 Co-ordinator, in Meeting of Special Committee with Foods Co-ordination 2, 27 Oct. 1964, AHK 1733–90122, UAR; Jones, 'Control, Performance and Knowledge Transfers', 459–60.

29. Meeting of the Special Committee with Food Co-ordination 2, 16 June 1965, AHK 1733–90122, UAR.

30. Meeting of the Special Committee with Food Co-ordination 2, 27 Oct. 1964, AHK 1733–90122, UAR.

31. Meeting of the Special Committee with Food Co-ordination 2, 16 June 1965, AHK 1733–90122, UAR.

32. Marketing Division, Unilever Soup Varieties (July 1974), EXCO, UAL.

33. See Ch. 10.

34. Meeting of the Special Committee with Foods 2 Co-ordination, 6 July 1967, AHK 1735–90122; Special Committee Meeting at Unilever Head Office Vienna, 24–6 Apr. 1972, AHK 1872–90122, UAR.

35. Special Committee meeting with Food and Drinks Co-ordination, 7 Aug. 1975. AHK 2225–90122, UAR.

36. H. F. van den Hoven to J.P. Erbé, A.W. P. Stenham, and C. Zwagerman, 24 Oct. 1973; Private Note of Discussion, 8 Feb. 1974; Private Note of Discussion, 20 Mar. 1974, EXCO, UAL; interview with Ernst Verloop, 27 Apr. 2000.

37. ISD-Raincoat, by F. A. Maljers, 12 Apr. 1974, Acc1993/71, UAL.

38. Unilever Meat Study Group report, July 1965, Report 3138, UAR.

39. Meeting of Special Committee with Foods 1 Co-ordination, 17 Sept. 1963, Meetings Box 2, 6/6, UAL.

40. Meeting of Special Committee with Foods 2, 3 Jan. 1968, Meetings Box 2, 6/4, UAL.

41. Meeting of Special Committee with Foods 2, 15 Apr. 1970, Meetings Box 2, 6/4, UAL.

42. 'The Unilever Wine Project', Rotterdam, Jan. 1976, Report 3464, UAR.

43. Meeting of Special Committee with Foods 2, 12 July 1968, Meetings Box 2, 6/4, UAL.

44. T. R. Gourvish and R. G. Wilson, *The British Brewing Industry 1830–1980* (Cambridge: Cambridge University Press, 1994), 478–9; The Monopolies Commission, *Unilever Limited and Allied Breweries Limited: A Report on the Proposed Merger* (London, 9 June 1969), Report 4396, UAR.

45. Extract from Directors' Conference, 29 Nov. 1968, Meetings Box 2, 6/6, UAL.

46. JFK/AS, 'Industrial Logic', 29 Nov. 1968, NF Box 9, 7/1, UAL.

47. Gourvish and Wilson, *British Brewing*, 478–9.

48. Lord Cole to Tony Crosland, June 1969, NF Box 9, 7/1, UAL.

49. 'Beer Report 11', 18 June 1971, Report 1411, UAR.

50. Wilson, *Unilever 1945–1965*, 160–1, 198–201.

51. Preparations and Perfumery Survey, 1950–1951, June 1951, Report 3508, UAR; Andrew M. Knox, *Coming Clean* (London: Heinemann, 1976), 155–61; 'Towards a More Beautiful Unilever', by Maurice Zinkin, Dec. 1970, Microfiche Vtext TR 70 006, UAR.

52. World Toilet Preparations Survey, 1959–1960, Report 3110; Toilet Preparations Co-ordination Forward Plans, 1972 and 1973, UAR; Peter Miskell, 'Cavity Protection or Cosmetic Perfection? Innovation and Marketing of Toothpaste Brands in the United States and Western Europe, 1955–1985', *Business History Review*, 78 (Spring 2004), 29–60; Dyer, Dazell, and Olegario, *Rising Tide*, ch. 7.

53. Wilson, *Unilever 1945–1965*, 199.

54. J. & E. Atkinson, Five-Year Plan 1968–1972 (Feb. 1968), UAL.

55. Worldwide Review of Rexona deodorant, Microfiche Vtext ES 81 220C, UAR.

56. Interview with Harold Hartog, 3 Aug. 1999.

57. L'Oréal: Private Note of Discussion held on 24 May 1966, AHK 1748–301410, UAR. Seamus Sweetman was the Co-ordinator.

58. Special Committee minutes E2581 and 2582, cited in H. Meij to Special Committee, 6 Mar. 1975, Unit Box 16, 24/7, UAL.

59. James Foreman-Peck, *Smith & Nephew in the Health Care Industry* (Aldershot: Edward Elgar, 1995), 217–19; Conference of Directors, 16 Apr. 1968, UAL.

60. See Ch. 7.

61. Transport Co-ordination, Review of 1981 Long Term Plan and the Strategic Value to Unilever of its Activities, July 1982, EXCO:Transport—General Matters 1982, UAL.

62. 'Unilever Transport: Going Places', *Unilever Magazine* (Nov./Dec. 1976).

63. Tom Trenchard to Special Committee, 27 June 1972, AHK 1887–101410, UAR.

64. Meeting of Special Committee with Foods 3 Co-ordination, 6 July 1972, AHK 2041–101410, UAR.

65. Transport Co-ordination, Norfolk Line—Acquisition, June 1973, AHK 2041–101410, UAR.

66. Len Sharpe, *The Lintas Story: Impressions and Recollections* (London: Lintas Ltd., 1964); Publication 4085, UAR; SSC7 B-Lintas International 1971 Longer Term Plan (July 1971), SD Box 11, 31/13; Lintas Longer Term Plans and Annual Estimates, 1974, 1977, and 1981, SD Box 5, 30/7, UAL.

67. D.K. Fieldhouse, *Merchant Capital and Economic Decolonization* (Oxford: Clarendon Press, 1994), 509–10.

68. Ibid. 681, 694–700.

69. Management Communication in Unilever, by Pieter Kuin, 28 July 1969, AHK 1960–060, UAR.

70. Christopher A. Bartlett and Sumantra Ghoshal, *Managing across Borders* (Boston: Harvard Business School Press, 1989), 48–50.

71. Dyer, Dazell, and Olegario, *Rising Tide*, 204–6.

72. Unilever Organization, 14 Dec. 1951, HA 123–439.11, UAR.

73. D. K. Fieldhouse, *Unilever Overseas* (London: Croom Helm, 1978), 55–7; Knox, *Coming Clean*, 208.

74. Interview with Floris Maljers, 27 June 1999.

75. Jones, 'Control, Performance, and Knowledge Transfers', 466–8; Geoffrey Jones and Lina Gálvez-Muñoz (eds.), *Foreign Multinationals in the United States* (London: Routledge, 2001); An Address to the Board by Mr Abe Fortas on Anti-Trust, 25 Sept. 1959, Special Committee supporting Documents, UAL; Klaw, 'The Soap Wars'.

76. Fieldhouse, *Merchant Capital*, 46–8.

77. Interview with Okko Mueller, 3 Aug. 1999.

78. 'The Organisation of Unilever' (1953), Publication 4241, UAR.

79. Geoffrey Heyworth, 'Unilever Organisation', 5 Dec. 1951, UAL.

80. Minutes of Directors' Conferences, 16 June 1961, UAL.

81. Functionally versus Regionally Controlled Organisation, by H. S. A. Hartog, 25 Sept. 1962, AHK 1575–01010, UAR.

82. Memorandum on Detergents Committee by J. F. van Moorsel, 13 Aug. 1958, AHK 1575–01010, UAR.

83. J. F. van Moorsel, 'The Future', memorandum to Special Committee, 29 Oct. 1962, AHK 1575–01010, UAR.

84. Circular on Co-ordination of Product Policy, 26 Jan. 1962, AHK 1575–01010, UAR.

85. Verbatim note of a discussion on Harold Hartog's memorandum dated 26 Aug. 1963 on operation of the Co-ordination System, Private Note of Discussion, 26 Aug. 1963, UAL.

86. Co-ordination, memorandum by J. P. Stubbs and WD, 1 and 28 Aug. 1963. UAL.

87. Interview by P. W. Klein and W. J. Reader with H. S. A. Hartog, 22 Mar. 1989.

88. Managers' Courses: Unilever on the Continent of Europe, 18 Nov. 1964, AHK 1720–01010, UAR.

89. Interview with Pieter Kuin, 16 Mar. 2000.

90. Memorandum to Special Committee by Sidney van den Bergh, 7 Nov. 1962, AHK 1575–01010, UAR.

91. Private Note of Discussion, 11 Aug. 1964, EXCO, UAL.

92. Unilever Information Bulletin No. 190, Oct. 1964, UAR.

93. Private Note of Discussion, 11 Aug. 1964, EXCO, UAL.

94. Board Memorandum on Organization (excluding USA), 22 Feb. 1966, Special Committee Supporting Documents, UAL.

95. Location of Co-ordinators, 25 June 1966, AHK1575–01010, UAR.

96. For the Record, a note in reply to Mr. Andrew Knox's paper, A. C. C. Baxter, 19 Oct. 1966, AHK 1720–01010, UAR.

97. Memorandum by P. A. Macrory on Food Co-ordination, 4 Nov. 1966, AHK 1720–01010, UAR; interview by P. W. Klein and W. J. Reader with Han Goudswaard, 24 May 1989.

98. Meeting of Special Committee re General Matters, 6 May 1968, Meeting Box 18, 36/15, UAL.

99. Notes on Discussion held on 11 Apr. 1962, NA Confidential Matters in Connection with North America, Basement Files; Corporate Development File Notes, 15 July 1968 and 25 Mar. 1969, Files on Unilever Visitors 1968 and 1969, UNUS CD, Boxes 18 and 19, UAL.

100. Dr E.G. Woodroofe's Visit to USA, Report to the Board, 17 Sept. 1971, UAL.

101. P. Kuin to E. G. Woodroofe, 'Management Communication in Unilever', 28 July 1969, SC Supporting Documents, Cupboard 4, Shelf 1, UAL.

102. Lewis and Van der Hoek Report, Mar. 1970; Meeting on Organization, 1 July 1970, UHP 43, UAR.

103. 'After Brighton Thoughts', Harold Hartog, 10 Nov. 1965, Corporate Relations Acc. 1997/50, UAL.

104. Channon, *Strategy and Structure*, 163–73.

105. Functionally versus Regionally Controlled Organization, by H.S.A. Hartog 25 Sept. 1962, AHK 1575–01010, UAR.

106. McKinsey & Co., Directing the Concern— A Top Management Framework (Feb. 1972), Report 289, 2183 UAR.

107. H.S.A. Hartog's Speech for Rotterdam Conference, Nov. 1970, UAL.

108. Interview with Cob Stenham, 18 Mar. 2002.

109. Hartog and Woodroofe speeches for Rotterdam Conference, Nov. 1970, UAL.

110. Edible Fats and Dairy Co-ordination, Annual Estimate 1970, UAL.

111. E.G. Woodroofe's speech to the Rotterdam Conference, Nov. 1970, UAL.

112. Paper by J. P. Erbé on Unilever 1961–71 for Special Committee, UAL.

113. Memorandum attached to Special Committee letter of 17 Dec. 1970, UAL.

114. Interview with Sir Ernest Woodroofe, 7 Feb. 2002.

115. Interview with Cob Stenham, 18 Mar. 2002.

Chapter 3 *New and Old Worlds 1974–1983*

1. Jan L. van Zanden, *The Economic History of the Netherlands 1914–1995* (London: Routledge, 1998), 46.

2. Interview with Frans van den Hoven, 24 Feb. 2000.

3. Dr Woodroofe's report to the Directors' Conference on 11 Dec. 1964 on his visit to Mr Tempel, Special Committee Supporting Documents, UAL.

4. 'Orr Finds his Man—Again', *The Times*, 1 June 1992.

5. Minutes of the Meeting of Special Committee on 12 June 1975 re Corporate Development, NOD Box 6, 4/8, UAL.

6. Chairman Review of the Year, 1975, Publication 4996, UAR. Unilever's strategy in Europe is examined in Geoffrey Jones and Peter Miskell, 'European Integration

and Corporate Restructuring: The Strategy of Unilever *c*1957–*c*1990', *Economic History Review*, 58/1 (2005).

7. Introductory Speech, Directors' Conference Amsterdam, EXCO, UAL.

8. Board Conference Papers No. 4, Problem Areas, Papers of Board Conference, 15 Jan. 1976, EXCO, UAL.

9. Meeting of Special Committee with Meat Products Co-ordination, 1 Aug. 1977, SD Box 11, 31/12, UAL.

10. Interview by W. J. Reader with D. Angel, 13 Dec. 1988.

11. Edible Fats and Dairy Co-ordination Five-Year Plan and Annual Estimate, SD Box 10, 31/9, UAL.

12. Meeting of Special Committee with Edible Foods and Dairy Co-ordination, 5 Aug. 1977, Meeting Box 13, File 34/7 UAL.

13. Detergents Co-ordination Longer Term Plans, 1975, 1981, 1985, and 1989, SD Box 9, 31/6, UAL; 'Competition in Detergents: Some Key Issues', Apr. 1985, Microfiche Vtext ES 85 020, UAR.

14. Interview with Antony Burgmans, 2 Apr. 2001.

15. Meeting of Special Committee with Frozen Products Co-ordination, 13 Dec. 1977, SD Box 11, 31/11, UAL.

16. These issues are examined further in Chs. 10 and 11.

17. Memo to Special Committee, Supplementary Proposal 1979/3, Lipton International purchase of tea bag machinery worldwide, EXCO, UAL.

18. Meeting of Special Committee with Toilet Preparations Committee, 10 Aug. 1976, Meeting Box 21, 37/1, Meeting of Special Committee with Toilet Preparations Committee, 13 Feb. 1979, Meetings Box 21, 37/1, UAL.

19. A. C. Emmerson to Special Committee, 13 July 1984, NF Box 11, 9/8, UAL; 'Coping with Retailer Power, Nov. 1982, Microfiche Vtext ES 82 262, UAR.

20. This issue is examined in Ch. 5.

21. Meeting of Special Committee with Edible Fats and Dairy Co-ordination, 13 July 1979, UAR.

22. Meeting of Special Committee with Frozen Products Co-ordination, 5 Aug. 1976, 9 Dec. 1975, Meetings Box 18, 36/12, UAL.

23. Paul Geroski and Tassos Vlasopoulos, 'The Rise and Fall of a Market Leader: Frozen Foods in the UK', *Strategic Management Journal*, 12 (1991).

24. M. Bucci, A. Richards, and K. R. Tinsley, 'Soap Manufacture in Europe: Introduction and Part 1', Soap Supply Group (Dec. 1974), Detergents Co-ordination, Production/R & D, Box 2, UAL.

25. Concern Manpower and Salaries/Wages at end 1973, UAL.

26. Salary and Appraisal Policy for Top Management, by D. Angel, 11 Feb. 1983, AHK 2665–06040, UAR.

27. Interview by P. W. Klein and W. J. Reader with M. L. Mogendorff, 24 May 1989.

28. Meeting of Special Committee with Detergents Co-ordination, 9 Aug. 1983, Unit Box 26, 26/13, UAL.

29. Meeting of Special Committee with Detergents Co-ordination, 22 May 1979, Unit Box 26, 26/10, UAL.

30. See Ch. 11.

31. Concern Longer Term Plans, 1972, 1974, 1979, 1983, SD Box 13, 32/6, 32/11, UAL.

32. Meeting of the Special Committee with Research International, 24 June, 8 Dec. 1981, EXCO: Marketing Division, UAL.

33. See Ch. 11.

34. Initial Thoughts on Expanding our US Toiletries Business, Michael Angus, 2 Apr. 1971, EXCO: Personal Products North America 1953–1986, UAL.

35. See Ch. 12.

36. Robert Heller and Norris Willatt, *The European Revenge* (London: Barrie and Jenkins, 1975), 138.

37. 'Unilever Fights Back in the US', *Fortune*, 26 May 1986.

38. Lever Brothers Company, USA Foods Division, Margarine Business proposal, Paper 7861 for Special Committee Meeting, 12 Dec. 1980, UAL.

39. See Ch. 10.

40. Geoffrey Jones, 'Control, Performance and

Knowledge Transfers in Large Multi-nationals: Unilever in the United States 1945–1980', *Business History Review*, 76 (Autumn 2002).

41. Ibid.

42. Conference of Directors, 30 July 1971, UAL.

43. Interview with Ernst Verloop, 27 Apr. 2000.

44. Anil K. Gupta and Vivay Govindarajan, 'Knowledge Management's Social Dimension: Lessons from Nucor Steel', *Sloan Management Review* (Fall 2000).

45. Interview with Ernest Verloop, 27 Apr. 2000.

46. Interview with Mike Dowdall, 22 Feb. 2000.

47. J. P. Erbé to M. R. Angus, 5 May 1972; J. P. Erbé to Special Committee, 5 Dec. 1973; J. P. Erbé to Special Committee, 29 Mar. 1974. Policy Documents, File 1, 1963–1975, UAL.

48. Board Conference, Paper No 4, Problem Areas, 29 Dec. 1975, Board Conference, 15 Jan. 1976, EXCO, UAL. Interview with Henk Meij, 12 Feb. 2000.

49. Memorandum by Special Committee to All Directors, 11 Feb. 1976, Board Conference, 15 Jan. 1976, EXCO, UAL.

50. Private Note of Discussion, 29 Apr. 1976, EXCO; Meeting of the Special Committee re North America, 29 Apr. 1976, Meeting Box 18, 36/20; Private Note of Discussion, 19 Nov. 1976, EXCO, UAL.

51. See Ch. 11.

52. Interview by Alison Kraft with Wallace Grubman, 20 Feb. 2001.

53. Private Notes of Discussion, 16 Feb. 14 Oct. 1976, 25 Aug. 1977, UAL.

54. See Chs. 7 and 11 for a further discussion of National Starch.

55. Private Note of Discussions, 27 July 1977, EXCO, UAL.

56. Interview with Sir Michael Angus, 11 Nov. 1999.

57. Interview with Sir Kenneth Durham, 10 Nov. 1999.

58. Paper by A. W. P. Stenham on UNUS Dividend Policy, 29 Apr. 1983, Special Committee Supporting Document No. 8492;

Memorandum by H. Eggerstedt on Financing the US Expansion, 17 Dec. 1984, EXCO: National Starch 1983–1986, UAL.

59. Private Note of Discussion, 30 Apr. 1979; Board Meeting, 26 Aug. 1982; Talk by Mr Angus, UAL.

60. McKinsey & Co., Assessing Strategic Alternatives for the Foods Division, 24 Sept., 21 Oct. 1980, Reports Box 10, 60/8, UAL.

61. Interview by David Grayson Allen with Floris Maljers, 27 June 1989.

62. Meeting of the Special Committee with North American Office, 12 Dec. 1980, Meeting Box 12, 34/2; Lever Brothers Company, USA Foods Division Margarine Business Proposal, Special Committee Supporting Document No. 7861, UAL.

63. Memo to Special Committee on Lever Brothers USA—Foods Division, 27 July 1983. EXCO: NAO-Lever Foods/Shedd Margarine Group 1983–, UAL.

64. Possible Acquisition of the Shedd Margarine Business from Beatrice Foods, 5 Aug. 1983. EXCO: NAO-Lever Foods/Shedd Margarine Group 1983–, UAL. Private Note of Discussion, 22 Dec. 1983, EXCO, UAL.

65. Lever Brothers Co. New Products Investment, Dec. 1983, Special Committee Supporting Document No. 8615, UAL.

66. P & G North America Appendices, July 1987, EXCO, Misc.Competitors, UAL.

67. Competition in the US Toothpaste Market 1960–1985, Economics Department, Feb. 1986, Microfiche Vtext ES 86 073, UAR.

68. Notes on Board Discussion, 29 Oct. 1976, UAL.

69. Geoffrey Jones, *Merchants to Multinationals* (Oxford: Oxford University Press, 2000).

70. See Ch. 7.

71. Report by A. M. Knox to the Conference of Directors, 19 Jan. 1968, UAL.

72. Detergents World Strategic Plan, Fourth Draft, July 1973, UAL.

73. See Ch. 6.

74. Overseas Companies—Annual Estimate 1968. Report by A. M. Knox, 19 Jan. 1968, UAL.

75. Charles Wilson, *Unilever 1945–1965* (London: Cassell, 1968), 250; Overseas Companies—Annual Estimate 1968. Report by A. M. Knox, 19 Jan. 1968; Draft Paper on Sundry Foods Overseas, 21 Apr. 1976, UAL.

76. Wilson, *Unilever 1945–1965*, 191–2, 224, 298.

77. Memo by N. F. Nicolson to Contact Directors, London, on Visit to Japan, Oct.–Nov. 1947, AHK 2130-932, UAR.

78. Memo on Lipton in Japan by Sundry Foods and Drinks Co-ordination, 5 Dec. 1979, EXCO: Japan 1977–1984, UAL.

79. Visit to Japan, 10–14 Feb. 1981, EXCO Japan 1977–1984, UAL.

80. Interview with Satoru Akaiwa, Takeshistu Seto, and Yoshio Ikeda, Tokyo, 20 Sept. 1999.

81. Meeting of the Special Committee with the Overseas Committee, 12 Aug. 1980 Meetings Box 11,3/14; Memorandum by D. F. Webb on 'The Failure of Sunsilk Mon Stylist', 30 July 1980, UAL.

82. Mark Mason, *American Multinationals and Japan* (Cambridge, Mass.: Harvard University Press, 1992).

83. 'Procter & Gamble (A)', Harvard Business School Case No. 9-391-003 (1990); Davis Dyer, Frederick Dazell, and Rowena Olegario, *Rising Tide: Lessons from 165 Years of Brand Building at Procter & Gamble* (Boston: Harvard Business School Press, 2004), ch. 10.

84. H. F. van den Hoven to G. E. Graham, 6 June 1973, Japan AHK 2130-932, UAR;

Interview with C. M. Jemmett, 3 May 2002.

85. See Ch. 11.

86. Overseas Committee Paper on Options for Unilever in Japan, circulated to Special Committee, 3 July 1978, Memorandum on Japan by Corporate Strategy Advisory Committee, Aug. 1984, EXCO: Japan 1977–1984, UAL.

87. Overseas Committee memorandum on Business Strategy for Japan, 12 Oct. 1979, Meetings Box 11, 33/14; Meeting of the Special Committee with the Overseas Committee, 13 Dec. 1979, Meeting Box 11, 33/14; Memorandum on Japan by the Overseas Committee to the Special Committee, 13 Feb. 1981, Meetings Box 12, 33/15; Meeting of Special Committee with Overseas Committee, 12 Jan. 1983, Meeting Box 12, 33/15 UAL.

88. Interview with Frans van den Hoven, 24 Feb. 2000.

89. Interview by W. J. Reader with C. F. Sedcole, 29 Nov. 1988.

90. Letter from H. F. van den Hoven, 26 July 1972; G. F. J. van der Gaag to A. W. J. Caron, 21 Mar. 1972; F. van den Hoven to A. W. J. Caron, 3 May 1972, AHK 1859-01010, UAR.

91. Terms of Reference, National Manager—European Countries; National Conference; European Liaison Committee, Mar. 1986, UAL.

92. Special Board Conference on the 1983 Concern Longer Term Plan, EXCO, UAL.

Chapter 4 *Rethinking Unilever 1984–1990*

1. C. K. Prahalad and Gary Hamel, 'The Core Competence of the Corporation', *Harvard Business Review*, 66 (May–June 1990).

2. CSAC, Unilever Performance: Regional and Industrial Balance, 4 Nov. 1983, Cupboard 1, 30/04, UAL.

3. Board Discussion—1 Dec. 1983, Meetings Box 24, 59/53, UAL.

4. Board Conference held on 6 Nov. 1980, UAL.

5. Conference of Directors, 22 July 1982, UAL.

6. Floris Maljers, 'Maintaining Strategic Momentum-Theses: Address to the World Conference of the Strategic Management Society in Paris', Sept. 1994.

7. Major Strategic Decisions—Transport Co-ordination, Transport Co-ordination, Rotterdam, 27 Apr. 1983, contained in Private Note of Discussion, 9 June 1983; Private Note of Discussion, 30 Nov. 1983, EXCO, UAL.

8. Private Note of Discussions, 14 Dec. 1983, EXCO, UAL.

9. In 1982 Orr recruited a British academic economist, David Stout, to head the department. Interview with Stout, 28 Nov. 2001.

10. Meeting of Special Committee with Corporate Strategy Advisory Committee, 16 Dec. 1982, EXCO: Corporate Strategy Advisory Committee, UAL.

11. CSAC Paper on Discontinuous Change, 23 Jan. 1984; Meeting of the Special Committee with CASC, 29 Feb. 1984, EXCO: CSAC, UAL.

12. John P. Kotter and James L. Heskett, *Corporate Culture and Performance* (New York: Free Press, 1992), ch. 7.

13. Interview with Floris Maljers, 27 June 1999.

14. Interview by W. J. Reader with Sir Michael Angus, 21 July 1989.

15. Minutes of Special Sitting Together at Marlow, 30 May 1984, Meetings Box 5,14/8, UAL.

16. Conference of Directors, 18 Apr. 1985, UAL.

17. Conference of Directors, 7 Feb. 1985, UAL.

18. Concern Longer Term Plan 1990–1994, Jan. 1990, EXCO, UAL.

19. Memo by A. W. P. Stenham to J. Louden and M. S. Perry, 2 Nov. 1984, Fieldhouse Papers, Box 6; Minutes of the Meeting of the Special Committee with UAC International, 18 June 1985, UAL.

20. OSC/UACI Report of the Study Group, Oct. 1986, Misc: Study Group—OSC/UACI 1986, EXCO, UAL; David K. Fieldhouse, *Merchant Capital and Economic Decolonization* (Oxford: Clarendon Press, 1994) 799–803.

21. Edible Fats and Dairy Co-ordination, Memorandum to Special Committee, Boursin, 1 May 1989; id., Note on the Acquisition of Boursin, 26 Sept. 1989, 3014.10, UAR.

22. Meeting of Special Committee with Frozen Products Co-ordination, 19 June 1981, Meetings Box 18,36/12, UAL.

23. OFF Performance and Pillar Strategy. Initial Review (Jan. 1987), Microfiche Vtext ES 87 050, UAR.

24. See Ch. 5.

25. Interview with Morris Tabaksblat, 25 Feb. 2000; Memorandum by M. Tabaksblat to Special Committee on 'The Role of Acquisitions in PPC', 25 Oct. 1985, EXCO, UAL.

26. Davis Dyer, Frederick Dazell, and Rowena Olegario, *Rising Tide: Lessons from 165 Years of Brand Building at Procter & Gamble* (Boston: Harvard Business School Press, 2004), ch. 13.

27. Economics Department Paper, Microfiche Vtext ES 88 078, Market Highlights: Personal Products, UAR.

28. Growth Opportunities for Personal Products in the 1990s, 18 Nov. 1988, EXCO: PPC, UAL. Interview with Sir Michael Perry, 10 Apr. 2002.

29. Interview with Sir Michael Perry, 10 Apr. 2002.

30. Conference of Directors, 1 Dec. 1988, 16 Mar. 1989, UAL.

31. 'Unilever Cancels Fabergé Deal', *Financial Times*, 29 Apr. 1989; Interview with Sir Michael Angus, 11 Nov. 1999.

32. Chemicals Co-ordination, Annual Estimate and Longer Term Plan 1990, UAL.

33. See Ch. 7.

34. See Chs. 7 and 10.

35. McKinsey & Co., *Defining New Sources of Profitable Growth* (Oct. 1988), EXCO, UAL.

36. Corporate Development and Economics, Corporate Strategy (Jan. 1990), Report 7035, UAR.

37. Growth Opportunities for Personal Products in the 1990s, 18 Nov. 1988, EXCO: PPC Chesebrough-Pond's 88/90; Meeting of the Special Committee with Personal Products Co-ordination, 29 Nov. 1988, EXCO: Personal Products, General Matters 1985–1988, UAL.

38. Report on P & G in North America, Economics Department, July 1985, EXCO, UAL.

39. US Review, 1990, UNI/CO/DT/D/2/8, UAL.

40. Detergents Co-ordination, 1990–1994 Longer Term Plan, EXCO: Detergents General Matters, 1990–1991, UAL.

41. Meeting of the Special Committee with North American Office, 2 Apr. 1986, Meetings Box 19,36/23, UAL.

42. Meeting of the Special Committee with North American Office, 1 July 1987, Meetings Box 19,36/23, UAL.

43. Detergents Co-ordination, 1990–1994 Longer Term Plan, EXCO: Detergents General Matters, 1990–1991, UAL.

44. Ibid.

45. Comments by Special Committee on Detergents Co-ordination—Longer Term Plan, 20 Nov. 1989, EXCO: Detergents General Matters 1988–89, UAL.

46. Meeting of Special Committee with Detergents Co-ordination, 21 Nov. 1990, EXCO: Detergents General Matters 1990–1991, UAL.

47. North America Office Memorandum on Good Humor Update, 30 July 1985, EXCO, UAL.

48. Minutes of Sitting Together, 12 June 1981; 23 June 1981; Memo by A. W. P. Stenham to Special Committee, 12 June 1981; Unit Box 37, 28/8, UAL.

49. Meeting of the Special Committee with Frozen Products Co-ordination, 13 Jan. 1987, EXCO: US Foods—Jan. 1987, UAL.

50. Meeting of Special Committee with North American Office, 1 Feb. 1989, EXCO, UAL.

51. North American Office, Proposal to Acquire Ganges, 9 Mar. 1989, EXCO, UAL.

52. D. W. Gill to Morris Tabaksblat, 19 Apr. 1989, EXCO, UAL.

53. McKinsey & Co., *Defining New Sources of Profitable Growth*, Oct. 1988, EXCO, UAL.

54. Meeting of the Special Committee with North American Office, 2 Feb. 1983, UAL.

55. Interview with Morris Tabaksblat, 25 Feb. 2000.

56. Meeting of the Special Committee with Overseas Committee, 9 Aug. 1984 Meetings Box 20,36/29; Nippon Lever KK, Strategy for Japan, Aug. 1984; Minutes of Conference of Directors, 27 Sept. 1984, UAL.

57. Meeting of the East Asia and Pacific Regional Management Group with the Special Committee, 10 Dec. 1987, EXCO: East Asia and Pacific Management Group 1987–, UAL.

58. Interview with Akaiwa, Seto, and Ikeda, 20 Sept. 1999.

59. Meeting of the East Asia and Pacific Regional Management with the Special Committee, 13 Dec. 1989; EAP-Japan. Surf Fabric Detergent Launch proposal, Oct. 1989, EXCO East Asia Pacific: Japan, UAL.

60. Meeting of the East Asia and Pacific Management Research Group and Special Committee, 12 Sept. 1990, EXCO East Asia Pacific: Japan, UAL.

61. Interview with Akaiwa, Seto, and Ikeda, 20 Sept. 1999.

62. Christopher A. Bartlett and Sumatra Ghoshal, *Managing across Borders* (Boston: Harvard Business School Press, 1989).

63. P & G: European Organization (Economics Department, Aug. 1988), Microfiche Vtext 88 070, UAR.

64. Economics Department, Nestlé SA. Old Rival with a New Face, Dec. 1985, Report 205, UAR.

65. Eastbourne Conference—Oct. 1988; Eastbourne Conference, Special Committee, 15 Feb. 1989. EXCO: Management Conference—Eastbourne, UAL.

66. Kurhaus Conference, 16/17 Apr. 1985, Board Discussion, 6 June 1985, UAL.

67. Special Committee Conclusions on Eastbourne Conference, 1 Mar. 1989, EXCO: Eastbourne Conference, UAL.

68. Foods Executive Study Group, EXCO: Foods Executive General Matters 1989–, UAL.

69. Detergents Co-ordination: Proposal to Change the Organization of DT Companies in Europe, 9 Mar. 1989, EXCO: Detergents Co-ordination. Lever Europe 3 1989–, UAL.

70. Lever Europe: Organization, 3 Oct. 1989, EXCO: Detergents Co-ordination. Lever Europe 3 1989–, UAL.

71. Conference of Directors, May 1990, EXCO, UAL.

Chapter 5 *Adding Value: Marketing and Brands*

1. Richard S. Tedlow, *New and Improved* (London: Heinemann, 1990), 7, 101.

2. Notes on Zinkin Film, Four Major Factors of Change in Modern Life, AHK 1944-102621, UAR.

3. The members were Maurice Zinkin (chair), J. G. Collingwood, S. R. Green, C. T. C. Heyning, M. Weisglas, and P. J. F. van der Sanden. W. B. Blaisse replaced Zinkin as chairman in 1972.

4. Consumer Change Committee, The Changing Consumer. Some Hypotheses, 5 June 1967, AHK 1735-02621, UAR.

5. E. G. Woodroofe, 'Research in the Market Place', Presented to the Society of Chemical Industry, 9 Apr. 1968.

6. Presentation to the Special Committee on Marketing Strengths, Nov. 1979, MD 1993/59, UAL.

7. Marketing, Organization, and Personnel Divisions, Closer Integration between Sales and Brands in Marketing (June 1973), Report 425, UAR.

8. Presentation to the Special Committee on Marketing Strengths (Nov. 1979), MD 1993/59, UAL.

9. Organization Division, 'Marketing Division: Terms of Reference' (11 Feb. 1958), MD 1995/13, UAL.

10. Marketing Division, 'Long Term Plan 1988–1990 Discussion Document: Marketing Networking—A Concept for the 1990s' (Nov. 1987), EXCO, UAL.

11. Maurice Zinkin, The Old People's Market, 11 Sept. 1970, AHK 1944-02621, UAR; Consumer Change Committee, The Challenge of the Upper Age Market, Jan. 1972, Reports Box 7, 47/3, Consumer Change Committee, The Multidimensional Consumer, Sept. 1972, Reports Box 2, 39/2, UAL; 'Marktverkenningen', *Op Eigen Terrein*, 26 (20 Dec. 1971), UAR.

12. Report on Tour of US Universities, by P. J. F. van der Sanden, Dec. 1967, AHK 1944-02621, UAR; V. Langholz to Henk Meij, 6 Jan. 1976, contains a summary of all the Consumer Change Committee papers, AHK 2426-02621, UAR.

13. Minutes of the Unilever International Market Research Conference, Crawley, Sussex, June 1970, AHK 1944-02620, UAR.

14. International Market Research Development Conference, Vierhouten, Holland, June 1969, MD 1998/20, UAL.

15. Market Research in Unilever 1988. Report on an International Audit by Marketing Division, Sept. 1989, Report 1105 UAR.

16. Meeting of Special Committee with Marketing Division, 11 Mar. 1969, EXCO: Marketing Division, UAL; D. B. Hurst, 'Unilever Value Added and Cost Structure' reports for the years 1984–7, Economics Department, ES 85 021, ES 87 025, ES 88 025, UAR.

17. Charles Wilson, *Unilever 1945–1965* (London: Cassell, 1968), 98–9.

18. Richard S. Tedlow, 'The Fourth Phase of Marketing', in Richard S. Tedlow and Geoffrey Jones (eds.), *The Rise and Fall of Mass Marketing* (London: Routledge, 1993), 16.

19. Marketing Division, 'The Management of Advertising in Unilever', Aug. 1979, MD 1997/50, UAL.

20. Ibid.

21. Wilson, *Unilever 1945–1965*, 92.

22. The Measurement of the Effect of Marketing Variables and Product Quality on Sales: Implications for Research and Advertising (Unilever Research, 1983), Vtext Report UD 84006, UAR.

23. Unilever Plan for Good Advertising (1979), MD 1997/50, UAL.

24. Conference of Directors, 15 Mar. 1979, UAL.

25. Marketing Division, 'The Management of Advertising in Unilever', Aug. 1979, MD 1997/50, UAL.

26. Conference of Directors, 10 Aug. 1989, UAL.

27. Monopolies Commission Report on Household Detergents, 1966.

28. 'The Controversy about Advertising: Unilever's View', 1970, Library, ADS664, UAL.

29. 'Advertising and Responsibility', Sept. 1973, MD 1997/66, UAL.

30. 'A Study of Advertising in the United Kingdom and the Federal Republic of Germany', Prepared by the Bureau Européen des Unions de Consommateurs for the Environment and Consumer Protection Service of the EEC, Nov. 1974, UAL.

31. Meetings of Special Committee with Marketing Division, 12 Mar., 23 Apr. 1968, EXCO: Marketing Division, UAL.

32. 'Advertising and Responsibility', Sept. 1973, EXCO: Marketing Division, UAL.

33. Mira Wilkins, 'When and Why Brand Names in Food and Drink?', in Geoffrey Jones and Nicholas J. Morgan (eds.), *Adding Value: Brands and Marketing in Food and Drink* (London: Routledge, 1994).

34. Jean-Noël Kapferer, *(Re)inventing the Brand* (London: Kogan Page, 2001), 32–3.

35. Marketing Division, Brand Positioning as a Marketing Discipline, Sept. 1975, UAL.

36. Toilet Preparations Co-ordination Brand Strategy, 'Sunsilk', Sept. 1973, Report 3266, UAR.

37. TPC Forward Plans, 1974 and 1977, SD Box 12, 31/16, UAL. Oldham, 'Brand Name Chart—Unilever Personal Products', Jan. 1983, chart 2, Economics Department London, ES 83 026, UAR.

38. 'Timotei Shampoo; Progress Report', Apr. 1982, Economics Department, ES 82 214S, UAR. Toilet Preparations Co-ordination Forward Plan, 1985, EXCO, UAL. R. Mader to R. M. Latham, Elida Gibbs Ltd Internal Memorandum, 10 Jan. 1986, Personal Products Co-ordination, Box 1, 'Timotei Background', UAL.

39. J. H. van Stuyvenberg, *Margarine: An Economic, Social and Scientific History, 1869–1969* (Liverpool: Liverpool University Press, 1969), 227–45.

40. Brands History File, AHK 2384-02110, 'Becel', UAR.

41. 'The Long Term Development of Fats', Unilever, June 1959, Report 869; 'How to Keep the Lead in the Margarine Business', Jan. 1965, Foods 1 Co-ordination, Report 3131, UAR.

42. Interim Brand Intentions—Margarine, Unilever World Co-ordination Foods 1, Policy Memorandum No. 3, June 1965, Report 3136, UAR.

43. Policy Memorandum No. 1; Fats, Heart Disease and Unilever, *c.*1964, Report 3120, UAR.

44. VdB&J News, Feb. 1972, p. 4.

45. Janet Wilkie, 'Analysis of the Margarine Market in the Netherlands—Discussion Draft', 15 May 1975, ES 75 042, UAR.

46. Du Darfst Advertising Brief 1989, ODF 128, UAR.

47. Personal Products Co-ordination, Longer Term Plan 1983, SD Box 12,31/16, UAL.

48. Interview with Nigel Clayton, 20 Nov. 2001.

49. 'The Impulse Story—SSC&B: Lintas Creative Guidelines', Personal Products Co-ordination, Box 40, UAL.

50. Nancy F. Koehn, *Brand New* (Boston: Harvard Business School Press, 2001), 194.

51. Economics Department, Worldwide Review of Rexona Deodorant, Apr. 1981, Micro-fiche Vtext ES 81 220C, UAR.

52. Pim Reinders, *Licks, Sticks and Bricks* (Rotterdam: Unilever, 1999), 480.

53. Sharon Skeggs, 'Cornetto: An Advertising Case History', 22 Nov. 1982, p. 3. Frozen Foods Co-ordination, Box 16, UAL.

54. Ibid. There were a number of versions of the lyric. The one cited here was used in an advert in 1981 and sung by a gondolier. Another advert of the same vintage substituted 'The great Italian dream' in the fifth line.

55. SSC&B: Lintas World-wide, 'Cornetto International Positioning: Review from Hamburg Ice Cream Conference', Mar. 1983, Frozen Foods Co-ordination, Box 25, UAL; Reinders, *Licks, Sticks and Bricks*, 614–15.

56. Project Renaissance Qualitative Research: Final Report, Jan. 1986, Frozen Products Co-ordination, 21/5/4/AA, UAL.

57. Reinders, *Licks, Sticks and Bricks*, 418.

58. Ibid. 621–22; Interview with Hans Eggerstedt, 8 May 2000.

59. Magnum Brand History.

60. 'Magnum: Love at First Bite', *Unilever Magazine*, 2nd issue (1995).

61. Commission of the European Communities, Evolution of Concentration in the Soap and Detergents Industry for the United Kingdom (Brussels, June 1978).

62. Comment by Nick Burstin from J. Walter Thompson, cited in press article on 'Learning from Lever', 26 July 1984, Detergents Co-ordination, Visits Box 3, UAL.

63. Meeting of Detergents Co-ordination with Special Committee, 19 Sept. 1984, Meeting Box 14, 35/6, UAL.

64. Economics Department, The Development of the Gum Health Segment and Progress of Unilever's Entry Mentadent, Aug. 1982, ES 82 257, UAR.

65. Ibid.; Peter Miskell, 'Cavity Protection or Cosmetic Perfection? Innovation and Marketing of Toothpaste Brands in the United States and Western Europe, 1955–1985', *Business History Review*, 78 (Spring 2004), 29–60.

66. Edible Fats & Dairy Co-ordination, EF & DC Becel Policy, June 1987, Report 5902, UAR.

67. Becel, Briefing for 1987–1988 Campaign, Report 2202, UAR.

68. Unilever Detergents Policy, Memorandum No. 9, Dove, Dec. 1964, UNI/CO/DT/1/3/4/1/9, UAL.

69. G. W. Hill, Unilever Research Port Sunlight Laboratory, to A. R. van Heemstra, 20 June 1990, UAL.

70. Brand Marketing Strategy Morgen, 14 July 1982; J. W. Eenhoorn, 'Morgen Margarine: A Brief Case History', Oct. 1983, AHK 2619-102110, UAR.

71. Tea Based Drinks—Study Group, Apr. 1985, Report 8596, UAR.

72. Economics Department, Opportunities for Iced Tea, Oct. 1988, ES 88 053, UAR.

73. Stephen J. Hoch and Shumeet Banerji, 'When do Private Labels Succeed?', *Sloan Management Review* (1993); Bridget Williams, 'Multiple Retailing and Brand Image: An Anglo-American Comparison 1860–1994', in Jones and Morgan (eds.), *Adding Value*; John A. Quelch and David Harding, 'Brands versus Private Labels: Fighting to Win', *Harvard Business Review* (Jan.–Feb. 1996); Philip Fitzell, *The Explosive Growth of Private Labels in North America* (New York: Global Books, 1998).

74. Bridget Williams, *The Best Butter in the World: A History of Sainsbury's* (London: Ebury Press, 1994), 86.

75. Economics Department, Competition in the UK Fish Finger Market, Nov. 1984, Microfiche Vtext ES 84 156, UAR.

76. Unilever's Policy on Supplying Distributor-Owned Brands and Guidelines for its Implementation, Marketing Division, Sept. 1974, Reports Box 8, 52/6, UAL.

77. Low Priced MOBs and DOBS in the Dutch Yellow Fats Market, Dec. 1979, Report 645, UAR.

78. MOBS, DOBS, and Generics, 'The Divine Right', Marketing Division, May 1982, Report 487, UAR.

79. D. B. Lewis, 'Covering Letter for Own Label Brands', see report by Marketing Division and Economics and Statistics Department (1961), Microfiche Vtext OS 61 010, UAR.

80. Unilever's Policy for Distributor-Owned Brands, May 1964, Report 3359, UAR.

81. Unilever Policy on Supplying Distributor-Owned Brands and Guidelines for its Implementation, Marketing Division, Sept. 1974 Reports Box 8, 52/6, UAL; 'Do we produce and market products which cater for the needs of all consumers, including those that want cheap products?', Paper for Amsterdam Conference, 1976, EXCO, UAL; Economics Department, Low Priced Competition in the DT Margarine Market (February 1981), ES 81 202, UAR.

82. Reinders, *Licks, Sticks and Bricks*, 508–11.

83. MOBS versus DOBS, 5 Jan. 1983, Report 4310, UAR.

84. Low Priced MOBs and DOBS in the Dutch Yellow Fats Market, Dec. 1979, Report 645, UAR.

85. Edible Fats and Dairy Co-ordination, Report of the EF and DC DOB Supply Policy Group, June 1989, Report 5894, UAR.

86. European Retailer Strategies, Apr. 1988, Economics Department, Microfiche Vtext ES 88 015, UAR.

87. Conference of Directors, 11 Nov. 1981, UAL.

88. Edible Fats and Dairy Co-ordination, Supplying Margarine, White Fats and Oils as DOBs. Should we or should we not?, June 1983, Report 4220, UAR.

89. Conference of Directors, 11 Nov. 1982; Board Discussion, 7 Dec. 1983, UAL.

90. 'Tough Times for Teeth', *Unilever Magazine* (1988), 68.

91. Economics Department, Worldwide Review of Rexona Deodorant, Apr. 1981, ES 81 220, UAR.

92. Interview with Hans Eenhoorn, 15 Aug. 2000.

93. Economics Department, The Structural Trends in the Ice Cream Market, Aug. 1978, Microfiche Vtext ES78174, UAR.

94. Economics Department. Premium Ice Cream: Carte d'Or and Mövenpick (June 1988), Microfiche Vtext ES88022, UAR.

95. S. R. Green, 'European Marketing', 12 Mar. 1958, AHK 1575-01010, UAR. Green was then Marketing officer, Rotterdam Group, and became chairman of Lintas Ltd in 1959.

96. Unilever Detergent Policy memorandum, International Brand Intentions, July 1964, Report 3127, UAR.

97. Foods 2 Co-ordination, Canned Soups: International Brand and Pack Policy, Jan. 1963, AHK 1590, UAR.

98. Economics Department, Product Profitability, May 1978, Microfiche Vtext ES 78 173, UAR.

99. Report of the Study Group on Detergents Research, 19 Apr. 1979, Unit Box 26, 26/10, UAL.

100. Marketing Division, Brand Positioning as a Marketing Discipline (Sept. 1975), UAL.

101. Toilet Preparations Co-ordination, Brand Policy Document. Close-Up Toothpaste, Oct. 1973, Report 3362, UAR.

102. Unilever Detergents Policy Memorandum No. 9, Dove, Dec. 1964, UNI/CO/DT/1/3/4/1/9, UAL.

103. Interview with Nigel Clayton, 20 Nov. 2001.

104. Minutes of the Meeting of Lever European Executive, 15 Sept. 1987, UNI/CO/DT/1/1/1/5/7, UAL.

105. Economics Department, The Development of the Gum Health Segment and Progress of Unilever's Entry Mentadent, Aug. 1982, Report 1387, ES 82 257, UAR.

106. Unilever/Nestlé: Comparison, May 1986, UAL.

107. Gale Lockhart Griffen, A Portrait of Bestfoods (the company, 2000), 32–3, UAR.

108. Edible Fats and Dairy Co-ordination, Report of the Becel Working Group, 22 Aug. 1989, Report 6176, UAR.

109. Food and Drinks Co-ordination, Report of the Working Party on the International Use of the Lipton Name and Pack Design, 25 July 1983, Report 2571; Food & Drinks Co-ordination, Policy for the Use and Application of the Lipton Name, June 1984, Report 1387; Food and Drinks Co-ordination, Draft Note for Overseas Companies Use of the Lipton Name and Quality Standards, 3 June 1988, Report 5203, UAR.

110. Corporate Development and Economics, Branding in F and DC. An Analysis of Competitors July 1989, Report 8601, UAR.

111. A. R. van Heemstra, 'Brand Policy in the Nineties' (Dec. 1989), EXCO, UAL.

112. Christopher Napier, 'Brand Accounting in the United Kingdom', in Jones and Morgan (eds.), *Adding Value*, 89–90.

113. Personal Products Co-ordination, 1985 Longer Term Plan, SD Box 12, 31/16, UAL; EXCO, Conference of Directors, EXCO, 7 Aug. 1986, UAL.

114. A. R. van Heemstra, 'Brand Policy in the Nineties', Dec. 1989, EXCO, UAL.

115. Corporate Development and Economics, Branding in F and DC. An Analysis of Competitors July 1989, Report 6594, UAR.

116. Marketing Division, The Management of Advertising in Unilever, Aug. 1979, MD 1997/50, UAL.

117. Report of a Study Group on the Strength and Quality of Marketing Resources in Unilever, Mar. 1984, Marketing Resources Study Group 1983–, EXCO, UAL.

118. Meeting of the Special Committee with Marketing Division, 22 Oct. 1986, Marketing Division, 1978–1986, EXCO, UAL.

119. D. B. Hurst, 'Unilever Value Added and Cost Structure (1985–1988)', ES 85 021, ES 87 025, ES 88 025, UAR.

120. Conference of Directors, 10 Aug. 1989, EXCO. Marketing Division, The Management of Advertising in Unilever, Aug. 1979, MD 1997/50, UAL; T. A. B. Corley, 'Best Practice Marketing of Food and Health Drinks in Britain 1930–70', in Jones and Morgan (eds.), *Adding Value,* 227–9.

121. 'Unilever is Dull but Brands Aren't', *Advertising Age Europe* (Jan. 1981).

Chapter 6 *Risk and Reward in Emerging Markets*

1. David Fieldhouse, *Unilever Overseas* (London: Croom Helm, 1978); Frans-Paul van der Putten, *Corporate Behaviour and Political Risk: Dutch Companies in China 1903–1941* (Leiden: CNWS, 2001).

2. Andrew M. Knox, *Coming Clean* (London: Heinemann 1976), 213.

3. Report by Andrew Knox to the Directors' Conference, 20 Jan. 1967, UAL.

4. Annual Estimate 1979. Overseas Summary, UAL.

5. OSC Memorandum on Regional Strategy, 3 Mar. 1980, Central Filing OSC 1980, UAL.

6. Paper on Shareholdings by J. P. Erbé, 13 June 1973, Special Committee Supporting Document No. 5860, UAL.

7. Meeting of the Special Committee with the Overseas Committee, 14 July 1970, Meeting Box 19, 36/24, UAL.

8. Discussion Paper on the Problems of Local Participation, 7 June 1973, Overseas Committee Supporting Document No. 5833, UAL

9. Conference of Directors, 27 Sept. 1984, UAL.

10. Meeting of Overseas Committee with Special Committee, 13 May 1969, Box 44, UAL.

11. Visit Report to Unilever-İş by F. Martin, 30 Jan.–3 Feb. 1978, AHK 2242-92802560, UAR.

12. Meeting of Special Committee with Overseas Committee, 20 Jan. 1971, Box 19,36/24, UAL.

13. Zwanenberg de Mexico, 5 July 1982, Zwan Mexico File, EXCO, UAL.

14. Extract from Minutes of Directors' Conference, 24 May 1974, OSC Papers, UAL.

15. Conference of Directors, 8 Apr. 1982, UAL.

16. N. A. Smith to S. L. Agarwal, 25 Nov. 1968, Special Committee Supporting Papers 22 56 AA, UAL.

17. Raymond Vernon, *In the Hurricane's Eye* (Cambridge, Mass.: Harvard University Press, 1998), 184–5.

18. Special Committee Minutes, 12 Apr. 1976, 22 56 AA, UAL.

19. Joint Secretaries' Memorandum on Irregular Payments—Policy, and Policy on Irregular Payments, Guidelines, 24 June 1980, EXCO Irregular Payment/Corporate Conduct, UAL.

20. D. K. Fieldhouse, *Merchant Capital and Economic Decolonization* (Oxford: Clarendon Press, 1994), 375–7; Geoffrey Jones, *British Multinational Banking 1830–1990* (Oxford: Clarendon Press, 1993), 217–21; id., *Merchants to Multinationals* (Oxford: Oxford University Press, 2000), 223–5.

21. Knox, *Coming Clean*, 161–71.

22. Overseas Committee, Mexico. An Evaluation of Unilever Opportunities, 4 Feb. 1980, EXCO LA and CA; Minutes of Sitting Together, 7 Feb. 1980, UAL.

23. Overseas Committee Annual Estimate, 13 Dec. 1982, UAL.

24. The Management of Unilever Interests in Mexico, Overseas Committee memorandum to the Special Committee, 3 Sept. 1985, EXCO, UAL.

25. Memorandum by A. W. P. Stenham to Special Committee, 2 Sept. 1986, EXCO, UAL.

26. Meeting of the Special Committee and the Overseas Committee, 5 Nov. 1979. EXCO: EAPM China/Hongkong 1971–1990, UAL.

27. Conference of Directors, 11 Aug. 1978, Memorandum by K. Durham on Discussions on China, 12 June 1979; Minutes of Sitting Together, 15 Feb. 1979. EXCO: EAPM China/Hongkong 1971–1990, UAL. Geoffrey Jones, *Multinationals and Global Capitalism* (Oxford: Oxford University Press, 2005), 217.

28. Minutes of the Meeting of the Special Committee with the Overseas Committee, 5 Nov. 1979. EXCO: EAPM China/Hongkong 1971–1990, UAL.

29. Meeting of the Special Committee with the Detergents Co-ordination, 26 June 1984, EXCO: EAPM China/Hong Kong 1971–1990, UAL.

30. Visit to China, 25–31 May 1988, F. Martin. File ICG 47-9330132, UAR.

31. Visit to the Far East, Sept. 1987, Note for the Special Committee, EAPM: China/Hong Kong 1971–1990, EXCO, UAL.

32. East Asia and Pacific Regional Management, Memorandum to the Special Committee, 1 Dec. 1988, EAPM: China/Hong Kong 1971–1990, EXCO, UAL.

33. Memo by F. Martin on Shanghai-Van den Berghs, 15 Mar. 1989, EXCO, UAL. Frank Martin, 'Oh Zenobia' (unpublished MS, 1989), 217. The Turkish manager was Rehan Perin.

34. Interview with Niall FitzGerald, 7 Mar. 2001, referring to his experience in South Africa in the 1980s.

35. Interview with Hans Eggerstedt, 8 May 2000.

36. Hellmut Schutte with Deanna Ciarlante, *Consumer Behavior in Asia* (New York: New York University Press, 1998).

37. The Next Five Years Overseas, 1 June 1971, UAL.

38. OSC and Research Division Executive Meeting, 27 Feb. 1980, Central Filing: OSC 1980, UAL.

39. Board Meeting, 13 Jan. 1983, UAL.

40. Thailand. Report to the Special Committee on 5 Nov. 1963 by F. M. L. Mann, OSC, UAL.

41. Unilever Review of Operations Overseas Companies, 1967, UAL; Interview by W. J. Reader with M. S. Perry, 19 Oct. 1988.

42. Meeting of the Special Committee with the Overseas Committee, 21/2 Dec. 1970, Meetings Box 19, 36/24, UAL.

43. CSAC 1 Background Paper: Detergents, 17 June 1983, ES 83 1738, UAR.

44. Meeting of the Special Committee with the Overseas Committee, 13 Dec. 1983, Meetings Box 20, 36/28, UAL.

45. Conference of Directors, 23 June 1988, UAL.

46. World Toilet Preparations Survey 1959–1960, Report 3110, UAR.

47. Report on Hindustan Lever, 1968, AHK 1745-935. 20132, UAR.

48. Overseas Companies—Annual Estimate for 1967. Report by Mr Knox to the Directors' Conference, 20 Jan. 1967, UAL.

49. Toilet Preparations Co-ordination Brand Strategy, 'Sunsilk', Sept. 1973, Report 3266, UAR.

50. Economics Department, Shampoo Overseas, Mar. 1983, ES 83111, UAR.

51. World Toilet Preparations Survey 1959–1960, Report 3110, UAR.

52. Toothpaste Strategy: An Economics Contribution, May 1987, ES 87 017, UAR; Economics Department, Colgate-Palmolive Report, Appendices Jan. 1988, Report 845 UAR.

53. Worldwide Review of Rexona Deodorant, 1979, ES 81 220C, UAR.

54. Toilet Preparations—5 Year Plan OSC (1975–1980), UAL.

55. Fieldhouse, *Unilever Overseas*, 428–35.

56. J. P. Erbé to H. A. Kinghorn, 19 Sept. 1977, AHK 2123-928, UAR.

57. Economics and Statistics Department, Turkey—Foods 1 Study, Apr. 1971, F1 71 024 UAR.

58. Meeting of the Special Committee with Overseas Committee, 26 June 1969, Meetings Box 20, 36/29, UAL.

59. The Next Five Years Overseas, 1 June 1971, Supporting Papers 5142 and 5143, UAL.

60. Conference on Innovation Overseas, 15 Mar. 1984, EXCO, UAL.

61. Meeting of Special Committee with Overseas Committee, 17 Dec. 1985, Meetings Box 20, 36/29, UAL.

62. Meeting of Special Committee with Overseas Committee, 26 June 1969, Meetings Box 19, 36/25, UAL. Interview with Sir Michael Perry, 10 Apr. 2002.

63. Interview with Ernst Verloop, 27 Apr. 2000.

64. Fieldhouse, *Unilever Overseas*, 148–81.

65. Meeting of the Special Committee with the Overseas Committee, 26 July 1967, UAL.

66. OSC memorandum to Special Committee on India—Corporate Strategy, 7 Jan. 1971, Special Committee Supporting Document No. 4945, UAL.

67. Fieldhouse, *Unilever Overseas*, 148–244.

68. G. D. A. Klijnstra, Some Notes on my Visit to Hindustan Lever Ltd, 4–11 Dec. 1968, AHK 1745-935.20132, UAR.

69. Meeting of Special Committee with Overseas Committee, 13 Apr. 1971, Meetings Box 19, 36/25, UAL. Annual Estimate 1973. Overseas Summary, AHK 1556, UAR.

70. Annual Estimate 1976. Overseas Summary, CAA 1528 UAR.

71. Conference of Directors, 24 Jan. 1980, EXCO: LACA, India 1980–1987.

72. Dennis J. Encarnation, *Dislodging Multi-nationals: India's Strategy in Comparative Perspective* (Ithaca, NY: Cornell University Press, 1989), 165.

73. Ibid. 111–12, 182.

74. Jack N. Behrman and William A. Fischer, *Overseas R & D Activities of Transnational Companies* (Cambridge, Mass.: Oelgeschlager, Gunn & Hain, 1980), 231–7.

75. The Etah Project, 6 Jan. 1970, Special Committee Supporting Document No. 4567, UAL. Annual Estimate 1972. Overseas Summary, UAL.

76. Memorandum to the Special Committee, 16 Dec. 1980, EXCO: LACA, India 1980–1987, UAL.

77. Private Note of Discussions held on 17 Dec. 1980, EXCO, UAL.

78. Overseas Committee Annual Estimate, 13 Dec. 1982, SD Box 5, 30/9, UAL.

79. Meeting of the Special Committee with the OSC, 11 Mar. 1987, SD Box 20, 36/29, UAL.

80. Meeting of the Special Committee with Foods and Drinks Co-ordination, 25 Feb. 1987; Meeting of the Special Committee with Latin American and Central Asian Group, EXCO, UAL.

81. Leslie Benthall (ed.), *Latin America: Economy and Society since 1930* (Cambridge: Cambridge University Press, 1998), 186.

82. Interview by D. B. Lewis with Paschoal Ricardo Netto, 26 Oct. 1988.

83. Interview with Harold Hartog, 3 Aug. 1999.

84. Interview with Tom Hoogcarspel, 17 Nov. 2001.

85. Conference of Directors, 28 Aug. 1970.

86. Interview with Morris Tabaksblat, 25 Feb. 2000.

87. Interview with Hans Eenhoorn, 15 Aug. 2000.

88. Report on a Visit to Brazil by O. Strugstad, 28 Nov.–6 Dec. 1978, AHK 2242-9150132, UAR.

89. Annual Estimate 1972: Overseas Summary, UAL.

90. Visit to Brazil, F. A. Maljers and J. H. Hulshof, Feb. 1977, Visit to Brazil, by F. A. Maljers and J. H. Hulshof, Jan. 1979, AHK 2242-9150132, UAR.

91. Visit to Industrias Gessy Lever Ltd., Brazil, Gelato Division, 6–15 Mar. 1978, AHK 2242-9150132, UAR.

92. Review of Kibon SA Brazil from OSC Files, 1977–81, CAH 2698-915, UAR.

93. Pim Reinders, *Licks, Sticks and Bricks* (Rotterdam: Unilever, 1999), 550–1.

94. Jan Peelen, Gessy Lever 1983–1986, Mar. 1986, CAH 2698-915, UAR.

95. Fieldhouse, *Unilever Overseas*, 96–146.

96. Interview with Nigel Clayton, 20 Nov. 2001.

97. Report on Visit to van den Bergh & Jurgens and Hudson & Knight, 28 Sept. to 9 Oct. 1970, AHK 1883-94/170132, UAR.

98. Meeting of the Special Committee with the Overseas Committee, 17 Dec. 1974, Meetings Box 19, 36/25, UAL.

99. Fieldhouse, *Unilever Overseas*, 139–42.

100. Overseas Committee, Brief on South Africa, 6 Apr. 1973, OSC Papers, UAL.

101. Interview with Sir Kenneth Durham, 10 Nov. 1999. Mike Dowdall, later to become Detergents Co-ordinator, also refused to work in South Africa.

102. OSC Brief on South Africa, 6 Apr. 1973, OSC Papers, UAL.

103. Report on Visit to South Africa by P. J. Keehan, 4–11 Dec. 1976, AHK 2006-94/17.0132, UAR.

104. Report on Visit to South Africa, Feb. 1980, AHK 2253-94/170132, UAR.

105. Annual Estimates 1978–1980. Overseas Summary, UAL.

106. Interview with Niall FitzGerald, 7 Mar. 2001.

107. See Ch. 12.

108. Visit to South Africa—Oct. 1982, Report to Unilever Board, 14 Oct. 1982, by F. A. Maljers, AHK 2253-94/170132, UAR.

109. Minutes of the Meeting of the Special Committee and the Overseas Committee, 16 June 1984, Meetings Box 20,36/28 UAL.

110. Memorandum by M. R. Angus to All Directors, 22 Apr. 1987, CRM 37, UAR.

111. Interview with Nigel Clayton, 20 Nov. 2001.

112. South Africa Longer Term Plan 1990–1994. Environmental Overview, UAL.

113. Co-ordination Visit; 1989. Mr R. Klages, ODF48-94/17013.2, UAR.

114. Visit Report van den Berghs & Jurgens Pty Ltd—South Africa, 10–18 Aug. 1989, EXCO, UAL.

115. South Africa. Longer Term Plan 1990–1994. Food and Drinks, EXCO, UAL.

116. Visit Report Melrose/Simonsberg, 3/7 Apr. 1989, EXCO, UAL.

117. Interview with Nigel Clayton, 20 Nov. 2001.

Chapter 7 *Trading, Plantations, and Chemicals*

1. Charles Wilson, *The History of Unilever*, (London: Cassell, 1954), i. 159–82; D. K. Fieldhouse, *Unilever Overseas* (London: Croom Helm, 1978), ch. 8; F. Pedler, *The Lion and the Unicorn* (London: Heinemann, 1974); D. K. Fieldhouse, *Merchant Capital and Economic Decolonization* (Oxford: Clarendon Press, 1994). Fieldhouse provides an in-depth account of UAC's history from its formation until 1987.

2. Wilson, *Unilever*, i. 125–34, 243–7; Wilson, *Unilever 1945–1965* (London: Cassell, 1968), 176–7; A. E. Musson, *Enterprise in Soap and Chemicals: Joseph Crosfield and Sons 1815–1965* (Manchester: Manchester University Press, 1965).

3. 'Vimms' was launched in 1941 and abandoned in 1946 after losing $5 million.

Meeting of the Special Committee, 15 Mar. 1946, UAL

4. Fieldhouse, *Unilever Overseas*, 62.

5. Fieldhouse, *Merchant Capital*, 6.

6. Fieldhouse, *Unilever Overseas*, 546.

7. Report of the Purchasing Committee. Part 2. Trade between Unilever Companies, 19 Jan. 1968, Report 3159, UAR.

8. Fieldhouse, *Merchant Capital*, 19–21.

9. Interview with Harold Hartog, 3 Aug. 1999; Interview with Sir Ernest Woodroofe, 7 Feb. 2002.

10. Fieldhouse, *Unilever Overseas*, 340–57.

11. Ibid. 384–5, 403–4; Wilson, *Unilever*, 220.

12. Memo on UAC Group Strategy, 2 Dec. 1970, Fieldhouse Papers, Box No. 4; Meeting with

Heineken, 15 Dec. 1968, Africa and Middle East Group Brewery Activity, 1968/1985, EXCO, UAL.

13. Fieldhouse, *Merchant Capital*, 509–10.

14. Ibid. 582–7.

15. Unilever in Indonesia and in Ghana, Aug. 1973, Ghana Report 694, 14, UAR.

16. Fact Sheets for Liphook 1, Fieldhouse Papers, Box No. 6, UAL.

17. 'The Golden Jubilee of UAC International', *Unilever Magazine* (May/June 1979).

18. Minutes of the Meeting of the Special Committee with UAC International, 29 July 1983; Minutes of the Meeting of the Special Committee with UAC International, 18 June 1985, EXCO, UAL.

19. J. O. Ihonvbere and T. M. Shaw, *Towards a Political Economy of Nigeria* (Aldershot: Avebury, 1988), 26.

20. Conference of Directors, 9 Nov. 1989, EXCO, UAL.

21. Minutes of Meeting of the Special Committee with Africa and Middle East Regional Management, 28 Nov. 1990, EXCO, UAL.

22. Briefing Document No. 1, 1984, for Liphook 2; Fieldhouse Papers, UAL.

23. H. A. J. Moll, *The Economics of the Palm Oil* (Wageningen: PUDOC, 1987); E. Graham with I. Floring, *The Modern Plantation in the Third World* (London: Croom Helm, 1984).

24. Taken from data tabled at Unilever Board Meeting, 24 July 1980, EXCO: Plantations—General Matters, 68/1985, UAL.

25. The initial recommendation was made in a document entitled 'Unilever 1961–69 (Some Lessons from the Past)', repeated in Han Goudswaard to David Orr, 4 May 1971, in EXCO: Plantations—General Matters, 1968–1985, UAL.

26. Conference of Directors, 1 Sept. 1972, UAL.

27. Corporate Development, 'Unilever 1961–1971', June 1972, UAL.

28. F. Sedcole and C. F. Black, 'Recommendations on the Future of Plantations Group', Dec. 1974, EXCO: Plantations—General Matters, 1968–1985, UAL.

29. Meeting of Special Committee with Overseas Committee, 20 Oct. 1976. EXCO: Plantations—General Matters, 1968–1985, UAL.

30. Overseas Committee Paper, 'Unilever Plantations Policy', May 1978, EXCO: Plantations—General Matters, 1968–1985, UAL.

31. Plantations Group, 'Results for Nine Months to 30 September 1971', EXCO: Plantations—General Matters, 1968–1985, UAL.

32. Plantations Group Longer Term Plan, 1979, EXCO: Plantations—General Matters, 1968–1985, UAL.

33. Meeting of Special Committee with Plantations Group, 14 Dec. 1983. EXCO: Plantations—General Matters, 1968–1985, UAL.

34. Meeting of Special Committee with Overseas Committee. EXCO: Plantations—General Matters, 1968–1985, UAL.

35. Meeting of Special Committee with Overseas Committee, 17 Dec. 1979. EXCO: Plantations—General Matters, 1968–1985, UAL.

36. Figures tabled at Unilever Board Meeting, 24 July 1980. EXCO: Plantations—General Matters, 1968–1985, UAL.

37. See 1983 Longer Term Plan. EXCO: Plantations—General Matters, 1968–1985, UAL.

38. Meeting of Special Committee with Plantations Group, 20 Sept. 1983. EXCO: Plantations—General Matters, 1968–1985, UAL.

39. Meeting of Special Committee with Overseas Committee, 7 Sept. 1978. EXCO: Plantations—General Matters, 1968–1985, UAL.

40. Possible Acquisition Opportunity in Indonesia, 12 June 1985; Meeting of Special Committee with Agribusiness Co-ordination, 1 May 1986, EXCO: Agribusiness—Plantations/BBG Estates, UAL.

41. Interview with Ernst Verloop, 27 Apr. 2000.

42. 'Agribusiness Strategy for Unilever,' Mar. 1985, EXCO: Agribusiness—Plantations/BBG Estates, UAL.

43. Meeting of the Special Committee with Agribusiness Co-ordination, 6 Apr. 1989, EXCO: Agribusiness—Plantations/BBG Estates, UAL.

44. Minutes of Directors' Conference, 8 Nov. 1984. EXCO: Plantations—General Matters, 1968–1985: 'Agribusiness Strategy for Unilever', Mar. 1985, UAL.

45. 'Palm Oil Producers' Response to Current Low Prices', 1 Sept. 1986, EXCO: Agribusiness—Plantations—General Matters 1986, UAL.

46. Conference of Directors, 13 Aug. 1987, UAL.

47. P. J. Croome to Special Committee, 3 Aug. 1990; Finance proposals put before Directors' Conference, 11 Oct. 1990; Meeting of Special Committee with Agribusiness Co-ordination, 22 Nov. 1990. EXCO: Agribusiness—Plantations/BBG Estates, UAL.

48. *Unilever Magazine*, 53 (1984).

49. Barrie Hall, *The Colworth Chronicles* (Bedford: Unilever, 1998), 63–6; Meeting of Special Committee with Overseas Committee, 29 Jan. 1980. EXCO: Plantations—General Matters, 1968–1985, UAL.

50. Minutes of Directors' Conference, 24 July 1980. EXCO: Plantations—General Matters, 1968–1985, UAL.

51. Meeting of Special Committee with Plantations Group, 20 Sept. 1983. EXCO: Plantations—General Matters, 1968–1985, UAL.

52. Meeting of Special Committee with Agribusiness Co-ordination, 1 May 1986. EXCO: Agribusiness—Plantations—General Matters 1986, UAL.

53. Unilever Plantations Conference, 3–5 July 1989, Acc 1992/65, Box 5, UAL.

54. Ken Durham to J. Collingwood, 24 Mar. 1964, RD 1992/32, Chemicals Folder, UAL.

55. The Study Group was chaired by Ronnie Del Mar, a graduate in chemistry who had been instrumental in the creation of Advita in the late 1940s, who was then a member of the Overseas Committee, having served as chairman of Unilever in South Africa. He became the first Chemicals Co-ordinator.

56. Report of the Chemicals Study Group, 1965, Reports Box 3, 41/2, UAL.

57. Interview by Alison Kraft with R. H. Del Mar, 30 Mar. 2001; Memorandum by R. H. Del Mar to Special Committee in Chemicals Co-ordination Annual Estimate 1975, UAL.

58. 'A Strategic Overview of Unilever Chemical Business', 1980, Blue File, UAL.

59. Meeting of the Central Research Planning Group, 27 June 1968, Box 2, Research Division, 1999/32, UAL

60. Conference of Directors, 12 Aug. 1977, UAL.

61. Musson, *Enterprise*, 362–5.

62. Interview by Charles Wilson and W. J. Reader with R. H. Del Mar, 11 Oct. 1988.

63. 'The Spice of Life', *Unilever Magazine* (Jan./Feb. 1979).

64. Strategy for Chemicals Business of Unilever, 1 Dec. 1980, Unit Box 37, 27/7, UAL.

65. Private Note of Discussion, 27 Jan. 1981; Minutes of Sitting Together, 30 Jan. 1981, EXCO, UAL.

66. Conference of Directors, 26 Mar. 1981. Management Group Review—Chemicals, EXCO, UAL.

67. Research Division Annual Estimates, UAL; 'Introducing Sir Geoffrey Allen', *Unilever Magazine*, 43 (1981).

68. Frank Greenwall, *Yesterday, Today, Tomorrow: The Story of National Starch and Chemical Corporation* (n.p., n.d.).

69. Interview by Alison Kraft with Wallace Grubman, 20 Feb. 2001.

70. Private Note of Discussion, 30 Nov. 1983, EXCO, UAL.

71. Interview by Alison Kraft with Wallace Grubman, 20 Feb. 2001.

72. Meeting between Chemicals Co-ordination and Special Committee, 27 Nov. 1987, EXCO: Chemical Co-ordination General Matters, UAL.

73. Naarden to W. Grubman, 2 Feb. 1987, EXCO: Quest 1981–1987 File, UAL.

74. Conference of Directors, 19 Apr. 1990, UAL.

75. Interview by Alison Kraft with Wallace Grubman, 20 Feb. 2001.

Chapter 8 *Human Resources*

1. Interview by Anna Tijsseling with Hans van der Hoek, 29 May 2001.

2. Booz Allen & Hamilton International, 'Study of Personnel Programmes and Organization: Unilever', 3 July 1967, Reports Box 7, 48/1, UAL.

3. Ken Wheeler was responsible for recruitment, development, and training, and Hans van der Hoek was responsible for management remuneration and structure.

4. Interview by Anna Tijsseling with Hans van der Hoek, 29 May 2001.

5. 'Recommendations of the UCMDS Fundamental Review Working Party' (1994), appendix IX. UK National Personnel Department, London.

6. '1987 Recruitment Statistics', appendix IV and appendix VII. UK National Personnel Department, London.

7. S. P. Keeble, *The Ability to Manage: A Study of British Management 1890–1990* (Manchester: Manchester University Press, 1992), ch. 3.

8. Comments by AJR on Unilever, 17 Dec. 1974, in Cambridge University Appointments Board. Cited by Mike Hicks, 'The Recruitment and Selection of Young Managers by British Business 1930–2000' (unpub. Oxford D. Phil. thesis, 2004), 191.

9. Meeting of Special Committee with Personnel Division, 13 Feb. 1968, Meetings Box 21, 37/3, UAL.

10. Basic Information of the Personnel Department Unilever Holland, 1961, HA 334-334.9, UAR.

11. De selectie procedure van APN, Werken bij Unilever, 1991, EXCO—Management Development—Rotterdam, UAL.

12. File on Academics, 1950–1970, APN 457, UAR.

13. Management Development Section, Werken bij Unilever (1991), Management Development—Rotterdam, EXCO, UAL.

14. Interview by Peter Miskell with Martin Duffell, 9 Jan. 2001.

15. Memorandum by K. H. Wheeler, Management Recruitment—Europe, 13 Feb. 1974, Correspondence between Wheeler and National Managers Europe, 13 Feb. 1974, UAL

16. Meeting of Special Committee with Personnel Division, 27 Apr. 1978 and 23 Apr. 1981, Meetings Box 21, 37/3, UAL.

17. Sundry Food and Drinks Co-ordination, Chairmen's Meeting with Personnel Division, Venice, 15 June 1979, File 5803, UAR.

18. Examination of Technical Resources, Acc 2000/145, Box 11, UK National Personnel Department, UAL.

19. Management Development Section, Werken bij Unilever (1991), Management Development—Rotterdam, EXCO, UAL.

20. Interview by Anna Tijsseling with Han Goudswaard, 26 June 2001.

21. Report of a Study Group on the Strength and Quality of Marketing Resources in Unilever, Mar. 1984, UNI/CO/DT/1/1/3/1/1/1, UAL.

22. Conference of Directors, 12 Jan. 1989, UAL.

23. Meeting of Special Committee with Personnel Division, 23 Apr. 1981, Meetings Box 21,37/3, UAL.

24. Interview by Anna Tijsseling with Huib Ketelaar, 16 May 2001.

25. Report of the Working Party on the Dutch Presence in Unilever, Apr. 1988, Report 2783, UAR.

26. Notes on the Netherlands National Personnel Review 1990, APN Files, UAR.

27. 'The Management of Mid Career Recruitment', Acc 2000/145, Box 5, UK National Personnel Department, UAL.

28. 'Joining Unilever in Mid-Career', Feb. 1989, Report 7770, UAR.

29. 'U.C.M.D.S. Intake List, 1952–1973', UK National Personnel Department, London.

30. Interview by W. J. Reader with Eleanor MacDonald (n.d. [*c*.1989]).

31. Collection of data and reports combined under the heading 'Recommended for putting forward to Dr. Goudswaard', 2 Nov. 1973, AHK 060, UAR.

32. 'De positie van de vrouw bij Unilever', *Op Eigen Terrein*, 14 (12 July 1957), UAR.

33. 'Recommended for putting forward to Dr. Goudswaard', 2 Nov. 1973. UHA Rotterdam, AHK 060, UAR.

34. 'Take Promotion, Miss Smith', *Unilever Magazine* (May/June 1979).

35. Thomas K. McCraw, *American Business, 1920–2000: How it Worked* (Wheeling, Ill.: Harlan Davidson, 2000), 64.

36. Report of a Study Group on the Strength and Quality of Marketing Resources in Unilever, Mar. 1984, UNI/CO/DT/1/1/3/1/1/1, UAL.

37. UCMDS/UEMTS—% Cumulative Losses by Sex and Years of Service, Acc 2000/145, Box 4, UAL.

38. Briefing Document No. 1, 1984, for Liphook 2, Fieldhouse Papers UAL. Hicks, 'Recruitment and Selection', 44.

39. Study on Central Head Office Resources and on Local Head Office Resources, May 1982, UAL.

40. Quoted in 'Four Acres: A Centre for Stretching People', *Unilever Magazine*, 32 (May/June 1979).

41. Meeting of Personnel Division with Special Committee, 13 Jan. 1983, Meetings Box 21, 37/3, UAL.

42. 'Come and Work for Us', *Unilever Magazine*, 64 (1987).

43. Interview by Anna Tijsseling with Hans van der Hoek, 29 May 2001.

44. Interview by Anna Tijsseling with Huib Ketelaar, 16 May 2001.

45. Extract from Minutes of Directors' Conference, 17 Jan. 1985, Meetings Box 21, 37/3, UAL.

46. Interview by P. W. Klein and W. J. Reader with Han Goudswaard, 24 May 1989.

47. Floris Maljers and Morris Tabaksblat respectively.

48. Interview with Sir Kenneth Durham, 10 Nov. 1999; Interview with Sir Ernest Woodroofe, 7 Feb. 2002; Interview with Niall FitzGerald, 7 Mar. 2001; Interview with Sir Michael Perry, 10 Apr. 2002.

49. 'Appraisal of Manager', (Personnel Division, Aug. 1969) PD 688, UAR.

50. Extract from Minutes of Directors' Conference, 24 Nov. 1978, Meetings Box 21, 37/3, UAL.

51. McKinsey, 'Strengthening Implementation of Unilever's Personnel Policies on Salaries and Management Appraisal', UAL.

52. Personnel Division, 'Unilever Management Salary Policy' (23 Aug. 1965), Special Committee Supporting Documents, No. 3178, UAL.

53. 'Employment Policies of Unilever', 1 Feb. 1977, AHK 2517, UAR.

54. Meeting of Special Committee with Personnel Division, 26 Apr. 1983, No. W. 473, Meetings Box 21, 37/3, UAL.

55. Management Remuneration—Annual Cash Awards, 25 June 1986, EXCO: Personnel Division, General Matters, 1984/86, UAL.

56. H. W. Kressler, 'Review of the Cash Award System', 11 Aug. 1988, appendix. EXCO: Personnel Division, General Matters—1987, UAL.

57. H. W. Kessler, 'Review of the Cash Award System', 11 Aug. 1988; Meeting of Special Committee with Personnel Division, 23 Aug. 1988; Kressler to Special Committee, 21 Oct. 1988; EXCO: Personnel Division, General Matters—1987, UAL.

58. Share Option Scheme—SAYE. A. H. C. Hill to W. B. Blaisse, 28 Apr. 1981, AHK 2665, UAR.

59. Meeting of the Special Committee with Personnel Division, EXCO: Personnel Division, General Matters—1984–86, UAL.

60. Meeting of Special Committee with Personnel Division, 31 Jan. 1990, EXCO: Personnel Division, General Matters—1987, UAL.

61. Interview by P. W. Klein and W. J. Reader with Han Goudswaard, 24 May 1989; Interview by Anna Tijsseling with Han Goudswaard, 26 June 2001.

62. 'The Unilever Traineeship on the Continent' July 1962, HA 333-333.3, UAR.

63. Conference of Directors, 8 Dec. 1978 and 3 Dec. 1981, Personnel Division, Management Salary Policy Documents, UAL.

64. Interview by P. W. Klein and W. J. Reader with Han Goudswaard, 24 May 1989.

65. Noordwijk Letter, 30 Oct. 1965, NUB 1135, UAR.

66. Korte notitie naar aanleiding bespreking met jonge managers, ondertekenaars van de brief dd. 30 Oct.1965 uit Noordwijk, NUB 1135, UAR.

67. Correspondence R. Nolen to National Management, 18 Nov. 1965, NUB 1135, UAR.

68. Meeting of Dutch Board Members and Advisory Members of Unilever, 30 June 1969, AHK 1944, UAR.

69. J. P. Windmuller, C. de Galan, and A. F. van Zweeden, *Arbeidsverhoudingen in Nederland* (Utrecht: Aula, 1985).

70. Initial Committee VHUP, 28 Aug. 1968, HA 306-306.3, UAR.

71. G.V. van Leeuwen VHUP, to H. P. H. Nitschmann, 31 Oct. 1972, HA 150-466.13, UAR.

72. R. Nolen to H. P. H. Nitschmann and P. J. B. Jongstra, 7 Feb. 1972, HA 150-466.13, UAR.

73. APN to VHUP, 30 Oct. 1970, HA 306-306.6, UAR.

74. In January 1970 a Study Group published a confidential report on Management Attitudes, AHK 1960, UAR.

75. Personnel Division, Competitive Management Structures and Greenfielding, July 1983, Report 1319, UAR

76. Greater Cost Effectiveness in Europe, Apr. 1985, paper for Kurhaus Conference, 16/17 Apr. 1985, EXCO, UAL.

77. Education and Training within Unilever (*c.*1980), Report 440, UAR.

78. Han Goudswaard to Special Committee, 20 Jan. 1976, AHK 2517-060, UAR.

79. Personnel Division, 'Guide to Courses' (Jan. 1978), AHK 2518-06010, UAR.

80. Personnel Division, 'Guide to Courses' (Jan. 1983), AHK 2518-06010, UAR.

81. Maurice Zinkin to Special Committee, 12 Aug. 1966, Special Committee Supporting Document, 3426, UAL.

82. Detergents Co-ordination, 'A Detergent Training Plan for Executive Countries' 27 Jan. 1970, AHK 1962, UAR.

83. Personnel Division, 'Guide to Courses' (Jan. 1978), AHK 2518-06010, UAR; 'Management Development and Training of Buyers', 1970, Report 557, UAR; D. S. Markwell, 'Strategies for Organisational Development Training', 4 Feb. 1970, AHK 1960, UAR.

84. Personnel Division 'Guide to Courses', Jan. 1978, AHK 2518-06010, UAR.

85. 'Education and Training in Unilever, *c.*1980, Report 440, UAR.

86. 'International Trade Unions and Unilever', a report by prepared by Personnel Division's International Committee on Industrial Relations, Sept. 1972, AHK 1960-060, UAR.

87. Conference of Directors, 11 June 1976, UAL.

88. 'International Trade Unions and Unilever', a report prepared by Personnel Division's International Committee on Industrial Relations, Sep. 1972, 15–16. AHK 1960-060, UAR.

89. Meeting of Special Committee with Personnel Division, 23 Aug. 1973. Meetings Box 21, 37/3, UAL; 'Unilever's Attitude Towards International Trade Unionism—Guidelines' 1 Sept. 1973, AHK 2517-060, UAR.

90. Summary of main points made at the Directors' Conference, 'Co-determination' (10 Nov. 1976), EXCO, UAL.

91. Memorandum on Participation and Co-determination, 23 Sept. 1976, EXCO: Directors' Conference, Oct. 1976, UAL.

92. Memorandum on Participation and Co-determination, 23 Sept. 1976, EXCO: Directors' Conference, Oct. 1976, UAL.

93. 'Notes on Meeting with Mr F. O. Gundelach, Commissioner for the Internal Market and Customs Union', 24 Feb. 1975, AHK 2529-060/18, UAR.

94. Directors' Conference Wolfheze, 23 Sept. 1976, appendix 2, HA-RVB-11455, UAR.

95. Unilever Submission to the Inquiry on Industrial Democracy, Feb. 1976, Special Committee Supporting Documents, 6610, UAL.

96. Conference of Directors, 1 Mar. 1977, UAL.

97. 'Discussion with Sir Christopher Soames, Vice-President of the Commission of the European Communities', 23 Jan. 1975, AHK 2529-060/18, UAR.

98. Memorandum by Joint Secretaries, 10 Nov. 1976, EXCO: Conference of Directors, Oct. 1976, UAL.

99. Secretaries of Unilever to Special Committee, 3 Oct. 1979, EXCO: Joint Secretaries Special Study, UAL.

100. Ibid.

101. Alec Cairncross, 'The Postwar Years, 1945–77', in Roderick Floud and Donald McCloskey (eds.), *The Economic History of Britain since 1700,* ii: *1860 to the 1970s* (Cambridge: Cambridge University Press, 1981), 383–4.

102. Meeting of Special Committee with UK Committee, 20 Aug. 1970, Unit Box 41, 52/2, UAL.

103. Meeting of Special Committee with United Kingdom Committee, 15 Aug. 1977, Unit Box 41, 52/3; Conference of Directors, 17 Aug. 1977, UAL.

104. Extract from Directors' Conference, 23 Sept. 1977, Unit Box 41, 52/3, UAL.

105. See Ch. 3. Meeting of Special Committee with Frozen Products Co-ordination, 14 Dec. 1976, Meetings Box 18, 36/12, UAL.

106. *Birds Eye News* (Dec. 1977, Feb. 1978), Library, UAL.

107. *Birds Eye News* (Dec. 1977).

108. *Birds Eye News* (Jan. 1978).

109. Conference of Directors, 7 Mar. 1978, UAL.

110. *Birds Eye News* (Mar. 1978).

111. Meeting of Special Committee with UK National Management, 30 May 1979, Unit Box 41, 52/3, UAL.

112. Conference of Directors, 16 Mar. 1989, UAL.

113. Conference of Directors, 9 Nov. 1989, UAL.

Chapter 9 *Corporate Culture*

1. Thomas J. Peters and Robert H. Waterman, Jr., *In Search of Excellence: Lessons from America's Best Run Companies* (New York: Harper and Row, 1982); Stanley Davis, *Managing Corporate Culture* (Cambridge: Ballinger, 1984); Joanne Martin, *Culture in Organisations: Three Perspectives* (New York: Oxford University Press, 1992); John P. Kotter and James L. Heskett, *Corporate Culture and Performance* (New York: Free Press, 1992).

2. E. H. Schein, 'Coming to a New Awareness of Organisational Culture', *Sloan Management Review* (Winter 1984); id., *Organisational Culture and Leadership: A Dynamic View* (San Francisco: Jossey-Bass, 1985).

3. E. H. Schein, 'Organizational Socialization and the Profession of Management', *Sloan Managament Review,* 30 (1988), 53–65.

4. Charles Wilson, *The History of Unilever* (London: Cassell, 1954), 293–4.

5. John Griffiths, ' "Give My Regards to Uncle Billy…": The Rites and Rituals of Company Life at Lever Brothers, c1900–c1990', *Business History,* 37/4 (1995), 25–45.

6. W. C. Frederick, J. E. Post, and K. Davis, *Business and Society: Corporate Strategy, Public Policy and Ethics* (New York: McGraw Hill, 1992); Ans Kolk and Rob van Tulder, 'Can Transnational Corporations Regulate Themselves', in Ans Kolk and Rob van

Tulder, *International Codes of Conduct* (Rotterdam: Erasmus University, 2002).

7. See also Ch. 12.

8. The quotes are from the four articles by Kuin on 'There's More to Management' published in the 1978 issue of *Unilever Magazine*. Kuin wrote a number of major works on his views after his retirement from Unilever in 1970. See especially Pieter Kuin, *Management is méér. De Sociale verantwoordelijkheid van de ondememerner* (Amsterdam: Elsevier, 1977).

9. 'What Unilever Is', *Progress: The Magazine of Unilever*, 47 (1959), 107.

10. RBL, 'A Qualitative Survey of How Unilever Communicates and is Perceived', Dec. 1972, vol. 2, Reports Box 7, 47/3, UAL.

11. 'The Morality of Business: Nuances of Good Behaviour', *Unilever Magazine*, 51 (1983).

12. Comments by D. Webb at International Public Relations Conference, 20 Oct. 1971, AHK 1894-0163, UAR.

13. Economics Department, Procter and Gamble's Strategy Overseas (1984), ES 84 139C, UAR.

14. Interview by P. W. Klein and W. J. Reader with Han Goudswaard, 24 May 1989.

15. Andrew Knox, *Coming Clean: A Postscript after Retirement from Unilever* (London: Heinemann, 1976), 243.

16. Rob Goffee and Gareth Jones, 'What Holds the Modern Company Together', *Harvard Business Review* (Nov.–Dec. 1996), 133–48.

17. 'Guide to Courses', Jan. 1978, AHK 2518-06010, UAR.

18. Floris A. Maljers, 'Inside Unilever: The Evolving Transnational Company', *Harvard Business Review* (Sept.–Oct. 1992), 46–51.

19. Chairmen's Review of the Year, 1992, UAL.

20. Interview with Nigel Clayton, 20 Nov. 2001.

21. Interview with Stephen Williams, 19 June 2002.

22. Goffee and Jones, 'What Holds the Modern Company Together', 133–48.

23. Interview with Stephen Williams, 19 June 2002.

24. Interview with Niall FitzGerald, 7 Mar. 2001.

25. Study on Central Head Office Resources and on Local Head Office Resources, Special Committee, May 1982, Report 2714, UAR.

26. Interview with Henk Meij, 12 Feb. 2000.

27. RBL, 'A Qualitative Survey of How Unilever Communicates and is Perceived', Dec. 1972, vol. 2, Reports Box 7, 47/3, UAL.

28. Product Innovation. Report of a Marketing Division Working Party, Mar. 1980, Report 1006, UAR.

29. 'Joining Unilever in Mid-Career: A Report to Unilever Personnel Division on the Experience of Senior Managers who have Joined Unilever in Mid Career', Feb. 1989, Report 7770, UAR.

30. This was widely ascribed to Maurice Zinkin, the secretary of the Special Committee for many years.

31. 'Joining Unilever in Mid-Career'. Report 7770, UAR.

32. 'The Rise of the Multi-Local Multi-national', Speech at Yale University by Sir Michael Perry, 30 Nov. 1995.

33. Ibid.

34. *Procter & Gamble: The House that Ivory Built* (Lincolnwood, Ill.: NTC Business Books, 1988), 88–9.

35. Pieter Kuin, 'The Magic of Multinational Management', *Harvard Business Review* (Nov.–Dec. 1972).

36. Interview by Kenneth Harris with George Cole, published in *The Observer*, 6, 13 Jan. 1963.

37. 'Joining Unilever in Mid-Career', Report 7770, UAR.

38. Interview with David Stout, 28 Nov. 2001.

39. Marketing Division, 'Company Marketing Organisation and Management' Dec. 1970, Reports Box 6, 45/1, UAL.

40. Corporate Development and Economics: Unilever's Use of Management Consultants Mar. 1990, ES 90037, UAR.

41. RBL, 'A Qualitative Survey of How Unilever Communicates and is Perceived', Dec. 1972, vol. 2, Reports Box 7, 47/3, UAL.

42. Meeting of Special Committee with Personnel Division, 23 Oct. 1985, EXCO:

Special Committee and Research Division, 12 Oct. 1978, Unit Box 33, 27/13, UAL.

20. Edgerton, *Science*, 33.

21. Meeting of Special Committee and Research Division, 15 July 1976; Minutes of the Research Division Executive Committee, Meetings Box 21, 34/14, UAL.

22. Research Division Review and Plans 1974–1983, UAL.

23. Research Division, Annual Estimate 1976, SD Box 6, 30/15, UAL.

24. Minutes of Marketing Directors' Meeting, Amsterdam, 22 Jan. 1976, IJs 18, UAR; Conference of Directors, 9 Oct. 1980, UAL.

25. Davit A. Hounshell, 'The Evolution of Industrial Research in the United States', in Richard S. Rosenbloom and William J. Spencer (eds.), *Engines of Innovation: US Industrial Research at the End of an Era* (Boston: Harvard Business School Press, 1996).

26. Kenneth Durham, Review of Unilever Research, 31 Aug. 1978; Meeting between Special Committee and Research Division, 12 Oct. 1978, Unit Box 33, 27/13, UAL.

27. W. J. Beek, *History of Research and Engineering in Unilever, 1911–1986* (Rotterdam: Unilever, 1996), 2.5.

28. Research Division, 'Research Contribution to Innovation, 1965–1980' (Aug. 1980), 7, UNI/CO/DT/D/6/3/2/2, UAL.

29. Interview with Morris Tabaksblat, 25 Feb. 2000.

30. Meeting of Special Committee with Research and Engineering Division, 10 July 1985, Meetings Box 21, UAL.

31. Meeting of Special Committee and Research Division, 15 Jan. 1980, 22 Sept., 15 Dec. 1982, Meetings Box 22, 34/14, UAL.

32. Meeting of Special Committee with Detergents Co-ordination, 9 Aug. 1983, Unit Box 26, 26/13, UAL.

33. SRU Ltd., Unilever R & D, 30 Oct. 1986, 47/1, Reports Box 7, 47/1, UAL.

34. François Dalle, *L'Aventure L'Oréal* (Paris: Éditions Odile Jacob, 2001), ch. 15; Economics Department, 'Competition in Detergents: Some Key Issues' (1985), ES

85020, UAR; Interview with David Stout, 28 Nov. 2001.

35. Report of the Study Group on Detergents Research, Apr. 1979, Unit Box 26, 26/10, UAL.

36. Keith Pavitt, 'Some Foundations for a Theory of the Large Innovating Firm', in Giovanni Dosi, Renato Giannetti, and Pier Angelo Toninelli (eds.), *Technology and Enterprise in Historical Perspective* (Oxford: Clarendon Press, 1992), 213–20.

37. Board Conference, 11 Nov. 1981, UAL.

38. McKinsey & Co., *Achieving Profitable Innovation: A Summary of Recommendations* (Aug. 1972), Report 5498, UAR.

39. Beek, *History*, 3.12.

40. R. J. Taylor, 'Research Establishments in Europe: URL Vlaardingen', Chemistry and Industry, 15 Jan. 1966; Research Division, Box 4, UAL; R. J. Taylor, *A Concise History of Unilever Research in Western Europe*, Dec. 1967, Publication 7293, UAR; J. Nieuwenhuis, Forty Years of Unilever Research Vlaardingen (unpublished MS, 1999).

41. Behrman and Fischer, *Overseas R & D Activities*, 222.

42. Interview with Sir Kenneth Durham, 10 Nov. 1999.

43. K. K. G. Menon, Report to Special Committee on Hindustan Lever Research Centre, 17 Oct. 1978, Y 294, 7343, UAL.

44. Behrman and Fischer, *Overseas R & D Activities*, 243.

45. Geoffrey Jones, 'Control, Performance, and Knowledge Transfers in Large Multinationals: Unilever in the United States 1945–1980', *Business History Review*, 76 (Autumn 2002), 449.

46. Interview with Sir Ernest Woodroofe, 7 Feb. 2002.

47. Detergents Co-ordination, '1985 Longer Term Plan', SD Box 9, 31/6, UAL.

48. 'Dairy Products Strategy 1969–1973 in Foods 1 Co-ordination' (Rotterdam, 6 May 1969), AHK 1931; Economics and Statistics Department, 'The Cheese and Yoghurt Markets in the EEC and the United Kingdom' (July 1969), AHK 1931;

G. Berwick, 'Yoghurt and Dessert Market' Feb. 1973, appendix 1, AHK 1931, UAR.

49. Interview by P. W. Klein and W. J. Reader with F. A. Maljers, 8 Sept. 1989. The Co-ordinator was Noud Caron.

50. J. C. Rolandus Hagedoorn, 'Marketing Dairy Products', Sept. 1969 for the National Counties Dairy Conference in Vlaadingen, AHK 1931, UAR.

51. Ibid.

52. Meeting of Special Committee with Edible Fats and Dairy Co-ordination, 28 Jan. 1976, Meetings Box 15, 35/8, UAL.

53. Meeting of Special Committee with Detergents Co-ordination, 12 July 1978, Unit Box 26, 26/10, UAL.

54. F. W. L. Mann and D. F. Webb, 'Notes on a Visit to Lever Sunlicht, Hamburg' (14–15 June 1977), Detergents Co-ordination, Visits Box 3, UAL.

55. D. F. Webb, 'Notes on Field Visit to Germany, 28/29 Sept. 1977', Visits Box 3, UAL.

56. Mann and Webb, 'Notes on a Visit to Lever Sunlicht'.

57. Meeting of Special Committee with Detergents Co-ordination, 11 Apr. 1978, Unit Box 26, 26/10, No. 194, UAL.

58. 'Co-ordination Brief to JWT International for Alternative Advertising for Apollo in Germany' (Oct. 1977), Detergents Co-ordination, Visits Box 3, UAL.

59. Meeting of Special Committee with Detergents Co-ordination, 11 Apr. 1978, Unit Box 26, 26/10, UAL.

60. Henk Meij to Special Committee, 'Hyacinth Project, Appendix 1: "Extracts Indicating the Progress of the Unilever interest in Disposables" ', Mar. 1975, Unit Box 16, 24/7, UAL.

61. J. P. Erbé to Special Committee, 28 Jan. 1974, AHK 2007-01410, UAR.

62. J. P. Erbé, 'Application of Research and Development to Disposables', June 1973, Unit Box 16, 24/7, UAL; B. Hall, *The Colworth Chronicles: A Golden Celebration 1947–1997* (Bedford: Unilever, 1998).

63. Private Note of Discussion, 5 Dec. 1973, Unit Box 16, 24/7, UAL.

64. 'Notes on Meeting about Hyacinth', 13 Mar. 1975, Unit Box 16, 24/7, UAL.

65. Minutes of Sitting Together, 25 Mar. 1975, Private Note of Discussion, 23 Apr. 1975, Unit Box 16, 24/7, UAL.

66. H. Meij to Special Committee, 'Hyacinth Project', 6 Mar. 1975, Unit Box 16, 24/7, UAL.

67. Private Note of Discussion, 10 Aug. 1976, Unit Box 16, 24/7, UAL.

68. Meeting of Special Committee with Toilet Preparations Committee, 14 Aug. 1979, Unit Box 16, 24/7, UAL.

69. Meeting of Special Committee with Personal Products Co-ordination, 4 Nov. 1980, Unit Box 16, 24/7, UAL; Hall, *Colworth Chronicles*, 140–2.

70. Meeting of Special Committee and Research Division, 19 Aug. 1980, Meetings Box 22, File 34/14, UAL. On the Rely crisis, see Davis Dyer, Frederick Dazell, and Rowena Olegario, *Rising Tide: Lessons from 165 Years of Brand Building at Procter & Gamble* (Boston: Harvard Business School Press, 2004), 113–16.

71. Detergents Co-ordination, 'Unilever Detergents Policy Memorandum No 19: Abrasive Cleaner Policy', July 1972, UNI/CO/DT/1/3/4/1/19, UAL.

72. Detergents Co-ordination, 'Unilever Detergents Business, 1958–1968' (Aug. 1969), UAL.

73. Interview with Sir Ernest Woodroofe, 7 Feb. 2002.

74. Unilever Detergents Policy Memorandum no. 21, UNI/CO/DT/1/3/4/1/19, UAL.

75. Ibid.

76. Pim Reinders, *Licks, Sticks and Bricks* (Rotterdam: Unilever, 1999), 618.

77. Minutes of the Viennetta Workshop at Colworth House, 16 Sept. 1987, ICG 56-02523, UAR.

78. 'Co-ordination Marketing and Technical Guidelines for Viennetta', 24 Feb. 1987, Frozen Foods Co-ordination, 215 4AA, UAL.

79. Reinders, *Licks, Sticks and Bricks*, 619.

80. 'Briefing "Viennetta" New TV Campaign', Hamburg, 9 Sept. 1987, Frozen Foods Co-ordination, Box 25, Viennetta, UAL.